LAW AND JUSTICE IN TOKUGAWA JAPAN

This series will consist of the following volumes:

PART I	INTRODUCTION
PART II	CONTRACT: CIVIL CUSTOMARY LAW
PART III	CONTRACT: LEGAL PRECEDENTS
PART IV	CONTRACT: COMMERCIAL CUSTOMARY LAW
PART V	PROPERTY: CIVIL CUSTOMARY LAW
PART VI	PROPERTY: LEGAL PRECEDENTS
PART VII	PERSONS: CIVIL CUSTOMARY LAW
PART VIII	PERSONS: LEGAL PRECEDENTS
PART IX	PROCEDURE: LEGAL PRECEDENTS
PART X	INDICES AND VOCABULARY

Comparative legal science teaches us how nations having a common origin may develop independently their original inheritance of legal ideas . . . and, on the other hand, how the legal systems of nations having no association in history may advance along common lines of development. . . . Investigations carried on in the region of a single system serve to smooth the path for the advent of comparative legal science. Each enlargement of our view, each addition to our available material, is a gain of the greatest moment for that science.

Bernhöft, in Zeitschrift für vergleichende Rechtswissenschaft, 1878

LAW AND JUSTICE IN TOKUGAWA JAPAN

Materials for the History of Japanese Law and Justice under the Tokugawa Shogunate 1603–1867

PART IV–C
Contract: Commercial Customary Law

Edited by
John Henry Wigmore

Translated and Published under the Auspices of
The Japan Foundation

UNIVERSITY OF TOKYO PRESS
1986

3-6 Kioi-cho, Chiyoda-ku,
Tokyo, Japan

ISBN 4-13-007508-4 / UTP 37312
ISBN 0-86008-404-3

Printed in Japan

Contents

BOOK III
CONTRACT

PREFACE BY THE EDITOR OF THE JAPANESE PRINTED EDITION

This work, *Collection of Commercial Customs*, consisting of three Books, is further subdivided into chapters on (1) merchants, commerce, and commercial account-books; (2) commercial mortgages and their liens; (3) agents for buying and selling; (4) buying and selling; (5) breach of contract; (6) vendors; (7) vendees; (8) transport (in Books I and II of the Printed Edition); (1) contracts; (2) performance of contracts; (3) restitution of price, damages, and discount; (4) damages for breach of contract; (5) agency; and (6) account current (Book III). It consists of reports, including verbatim notes, submitted by merchants, business organizations, and provincial governments, in answer to questionnaires about the commercial customs that obtained in the various parts of Japan in the period from the closing years of the Tokugawa regime to the early years of Meiji. It forms a good reference volume for all the commercial customs that generally prevailed in the country in the days preceding the Meiji era.

As there is no explicit enumeration of the names of those issuing and answering the questionnaires, their identity cannot be definitely stated. But as there is a recital at the end of Book I, "Published in July in the 16th year of Meiji [1883]" and at the end of Book II "Published in February in the 17th year of Meiji [1884]," we are inclined to believe that these Books were the work of the Compilation Committee on a Code of Commerce[1] that had been organized under the then Central Government[2] and which was later replaced by a reorganized body known by the name of "Committee for the Investigation of Commercial Law."[3] Our belief is: that these Committees, organized for the purpose of expediting the speedy enactment of a commercial code as a part of the policy of the then government, sent out questionnaires to all the parties concerned with a view to obtain helpful information for drafting the commercial code, and after arranging and classifying the reports thus obtained, to publish them. The result was these Books. The party who was in

[1] Shôhô Hensan Iin. [2] *Dajôkan.* [3] Shôhô Torishirabe Iin.

charge of drafting the Commercial Code was the eminent German scholar Dr. Hermann Roesler,[1] and his bulky draft code was completed at about this time (in January of the 17th year of Meiji [1884]). In his report on his draft code, he says, "The native commercial customs have not been incorporated in this Draft Code, because they were not made definitely known at the time the work of drafting was in progress." He also says in his report, "It would not have been unsuitable to preserve the old Japanese legal conceptions and customs, and to adopt in the Code those which do not conflict with the general principles of commercial law. Although it is regrettable that these Japanese legal ideas and customs have not so far been brought to the notice of the draftsman of the Code, yet it is earnestly hoped that this may still be done." Considering that this report of Dr. Roesler was presented to the Emperor in the month preceding the one when this work (that is, Book II of the Collection of Commercial Customs) was completed and printed (Book II of the Collection being printed in February of the 17th year of Meiji [1884] and Dr. Roesler's report being dated January 19th of the same year), it seems incomprehensible that the Japanese Committee for the Investigation of Commercial Laws should not have informed the German jurist of the materials thus collected. But that this Collection was made with the object of supplying materials for drafting the code, there can be no doubt. In the light of today's knowledge, there is not a little contained in it which is mere speculation or guessing on the part of those who furnished the answers to the questionnaire, and is hardly worthy of classification as statements of facts. But there is also much reliable information that was clearly based on the memory of the older generation. The use of the Volumes, therefore, needs some care on the part of the reader; but those who make use of them, using such care, though they may find some answers not to be depended upon, yet will reap not a little profit. That is the reason why the present editor has put the whole materials, as they were originally collected, into the present Collection, in spite of their being somewhat confused and crude in their composition.

1930 Takimoto Seiichi

[1] Karl Friedrich Hermann Roesler (1834–94). He was invited by the Japanese Government in 1878 and stayed in Japan for about 15 years.

EDITORIAL NOTE
by
Dr. John Henry Wigmore

A complete account of the sources from which this Series is translated will be found in the Editorial Notes (pp. xxix–xxxii) and Appendix A and B (pp. 145–156) to Part I of the Series.

This Part IV is translated from a printed Japanese volume of which the exact title is as follows:

[Title Page]
法学博士　瀧本誠一編纂
日本経済大典
第四十九巻，第五十巻
[Translated:
Edited by Takimoto Seiichi, Juris Doctor.
Collection of Economic Materials of Japan
(*Nihon Keizai Taiten*)
Volumes 49 & 50]
[Sub-title Page]
日本経済大典
第四十九巻，第五十巻
商事慣例類集
[Translated:
Collection of Economic Materials of Japan
Vols. 49 & 50
Collection of Commercial Customs
(*Shôji Kanrei Ruishû*)]

The work is printed in two volumes, dated 1930 (Shôwa V). Tokyo; the first volume contains Books I and II (236 and 496 pages); the second volume contains Book III (498 pages); the Books are paged consecutively to 1130, and the treatise "Minji Kanrei Ruishû," is translated as Part VII of this Series. This Japanese edition was a printing of a work in three volumes, prepared about 1880 by an official Commission under Count Terajima Munenori (1833–1893), that had been charged with collecting and reporting on the commercial customs, with a view to assisting the preparation of a Commercial Code. A translation of it was begun for him in

1892, but only a fragment of the first draft was done. At that time the volumes consulted for the purpose in the Department of Justice were in manuscript; there were five volumes in all, one of Book I, two of Book II, and two of Book III. The Preface of the printed edition of 1930 refers to the Commission's report as having been "published" in Meiji 16 and 17 (1883–84); but that printed edition has not been seen by the Editor.

It may here be noted that though the Japanese work is divided into three parts, here termed "Books," the topics reported on in Books I and II are identical; the answers reported, however, represent answers from different parties—in Book I, the regional commercial committees, Book II, the local officials and trades. Both are useful. But for clearness' sake, the answers from the two Books have here been placed together under the respective topics.

LIST OF THE TOPICS OF THE QUESTIONNAIRES IN BOOKS I & II[1]

Chapter I Merchants, Commerce, and Merchants' Books

Topic 1: Is there any customary standard by which to distinguish between a merchant and non-merchant?

Topic 2: Is any distinction made between civil and commercial matters according to the nature of the enterprise or contract?

Topic 3: Does a married woman trade apart from her husband? If so, what will be her relation to her husband with respect to her property?

Topic 4:

Sub-topic 1: How many kinds of trade books are there? What are their respective names, their uses; and how long are they supposed to be preserved?

Sub-topic 2: Is there any fixed form of entries? Are different kinds of books used in different trades?

Sub-topic 3: Is the Occidental method of bookkeeping by single and double entry becoming prevalent?

Topic 5: Have merchants' trade books any legal force as evidence against another person?

Topic 6:

Sub-topic 1: Is there any difference of treatment in legal proceedings depending upon whether the trade books are properly kept?

Sub-topic 2: Is it desirable to have some fixed rules for the supervision of a merchant's books? If so, what should be the principles?

Chapter II Commercial Mortgages and Liens

Topic 1: Is there any difference between commercial and civil mortgages?

Topic 2: When an obligor does not pay his debt at the expiration of the agreed term, payment being secured by a

[1] The divisions of Book II are identical with those of Book I. See Translation Editor's Note.

mortgage, is it the usual practice for the creditor to appropriate the entire property to compensate for the loss he incurs, even when the value of the mortgaged property exceeds the amount of the debt, including its principal and interest? Or is it the custom for the creditor to sell the mortgaged property, reimburse himself out of the money received from the sale, and return the balance to the obligor?

Topic 3: When an obligor becomes insolvent, does any obligee besides the holder of a mortgage take priority[1] over other (general) creditors? (For example, is there any custom according to which a land rent,[2] a house rent,[3] an employee's wage, or money due for food supplied to the obligor, etc., takes priority over other general claims?)

Topic 4: May a merchant who is holding a mortgage given by another merchant, execute a second mortgage[4] on the security in favor of a third merchant, without obtaining the consent of the second merchant?

Chapter III Agents for Sale

Topic 1: What marks the difference between the trade of a *toiya* and that of a *nakagai*?[5]

Topic 2: Is there any class of persons who, acting as agents for sale between two parties, receive a commission, other than those who are publicly called *toiya* and *nakagai*? If there are, what are the varieties?

Topic 3: Does the agent[6] make contracts with other parties in his own name, when executing any sale or purchase transaction committed to him? Or does he act as representative of his principal[7] concluding a contract in the name of his principal?

Topic 4: If the agent advances money to his principal on goods

[1] *Sakidori-tokken.*

[2] *Jidai.*

[3] *Yachin.*

[4] *Fuku-teitô.*

[5] Literally, "middle-man."

[6] *Baikainin.*

[7] *Iraisha.*

with whose sale he is entrusted, does he have any prior claim on the proceeds to reimburse himself for the money he has advanced?

Topic 5: Is there any sort of business transaction that cannot be done except through the agency of an intermediary?

Topic 6: Are there any intermediaries who act as agents for a consignor in connection with transportation of goods, such as those who make a contract, on behalf of a consignor,[1] with a shipowner[2] or a wagon-owner?[3]

Chapter IV Selling and Buying[4]

Topic 1: Are there any practices peculiar to sales in the commercial sense, as compared with sales in the civil sense?

Topic 2: What constitutes the proof of a contract of sale? Is there any distinction between a contract for which a written instrument[5] is invariably required and one which requires none?

Topic 3: Must a sales-contract be confirmed by the payment of earnest-money?

Topic 4: When a contract of sale is made, at what time does the title to the goods pass to the vendee? And from what moment does the vendee bear the risk of loss in connection with the goods? Does it make any difference on these points whether they are specified goods [that is, goods that have specifically been designated by the vendee] or unspecified goods?

Topic 5: Is there any practice of a buyer reselling[6] goods to another merchant, by means of a manifest[7] or an invoice,[8] before the goods come into his possession?

Topic 6: Is there any practice whereby the price of goods is fixed by the parties not at the moment when a contract

[1] *Ninushi.*
[2] *Senchu.*
[3] *Shaba-mochinushi.*
[4] *Baibai.*
[5] *Shôsho.*
[6] *Matauri.*
[7] *Tsumini-mokuroku.*
[8] *Unsô-jô.*

of sale is concluded, but after the delivery of the goods? If so, how is the price fixed?

Topic 7: If the time of delivery of goods or the term of payment is not set at the time of the formation of a contract of sale, when should the delivery or payment be made?

Topic 8: Does it sometimes occur that a creditor who has a debtor's loan receipt[1] or a bill of sale[2] in his possession endorses the document and transfers his creditor-right[3] to others? In such a case, what form[4] is used? What advantages and disadvantages are derived from such a practice?

Topic 9: How many sorts of notes,[5] tickets,[6] and the like are used in commerce? Are those notes or tickets issued with government permission or by private individuals?

Topic 10: What is the ordinary time limit for the payment[7] of a commercial debt? What is the maximum time limit? What is the minimum time limit?

Topic 11: Is there any custom, in the case of several obligors in connection with a commercial sale or loan,[8] of the whole liability being jointly assumed?[9]

Topic 12: Does the word *torihiki* (transaction) in commerce include everything from the making of a sale contract to the delivery of the goods and the payment of the price? Or does it refer only to the acts carried out at the time of the delivery of the goods or the payment of the price?

Topic 13: What is the difference between a wholesale merchant[10] and a retail merchant?[11] Are there any wholesale merchants who deal only with retailers, but never directly with ordinary customers?[12]

Appendix to Chapter IV Sample forms of commercial instruments

1 *Shakuyo-shôsho.*
2 *Kaiuke-shôsho.*
3 *Saishu-ken.*
4 *Shoshiki.*
5 *Tegata.*
6 *Kitte.*
7 *Harai-kigen.*
8 *Taishaku.*
9 *Rentai-tantô.*
10 *Oroshiuri.*
11 *Kouri.*
12 *Tsûjô-nin.*

Chapter V Rescission of Contract[1]

Topic 1: When the earnest-money[2] for a sale is forfeited,[3] does the sale contract become rescissible?

Topic 2: If the amount of damages for breach of contract has not been fixed beforehand, how is the amount to be determined when such a breach takes place?

Topic 3: If the seller does not deliver goods[4] to the buyer, or the buyer does not take delivery[5] of them when the time limit is due, is the sale contract rescissible, or is it still in force?

Chapter VI Seller[6]

Topic 1: If the specifications of the goods, including their quality[7] and grade,[8] have not been named in the sales contract, what kinds[9] of goods are to be delivered by the seller to the buyer?

Topic 2: If a seller accepts an offer of a customer to buy some goods after examining the samples or the actual merchandise, is the seller under obligation not to sell the goods to another person before they have been examined by the first customer?

Topic 3: If the buyer forfeits his earnest-money when he breaks a contract, may not the seller claim damages?

Topic 4: Is the seller implied to be held to a warranty that the goods he sells are perfectly fit for use? Or does such a warranty arise only when it is expressly provided in the contract?

Topic 5: Is the sales contract valid when the vendor sells an article to which he has no title (for example, stolen goods)?

[1] *Hayaku.*
[2] *Tetsuke-kin.*
[3] *Nagareru.*
[4] *Hikiwatasu.*
[5] *Hikitoru.*
[6] *Urinushi.*
[7] *Seishitsu.*
[8] *Hin-i.*
[9] *Shinagara.*

Chapter VII Vendee

Topic 1: When the goods delivered turn out to differ from the samples on which a contract of sale has been based, is the buyer entitled, at any time, to claim replacement[1] of the goods by proper ones, or to rescind the contract?

Topic 2: Is a buyer who has offered to buy a specified article[2] from a seller free to buy it from another without the consent of the first seller before he receives the latter's reply to his offer, and then to cancel the offer with the first seller?

Topic 3: If payment of the price of an article is overdue, does any interest[3] accrue thereon? If so, from what date is the interest computed?

Topic 4: If goods which have been warranted by the seller are found to be defective,[4] is the buyer entitled, at any time, to claim replacement of them by other goods, or to rescind the sales contract?

Chapter VIII Transportation[5]

Topic 1: Is it always the practice to set a time limit for the arrival of goods in a contract of transportation? If so, what are the responsibilities of the forwarding agent?[6] If otherwise, what are his responsibilities?

Topic 2: When goods in transit are transshipped[7] from one vessel to another due to unavoidable circumstances before they reach their destination, what are the responsibilities of the second vessel?

Topic 3: When the buyer refuses to take delivery of the goods on arrival, how shall the goods be disposed of if the seller or the forwarding agent is not present on the spot?

1 *Torikae.*
2 *Kakutei-butsu.*
3 *Rishi.*
4 *Furyô.*
5 *Unsô.*
6 *Unsônin.*
7 *Tsumikae.*

Appendix to Book I. Items Not Included in the Questionnaires on Commercial Customs

(A) On Guilds of the Same Trade[1]
(B) On Negotiable Instruments[2]
  (1) Bill of Exchange[3]
  (2) Deposit Certificate for Money[4]
  (3) *Seki-dashi-tegata* (Check Addressed to Exchange Broker)
  (4) *Furisashi-gami* (Note Issued by Exchange Broker)
  (5) *O-tegata* (Bill Used for Clearing Balance)
  (6) Promissory Note[5]
  (7) Warehouse Certificate[6]
(C) On Sales and Purchases on Credit[7]
(D) Disposal of Shipwrecked Goods[8]
(E) On Employees of a Commercial House
(F) On Merchants' Books

[1] *Kabunakama.*
[2] *Tegata-ryûtsû.*
[3] *Kawase-tegata.*
[4] *Azukari-tegata.*
[5] *Nobe-tegata.*
[6] *Kura-azukari-tegata.*
[7] *Nobe-baibai.*
[8] *Nampa-sen.*

LIST OF THE TOPICS OF THE QUESTIONNAIRES IN BOOK III

Chapter I Contract[1]

Topic 1: In the absence of an express oral agreement, or a written contract between two parties, does one party's silence imply acceptance[2] of the other party's proposal in such a way as to become a binding contract?

Topic 2: What degree of care must be exercised in commercial transactions in order to protect the interests of another party?

Topic 3: 1. When a party (the first) fails to receive acceptance of his offer from another party (the second), either at once, within a specified period, or within a supposedly reasonable time,[3] should the offer be regarded as rejected?

2. If, however, the parties have been dealing with each other for a long time, may not the second party's failure to reject the offer signify, in fact, his acceptance?

Topic 4: When an offer of contract is made by one party, does it become binding from the moment when the offeree accepts it, or from the moment when the offeror[4] receives the notification of acceptance?

Topic 5: Suppose a notice of acceptance of an offer is sent to the offeror. Can the notification of acceptance be cancelled if this is done before the notice has reached the offeror, or at the same time the notice is received by the offeror?

Topic 6: When a party who receives an offer accompanied by samples, or the goods themselves, finds that the samples or goods cannot be returned to the offeror due to certain circumstances, what should the offeree do?

If the samples or goods left with the offeree cost him some expense or are lost, what should he do? If the goods are liable to perish, may the offeree sell them and keep

[1] *Keiyaku.*
[2] *Mokudaku.*
[3] *Mihakarai-kigen-nai.*
[4] *Môshikomi-nin.*

the money for the offeror?

Topic 7: After approval[1] has been given to an account, or payment based on it has been made, is it permissible to raise an objection[2] if some error of computation or some misrepresentation is subsequently found?[3]

Chapter II Performance of Contract[4]

Topic 1: It is a matter of course that the obligor must obtain the permission of the obligee[5] to fulfill a contract by delivery of goods other than those agreed upon in the contract—by fulfilling,[6] for instance, a contract for grain by delivery of dry goods; but is there any situation in which permission of this nature, though not expressed, is implied?

Topic 2: When the obligee refuses to accept without any sufficient reason an article the obligor[7] duly[8] delivers in fulfillment of a contract, how should the obligor dispose of said article? If the article is money, how should the interest accruing to it after its rejection by the obligee be treated? If it is something other than money and is impaired by delay, whose loss is it deemed to be?

Topic 3: When the obligor makes only part payment[9] without previous agreement to that effect, is the obligee allowed to reject it?

Topic 4: If the time limit set in a contract is indicated by such expressions as "for a certain number of days,"[10] "for a certain number of months,"[11] or "for a certain number of years,"[12] what date should be set as the time for

[1] *Shôdaku.*

[2] *Koshô-o-môshitateru.*

[3] *Itsuwari.*

[4] *Keiyaku-no-rikô.*

[5] *Kenrisha.*

[6] *Hensai.*

[7] *Gimusha.*

[8] *Tôzenni.*

[9] *Uchibarai.*

[10] *Nankanichi-kan.*

[11] *Nankagetsu-kan.*

[12] *Nankanen-kan.*

performing the contract? If the time limit is indicated by such expressions as "within the period of a certain number of days," or "within the period of a certain number of months," or "within the period of a certain number of years," can the contract be performed at any time within the period thus indicated, and is the obligee entitled to demand the performance of the contract at any time within the period?

Topic 5: Is the time limit set in a contract computable from the day when the contract is made, or from the day following the day when the contract is made?

Topic 6: In commercial transactions, is the period of one month or half a month computable by the number of days? Or is there any other method for its computation?

Topic 7: If the time limit set in a contract is due on a general holiday, or a local holiday, or the holiday of the store (that is, one of the parties to the contract), how should the transaction be handled?

Topic 8: In commercial transactions, is the period of one day computable by the number of hours? Or is there any other method for its computation?

Topic 9: If an extension[1] of the time limit for a contract is agreed upon but there is no stipulation as to the time when the computation of the extended period should start, is it computable from the day when the new contract about the extension is made, or from the day when the time limit set in the original contract expires?

Topic 10: If no stipulations have been made in the contract as to the place where payment should be made and received, or where the goods should be delivered or taken delivery of, where should the payment or the delivery take place?

Topic 11: If there is no specific stipulation in the contract regarding the obligation on the part of an obligor to forward goods, should the goods be forwarded to the dwelling[2] of the obligee, or to the ordinary unloading place[3] in the

[1] *Enki.*

[2] *Jûsho.*

[3] *Nioroshiba.*

locality of his abode?[1] Or is it regarded as adequate for the obligor to deliver the goods to the obligee at the ordinary unloading place of the locality of the former's abode?

Topic 12 If there is no stipulation in the contract as to the details of the method of delivery, such as weights,[2] measures,[3] tare,[4] and the like, should the customs[5] of the place of delivery[6] be followed; or should the usual practices of the forwarder,[7] or the practices usually observed in connection with goods to be delivered, be followed?

Topic 13: If one party (the first party) should happen to incur a debt to another party (the second party), and there has been no specific agreement as to how the debt should be repaid, is the first party free to repay the debt with any kind of goods he prefers? Or may the second party dictate the commodity for repayment to the first party?

Moreover, if there is a contract which specifies two articles, either of which would satisfy the terms for repayment, and both articles have been lost by the first party, how should a substitute article be decided upon?

Chapter III Restitution of Price,[8] Damages,[9] and Discount[10]

Topic 1: If the obligor does not fulfill his obligation within a prescribed time,[11] is the obligee free to rescind[12] the contract, or demand restitution of price from the obligor? If any loss results, is he entitled to demand damages for it?

Topic 2: Is any interest supposed to accrue on the recovery of the price referred to in Topic 1? If it does, from what date

[1] *Jûchi.*
[2] *Ryômoku.*
[3] *Masume.*
[4] *Fûtai.*
[5] *Shikitari.*
[6] *Hikiwatashi-chi.*
[7] *Hikiwatashi-nin.*
[8] *Kakaku-hoshô.*
[9] *Songai-baishô.*
[10] *Waribiki.*
[11] *Teiki.*
[12] *Hayaku.*

should the computation of interest commence?

Topic 3: Is any interest supposed to accrue to money one has paid on behalf of another or money advanced on behalf of another?

Topic 4: Whenever damage has been done, whether intentionally[1] or not, may compensation be claimed for it?

Topic 5: Is compensation limited to the amount of damage actually done, or does it include the probable profit that would have accrued were it not for the damage?

In the latter case, how is the amount of damage to be estimated?

Topic 6: When it is found that the amount of the price[2] or of the damages to be recovered, an amount[3] which has been agreed upon beforehand, does not conform to the current prices, what should be done?

Topic 7: If an obligor repays his debt before it falls due, is he still supposed to pay the interest that would accrue between the date of the repayment and the original date of maturity?

Or is the obligation of the payment of interest supposed to extend no further than the day when the repayment is made?

Topic 8: When a contract is rescinded due to negligence[4] on the part of an obligor, and goods which have already been delivered to the obligee are returned to the obligor, is he bound to accept the goods, as they are returned, if they are fewer than the amount delivered or if they are impaired through no fault of the obligee; or may compensation be claimed for the damage?

If the goods are to be returned to the obligee by the obligor, are goods which are reduced in quantity or damaged to be returned as they are; or should compensation be paid for the damage?

Appendix: If any expense is incurred through negligence[5] on the

[1] *Koi.*

[2] *Kakaku-hoshôgaku.*

[3] *Sonshitsu-kakaku.*

[4] *Okotari.*

[5] *Okotari.*

part of the obligor, should the amount be added to the price as provided in Topic 2? Or should a separate claim be made?

Chapter IV Penalty for Breach of Contract[1]

Topic 1: May payment of penalty for breach of contract be demanded only when it has been stipulated beforehand in the contract? When there is no previous agreement to the effect, may such penalty be demanded when an occasion therefore occurs? May it happen that penalty for breach of contract and compensation for damage in general[2] are cumulative and the use of one remedy is not taken to exclude or waive the use of another?

Topic 2: When the obligee receives penalty for breach of contract, does he still have the right to demand performance of the contract, or is this right nullified?[3]

Chapter V Agency[4]

Topic 1: Is there any situation in which agency in a commercial transaction may be assumed by one to whom no letter of attorney[5] has been issued?

Topic 2: In a business transaction in which an agent is acting on behalf of his principal,[6] which one of the two, the agent or the principal, is supposed to assume directly the rights and the obligations toward the other party?[7]

In the case of the other party concluding a transaction with an agent without knowledge of the status of the latter, what rights and obligations should the principal assume toward the other party?

Topic 3: When an agent acts beyond his powers,[8] but the other party is not aware of this, is a contract thus concluded

[1] *Iyaku-kin.*
[2] *Songai-baishô.*
[3] *Shômetsu.*
[4] *Dairi.*
[5] *Ininjô.*
[6] *Honnin.*
[7] *Aitekata.*
[8] *Kengen-o-koeru.*

between the two parties valid? If it is, what should be done about a loss incurred by the principal as a result of his agent having acted in excess of his power?

Topic 4: When an agent alone is held responsible for a business transaction which has been conducted in the name of his principal, is the principal entitled to retain the goods, if any, which have already come into his possession, or may he be dispossessed of such goods?

Although it seems apparent that the restoration of the goods to the other party should be made by the agent, does it ever happen that the other party tries to recover the goods for himself?

Topic 5: Does the delegation of authority[2] (to an agent) terminate automatically when the principal or the agent dies?

Topic 6: Is it possible for an agent to delegate to somebody else the authority which has been committed to him?

Is this possible only when the consent of the principal is obtained?

Chapter VI Account Current[3]

Topic 1: Is there any practice whereby merchants who are engaged in continuous transactions with one another, assuming in turn the roles of a creditor or a debtor, settle their accounts not at each transaction but after several months or half a year of transactions, balance and settle accounts for the whole period, or carry the balance over into next term's account?

Is this method of balancing accounts[4] (at one time for a whole period) practiced only when it is stipulated beforehand in a contract, or is it observed, even if there is no stipulation to that effect, when the mutual accounts reach a large amount?

When this practice is stipulated in a contract, what is the usual length of period for settling an account?

Is any interest supposed to accrue on this account?

[1] *Torimodosaru.*

[2] *Dairi-no-inin.*

[3] *Sogo-keisan.*

[4] *Sashihiki-kanjô.*

Appendices: (a) Time limit for initiating a lawsuit[1] (Chiba Prefecture)

(b) Conditions for the circulation of bills[2]; Advantages of bills; Disadvantages of bills (Tochigi Prefecture).

Topic 2: What degree of care must be exercised in commercial transactions in order to protect the interests of another party?

[1] *Shusso-kigen.*

[2] *Tegata.*

Law and Justice in
Tokugawa Japan

PART IV-C

CONTRACT: COMMERCIAL CUSTOMARY LAW

MATERIALS FOR THE STUDY OF PRIVATE LAW IN OLD JAPAN

PART IV
CONTRACT: COMMERCIAL CUSTOMARY LAW

BOOK III

CHAPTER I
CONTRACT

Topic 1: In the Absence of an Express Oral Agreement, or a Written Contract between Two Parties, Does One Party's Silence Imply Acceptance of the Other Party's Proposal in Such a Way As to Become a Binding Contract?[1]

Tokyo Metropolis

Prefectural Office.

Soy Wholesalers.

Silence on the part of one party is construed as rejection of the offer. Of course a contract cannot be formed.

Sugar Wholesalers.

In the case of trade with merchants in nearby districts, the contract is formed when we receive their order by mail. In trade with merchants of other prefectures, it is concluded when we receive their acceptance in writing.

Dried Bonito Wholesalers.

The silence of one party upon receipt of an offer for a contract, will be regarded as implied acceptance, on the basis of which the contract is made.

Medicine Wholesalers.

A contract is formed when two parties agree with each other clearly. Agreement is not made if one party keeps silent.

Paper Wholesalers (*Kiu-kumi*).[2]

[1] *Mokudaku;* Implied assent.

[2] *Kiu-kumi kami-donya.*

A contract is formed when an acceptance is made in writing. It cannot be formed otherwise.

Oil Wholesalers.

We have never heard of the practice of implied assent.

Stone Wholesalers.

When one party regards the other party's silence as an implied acceptance of his offer, a contract may sometimes be formed. However, this may not hold true according to the circumstances.

Fuel Wholesalers.

As some cases, it seems that the silence on the part of one party may be regarded as an implied acceptance of an offer. But this is a business tactic. And it cannot be regarded as the prevailing practice here.

Porcelain Wholesalers.

Silence is usually regarded as an implied agreement. A contract can be formed. Even if the other party rejects it several days later, he will only find it ineffective. In such cases, therefore, both parties must compromise to some degree.

Paper Wholesalers (*Shôkai-kumi*).[1]

Unless specially acknowledged in a written agreement or by express oral agreement, the silence on the part of one party cannot be regarded as implied assent. Of course a contract cannot be formed by mere silence. Under some special circumstances, however, it seems that it can be. But we have not heard of such a case here.

Rice Traders.[2]

A contract has been, and still is, formed by implied agreement. When one party fails to fulfill the contract, it becomes ineffective, unless specially provided for by an agreement in writing. The contract in the present topic of course can be formed only due to the confidence of each party in the other.

Salt Wholesalers.

A contract is regarded as binding only when each party has received the other's acknowledgement in writing.

Timber Wholesalers.

Even a commercial contract is not formed. In such cases, the

[1] *Shôkai-kumi kami-donya.*

[2] *Beikoku sangyô-kumiai.*

contract cannot be regarded as binding on a business basis without the express acceptance of the offer.

Timber Traders.[1]

In such cases, the contract cannot be considered legal or effective.

Timber Traders (*Senju*).[2]

Same as timber trader's reply immediately above.

Saké Wholesalers (*Kudari*).[3]

Every business contract must be formed by an express oral agreement or a written agreement. Silence on the part of one party can never be regarded as implied agreement by the other party.

Mosquito Net Wholesalers.

One's silence is regarded as opposition to the agreement.

Lime and Shell Wholesalers.

Unless an agreement is made in an express oral agreement or a written document, no business contract can be formed.

Copper and Iron Wholesalers.

A contract is formed either through express oral agreements or written documents. Once concluded, the stipulations of the contract should be observed and never cancelled. Cancellation would be a disgrace to all merchants. Therefore, there has never been a cancelled contract. The nonfulfillment of a contract can occur only when the goods delivered are different from those prearranged. There can be no implied agreements.

Saké Wholesalers.

In some special cases the obligor may regard his own silence as implied agreement.

Matting Wholesalers.

Silence is regarded as disagreement.

Drapery Wholesalers.

Regarding the present topic, the silence is not regarded as implied assent, and no contract will be formed.

Fuel Wholesalers (*Umite-kumi*).[4]

A contract can be formed only when the two parties give oral or written consent. When one party keeps silent, there can be no con-

[1] *Zaimoku tôsei-kumiai.*

[2] *Senju zaimoku-donya.*

[3] *Kudari sake-donya.*

[4] *Umite-kumi shintan-donya.*

tract formed.

Tobacco Wholesalers.

Every contract can be formed only through talks between the two parties, according to the circumstances at the time. There is no established practice.

Kôjimachi Ward.

Implied agreement is sometimes considered acceptable between merchants who have been engaged in continuous transactions therefore. But it has never been considered legally binding.

Nihombashi Ward.

In business transactions, silence on the part of one party has never been regarded as an implied agreement.

Kyôbashi Ward.

Unless the two parties agree with each other, there can be no contract.

Yotsuya Ward and Ushigome Ward.

There can be no contract unless the two parties agree with each other orally or in writing.

Asakusa Ward.

Silence cannot be regarded as implied agreement and no contract can be formed.

Honjo Ward.

Silence can never be regarded as implied agreement, and no contract can be formed in the absence of an express oral or written agreement between the parties.

Ebara *kôri*.

Silence can never be regarded as implied agreement, and no contract can be formed without an express oral or written agreement between the parties.

Higashi-tama *kôri* and Minami-toshima *kôri*.

When one party keeps silent from the beginning of a transaction, the silence cannot be interpreted as implied agreement.

Kita-toshima *kôri*.

Unless the two parties (the contractors themselves or their employees) agree orally or in writing, no contract can be formed. Even after they have exchanged letters, no contract can be formed if either of them fails to get approval from the other.

Minami-adachi *kôri*.

Such a practice is not known here.

Shitaya Ward.

Although one party may fail to obtain an answer from the other party within a certain period of time, such silence on the part of the other party cannot be regarded as an implied agreement unless specially provided for beforehand.

Kanda Ward.

Silence cannot be regarded as an implied agreement and no contract can be formed.

Akasaka Ward and Azabu Ward.

Silence can sometimes be regarded as implied agreement and it is possible to conclude a contract on such consent.

Hongô Ward.

Silence can be regarded as implied agreement and the contract can be formed.

CHIBA PREFECTURE

Awa *kôri*, Hei *kôri*, Asai *kôri* and Nagasa *kôri*.

The contract in business is considered concluded when one party pays the other party a deposit. Merchants of good faith conscientiously fulfill their agreement even if they have made it only in speech or, sometimes, not in speech but only by clapping their hands. When one party keeps silent, a contract cannot be formed. This may sometimes occur, but such a case has never been heard of.

Katori *kôri*.

According to our practice, a contract cannot be formed if one party remains silent.

Yamabe *kôri* and Muza *kôri*.

A contract cannot be formed if one party remains silent.

Higashi-katsushika *kôri*.

Silence is sometimes regarded as implied agreement.

Unakami *kôri* and Sôsa *kôri*.

A contract cannot be formed when one party remains silent.

IBARAKI PREFECTURE

Nishi-katsushika *kôri* and Sashima *kôri*.

A contract cannot be formed unless the two parties agree in speech or in writing.

KANAGAWA PREFECTURE

Miura *kôri*.

In business transactions, the contract can be formed only when it is agreed upon in speech. Silence cannot be regarded as implied agreement.

Tachibana *kôri*.

If one party remains silent, such silence cannot be regarded as implied agreement.

Kita-tama *kôri*.

If one party remains silent, such silence cannot be regarded as implied agreement.

Ashigara-shimo *kôri*.

According to local practice, a contract can be formed when two parties agree in speech or in writing. If one party remains silent, it cannot always be regarded as implied acceptance. But we hear that it sometimes can be.

Prefectural Industrial Bureau.

A business contract can be formed only when two parties agree in speech or in writing. When the parties are in a hurry, a contract is usually formed by oral agreement. If one party remains silent, the other party does not regard the silence as implied acceptance to create a binding contract.

TOCHIGI PREFECTURE

Prefectural Office.

A contract cannot be formed unless the two parties express their agreement.

Shimo-tsuga *kôri* and Samukawa *kôri*.

According to our practices today, silence can never be regarded as implied agreement.

Ashikaga *kôri* and Yanada *kôri*.

Silence can never be regarded as implied agreement.

MIE PREFECTURE

Suzuka *kôri*.

A commercial contract can be formed only when two parties reach agreement in speech or in writing. Silence on the part of one party cannot be regarded by the other party as implied agreement upon which a formal contract can be concluded.

Ichishi *kôri*.

A contract cannot be formed.

Nabari *kôri* and Iga *kôri*.

A commercial contract is usually made when two parties agree with each other either verbally or in writing. Regarding implied assent, suppose a seller has sent his goods at his own judgement to his buyer without waiting for the latter's order. At such times the buyer often, without taking the trouble of making acceptance or rejection, receives the goods at the seller's own limits. Let us suppose, too, that a seller who has received an order from his buyer has sent the latter the goods, but has only informed him of his willingness to send a list of prices in a few days. Does this mean an implied agreement on the part of the buyer?

Kita-muro *kôri*.

Even when one party remains silent, in the case of trade between the mechants of long standing, the silence may sometimes be regarded as an implied assent on which a contract is made. But, in other cases, a contract cannot be formed.

AICHI PREFECTURE

Nakajima *kôri*.

A contract can be formed.

Nagoya Ward.

When one party keeps silent, the other party cannot regard this as implied agreement upon which a contract can be concluded.

Chita *kôri*.

The contract can never be formed; the silence cannot be regarded as an implied agreement.

Minami-shidara *kôri*.

Such a case of tacit consent has never been heard of. Probably the agreement will not be recognized as a binding contract.

Atsumi *kôri*.

A contract can be formed only when the two parties agree in speech or in writing.

Kaitô *kôri* and Kaisai *kôri*.

When one party remains silent, the other party cannot regard such silence as implied agreement to the contract.

Aichi *kôri*.

When one party remains silent, such silence cannot be regarded as implied agreement. The contract cannot be formed.

Niwa *kôri* and Haguri *kôri*.

In commercial transactions, silence on the part of one party cannot be regarded as implied agreement. There can be no contract if either party is silent.

SHIZUOKA PREFECTURE

Prefectural Office.

According to local practice, such behavior cannot be regarded as implied agreement.

Udo *kôri* and Abe *kôri.*

In the case of joint obligation, when one or two of the joint debtors present remain silent, the silence is sometimes regarded as an implied assent to create a contract.

Inasa *kôri* and Aratama *kôri.*

The silence cannot be regarded as an implied agreement. No contract can be formed.

Kamo *kôri* and Naka *kôri.*

In one situation an agent may be asked by a seller or a buyer to draw up the contract in the presence of the two parties. However, in watching the agent draw up the contract, silence on the part of either the seller or the buyer will be regarded as implied assent. In a second situation, two groups of sellers and buyers meet in order to conclude a contract. While the two persons representing the groups are acting, all others in attendance remain silent, and such silence is also regarded as implied assent.

Saya *kôri* and Kitô *kôri.*

With only a few exceptions, a contract cannot be formed when either of the two parties remains silent. In addition to agreements by speech or in writing, a contract can be agreed upon by two parties if they agree on the price as expressed by finger-signals or on the abacus,[1] such consent being demonstrated by clapping hands.

GIFU PREFECTURE

Mugi *kôri.*

A contract can be formed only when the two parties agree in an oral statement or in a written document.

Ampachi *kôri.*

A contract cannot be agreed to by silence. Silence does not represent implied agreement, in ordinary usage.

Fuwa *kôri.*

A contract cannot be formed unless the two parties agree with each other expressly.

Atsumi *kôri*, Kagami *kôri* and Katagata *kôri.*

[1] This is a traditional business practice used to show the price when the two parties concerned do not want the details of their agreement known to the other people present.

In the case when merchant A sends goods and a bill to merchant B, if the latter receives them without making any reply, his silence is to be regarded as acceptance.

Tagi *kôri* and Kami-ishizu *kôri.*

In business, silence cannot be regarded as implied agreement.

Ôno *kôri* and Ikeda *kôri.*

A business contract can usually be formed when two parties agree in an oral statement or a written document. In the case of trade of long standing, however, the one party sometimes regards the other party's silence as implied agreement.

Haguri *kôri* and Nakajima *kôri.*

The silence is, in most cases, regarded as implied assent.

Ena *kôri.*

Besides verbal or written consent, merchants enter into a contract for sale by clapping their hands. Mere silence is not construed as acceptance.

Kamo *kôri.*

A contract can usually be formed when two parties agree in either an oral or written statement. Sometimes, however, silence is regarded as implied agreement between two parties that have been engaged in transactions for many years and know each other closely, provided the prices of the goods have not been fluctuating greatly.

Kani *kôri.*

We have never heard of a case in which silence was regarded as indicative of implied assent.

Atsumi *kôri*, Gifu Township.

In most cases, the contract is not formed. However, suppose merchant A has sent goods to a second merchant B, together with a list of the prices of the goods and the message: "Is it possible for you to buy these goods? If it isn't, can you transfer them to C immediately? If you cannot do either, please send them back to me." If B fails to answer within the period of time specified by A, B is considered to have accepted the goods unconditionally, and the contract is considered binding. Let us look at another case. Merchant A, offering prices, has ordered some goods from merchant B. And let us further suppose that A writes to B: "If you cannot fill my order, please answer as early as possible." If B fails to answer, B is understood to have agreed to supply A, and the contract is formed.

Ôgaki.

We usually do not form a contract on the basis of silence.

Ena *kôri*, Nakatsugawa Village.

Even in the case when the offeree keeps silent without making any oral express, if he makes some gesture of assent, for instances, giving a nod or clapping the hands, his silence is construed as the implied acceptance to make the contract.

Shimo-ishizu *kôri*, Takasu Township.

Silence cannot be regarded as implied acceptance to form a contract.

Haguri *kôri*, Takegahana Village.

We have never heard of silence being regarded as an implied acceptance.

Yamagata *kôri*, Takatomi Village.

If one party remains silent, a contract cannot be formed.

Mugi *kôri*, Kôzuchi Village.

Only when two parties agree in an oral or written agreement can a contract be formed. The silence of one party cannot be taken as an implied assent, and a contract cannot be formed.

Haguri *kôri*, Kasamatsu Village.

We can usually enter into a contract by silence as a form of implied assent.

Fuwa *kôri*, Tarui Village.

A contract can never be formed unless the offeree makes an express acceptance.

Ôno *kôri*, Miwa Village.

If one party remains silent, not making any spoken or written statement, such silence can be regarded as implied assent, and a contract can be formed.

Ampachi *kôri*, Gôdo Village.

Such silence cannot be regarded as implied acceptance, and the contract cannot be formed.

Tagi *kôri*, Shimada Village.

Such practices of implied assent cannot be found here.

Ena *kôri*, Iwa Village.

Such silence cannot be regarded as implied acceptance.

Kamo *kôri*, Hosome Village.

Such cases of tacit consent can sometimes be found between merchants who have dealings of long standing with each other unless the goods in question are of a special kind. A contract cannot be formed, however, if the prices of the goods fluctuate irregularly. The transaction must then be done in cash.

Toki *kôri*, Takayama Village.

The silence is sometimes regarded as implied assent to a contract, according to the local practice.

Kani *kôri*, Mitake Village.

Silence can be regarded as implied acceptance of the offer.

Ena *kôri*, Akechi Village.

A contract is occasionally formed by hand-clapping, besides express oral or written acceptance. Mere silence, however, cannot be regarded as implied assent.

Mugi *kôri*, Seki Village.

When one party keeps silent, it is assumed that he disagrees. A contract can never be formed on the basis of silence.

Ôno *kôri*, Takayama Township.

A contract can be formed only when the two parties agree by verbal or written agreement. In case of silence as an implied assent, the acceptance should be recorded in a written instrument.

Motosu *kôri*, Kitagata Village.

In commercial transactions, a contract is usually formed when two parties agree in speech or in writing. However, even if one party remains silent, a contract is occasionally formed, and in such cases silence is regarded as implied assent.

Kamo *kôri*, Ota Village.

A contract is usually formed by an oral or written agreement. Silence on the part of one party may be regarded as implied agreement by the other party, if the two have had a business relationship of long and close standing. However, this does not apply if the goods they handle are of a special category.

Kaisai *kôri* and Shimo-ishizu *kôri*.

In such cases, silence cannot be regarded as an implied acceptance. A contract cannot be formed.

Gujô *kôri*.

A contract can be formed only when two parties make an oral or written agreement. If one party remains silent, a contract cannot be formed; silence cannot be regarded as an implied assent.

Topic 2: What Degree of Care Must Be Exercised in Commercial Transactions in Order to Protect the Interests of Another Party?

Tokyo Metropolis

Prefectural Office.

Paper Wholesalers (*Kiu-kumi*).

In the case of trade with merchants in the Tokyo metropolis, the buyer and seller take 70 percent of the responsibility for damage in transit, and the carrier, 30 percent.

Oil Wholesalers.

When the seller is in charge of the carriage of the goods, damage in transit is made good by him. If the buyer is in charge, the responsibility rests with him.

Stone Wholesalers.

Suppose a merchant has sold a customer 100 stone pillars, and a few pillars suffer some damage in transit. The seller sometimes exchanges the damaged pillars for new ones. However, when the seller makes delivery of the goods to the buyer at the seller's shop, the seller is free from any responsibility.

Medicine Wholesalers.

According to the practice prevailing here in the Tokyo area, the loss should be covered by the seller.

Sugar Wholesalers.

As long as the seller has not yet secured the impress of the buyer's seal in the *hantori-chô*, which is used to be sealed upon receipt of goods delivered, the loss should be covered by the seller. If the delivery of the goods has been made at the seller's shop, the buyer assumes responsibility for damage in transit.

Dried Bonito Wholesalers.

In the case of goods to be delivered to the buyer's shop by the seller (*okuri-tsuke-buppin*), the seller assumes responsibility for damage in transit. In the case of goods whose delivery is made at the seller's shop (*kai-tsuke-buppin*), the buyer is to assume the damage. According to the circumstances, the two may share the responsibility through talks between them. The carrier sometimes takes a part of the responsibility.

Soy Wholesalers.

Suppose a seller has concluded a contract with a buyer. If the cart for the carriage is the seller's, he is to be blamed for the damage done to the goods in transit. If the cart belongs to the buyer, he will bear the responsibility. When the forwarding agent acts for the two, he is to bear responsibility for the damage.

Timber Wholesalers.

Suppose some cargo is damaged in transit, for instance, at sea. If the buyer has not taken delivery of the cargo, the responsibilities for the damage rest with the seller. However, if the buyer has already taken delivery, he is to bear the responsibilities. The conveyer, boatman or cartman, occasionally will be held responsible according to the degree to which he caused the damage, or according to the degree to which the consignee has agreed to share the responsibility. In the case of unavoidable damages, a special meeting will be held among the seller, the buyer and the forwarding agent, with a view to making settlement jointly.

Timber Traders.

Those in the timber trade all make it a guiding principle to do business sincerely and to do their best in handling goods and making transactions. As timber is not easily damaged, there is no settled practice about the matter queried in the present topic. If the goods should be damaged in transit, either by cart or by ship, the damages are borne as follows. If the goods have not yet been delivered to the buyer, the responsibility is solely upon the seller. According to the circumstances, there may be deliberations between the two parties. In some cases, the conveyer, a boatman or a cartman, is to be blamed to some extent.

Timber Traders.

Even after the sales contract of the goods has been concluded, the seller shall assume responsibility for damages in transit. However, if goods are carried by the buyer's cart or ship, the responsibility rests with the buyer. The forwarding agent is free from any responsibility. But sometimes he may be blamed for the loss, as the case may be.

Fuel Wholesalers.

With regard to the present topic, the wholesaler makes the delivery and the receipt of the goods at his yard (*tonya-okiba*), according to the practice here. Hence, when goods are delivered from the place of production to the wholesaler, transit damage caused by accident, for instance at sea, as well as the cost for the transportation rests not with the wholesaler, but with the consignor and the carrier (*sendô*). If a small quantity of the goods are found to be missing when the shipment is landed at the port, the wholesaler receives compensation money for the damage (*benshô-kin*) from the carrier, then hands it to the consignor, at the time of settling the account. If a great quantity of the goods are found to be missing, according to custom a final settlement about the loss is reached after he informs the consignor of the fact. The delivery of the goods from the wholesaler to the retail merchant also has long been made at the wholesaler's yard, which is called the *niwa-barai*. If goods are missing, lost or found short due to shipwreck, collision or theft, etc., while being transported by the wholesaler (seller), the responsibility is solely upon the seller. If the goods are being transported by the buyer, he is solely liable for the kinds of damage mentioned above. Unless such damage is caused by deliberate negligence, the conveyer will not be blamed.

Porcelain Wholesalers.

The obligations under a contract are stipulated in the contract itself. So it is rather impossible to make a general statement about the matter. However, there are some old customs. In the case when goods in straw bags are to be delivered from the seller to the buyer, sometimes there is a breakage allowance of 7, 5 or 3 percent of the original price. The discount rate, however, is fixed according to the case, and there is no established practice. If the goods suffer any damage in transit due to shipwreck, etc., the two parties bear the loss equally, although sometimes only one of them covers it. This is also a matter to be settled by deliberations between the two and no definite practice seems to be established.

Paper Wholesalers (*Shôkai-kumi*).

When the wholesaler enters into a contract with the buyer and delivers goods to him, if the buyer is in Tokyo metropolis, the former is held responsible for the damage in transit. But sometimes the carrier also bears a part of the responsibility. If a contract of sale is formed with a local customer of many years (a buyer coming from a distant village, town, or province to renew his stock), the seller is obliged to convey the goods to a transporting agent in the metropolis named by the buyer. (This way of delivery is called *ibarai* for selling, and *niwa-chaku* for buying.) When the wholesaler concludes a contract with the consignor in the local district (the merchant who carries the goods from the place of production to the wholesalers in Tokyo and settles the account), damage in transit, on either sea or land, caused by an unavoidable accident is borne by the two in accordance with the contract (the consignor is held responsible for 60 or 70 percent of the damage, and the wholesaler 30 or 40 percent). Even when not clearly stipulated, the division of responsibility seems to fall within the above guidelines, judged by recent practice. If the damage is small, it will be borne by the boatman.

Rice Traders.

The role of the rice trader, inasmuch as he concludes the contract for sale with the buyer, is to ascertain the receiver or receiving agent of the buyer, and the unit of measurement, then to deliver the goods at his storehouse or shop front. Any damage to the goods thereafter due to accidents on land does not rest with the seller. In the case of a reduction in weight, the loss is shared by the two evenly. As for the retail merchant, the wholesaler sometimes allows him to take away a little more than the stipulated weight, if there is some prospect of the price rising.

Salt Wholesalers.

We need not assume such responsibility.

Saké Wholesalers.

Theoretically, the carrier should assume such responsibility. However, being unable to do so in most cases, he discusses the settlement in deliberations with the seller or the buyer, or sometimes both of them. In general, the consignor assumes responsibility.

Tobacco Wholesalers.

If there is any damage in transit, the two parties will deliberate on how to settle the matter, much as they did in concluding the contract.

Kudari Saké Wholesalers.

In as much as a contract has been concluded, the title to the goods has been transferred to the buyer. Theoretically, therefore, the seller is not responsible for the damage in transit. Since the goods are delivered, by land or sea, the carrier should be held responsible. However, the seller and buyer sometimes bear the loss evenly, depending on the case.

Mosquito Net Wholesalers.

According to Clause XIV of the articles of our association, when goods are sold and delivered, any damage in transit should be covered by the buyer, not the wholesaler.

Lime and Shell Wholesalers.

When the buyer and seller enter into a contract of sale and the goods are delivered by land, if the seller is in charge of the transportation, he is held responsible for the damage in transit. On the other hand, if the buyer is in charge of the carriage, the loss rests with him. In the case of conveyance by river boat, the forwarding agent assumes responsibility for damage due to his own negligence. However damage done to the goods due to an accident beyond his control, a storm, for instance, rests with both seller and buyer. Or, it is borne equally by the conveyer and the merchant, when moral obligation so dictates. Even in a case when only one party is liable to bear the full loss, the other party will bear a part of loss. However, in cash trading, the seller assumes no responsibility after he delivers the goods to the buyer.

Copper and Iron Wholesalers.

When a wholesaler receives an order from a cutomer of long standing who lives in or outside Tokyo, he selects the goods, packs and delivers the same by sea or by land at the current price. Furthermore he immediately sends a detailed current price list to the buyer. As for payment, there are some cases of partial payment, namely, in the case of payment by cash, as well as payment on credit. Regarding damage in transit, we wholesalers, called *Kyûten-gumi*, carry the goods to forwarding agents by sea or by land, or, at the convenience of the buyer, load the same on the buyer's cart. In either case, once the goods have left our yards, the buyer assumes any responsibility, according to the old custom in our trade, called *niwa-barai*. However, sometimes we may bear some responsibility, according to the circumstances. The forwarding agent may also bear a part of the loss, as the case may be.

Matting Wholesalers.

Clause XIII of the articles of our association states: "Whatever loss may occur in transit, if it occurs after the goods have been sold and delivered, the buyer alone is to assume responsibility." The buyer, therefore, has to bear the total loss.

Drapery Wholesalers.

Total responsibility for the loss referred to in the present topic rests with the buyer. However, depending on the case, the seller may share some responsibility with the buyer. If the damage results from the negligence of the forwarding agent, he becomes responsible.

Fuel Wholesalers (*Umite-kumi*).

Accidental damage in transit is to be borne by the party who is in charge of the transportation. In special cases, however, the seller and the buyer may share the responsibility. The circumstances being different in each case, it is impossible to establish a definite rule. If the damage is due to the intent or negligence of the forwarding agent, responsibility is to be borne by him.

Kôjimachi Ward.

The duty of the seller to take care of the goods ends when he completes the delivery of the same to the buyer.

Nihombashi Ward.

There is no definite, established rule. However, the seller has the duty to inform his customer of such things as, for instance, that the goods are well packed for shipment, and that the ship that will carry them is safe, as well as of the length of time the goods will remain unspoiled, if they are perishable.

Kyôbashi Ward.

There is a great variety of customs in such dealings, so a definite rule cannot be established. We cannot give any definite answer.

Yotsuya Ward and Ushigome Ward.

Answer missing.

Asakusa Ward.

No definite rule can be established; the circumstances differ according to the situation.

Honjo Ward.

Sincerity should be a guiding principle for all merchants in trading their goods.

Ebara *kôri*.

No definite rule can be found; the duties vary according to the circumstances under which people are placed.

Higashi-tama *kôri* and Minami-toshima *kôri*.

We cannot give a clear statement regarding the present topic. The seller always pays attention to the market, and when, for instance, he finds prices are climbing, he advises the buyer to buy the goods as soon as possible. If he finds that prices are declining rapidly, he advises the buyer to sell his stock as soon as possible.

Kita-toshima *kôri.*

If the pawnshop loses something by fire, the pawn-broker will lose the money which otherwise he would have gotten, and the borrower will lose his article. This is an established practice and applies to the case of a person borrowing money by placing something for security which is subsequently lost.

Minami-adachi *kôri.*

No definite answer can be given.

Shitaya Ward.

There is no settled practice about the extent of care in commercial affairs that one is supposed to take in connection with another's interest. It depends on the moral sense of each merchant.

Kanda Ward.

In the case of dealings in dangerous or perishable goods, the seller must maintain such goods carefully and deliver them to his buyer with a clear statement about their condition.

Akasaka Ward and Azabu Ward.

The goods of others should be handled in the same way as we treat our own goods.

Hongô Ward.

In general, the responsibility rests with the seller until the time when the goods are delivered to the buyer. The extent of responsibility differs according to the time and the place.

CHIBA PREFECTURE

Awa *kôri*, Hei *kôri*, Asai *kôri* and Nagasa *kôri.*

Answers missing.

Katori *kôri.*

Answer missing.

Yamabe *kôri* and Muza *kôri.*

Answers missing.

Higashi-katsushika *kôri.*

There is no definite responsibility, although there may be some responsibility involved.

Unakami *kôri* and Sôsa *kôri.*

Answers missing.

IBARAKI PREFECTURE

Nishi-katsushika *kôri* and Sashima *kôri.*

In connection with the other's interests the seller's duty is limited to paying attention to the current prices and market situation.

KANAGAWA PREFECTURE

Miura *kôri*.

Every transaction should be conducted with sincerity.

Tachibana *kôri*.

Responsibility rests with the seller until the time when the goods are received by the buyer. Suppose a fodder broker, acting on behalf of his principal, promises to buy fodder at a certain price and, after checking the weight delivers the goods to the principal. Upon receipt of the goods, the seller's responsibility ends.

Kita-tama *kôri*.

To what degree such responsibility should be assumed is not definitely known, because there are various customs which differ from one another. As a general rule, it is not very different from what is seen in civil affairs.

Ashigara-shimo *kôri*.

Regarding the present topic of the care the seller is supposed to take, firstly he must be sincere not to loose his credit in commercial transactions. Hence, he pays attention to the selection and warranty of the goods.

Prefectural Industrial Bureau.

Goods which are to be delivered to the buyer or goods on consignment[1] must be securely kept with ordinary care, regardless of whether such care profits only the seller or only the consignee, or both of them.

TOCHIGI PREFECTURE

Prefectural Office.

When a buyer receives goods with which he is dissatisfied, he can ask the seller to exchange them for others within a period of three days. In the case of goods made to order, the two parties concerned make the necessary arrangements in advance, and at the time the contract is concluded they clarify how the goods are to be treated. Great care must be taken in packaging to prevent the goods from getting wet from rain in transit.

Shimo-tsuga *kôri* and Samukawa *kôri*.

It is a guiding principle among us traders that credit with the public must be maintained and no damage of any kind shifted to

[1] Such commodities as silk or tea.

the customers.

Ashikaga *kôri* and Yanada *kôri*.

There is no established practice regarding the degree of care one is obliged to take. Even if one should fail to carry out his responsibility, none coud blame him. What we can say about this is that a man of honesty is able to enjoy prosperous business, while a dishonest man is not. Although there is a variety of different cases, let us give one particular example. Suppose a textile broker is asked by a merchant to conclude a contract to buy with a certain maker. At some point the broker may tell the merchant by telegram or mail not to buy the product from a maker A, with whom he has had business for many years, but to buy it from a second maker, B,[1] because the product of maker A is inferior to that of maker B. In another case, the broker may inform the merchant of recent market trends, and tell him to cancel an order with a maker. In general, the textile broker, as stated above in Business Procedures, makes it a rule to deliver the goods ex seller's yard,[2] after which he is free from all responsibility for any possible loss in transit. And yet the broker will spare no trouble to carry the goods to a place of loading or port several miles away, if the buyer wishes to receive them as early as possible.[3] In a word, it is the broker who is most careful in doing business.[4]

MIE PREFECTURE

Suzuka *kôri*.

No definite rule will be established, unless there is an agreement between the two. The goods, even if they are owned by others, should be handled with the same caution as that given goods owned by oneself.

Ichishi *kôri*.

We cannot give a definite answer, as the circumstances differ from one party to another. It depends, apart from the commodities that are being handled, on how and when the contract is concluded.

[1] Merchants usually issue an order for a product which they refer to as the product of maker so-and-so.

[2] *Niwa-barai*.

[3] This case is often seen in dealings in silk thread.

[4] This case is rarely seen among brokers who themselves are engaged in selling and buying.

Nabari *kôri* and Iga *kôri*.

Even after concluding a contract with the buyer, the seller has a duty to keep the goods in the best possible condition, if he has not yet delivered them. If the goods are delivered to the buyer before the specified time, the buyer also has a duty to keep the same in the best possible position. In addition, the seller and the buyer must inform each other moment by moment about price fluctuations. However, there is no definite rule concerning extent of care to be taken.

Kita-muro *kôri*.

A seller should never do anything wrong and should endeavor not to deliver to his buyer any crude goods or fakes, even if the latter is not aware of what he is being sold.

AICHI PREFECTURE

Nakajima *kôri*.

All kinds of information about the business transaction should be exchanged between the two parties.

Nagoya Ward.

Of course, there are obligations to be met. No definite rule, however, can be established; people vary greatly in their opinions.

Chita *kôri*.

The guiding principle for us is fulfillment of the contract—completing delivery within the specified period of time and paying the utmost care to preserving the goods from damage or decay. Needless to add, attention should be given to preventing fire, flooding and theft.

Minami-shidara *kôri*.

No definite rule can be set since there are so many cases, each different from the other.

Atsumi *kôri*.

If we see someone falling into a trick, or making a dangerous contract due to his poor knowledge of the market, we shall warn him against such dangers and thereby help make the work happier and more pleasant.

Kaitô *kôri* and Kaisai *kôri*.

In the commercial world, of course, there is something known as duty. But no definite rule exists.

Aichi *kôri*.

No definite rules exist here. The most important thing for us, as traders, to remember, however, is that the goods should always be kept safe and secure so that the buyer can conduct his business with the utmost convenience. But no standard rules have been set up.

Niwa *kôri* and Haguri *kôri*.

Sincerity is the most important thing in business affairs.

SHIZUOKA PREFECTURE

Prefectural Office.

No clear-cut rule exists regarding duties not specified in the contract.

Udo *kôri* and Abe *kôri*.

There is no fixed custom in this regard.

Inasa *kôri* and Aratama *kôri*.

No standard practice exists.

Kamo *kôri* and Naka *kôri*.

The seller's duties include: (1) clarification of quality; and (2) oral and written statements on how to use and keep the articles being sold.

Saya *kôri* and Kitô *kôri*.

The seller's duties here are: (1) the fulfillment of the contract without fail; (2) the maintenance in good condition of the articles under contract; (3) the preservation of qualitative similarity between the merchandise and the sample; (4) the clarification of quality differences; (5) the avoidance of any tacit damage to the other party; and (6) fulfillment of one's duties to the end if something goes wrong with regard to one's business.

GIFU PREFECTURE

Mugi *kôri*.

No definite rule can be established; there are many different cases, according to the person and the time.

Ampachi *kôri*.

People do not agree, and thus no definite rule exists. But it is generally thought that the seller ought to: (1) keep his merchandise in good condition; (2) make efforts to improve it; (3) let the other party know how prices are fluctuating; (4) pay attention to the other party's attitude; and (5) take care that a safe means of conveyance is provided.

Fuwa *kôri*.

A trader's duties with respect to his business are so wide ranging that they cannot be stated simply. But generally they will involve: (1) restraint in handling bad articles; (2) fulfillment of credit obligations with the public without fail and utmost effort to achieve his final aim; (3) thinking not only of the present in the pursuit of profits; and (4) the maintenance of merchandise in good condition. There are no special responsibilities unless otherwise provided.

Atsumi *kôri*, Kagami *kôri* and Katagata *kôri*.

No definite rules are known here.

Tagi *kôri* and Kami-ishizu *kôri*.

Examples are refusal to handle bad merchandise and the conduct of business in a fair way.

Ôno *kôri* and Ikeda *kôri*.

No definite rule exists. There are many cases and many opinions, each different from the other. As a matter of principle, however, the trader must respect his credit relationships with others. It is most unworthy of a trader to use any trick for his own benefit, or to look only to his own interests.

Haguri *kôri* and Nakajima *kôri*.

The most important duty for a trader is to let the other party know about the market each day. He should not think only of his own commission.

Ena *kôri*.

A trader should make it a practice to do business in a fair way, not thinking only of his own income.

Kamo *kôri*.

The duty of a trader toward the public is restricted to narrow limits. For example, if someone's merchandise sustains damage due to fire, flooding, or theft, the trader in charge of the merchandise should notify the owner without delay.

Kani *kôri*.

Articles should be well packed lest they be damaged in transport, and proper steps should be taken to have a reliable forwarding agent handle them. If one knows that the articles have not reached the other party, one should make an immediate investigation.

Atsumi *kôri*, Gifu Township.

There is no definite rule.

Ôgaki.

People differ greatly in their opinions. Thus, no definite rule can be stated. In these parts one must generally (1) keep articles in good condition; (2) make efforts to improve them; (3) let the other party know how the prices are fluctuating; (4) pay attention to the other party's action; (5) provide safe conveyance.

Ena *kôri*, Nakatsugawa Village.

One's duty is limited to keeping the articles in good condition.

Shimo-ishizu *kôri*, Takasu Township.

Regarding the present topic, one is supposed to treat other's goods as carefully as he treats his own.

Haguri *kôri*, Takegahana Village.

With regard to the present topic the extent of care one is supposed to take is not defined. Hence, we cannot state anything about this matter.

Yamagata *kôri*, Takatomi Village.

No limits can be placed upon one's duties.

Mugi *kôri*, Kôzuchi Village.

Such cases are unknown in this area.

Haguri *kôri*, Kasamatsu Village.

One of the most important duties is to let the other party know the market situation each day. A merchant should never think only of his own commission.

Fuwa *kôri*, Tarui Village.

Let us inform you of the following example. Suppose a trader, who deals in textile or tea, is on the brink of bankruptcy because he does not take much interest in trade and only attends to routine business. Such poor management will be a heavy blow not only for the district itself, but also for the whole country. However, another person decides to make every effort to revive the business once more, perhaps making his own investments for better management and a more extensive market. With a loan at a lower interest rate, he starts out by himself to take over the firm's management. Can this be called his "obligation"? Another example involves two traders, A and B, who are about to stop negotiations because A wishes to sell something for ¥5.00, and B insists that A reduce the price to ¥4.50. Just then, a third person intervenes and suggests that the dispute be settled with ¥0.15 of the difference between the two prices being made up by the seller, ¥0.15 by the buyer, and ¥0.20 by the third person himself. Is this also another example of duty? A third example supposes two dealers who are handling groceries and sugar. Both are going to Osaka to stock up on goods.

Then the price of silver abroad rises sharply, making it impossible for the grocer to buy. Just at that time, the grocer hears that the price of sugar is going down, an opportune development for the sugar dealer who is then short of funds. The sugar dealer, with a loan from the grocer, takes a chance and buys sugar in great quantity. A few days afterwards, sugar prices sharply rise, enabling him to make a good profit. This obligation applies to the public, too.

Ôno *kôri*, Miwa Village.

We have never heard of this kind of example here.

Ampachi *kôri*, Gôdo Village.

People differ in their opinions, no definite rule having been established.

Tagi *kôri*, Shimada Village.

Such examples are unknown here.

Ena *kôri*, Iwa Village.

Outside the realm of financial affairs, too, there are duties to be performed.

Kamo *kôri*, Hosome Village.

Each party is duty bound to inform the other of fluctuations in prices, to deliver messages for persons on a trip, and to help in case of fire or flood, if he happens to be there at the time.

Toki *kôri*, Takayama Village.

Of course each party is duty bound to help the other. However, there is no definite clarification of extent.

Kani *kôri*, Mitake Village.

We can reach no conclusion.

Ena *kôri*, Akechi Village.

Regardless of his profit and loss, it is the duty of the one party to inform the other party of an accident.

Mugi *kôri*, Seki Village.

Duties arising from a commercial affair include: (1) the avoidance of articles of poor quality so as not to swerve from his obligation, and lose a final aim; (2) the pursuit of the long-run profits without thinking only of the present; (3) care in packing;[1] (4) the fulfillment of contracts; (5) the repayment of loans; (6) the supply of information about market fluctuations to the other party.

[1] *Nizukuri.*

Ôno *kôri*, Takayama Township.

Most important in business affairs is the close relationship based upon friendship. If asked by the other party for some business, we should make every effort to do it successfully. Negotiations should be stopped only when no agreement can be reached in spite of each other's repeated efforts.

Motosu *kôri*, Kitagata Village.

Duties or obligations arising in commercial affairs cannot be so clearly defined. It is quite enough to do one's business in a fair way as provided for in the commercial law.

Kamo *kôri*, Ôta Village.

When some damage to articles owned by another party occurs, due to fire, flooding, or theft, the party taking charge of the articles should inform the owner without a moment's delay. Such are the customs here.

Kaisai *kôri* and Shimo-ishizu *kôri*.

One is to make every effort to avoid goods of poor quality and loss each other and to fulfill his contract successfully.

Gujô *kôri*.

We have no answer.

Topic 3:

Subtopic 1: When a Party (the First) Fails to Receive Acceptance of His Offer from Another Party (the Second), Either at once, within a Specified Period, or within a Supposedly Reasonable Time,[1] Should the Offer Be Regarded as Rejected?

Subtopic 2: If, However, the Parties Have Been Dealing with Each Other for a Long Time, May Not the Second Party's Failure to Reject the Offer Signify, in Fact, His Acceptance?

TOKYO METROPOLIS

Prefectural Office.

Paper Wholesalers (*Kiu-kumi*).[2]

Regarding the former half of the topic, if one party makes an offer, and the other party fails to notify the first party of his acceptance, the offer should be regarded as rejected. But, with regard to the latter half of the topic, if the offeree fails to express his rejection, the offer should be regarded as accepted.

Oil Wholesalers.

As for the first half of the topic, it is regarded as rejected. As for the second case, it is also regarded as rejected.

Stone Wholesalers.

It is regarded as rejected.

Medicine Wholesalers.

The offer is regarded as rejected if the other party does not accept. In the second case, also, the same can be said.

Sugar Wholesalers.

In the first case, if the offeror fails to receive a notice of acceptance, the offer should be regarded as rejected. If the offeree is to a long-time customer, it sometimes is regarded as accepted just as suggested in the latter half of the topic.

Dried Bonito Wholesalers.

In the first case, if the party fails to receive notification that his offer was accepted, the offer should be regarded as rejected. In the

[1] *Mihakarai-kigen-nai.*

[2] *Kiu-kumi kami-donya.*

second case, if the offeree fails to express his rejection, the offer should be regarded as accepted. But the offeree makes it a rule not to fail in expressing his acceptance or rejection.

Soy Wholesalers.

In either case, if the recipient of the offer fails to express his acceptance, the offer should be regarded as rejected. Thus, in the second case as well, the offer is not regarded as accepted.

Timber Wholesalers.

Unless expressly accepted, it should be regarded as rejected. However, there may be the exceptional case when the parties know each other well and the other party's silence is regarded as acceptance.

Timber Traders.[1]

As stated above.

Timber Traders (*Senju-kumi*).[2]

Same as stated above.

Fuel Wholesalers.

No definite answer can be given to the present topic, because there are many cases, each one different from the other. In general, however, if either of the two parties fails to inform the other party of his intention, the offer cannot be regarded as accepted.

Porcelain Wholesalers.

When the first party (a Tokyo wholesaler) fails to receive a notice of acceptance from the other party (the maker or the consigner), the offer is regarded as rejected. As for the second question: if the offer is made from a customer (a buyer) to the wholesaler, it will be regarded as accepted, as long as it is not rejected in an definite answer.

Paper Wholesalers (*Shôkai-kumi*).[3]

If the first party fails to receive a notice of acceptance, the offer is regarded as rejected.

Rice Traders.[4]

If one party fails to receive a notice of acceptance, it is regarded as rejected. As for the second question, the second party should still inform the first party of his rejection. He should make it a

[1] *Zaimoku-tôsei-kumiai.*

[2] *Senju-kumi zaimoku-tôsei-kumiai.*

[3] *Shôkai-kumi kami-donya.*

[4] *Beikoku sangyô-kumiai.*

practice to reply in writing. A trader who always remains silent when approached by his customer will soon be shunned as a man unworthy of trust.

Salt Wholesalers.

When the other party fails to express his acceptance, the offer should be regarded as rejected. As for the second question, there are some cases as stated in the topic.

Copper and Iron Wholesalers.

As for the first situation, the offer should be regarded as rejected. However, in the second case, no definite custom has been established; there are many cases, each one different from the other, according to the time and place.

Kudari Saké Wholesalers.

An offer should be made explicit by one party to the other. If the second party then fails to express his acceptance, the offer should be regarded as rejected. As for the second situation, the custom is just as stated above.

Lime and Shell Wholesalers.

In the first case it should be regarded as rejected; but in the second case it should be regarded as accepted.

Mosquito Net Wholesalers.

When the first party fails to receive the acceptance within a reasonable period of time, the offer should be regarded as rejected. After receiving an offer from his customer, his failure to express his acceptance should not be regarded as acceptance.

Saké Wholesalers.

As each case is different, there are no definite, established rule.

Matting Wholesalers.

When the first party fails to receive a notice of acceptance within a reasonable period of time, the offer should be regarded as rejected. After receiving the offer from the first party, one's failure to express his acceptance should not be regarded as acceptance.

Drapery Wholesalers.

Regarding the former half of the present topic, when the party who makes an offer fails to receive an express acceptance, his offer should be regarded as rejected. If an offer is made from an old customer with whom one has been accustomed to dealing, however, it is almost always regarded as accepted even if the other party has failed to express his acceptance.

Fuel Wholesalers (*Umite-kumi*).[1]

If one party has failed to receive a notice of acceptance either at once, within a specified period, or within a supposedly reasonable time, the offer should be regarded as having been rejected. When one party receives an offer from his customer and fails to express his rejection, he should be regarded as having accepted it. But, in some special cases and circumstances, it occasionally is regarded as rejected.

Tobacco Wholesalers.

Under some special circumstances the two parties reach their agreement through negotiations. Hence no definite rule can be found.

Kôjimachi Ward.

The failure to express one's acceptance occasionally means that the offer has been accepted, if the offer is made from a customer with whom he has been accustomed to dealing.

Nihombashi Ward.

In the first case it should be regarded as rejected. It should be regarded as accepted, however, when the offer is from a customer with whom one has been dealing for a long time.

Kyôbashi Ward.

As for the first question, the offer is not necessarily rejected. In the second case, when the second party fails to express his rejection, the offer should be regarded as accepted.

Yotsuya Ward and Ushigome Ward.

Even when the offer is made by a long-standing customer, it cannot be regarded as accepted unless a definite acceptance is given each time.

Asakusa Ward.

It should not be regarded as accepted even if no definite expression of rejection is made.

Honjo Ward.

When the first party fails to receive the other party's acceptance either at once, within a specified period, or within a supposedly reasonable length of time, the offer should be regarded as rejected. When it is from a customer with whom he has been accustomed to dealing, it should not be regarded as accepted if the other party

[1] *Umite-kumi shintan-donya.*

fails to express his rejection.

Ebara *kôri.*

When the offeror fails to receive the other party's acceptance either at once, within a specified period, or within a supposedly reasonable length of time, the offer should be regarded as rejected. When it is from a regular customer, it occasionally is regarded as accepted.

Higashi-tama *kôri* and Minami-toshima *kôri.*

When an offer is made by one party, the offer should be regarded as rejected if the other party fails to express his acceptance either at once, within a specified period, or within a reasonable time period. If the offer is from a regular customer, with whom he has long been accustomed to dealing and who has a full knowledge of the business, it occasionally is regarded as accepted even when the other party fails to express his rejection.

Kita-toshima *kôri.*

If one party fails to express his acceptance, the offer can be regarded neither as rejected nor as accepted. The offer is still open and it is settled by the express reply made by the offeree. When an offer is made by a customer with whom one has been accustomed to dealing for many years, one's silence is often regarded as the acceptance.

Minami-adachi *kôri.*

As for the first situation: the offer should be regarded as rejected. In the second case: when the second party fails to express his rejection, the offer will be regarded as accepted if he has been a regular customer who has so far followed the same practice.

Shitaya Ward.

The offer by one party should be regarded as rejected unless a definite assent is given by the other party. Even when it is from a regular customer, unless provided for in advance, it should not be regarded as accepted.

Kanda Ward.

When the first party fails to receive a notice of acceptance within a specified period, the offer should be regarded as rejected. However, it is regarded as accepted from time to time, even if the second party fails to express his rejection.

Akasaka Ward and Azabu Ward.

When the first party who makes an offer fails to receive an acceptance from the other party, the offer should be regarded as rejected. But the offer occasionally will be regarded as accepted if it is from a regular customer. Thus, this situation is almost the same as stated in first topic.

Hongô Ward.

When a notice of acceptance does not arrive within a specified period of time, the offer should be regarded as rejected. In some cases, even after the offer has been regarded as rejected, it occasionally may be accepted afterwards in talks between the two. On the contrary, even when the offeree fails to express his rejection, if he has for a long time had business connections with the offeror, it sometimes is regarded as accepted.

Chiba Prefecture

Awa *kôri*, Hei *kôri*, Asai *kôri* and Nagasa *kôri*.

When one party who has made an offer fails to receive a notice of acceptance from the other party, with whom he has not been accustomed to dealing, he should regard the offer as rejected. In reality, however, there are few who fail to clearly express reply of their assent or rejection. If one cannot afford to accept the offer, he expresses his rejection so as not to trouble the other party. When the offeree fails to express his rejection, it occasionally is regarded as signifying his acceptance if he has been a regular customer. Otherwise it is expected that he will express his rejection at the earliest possible opportunity.

Katori *kôri*.

When the second party fails to express his acceptance, the offer should be regarded as rejected. However, when he fails to make any declaration of intent, it sometimes may be regarded as a sign of his acceptance if he has had business connections with the first party for a long time.

Yamabe *kôri* and Muza *kôri*.

Regarding the first question, when a notice of acceptance fails to reach the first party within a specified period of time, the offer should be regarded as rejected. As for the second question, when a notice of rejection fails to reach the first party within some period, it should be regarded as accepted.

Unakami *kôri* and Sôsa *kôri*.

Regarding the first question, when the notice of acceptance fails to reach the offeror within a specified period, the offer should be regarded as rejected. As for the second question, unless a notice of rejection is received by the offeror, it should be regarded as accepted.

Higashi-katsushika *kôri*.

When the first party does not receive any express acceptance from the other party, the offer should be regarded as rejected. However, when the offer is made by him to a regular customer, the latter's silence occasionally is regarded as signifying his acceptance.

IBARAKI PREFECTURE

Nishi-katsushika *kôri* and Sashima *kôri*.

The offer is regarded as rejected. However, if one party receives an offer from a customer with whom he has long been accustomed to dealing, he will make every effort to supply him with the goods, even if the goods are not presently in stock. The customer will consider his order accepted unless he receives a notification of its rejection from the other party.

KANAGAWA PREFECTURE

Miura *kôri*.

If one is not notified that his offer has been accepted, his offer should be regarded as rejected. In the second case, it should be regarded as accepted unless a notice of rejection is received.

Tachibana *kôri*.

In the first case, the offer should be regarded as rejected. In the second case, however, it should be regarded as accepted unless a notice of rejection is received.

Kita-tama *kôri*.

As for the first question, if one party fails to receive the other party's notice of acceptance, the offer should of course be regarded as rejected. In the second case, the case of an old customer, he will regard his offer to have been accepted even if he receives no answer.

Ashigara-shimo *kôri*.

When two parties fail to reach an agreement, there cannot be any contract. Naturally the offer is not accepted. In the second case, the answer is the same as in the first case.

Prefectural Industrial Bureau.

When one party makes an offer but fails to receive notification of the other party's acceptance either at once, within a specified period, or within a supposedly reasonable time, the offer should be regarded as rejected. When the offer is made by a customer of long standing, however, it occasionally is regarded as accepted unless the second party expresses his rejection, because the two are closely related to each other and are on friendly terms.

TOCHIGI PREFECTURE

Prefectural Office.

If the second party fails to express his acceptance, the offer should be regarded as rejected. There are no exceptions even for customers of long standing. Upon receiving an offer from another party, one is obliged to make an express acceptance or rejection.

Shimo-tsuga *kôri* and Samukawa *kôri*.

When one party makes an offer to the other party and fails to receive a notice of acceptance, the offer is sometimes regarded as rejected. Between parties long accustomed to dealing with each other, the offer occasionally is regarded as accepted even if the second party fails to convey his express acceptance.

Ashikaga *kôri* and Yanada *kôri*.

An agreement to start negotiations, like the payment of a deposit, cannot be regarded as a formal contract. This case can usually be seen in the textile industry. Here in this district, a merchant and a regular customer do not exchange written contracts. When a merchant receives an order from a customer, he immediately gets together the goods for him (the buyer), and sends him an invoice to let him know that his order is being filled. The seller need not reply to the buyer unless he feels there will be some inconvenience or delay in filling the order. When the seller fails to answer the buyer, the former is regarded as having accepted the offer; otherwise the former would inform the latter of his inability to fill the order. (This case can be seen only in transactions between a merchant and his regular customers.) In the silk industry also, it is necessary to conclude a contract. In the case of long time acquaintances, the case is the same as given above for the textile industry.

MIE PREFECTURE

Suzuka *kôri*.

When a notice of acceptance from the second party is not received either at once, within a specified period, or within a supposedly reasonable time, the offer should be regarded as rejected. When the offer is made by an old customer, the offeree may be sometimes regarded as accepted, unless the offeree expressly rejects it.

Ichishi *kôri*.

It is a practice here to wait for the other party's answer unless there is an agreement in advance that the offer will be regarded as rejected, if no answer is made.

Nabari *kôri* and Iga *kôri*.

The acceptance of an offer between two parties depends upon what the offer includes, and whether the two agree or not. It is hard to say at present which interpretation is right and which is wrong. The other matters are the same as stated in the answer to Topic I.

Kita-muro *kôri*.

Regardless of whether a time period is specified or not, no offer should be regarded as rejected because the second party has failed to express his reply. However, the first party should again ask the other party for an answer. When one party makes an offer, for example, to purchase some articles from a merchant with whom he has long been accustomed to dealing, the second party's failure to express his acceptance is itself occasionally regarded as acceptance.

AICHI PREFECTURE

Nakajima *kôri*.

Regarding the first half of the topic, the offeree's silence is regarded as rejection. On the contrary when the one party receives the offer from his customer and fails to express his rejection, the offer, as a rule, should be regarded as having been accepted.

Nagoya Ward.

If a notice of acceptance has not been received within some such specified period, the offer should be regarded as having been rejected. Even if the rejection is not expressly stated, the offer cannot be regarded as accepted.

Chita *kôri*.

As a general rule of business, an offer made by one party should be regarded as rejected unless it is expressly accepted by the other party. Indeed, the offeree is sometimes asked again to answer if he is not a regular associate of the offering party. In a transaction between businessmen with a long standing relationship, the failure to answer may be regarded as acceptance. This also holds true when the goods handled are small in quantity and are not subject to fluctuations in price.

Minami-shidara *kôri.*

According to the local usage, the acceptance or rejection is always expressly made. Hence, even if the offeree fails to answer, the offer should not be regarded as rejected. This also applies to regular customers as well.

Atsumi *kôri.*

If the second party fails to express his acceptance, the offer will always be regarded as rejected. This holds true even when he is a regular customer.

Kaitô *kôri* and Kaisai *kôri.*

When the second party fails to answer within a specified period, the offer is regarded as rejected. If he is a regular customer, it sometimes is regarded as accepted, as stated in the latter half of the topic.

Aichi *kôri.*

When one party makes an offer to the other party, and fails to receive notification of the latter's acceptance, the offer should be regarded as rejected. If the latter is a regular customer, and fails to express his rejection, the offer is sometimes regarded as accepted.

Niwa *kôri* and Haguri *kôri.*

If one party makes an offer and fails to receive a definite answer from the other party within a specified period of time, the offer should be regarded as rejected. When the offer involves a small amount so as not to require a written document or deposit, the offer sometimes is regarded as accepted if the second party has been a customer of long standing, according to the local usage.

Shizuoka Prefecture

Prefectural Office.

If one party makes an offer and fails to receive notification of the other party's acceptance, the offer should be regarded as rejected. However, if the other party is a long-standing customer, the offer should be regarded as accepted.

Udo *kôri* and Abe *kôri.*

In the first instance the offer should be regarded as rejected. In the second case it is sometimes regarded as accepted.

Inasa *kôri* and Aratama *kôri.*

If a notice of acceptance is not received within a specified period of time, the offer should be regarded as rejected. Even if the offer is made to a regular customer, the offeree's silence cannot be regarded as acceptance.

Kamo *kôri* and Naka *kôri*.

The answer in the first case is yes. In the second case, when the offer is made to a regular customer, it is sometimes regarded as accepted. Even at that time, however, one should not regard the offer as definitely accepted.

Saya *kôri* and Kitô *kôri*.

If the second party fails to express his acceptance within a specified period of time, the first party is free to make a contract with a third party. The revocation of the offer to the second party should be made only after the offer has been accepted by the third party.

GIFU PREFECTURE

Mugi *kôri*.

If the party receiving an offer fails to express his acceptance either within a specified period of time or within a supposedly reasonable length of time, the offer should be regarded as rejected. When the offer made to a regular customer goes unanswered, the offer will be regarded as accepted, according to the custom here.

Ampachi *kôri*.

In the first case stated above, the offer should be regarded as rejected. In the second case, it sometimes will be regarded as accepted if the parties have long been accustomed to dealing with each other.

Fuwa *kôri*.

If a notice of acceptance is not received within a specified period, the offer should be regarded as rejected. When the offer is made to a regular customer, the offer is regarded as accepted if not expressly rejected, according to the local usage.

Atsumi *kôri*, Kagami *kôri* and Katagata *kôri*.

As for the first question, the offer should be regarded as rejected. As for the second, in some cases, the offer is regarded as accepted.

Tagi *kôri* and Kami-ishizu *kôri*.

If a notice of acceptance is not received within a specified period, the offer should be regarded as rejected. When the offer is made to an old customer of many years, and no rejection is expressed, the offer should be regarded as accepted.

Ôno *kôri* and Ikeda *kôri*.

The answer is exactly as stated in the first situation. When the offer is made to a customer of long standing, it is hard to give a definite answer.

Haguri *kôri* and Nakajima *kôri.*

Yes.

Ena *kôri.*

The answer to the first question is yes. In the second case, if no notice expressly rejecting the offer is received by the first party, the offer is sometimes regarded as accepted.

Kamo *kôri.*

If one party makes an offer to another party, and fails to receive the latter's answer either at once, within a specified period, or within a supposedly reasonable length of time, the offer is regarded as rejected. When the other party has long been accustomed to dealing with the first party, his failure to express his acceptance should itself be regarded as a sign of acceptance.

Kani *kôri.*

As for the first question, the offer should be regarded as rejected. In the second case, however, it is accepted.

Atsumi *kôri,* Gifu Township.

Our answer here is the same as that given to Topic I.

Ôgaki.

As for the first question, the offer should be regarded as rejected. In the second case, it often is regarded as accepted, according to the custom here, if the offer is made to one who has been a long-time customer.

Ena *kôri,* Nakatsugawa Village.

As for the first question, the offer should be regarded as rejected. In the second case, the offer is occasionally regarded as having been accepted, according to the custom here.

Shimo-ishizu *kôri,* Takasu Township.

When one party receives an offer from another party, and fails to make any answer within a specified period because of the distance between the two, the offer is regarded as rejected. When the offer is made to a customer of long standing, the offer is regarded as accepted if no answer is made within a specified period of time.

Haguri *kôri,* Takegahana Village.

When the recipient of an offer fails to answer within a specified period, the offer should always be regarded as rejected. The recipient of an offer, even if he is a customer of long standing, is obliged to inform the first party immediately if he wishes to accept the offer.

Yamagata *kôri*, Takatomi Village.

When one party receives an offer and fails to express his acceptance, the offer will always be regarded as rejected. However, as for a customer of long standing, the offer occasionally is regarded as accepted.

Mugi *kôri*, Kôzuchi Village.

If a notice of acceptance is not received within a supposedly reasonable period of time, the offer should be regarded as rejected. This is the same for a regular customer, also. The offer will never be regarded as accepted unless expressly so indicated.

Haguri *kôri*, Kasamatsu Village.

It is just as you have stated.

Fuwa *kôri*, Tarui Village.

If a notice of acceptance is not received, the offer should be regarded as rejected.

Ôno *kôri*, Miwa Village.

As for the first question, the offer should be regarded as rejected. As for the second, it is, on the contrary, often regarded as accepted.

Ampachi *kôri*, Gôdo Village.

The offer should be regarded as rejected. It should never be regarded as accepted unless the second party expressly accepts it.

Tagi *kôri*, Shimada Village.

Answer missing.

Ena *kôri*, Iwa Village.

As for the first question, the offer should be regarded as rejected. In the second case, it should be regarded as accepted.

Kamo *kôri*, Hosome Village.

When one party makes an offer and fails to receive a notice of acceptance from the other party, the offer should be regarded as rejected as stated in the first half of the topic. If the offer is made to a customer of long standing, and no notice of rejection is received, the offer occasionally is regarded as accepted. If the price of the articles offered fluctuates irregularly either up or down, the offer should be regarded as rejected and subject to negotiation.

Toki *kôri*, Takayama Village.

The answer to the first question is yes. As for the second, in the case of a business customer of long standing, the offer will be regarded as accepted, even when no answer is made.

Kani *kôri*, Mitake Village.

As for the first case, the offer should be regarded as rejected. In the second case, it occasionally is regarded as accepted.

Ena *kôri*, Akechi Village.

The answer to the first question is yes. As for the second, if one party fails to expressly reject the offer, it occasionally will be regarded as accepted.

Mugi *kôri*, Seki Village.

The offer is regarded as having effect. In the case of a customer of long standing, his failure to express his rejection will be regarded as implied acceptance.

Ôno *kôri*, Takayama Township.

When the recipient of an offer fails to express his acceptance, the offer is of course regarded as rejected. When the one party asks for an answer, and fails to receive any notice of acceptance, the offer of course should be regarded as rejected. When one is asked to answer within a specified period and fails to do so, the offer should be regarded as accepted. If no time limit is set for the answer, however, it is regarded as rejected.

Motosu *kôri*, Kitagata Village.

When a party making an offer fails to receive another party's acceptance, either at once, within a specified period, or within a supposedly reasonable length of time, the offer should be regarded as rejected. In the case of trade with a regular customer, failure to express one's rejection, on the contrary, means that the offer has been accepted.

Kamo *kôri*, Ôta Village.

When a party making an offer fails to receive another party's notice of acceptance, either at once, within a specified period, or within a supposedly reasonable period of time, the offer should be regarded as rejected. In case of business with an old customer, failure to make an answer may sometimes be regarded as a sign of acceptance.

Kaisai *kôri* and Shimo-ishizu *kôri*.

When a party making an offer fails to receive another party's notice of acceptance, either at once, within a specified period, or within a supposedly reasonable time period, the offer should be regarded as rejected. In a case when the offer is made to a regular customer, failure to make an express rejection of the offer occasionally will be regarded as a sign of acceptance.

Gujô *kôri.*

In these cases the offer should be regarded as rejected.

Topic 4: When an Offer of Contract Is Made by One Party, Does It Become Binding from the Moment When the Offeree Accepts It, or from the Moment When the Offeror[1] Receives the Notification of Acceptance?

TOKYO METROPOLIS

Paper Wholesalers (*Kiu-kumi*).

The offer becomes binding from the moment when the offeror receives the other party's notification of acceptance.

Oil Wholesalers.

As stated above.

Stone Wholesalers.

It becomes binding from the moment when the offeree accepts the offer. The buyer need not wait for the notification of acceptance to arrive.

Medicine Wholesalers.

It becomes binding from the day on which the offeree sends out his notification of acceptance.

Sugar Wholesalers.

The offer becomes binding from the moment when the offeree accepts it.

Dried Bonito Wholesalers.

As a rule, it becomes binding from the moment when the offeree accepts it. In some cases, however, it starts at the moment when the offeror receives the notification of acceptance.

Soy Wholesalers.

The offer becomes binding from the moment when the offeree accepts it.

Timber Wholesalers.

It becomes binding from the moment when the offeror receives the notification of acceptance.

Timber Traders (*Senju-kumi*).[2]

As stated above.

Timber Traders.[3]

[1] *Môshikomi-nin.*

[2] *Senju-kumi zaimoku-tôsei-kumiai.*

[3] *Zaimoku-tôsei-kumiai.*

As stated above.

Fuel Wholesalers.

Regarding the present topic, the moment when the contract becomes binding depends on the contents of the letter of acceptance.

Porcelain Wholesalers.

From the moment when the offeror receives the notification of acceptance.

Paper Wholesalers (*Shôkai-kumi*).[1]

From the moment when the offeror receives the notification of acceptance.

Rice Traders.[2]

When one party has made an offer and agreed with the other party on the price, the contract is made when the latter sends out the notification of acceptance.

Salt Wholesalers.

From the moment when the offeror receives the notification of acceptance.

Copper and Iron Wholesalers.

It becomes binding from the moment when the offeree accepts it, or sometimes from the moment when the offeror receives the notification of acceptance.

Kudari Saké Wholesalers.[3]

It becomes binding from the moment when the offeror receives the notification of acceptance.

Mosquito Net Wholesalers.

The offer becomes binding from the moment when the seller sends out notice of his acceptance.

Lime and Shell Wholesalers.

From the moment when the buyer receives the notification of acceptance.

Saké Wholesalers.

As stated above.

Matting Wholesalers.

The contract becomes binding from the moment when the offeree receives it and sends out notice of acceptance.

Drapery Wholesalers.

[1] *Shôkai-kumi kami-donya.*

[2] *Beikoku sangyô-kumiai.*

[3] *Kudari-sake-donya.*

From the moment when the offeree accepts it.

Fuel Wholesalers (*Umite-kumi*).[1]

Regardless of whether or not the notification of acceptance arrives, the offer becomes binding from the moment when the offeree accepts it.

Tobacco Wholesalers.

We usually reach agreement through negotiations. There is no established rule.

Kôjimachi Ward.

Both practices are followed, depending on the particular case.

Nihombashi Ward.

In most cases it becomes binding from the moment when the offeror receives the notification of acceptance.

Kyôbashi Ward.

It becomes binding from the moment when the offeree accepts it.

Yotsuya Ward and Ushigome Ward.

The offer becomes binding from the moment when the offeror receives the notification of acceptance.

Asakusa Ward.

It becomes binding from the moment when the offeree accepts it.

Honjo Ward.

Both practices are followed.

Ebara *kôri*.

From the moment when the offeree accepts it.

Higashi-tama *kôri* and Minami-toshima *kôri*.

As a rule it becomes binding from the moment when the offeror receives the notification of acceptance.

Kita-toshima *kôri*.

From the moment when the offeror receives the notification of acceptance.

Minami-adachi *kôri*.

From the moment when the offeror receives the notification of acceptance.

Shitaya Ward.

It is our practice that it becomes binding from the moment when

[1] *Umite-kumi shintan-donya.*

the offeror receives the notification of acceptance.

Kanda Ward.

From the moment when the offeror receives the notification of acceptance.

Akasaka Ward and Azabu Ward.

As stated above.

Hongô Ward.

As a rule it becomes binding from the moment when the offeror receives the notification of acceptance, but occasionally the other practice occurs.

CHIBA PREFECTURE

Awa *kôri*, Hei *kôri*, Asai *kôri* and Nagasa *kôri*.

When an offer is made in person by one party, or by his agent, it becomes binding as soon as the offeree expresses his acceptance. When an offer is made by mail or messenger, it does not become binding until the notification of acceptance reaches the offeror.

Katori *kôri*.

It beomes binding from the moment when the offeree accepts it. Even when the offeror does not receive a written notice of acceptance, the offer becomes binding and enables the offeree to act.

Yamabe *kôri* and Muza *kôri*.

It becomes binding from the moment when the offeror receives the notification of acceptance.

Unakami *kôri* and Sôsa *kôri*.

From the moment when the offeror receives the notification of acceptance.

Higashi-katsushika *kôri*.

As a rule it becomes binding from the moment when the offeror receives the notification of acceptance. In some cases it becomes binding from the moment when the one party makes the offer.

IBARAKI PREFECTURE

Nishi-katsushika *kôri* and Sashima *kôri*.

The offer becomes binding from the moment when the offeror receives the notification of acceptance.

KANAGAWA PREFECTURE

Miura *kôri*.

It becomes binding from the moment when the offeror receives the notification of acceptance.

Tachibana *kôri*.

It becomes binding from the moment when the offeree accepts it.

Kita-tama *kôri.*

When receiving an offer, the offeree will express his acceptance either verbally or in writing. But even when both parties reach agreement, a verbal contract is not definitely binding and cannot be set up against any act in the future. An offer in writing carries more weight than a verbal one. Therefore, the offer becomes binding from the moment when the offeror receives the written notification of acceptance.

Ashigara-shimo *kôri.*

It is our practice that it becomes binding from the moment when the offeror receives the notification of acceptance. But this cannot yet be regarded as a formal contract for buying or selling.

Prefectural Industrial Bureau.

The offer becomes binding from the moment when the offeree accepts it, or when he posts a letter of acceptance. Therefore, the contract can not be invalidated even if the letter should be delayed or lost in the mail. It is usually sent by registered mail so that it may be used as evidence in the future.

Tochigi Prefecture

Prefectural Office.

It is our practice that the offer becomes binding from the moment when the offeree accepts it. This applies even when the one party makes an offer by mail to another party, either at a distance or in the neighborhood. However, even in such cases, the offer becomes binding from the moment when the offeree writes a letter of acceptance to the buyer, or from the moment when he states acceptance orally, for instance, to a messenger from the offeror.

Shimo-tsuga *kôri* and Samukawa *kôri.*

The offer becomes binding only when the offeror receives the offeree's notification of acceptance.

Ashikaga *kôri* and Yanada *kôri.*

In the case of a contract for the sale of textiles, it is the practice here to execute the contract as soon as the offer arrives, without informing the offeror that his offer has been accepted. So the offer becomes binding from the moment when the offeree receives it. Even in a case where the offeror fails to receive the notification of acceptance, if he wants to revoke the offer already made, he must inform the offeree immediately to the effect that he wants to revoke it if the offeree does not object. In the silk trade, the offer becomes binding from the moment when the offeree accepts it. In the field of drapery, the offeror, or a retailer, takes the initiative in transactions. In many cases, therefore, he determines that the offer becomes binding when he receives the offeree's notification of acceptance.

MIE PREFECTURE

Suzuka *kôri.*

One party's offer becomes binding from the moment when the other party accepts it. But the offeror can cancel the offer as long as the articles offered still remain in his hands.

Ichishi *kôri.*

The offer becomes binding from the moment when the offeror receives the offeree's notification of acceptance.

Nabari *kôri* and Iga *kôri.*

An offer made by one party becomes binding from the moment when the other party accepts it.

Kita-muro *kôri.*

Even if the offeree has accepted the offer, it is impossible for the offeror to know that at the time. So the offer becomes binding only when the offeror receives the notification of acceptance.

AICHI PREFECTURE

Nakajima *kôri.*

Same as stated in the second situation.

Nagoya Ward.

In business, it is the practice that the offer becomes binding from the moment when the offeree accepts it.

Chita *kôri.*

It is the practice here that the offer does not become binding unless a notification of acceptance reaches the buyer.

Minami-shidara *kôri.*

If the offeree keeps silent, the offer is regarded as accepted. The offer becomes binding, therefore, even if the offeror has not received the notification of acceptance.

Atsumi *kôri.*

It becomes binding from the moment when the notification of acceptance reaches the offeror.

Kaitô *kôri* and Kaisai *kôri.*

The offer becomes binding from the moment when the notification of acceptance reaches the offeror.

Aichi *kôri*.

It becomes binding from the moment when the offeree accepts it.

Niwa *kôri* and Haguri *kôri*.

Every offer becomes binding from the moment when the notification of acceptance reaches the offeror; this is because such procedures as the exchange of written forms of contract or the payment of a deposit are required.

SHIZUOKA PREFECTURE

Prefectural Office.

As stated in the second situation.

Udo *kôri* and Abe *kôri*.

Acceptance is expressed by a written notification by the other party. The offer, therefore, becomes binding from the moment when the offeror receives the other party's notification of acceptance. A case such as that described in the second situation means that the other party has accepted, but this cannot be called a definite contract.

Inasa *kôri* and Aratama *kôri*.

It becomes binding from the moment when the offeror receives the other party's notification of acceptance.

Kamo *kôri* and Naka *kôri*.

It becomes binding from the moment when the offeree accepts it.

Saya *kôri* and Kitô *kôri*.

There are two different cases. In some cases it becomes binding from the moment when a notification of acceptance reaches the offeror, but in other cases it becomes binding even when the reply does not reach him. It depends solely on the sort of trade involved. For instance, a buyer who handles corn, tea, silk, etc., will wait for the reply, but a buyer who is, for instance, a drapery wholesaler or a retail dealer sometimes will not.

GIFU PREFECTURE

Mugi *kôri*.

The offer becomes binding from the moment when the offeror receives the other party's notification of acceptance.

Ampachi *kôri*.

Every offer becomes binding from the moment when the offeree accepts it, according to the local practice.

Fuwa *kôri.*

It becomes binding from the moment when the other party accepts it.

Atsumi *kôri*, Kagami *kôri* and Katagata *kôri.*

It becomes binding from the moment when the other party accepts it.

Tagi *kôri* and Kami-ishizu *kôri.*

The offer becomes binding from the moment when the other party accepts it. However, with regard to the case of silence as acceptance in the preceding topic, the offer becomes binding when it reaches the offeree.

Ôno *kôri* and Ikeda *kôri.*

It becomes binding only after the offeror receives the other party's notification of acceptance.

Haguri *kôri* and Nakajima *kôri.*

Either practice may be followed, depending on the relationship between the two parties and the goods they handle.

Ena *kôri.*

The offer becomes binding from the moment when the offeror receives the notification of acceptance.

Kamo *kôri.*

It becomes binding from the moment when the offeror receives the notification of acceptance.

Kani *kôri.*

As stated above.

Atsumi *kôri*, Gifu Township.

The offer becomes binding from the moment when the seller definitely expresses his acceptance orally, or when he gives notice of his acceptance either by mail or by telegraph.

Ôgaki.

Every offer becomes binding from the moment when the offeree accepts it.

Ena *kôri*, Nakatsugawa Village.

As stated above.

Shimo-ishizu *kôri*, Takasu Township.

It becomes binding from the moment when the buyer receives the notification of acceptance.

Haguri *kôri*, Takegahana Village.

At first it would seem that the offer becomes binding at the time when the offeree accepts it. But the offer cannot always be regarded as definitely accepted unless the offeror receives written notice of acceptance. This is because, in some circumstances, an offer made by one party may be rejected by the other party.

Yamagata *kôri*, Takatomi Village.

The offer becomes binding when the buyer receives the notification of acceptance.

Mugi *kôri*, Kôzuchi Village.

It becomes binding from the moment when the offeree accepts it.

Haguri *kôri*, Kasamatsu Village.

Either procedure may be followed, according to how closely the two parties are connected with each other and what sort of articles they handle.

Fuwa *kôri*, Tarui Village.

The offer becomes binding from the moment when the offeree accepts it.

Ôno *kôri*, Miwa Village.

As stated above.

Ampachi *kôri*, Gôdo Village.

It becomes binding from the moment when the offeree accepts it, or when the offeror receives the offeree's notification of acceptance.

Tagi *kôri*, Shimada Village.

No answer is given.

Ena *kôri*, Iwa Village.

It becomes binding from the moment when the notice of acceptance reaches the offeror.

Kamo *kôri*, Hosome Village.

It becomes binding from the moment when the offeree accepts it.

Toki *kôri*, Takayama Village.

The offer becomes binding from the moment when the offeree expresses his acceptance, even if he fails to reply in writing.

Kani *kôri*, Mitake Village.

It becomes binding from the moment when the offeree accepts it.

Ena *kôri*, Akechi Village.

It becomes binding from the moment when the offeror receives the notification of acceptance.

Mugi *kôri*, Seki Village.

As stated above.

Ôno *kôri*, Takayama Township.

It becomes binding from the moment when the offeree expresses his acceptance.

Motosu *kôri*, Kitagata Village.

The offer becomes binding from the moment when the offeror receives the other party's notification of acceptance.

Kamo *kôri*, Ôta Village.

It becomes binding from the moment when the offeror receives the notice of acceptance.

Kaisai *kôri* and Shimo-ishizu *kôri*.

As a general rule, it becomes binding from the moment when the offeror receives the notice of acceptance. But it is not unusual for it to become binding from the very moment when the offeror accepts it. The choice of procedure depends on how closely the two parties are connected with each other.

Gujô *kôri*.

The offer becomes binding from the moment when the offeror receives the notification of acceptance.

Topic 5: Suppose a Notice of Acceptance of an Offer Is Sent to the Offeror. Can the Notification of Acceptance Be Cancelled if This Is Done before the Notice Has Reached the Offeror, or at the Same Time the Notice Is Received by the Offeror?

TOKYO METROPOLIS

Paper Wholesalers (*Kiu-kumi*).[1]

Once notification has been given, it should be strictly observed. But sometimes it can be revoked under unavoidable circumstances.

Oil Wholesalers.

It can be cancelled.

Stone Wholesalers.

It can be cancelled.

Medicine Wholesalers.

In trade involving ordinary goods it can be cancelled. In trade involving a special class of goods or in an emergency, it cannot always be cancelled.

Sugar Wholesalers.

It can be cancelled.

Dried Bonito Wholesalers.

It can be cancelled if this is done before the notice has reached the offeror, or at the same time that the offeror receives the notice.

Soy Wholesalers.

It can be cancelled before the notice has reached the offeror, but it cannot be cancelled at the same time the offeror receives the notice.

Timber Wholesalers.

It can be cancelled if necessary before the notice has reached the offeror or at the same time that the notice is received by the offeror. In the case of unavoidable circumstances, the two parties should hold talks.

Timber Traders.[2]

As stated above.

Timber Wholesalers (*Senju-kumi*).[3]

[1] *Kiu-kumi kami-donya.*

[2] *Zaimoku tôsei-kumiai.*

[3] *Senju-kumi zaimoku-donya.*

As stated above.

Fuel Wholesalers.

If the goods have already been prepared for transport, the notice of acceptance occasionally cannot be cancelled. But it cannot be said that we have a common practice, since each case is handled differently.

Porcelain Wholesalers.

It can be cancelled.

Rice Traders.[1]

It cannot be cancelled after the offeree has sent the buyer a notice of acceptance.

Salt Wholesalers.

It can be cancelled if this is done before the notice has reached the offeror.

Paper Wholesalers (*Shôkai-kumi*).[2]

It can be cancelled.

Copper and Iron Wholesalers.

Suppose a buyer who has accepted the offer of a seller decides to cancel the acceptance soon after sending out the notice of acceptance. If the seller does not reply to the notice of cancellation the acceptance can be cancelled. If the cancellation causes damage to the seller, the two should hold talks to reach a satisfactory settlement.

Mosquito Net Wholesalers.

It can be cancelled if this is done before the notice has reached the offeror, or at the same time the notice is received by the offeror.

Kudari Saké Wholesalers.[3]

It can be cancelled.

Lime and Shell Wholesalers.

As stated above.

Saké Wholesalers.[4]

On some occasions it can be cancelled by negotiation.

Matting Wholesalers.

It can be cancelled if this is done before the notice has reached the offeror or at the same time that he receives the notice.

1 *Beikoku sangyô-kumiai.*

2 *Shôkai-kumi kami-donya.*

3 *Kudari Sake-donya.*

4 *Sake-rui-donya.*

Drapery Wholesalers.

It can be cancelled if this is done before or at the same time that the notice reaches the offeror. If this is done later than that, it can be cancelled only through negotiation between the two.

Fuel Wholesalers (*Umite-kumi*).[1]

It can be cancelled. But if there is any fear that one party will suffer a loss, the two parties should negotiate.

Tobacco Wholesalers.

Since circumstances vary, the settlement should be made through negotiation. There is no established practice.

Kôjimachi Ward.

It depends on the kind of goods involved.

Nihombashi Ward.

It can be cancelled before the notice has reached the offeror.

Kyôbashi Ward.

It cannot be cancelled.

Yotsuya Ward and Ushigome Ward.

It can be cancelled before the notice has reached the offeror. But it cannot be cancelled without negotiation after the notice has reached him.

Asakusa Ward.

Of course it can be cancelled.

Honjo Ward.

It can be cancelled, if this is done before or at the same time that the notice reaches the buyer.

Ebara *kôri.*

It can be cancelled, if this is done before or at the same time that the notice reaches the buyer.

Higashi-tama *kôri* and Minami-toshima *kôri.*

The offeree who has sent the notice of acceptance often revokes it owing to circumstances, regardless of whether the notice has reached the offeror.

Kita-toshima *kôri.*

It can be cancelled before or at the same time that the notice reaches the offeror. If the offeree has received any samples or articles with an offer, he should return them to the offeror. If any money is spent while they are in his hands, it must be settled, but

[1] *Umite-kumi shintan-donya.*

there is no generally established practice. If the samples or articles are perishable, the offeree is usually bound to sell them and to keep the money for the offeror. In such a case, the offeree is obliged to notify the offeror immediately.

Minami-adachi *kôri.*

In such cases, the acceptance can be cancelled.

Shitaya Ward.

It can be cancelled before the notice has reached the offeror. If, however, this is done, at the same time that the buyer receives the notice, settlement will be reached through deliberations between the two for which there is no established rule.

Kanda Ward.

The acceptance can be cancelled before the notice has reached the offeror, or at the same time that the notice is received by the buyer.

Akasaka Ward and Azabu Ward.

The acceptance can be cancelled.

Hongô Ward.

It can be cancelled.

CHIBA PREFECTURE

Awa *kôri*, Hei *kôri*, Asai *kôri* and Nagasa *kôri*.

The acceptance occasionally can be cancelled before or at the same time that the notice reaches the offeror. Such a case will probably occur when an offeree is hoping for larger profits, either because of irregularly fluctuating prices, or by finding another buyer. No honest trader will act in this way, looking only to his own selfish interests. Except for unavoidable cases, for instance, a case of articles being lost, such a situation is very rare between merchants.

Katori *kôri*.

An acceptance once made by one party (an obligator) cannot be cancelled unless the other party (an upright person), who has received a notice of cancellation, regards it as unavoidable.

Yamabe *kôri* and Muza *kôri*.

The offer can be cancelled.

Unakami *kôri* and Sôsa *kôri*.

The offer can be cancelled if this is done before the notice has reached the offeror, or at the same time that the notice is received by him.

Higashi-katsushika *kôri*.

It can be cancelled.

IBARAKI PREFECTURE

Nishi-katsushika *kôri* and Sashima *kôri*.

The acceptance can be cancelled.

KANAGAWA PREFECTURE

Miura *kôri*.

Once the offeree has notified the offeror of acceptance, he cannot cancel it, even if this is done before the notice has reached offeror.

Tachibana *kôri*.

The acceptance can be cancelled.

Kita-tama *kôri*.

The acceptance can be cancelled if this is done at the same time that the notice is received by the offeror.

Ashigara-shimo *kôri*.

It is the practice here that it can be cancelled through negotiation between the two parties.

Prefectural Industrial Bureau.

The offeree who has sent a notice of acceptance can revoke the acceptance, if the notice of revocation reaches the offeror before or at the same time the notice of acceptance reaches him.

TOCHIGI PREFECTURE

Prefectural Office.

The acceptance can be cancelled.

Shimo-tsuga *kôri* and Samukawa *kôri*.

The acceptance can be cancelled if this is done before or at the same time that the notice reaches the offeror.

Ashikaga *kôri* and Yanada *kôri*.

Between merchants handling silk or cotton thread,[1] the acceptance can be cancelled. In most cases this occurs when prices are rising sharply and the market is prosperous. The offeror will allow the offeree to cancel the original notice, even if he has just received it, saying that it failed to reach him in time. Such cases rarely occur among textile traders, though they seldom give notification of acceptance.

MIE PREFECTURE

Suzuka *kôri*.

[1] *Karaito.*

The acceptance can be cancelled if this is done before or at the time that the notice reaches the offeror.

Ichishi *kôri*.

It can be cancelled.

Nabari *kôri* and Iga *kôri*.

The acceptance can be cancelled if this is done before or at the same time that the notice has reached the offeror. As stated in Topic 4, the offer becomes binding from the moment when the offeree expresses his acceptance. However, naturally, the offeror knows nothing until he receives the notice.

Kita-muro *kôri*.

Regardless of whether or not it has been done before the notice reaches the buyer, or at the same time that the notice is received by the offeror, it is possible to cancel the acceptance under unavoidable circumstances.

AICHI PREFECTURE

Nakajima *kôri*.

Yes. That is right.

Nagoya Ward.

Regardless of whether the notice has reached the offeror or not, the acceptance cannot be cancelled once it is made. Under unavoidable circumstances, however, it can be cancelled through negotiations between the two.

Chita *kôri*.

The acceptance can occasionally be cancelled if this is done before or at the time that the notice reaches the offeror. However, the practice varies in each case according to what is handled and when it is done.

Minami-shidara *kôri*.

It is very difficult to cancel acceptance regardless of whether the notice arrives or not.

Atsumi *kôri*.

It can be cancelled. But if the offeror has already sent out the goods, or bought them, cancellation is sometimes impossible.

Kaitô *kôri* and Kaisai *kôri*.

The acceptance can be cancelled if this is done before or at the same time that the notice reaches the offeror.

Aichi *kôri*.

It can be cancelled.

Niwa *kôri* and Haguri *kôri*.

The acceptance can be cancelled if this is done before or at the time that the notice reaches the offeror. Even a few seconds later, however, it cannot be cancelled.

SHIZUOKA PREFECTURE

Prefectural Office.

Yes.

Udo *kôri* and Abe *kôri*.

It can be cancelled.

Inasa *kôri* and Aratama *kôri*.

It can be cancelled.

Kamo *kôri* and Naka *kôri*.

In such a case it can be cancelled.

Saya *kôri* and Kitô *kôri*.

In the first situation, acceptance once made cannot be cancelled. In the second, it can be cancelled, because prices are apt to fluctuate.

GIFU PREFECTURE

Mugi *kôri*.

The acceptance can be cancelled if this is done, at the latest, at the same time that the notice is received by the offeror.

Ampachi *kôri*.

In such a case it can be cancelled. But in some circumstances it cannot be cancelled.

Fuwa *kôri*.

The acceptance can be cancelled if this is done at the same time that the notice is received by the offeror.

Atsumi *kôri*, Kagami *kôri* and Katagata *kôri*.

It can be cancelled.

Tagi *kôri* and Kami-ishizu *kôri*.

Regardless of whether the notice has reached the offeror or not, acceptance can occasionally be cancelled if the goods have not yet been sent out by the offeror.

Ôno *kôri* and Ikeda *kôri*.

If the notice of acceptance has already reached the offeror, the acceptance cannot be cancelled.

Haguri *kôri* and Nakajima *kôri*.

Yes.

Ena *kôri*.

The acceptance can be cancelled if this is done before the notice has reached the offeror, but it cannot be cancelled at the same time that the notice is received by him.

Kamo *kôri.*

The acceptance can usually cancelled before or at the time that the notice reaches the offeror.

Kani *kôri.*

Acceptance once made cannot be cancelled unless settlement can be reached through negotiations. If circumstances require, however, this does not apply.

Atsumi *kôri*, Gifu Township.

Acceptance cannot be cancelled.

Ôgaki.

In such a case it can be cancelled. But in some circumstances it cannot be.

Ena *kôri*, Nakatsugawa Village.

It cannot be cancelled.

Shimo-ishizu *kôri*, Takasu Township.

The acceptance can be cancelled if this is done before or at the same time that the notice reaches the offeror. It cannot be cancelled after this time limit.

Haguri *kôri*, Takegahana Village.

Such cases have occurred from time to time in local practice.

Yamagata *kôri*, Takatomi Village.

If the offeree receiving an offer has notified the offeror of acceptance after making a close check on the quantities in stock, the offer cannot be cancelled. If there are mistakes on the part of the offeror's (the seller's) employee, and if the mistakes have no relation to price fluctuations, the acceptance, needless to say, can be cancelled.

Mugi *kôri*, Kôzuchi Village.

It can be cancelled.

Haguri *kôri*, Kasamatsu Village.

Yes.

Fuwa *kôri*, Tarui Village.

The acceptance can occasionally be cancelled if this is done at the same time that the notice is received by the offeror.

Ôno *kôri*, Miwa Village.

It cannot be cancelled.

Ampachi *kôri*, Gôdo Village.

The acceptance can be cancelled if this is done before or at the time that the notice reaches the offeror.

Tagi *kôri*, Shimada Village.

No answer is given.

Ena *kôri*, Iwa Village.

The acceptance can be cancelled before or at the time that the notice reaches the offeror.

Kamo *kôri*, Hosome Village.

Even if done before the notice has reached the offeror, it cannot be cancelled if the offeror has already sent out the goods.

Toki *kôri*, Takayama Village.

It can be cancelled.

Kani *kôri*, Mitake Village.

The acceptance can be cancelled if this is done before the notice has reached the offeror. If it is done at the same time that the offeror receives the notice, he will settle the matter according to his own judgement.

Ena *kôri*, Akechi Village.

The acceptance can be cancelled if this is done before the notice has reached the offeror.

Mugi *kôri*, Seki Village.

The acceptance can usually be cancelled if this is done before or at the same time that the notice reaches the offeror. But the settlement is solely up to the offeror himself.

Ôno *kôri*, Takayama Township.

The acceptance can be cancelled if this is done before the notice has reached the offeror. If it is done at the same time that the notice is received by him, it can be cancelled only through negotiations between the two.

Motosu *kôri*, Kitagata Village.

The acceptance can be cancelled before or at the time that the notice reaches the offeror.

Kamo *kôri*, Ôta Village.

The acceptance can be cancelled if this is done before or at the same time that the notice reaches the offeror.

Kaisai *kôri* and Shimo-ishizu *kôri*.

The acceptance can be cancelled if this is done before or at the time that the notice reaches the offeror. But occasionally it cannot be cancelled if cancellation is done a short while after the notice has reached him. Although it can be cancelled in either situation given in the present topic, the offeree should ask the offeror's pardon by explaining the circumstances.

Gujô *kôri*.

It can be cancelled.

Topic 6: When a Party Who Receives an Offer Accompanied by Samples, or the Goods Themselves, Finds That the Samples or Goods Cannot Be Returned to the Offeror due to Certain Circumstances, What Should the Offeree Do?

If the Samples or Goods Left with the Offeree Cost Him Some Expense or Are Lost, What Should He Do? If the Goods Are Liable to Perish, May the Offeree Sell Them and Keep the Money for the Offeror?

TOKYO METROPOLIS

Paper Wholesalers (*Kiu-kumi*).[1]

The holder need not return the samples, etc. They cause him no expense. If the samples, etc. are lost, the holder indemnifies the owner for the loss.

Oil Wholesalers.

The goods we handle are sold by brand. No samples are used.

Stone Wholesalers.

We have no custom of returning samples. The expense will be covered according to an agreement arranged beforehand.

Medicine Wholesalers.

If the samples or goods cannot be returned, the expense should be borne by the holder. If they are to be returned, the cost of keeping them should be borne by the owner. If they have been lost, the loss should be covered by the holder. If they have gone bad, the loss should be borne by the owner. If they are liable to perish, the holder should sell them and keep the money, informing the owner of the fact immediately.

Dried Bonito Wholesalers.

If the holder has been reimbursed for all expenses while he kept the samples or goods, he should send them back to the owner without delay. If they have been lost or damaged, the loss occasionally will be covered by the holder. If they are liable to perish, the holder will sometimes sell them, and keep the money.

Sugar Wholesalers.

The goods we handle are sold by brand. There is no practice of handing over the goods in advance as a sample. On some occasions,

[1] *Kiu-kumi kami-donya.*

we use a small bag of sugar as a sample, but it weighs only five *momme* (about 19 grams). Whether the contract is concluded or not, the sample is usually left with the holder.

Soy Wholesalers.

Why does the situation described in the first question—the holder keeping the goods—occur? It is a matter of course to return them as early as possible. We do not know why. Regarding the second question, if some expense is incurred while the samples are in the holder's hands, the consignor (owner) should cover it. If the samples received from the holder of the goods are lost, the loss should be covered by the wholesaler. With regard to the third question, if the goods are liable to perish, the holder will sell them and keep the money.

Timber Wholesalers.

We don't use samples.

Timber Traders.[1]

We don't use samples.

Timber Traders (*Senju*).[2]

As stated above, we don't use samples.

Fuel Wholesalers.

Such a case is unknown among us.

Porcelain Wholesalers.

If the samples or goods are left in our hands, we must be responsible for them. Expenses incurred should be defrayed by the owner, unless otherwise provided for in advance. If they are lost or damaged, the holder should make an apology to the owner and pay him a half or a third of the estimated loss.

Paper Wholesalers (*Shôkai-kumi*).[3]

If one party has asked another party to buy his wares by sending the latter a sample or the article itself, it is quite natural that the holder should return it immediately if he cannot accept the offer. However, if the holder incurs some expense in returning the sample or goods, the owner will reimburse him or not require him to return the item. If the holder requested the sample or the article, the owner need not assume responsibility. It is our practice that

[1] *Zaimoku tôsei-kumiai.*

[2] *Senju zaimoku tôsei-kumiai.*

[3] *Shôkai-kumi kami-donya.*

one who receives a sample need not return it. If the sample or the article causes the holder some expense, the owner should reimburse him if this has been agreed on beforehand. Therefore, the expense need not be reimbursed by the owner if he is not responsible for the payment. Damage resulting from loss of the samples or articles should be borne by the owner. If the sample or the article is perishable, the two parties should consider it a deposit against the payment. If it is lost, the loss should be paid by the holder.

Rice Traders.[1]

In dealings between parties anywhere in the country, we use a small paper bag of rice, which contains only one or two *gô* (about 0.18 to 0.36 litres), as a sample. It need not be returned. Even if it is lost or spoiles, the holder is free of responsibility.

Salt Wholesalers.

We have no such practice.

Copper and Iron Wholesalers.

When the offeree receives a sample along with an offer, he should buy it at the current price. If the goods are different from the sample, they will be returned to the owner. If some expense is incurred due to the sample, it will be paid by the owner. If the sample is lost, the damage will be covered by the holder.

Kudari Saké Wholesalers.[2]

We have no such practice.

Mosquito Net Wholesalers.

If a sample cannot be returned due to unavoidable circumstances, the owner will let the holder make the payment either at a price they have agreed on[3] or at the current price. Expenses incurred, if any, will be the owner's responsibility. If the sample is lost, the loss will be borne by the holder. As for perishable goods, the holder occasionally sells them and keeps the money.

Lime and Shell Wholesalers.

As the goods we handle are low-priced, there is no question of returning small samples. If the sample is fairly large, it should be paid for at a reasonable price. If the sample is lost, the loss should be covered in the way stated above.

[1] *Beikoku sangyô-kumiai.*

[2] *Kudari sake-donya.*

[3] *Sashi-date.*

Saké Wholesalers.[1]

If the sample cannot be sent back due to unavoidable circumstances, the owner will immediately bargain with the holder for it either orally or in writing. If it should be lost by theft or fire, the two parties will negotiate about the responsibility. If it is something fresh, liable to perish, the holder sometimes sells it and keeps the money for the owner.

Tobacco Wholesalers.

Regarding the first question, if the sample is to be left with the holder, or if it is lost, he should buy it at a reasonable price. Expenses incurred referred to in the second question should be borne by the owner, if the sample is to be left with the holder in behalf of the owner. Of course it should be borne by the holder if it is to be left with him in his own behalf. We have nothing to answer with regard to the third question.

Matting Wholesalers.

If the holder cannot return the sample due to unavoidable circumstances, he will buy it at the owner's price.[2] If he cannot buy it at that price, he will buy it at the current price. Expenses incurred, if any, will be the owner's responsibility. If the sample is lost, the loss will be covered by the keeper of the goods. If the sample is perishable, the holder will sell it and keep the money for the owner.

Drapery Wholesalers.

In such a case, the keeper of the goods should buy the sample at a reasonable price. The same steps will be taken if it is lost. We incur no expenses for custody; we handle nothing liable to perish.

Fuel Wholesalers (*Umite-kumi*).[3]

The holder should return the goods to the owner, and any expense incurred in keeping them should be covered by the owner. However, since particular cases differ, there is no established rule for settling expenses. We handle nothing liable to perish.

Kôjimach Ward.

Such cases are not encountered in this district.

Nihombashi Ward.

[1] *Sake-rui-donya.*

[2] *Sashine-de-shikiru.*

[3] *Umite-kumi shintan-donya.*

There is no established rule in this district.

Kyôbashi Ward.

We have nothing to say in reply.

Yotsuya Ward and Ushigome Ward.

No answer is given.

Asakusa Ward.

Regarding the first question, unless the loss is the result of an unavoidable accident, such as a fire which spread from another burning house, it should be paid for by the holder at the price offered beforehand by the owner. Regarding the second, any expense incurred in keeping the samples or goods will be paid by the owner. If the samples or goods are lost, the loss will be borne by the holder. If they are perishable, they will be sold off by the holder, who will then inform the owner of the disposal.

Honjo Ward.

When a party receives an offer accompanied by samples or by the goods, but is unable to return them due to unavoidable circumstances, he should inform the owner of the facts immediately, and upon hearing from him, should take appropriate measures. If the samples or goods have caused the holder any expense, responsibility is determined according to the situation at the time. If they are lost due to carelessness on the part of the holder, he should make up the loss with a reasonable amount of money. If the loss is due to a natural disaster, and the holder cannot be blamed for it, the owner bears the loss. If the samples or goods are perishable, they will be sold off and the money will be kept by the holder.

Ebara *kôri.*

When a party receives an offer accompanied by samples or goods and is unable to return them due to unavoidable circumstances, the owner is obliged to assume the loss. If the holder incurs any expense for keeping the samples or goods, or if he finds them damaged or lost, the owner should bear the loss. If the samples or goods are perishable, they will be sold off and the money kept by the holder.

Higashi-tama *kôri* and Minami-toshima *kôri.*

If a party receives an offer accompanied with samples or goods, and finds himself unable to return the samples or goods due to unavoidable circumstances, the holder should inform the owner of the facts immediately in writing or by messenger. If the samples or the goods have cost the holder some expense, the owner of the samples or the goods is obliged to pay. If they are lost, the two parties will negotiate. As for perishable items, the holder occasionally sells them off and keeps the money. Even if the things rot, the holder is not responsible if it is the result of something beyond his control.

Kita-toshima *kôri*.

The answer is the same as stated in Topic 5.

Minami-adachi *kôri*.

Regarding the first question, after informing the owner of the situation, the holder keeps the goods until he hears from the owner. Regarding the second, the holder can be reimbursed for the expense. If the goods are lost, the holder is responsible. As to the third question, the greatest possible care will be taken so that the holder's loss will be as little as possible.

Shitaya Ward.

Regarding the first question, in a case where samples cannot be returned due to unavoidable circumstances, the two parties will discuss the settlement. There is no established practice. Regarding the second, if the samples cause the holder some expense, the owner should cover it. If they are lost, the holder should compensate for the loss. As to the third question, even if the things are perishable, the holder cannot dispose of them at his convenience, unless he has the consent of the owner.

Kanda Ward.

When samples or goods cannot be returned, the holder occasionally makes a rough appraisal of them and sends the owner the money. Since samples are usually only worth about one yen, we have never heard of them being returned. If the holder incurs expenses in keeping the goods, the two parties often jointly share them. If the goods are lost, the holder is responsible. If they are perishable, the holder occasionally sells them off and keeps the money.

Akasaka Ward and Azabu Ward.

Regarding the first question, if the owner asks the holder to return the goods, the holder should send him substitutes or money equivalent to the value of the goods. Regarding the second, any expense incurred will be borne by the owner. If the goods are lost, the loss will be covered by the holder. As to the third question, there is no established practice.

Hongô Ward.

We cannot say how the offeree should act, for we do not know why the goods cannot be returned. As to the second question, expenses incurred should be borne by the owner. If the goods are lost, the loss will be covered by the holder. Regarding the third question, even if the goods are perishable, the holder cannot sell them off and keep the money, unless the owner asks him to do so. But fish wholesalers are an exception.

CHIBA PREFECTURE

Awa *kôri*, Hei *kôri*, Asai *kôri* and Nagasa *kôri*.

If the holder fails to accept the offer, he should return the samples to the owner, regardless of the quantity. Even if he himself has no intention of buying the goods, however, he may want to expand the sale of the goods in his district. In this case he will ask the owner to leave some samples in his hands. Since the sample is usually small, it causes him no expense. If the samples are lost, the owner pays for them. In cases involving certain kinds of goods, the two parties discuss warehouse rates and other terms, and the owner is responsible for payment. When the two parties are accustomed to dealing with each other, it is rare that troubles arise over the custody of goods, even if the holder cannot accept the goods received. Depending on the situation, the holder may keep the goods untouched, without asking for any compensation, or may send them back and pay the freight. For merchants who have dealings with each other have a very close relationship. If the goods kept in custody are lost, unless the loss occurs in a great accident, such as a flood or a fire, the holder, needless to say, cannot be so indifferent to the loss as to do nothing. He will immediately ask the owner to discuss the loss. If the goods are liable to perish, a holder who is closely related to the owner will sometimes sell them off, even at lower prices than those originally offered, and keep the money. If the holder does not have such a close relationship to the owner, he will keep the goods untouched until he receives the latter's directions for their disposal.

Katori *kôri*.

Suppose one party has received an offer accompanied by samples but cannot accept the offer due to unavoidable circumstances. According to the local practice, he should immediately send the samples back to the owner. If any expense is involved, the payment should be made by the owner. If the samples are lost, the loss should be covered by the owner, with the holder sometimes sharing part of the loss. If the goods are perishable, the holder cannot sell them off at his convenience unless he is allowed to do so by the owner.

Yamabe *kôri* and Muza *kôri*.

It is common practice for us to return the samples to the owner immediately. If they are low-priced, they need not be returned. Expenses for transport, etc., should be paid by the owner. If the samples are lost in transit, the owner will cover the loss. If they are lost while being kept by the holder, he will bear the loss. If they are perishable, the holder occasionally sells them off and keeps the money, afterwards informing the owner.

Unakami *kôri* and Sôsa *kôri*.

It is our practice to return the samples to the owner without delay, if we cannot accept the offer. If the samples cannot be returned without paying for transport, for instance, the resulting expense should be borne by the owner. If they are lost, the two parties will negotiate a settlement. If they are perishable and cannot be returned because of transport difficulties, the holder should inform the owner immediately. He cannot sell them off without the owner's consent.

Higashi-katsushika *kôri*.

The reason why the samples cannot be returned is not clear. However, if the holder incurs any expense in keeping the samples, or if they are lost, the responsibility should be taken by the owner alone. If the samples are perishable, the holder should turn them into money and return this to the owner. They will always be disposed of, regardless of whether the offer has been accepted or not.

IBARAKI PREFECTURE

Nishi-katsushika *kôri* and Sashima *kôri*.

It is enough for the holder to inform the owner of the reason why they cannot be returned. Expenses which he incurs while they are in his hands will be covered by the owner. If they are lost, the loss should be made up by the holder, unless it was caused by fire, flood, or robbery. As for the third question, the holder cannot do such a thing if it has not been agreed on in advance.

KANAGAWA PREFECTURE

Miura *kôri*.

No such business practice is known here.

Tachibana *kôri*.

Regarding the first question, since the reason is not clear why they cannot be returned, it is difficult to make a definite answer. As to the second question, if the holder incurs any expense, or if the goods are lost, the owner will cover the loss. On the third question, in the case of a commodity such as saké, the holder occasionally sells it and keeps the money.

Kita-tama *kôri*.

When a holder fails to return samples which he is expected to return, he should deliberate with the owner. If he incurs some expense, or if the samples are lost, he should do the same. If the goods are perishable, the holder sometimes sells them and keeps the money.

Ashigara-shimo *kôri*.

On the first question, if the holder fails to return the samples, he will be asked for payment. Regarding the second, the holder is responsible for expenses due to the samples, and he will compensate for accidental loss. As to the third question, the holder[1] will take proper steps, according to the owner's decision.

Prefectural Industrial Bureau.

When one party receives an offer accompanied by samples or goods, and finds that the samples or goods cannot be returned to the owner due to some circumstances, as for instance, in the case of samples of silk thread which become soiled, the holder should compensate for the loss. If the samples or goods cause the holder any expense, for example, warehouse charges or insurance premiums, the owner should make up the loss. The holder assumes liability if the samples are lost through his failure to take ordinary care. If the damage occurs in unavoidable circumstances, such as fire, theft, or some other unforeseeable event, this rule cannot be applied. If the samples are perishable, the holder should inform the owner of the fact and wait for the owner's directions. If the owner fails to reply, the holder can sell them at auction and keep the money. Suppose there are signs that the samples are about to perish. If the holder has no time to ask for the owner's directions, the holder can auction them off and inform the owner of the fact after-

[1] *Mihon-nin.*

wards.

Tochigi Prefecture

Prefectural Office.

If the holder finds that he cannot return the samples, because, for instance, they have been lost through fire, robbery, or accident, the owner is responsible for the loss, according to the old usage. If the samples or goods cause the holder any expense, the owner should cover it. If the samples are perishable, the holder will sell them off and keep the money.

Shimo-tsuga *kôri* and Samukawa *kôri*.

Regarding the first question, if there is any reason why the holder cannot return the goods or samples, he may keep them, and if any loss occurs he will not be blamed. However, he should compensate for damage if he has failed to return the samples out of negligence. Regarding the second, ordinary expenses incurred due to the samples should be paid by the holder. If the samples are lost, the holder assumes the responsibility. On the third question, if the samples are perishable, the holder will sell them off at current prices and keep the money.

Ashikaga *kôri* and Yanada *kôri*.

As to the first question, Ashikaga textile merchants have never used valuable samples. Our sample, called *kiri-bon*, is a collection of small pieces of cloth. As for silk thread, even if the goods are slightly damaged or returned after a delay, samples or goods will be returned as they are. If they are seriously damaged, the samples or goods will be bought by the holder at reasonable prices. Regarding the second question, the samples or goods will not cause us any expense, no matter how long we may keep them. (We don't handle goods in quantities which require warehousing.) While acting at someone's request, we sometimes may be obliged to incur expenses, for instance, in transit. The person who has asked us for the business is responsible for such expenses. If samples of silk thread, or goods, are lost, the holder will cover the loss at reasonable prices. We do not know of the case referred to in the third question.

Mie Prefecture

Suzuka *kôri*.

When a party receives an offer accompanied by samples or goods and cannot return them due to unavoidable circumstances, he will negotiate a satisfactory settlement with the other party. Anyway, cases differ. If the samples or goods cause the holder some expense or if they are lost, the two parties also discuss the settlement. If they are liable to perish, the holder sometimes sells them and keeps the money in hand.

Ichishi *kôri*.

If the holder finds that the samples or goods cannot be returned, he will inform the offeror of the fact and will compensate for the loss either in money or in goods. The holder usually covers his own expenses. If the samples are lost, the holder will bear all or half of the loss, depending on his agreement with the owner. On some occasions, the owner will defray the loss in full. Regarding the third question, our practice is the same as stated in the topic.

Nabari *kôri* and Iga *kôri*.

When the samples or the goods cannot be returned, the holder will talk with the owner and then dispose of them. The holder's expenses will be paid by the owner. If the samples are lost, the owner should bear the loss. As for goods sent out just after an order had arrived, the holder is obliged to take charge of them. If the samples or goods are liable to perish, the holder is largely responsible for their preservation. Therefore, the holder will put them on sale if circumstances warrant.

Kita-muro *kôri*.

If the party receiving an offer finds there are good reasons why the samples or goods cannot be returned, he should send out the samples or goods after informing the holder in advance of what steps should be taken afterwards. As for other goods, the holder should inquire of the owner about the matter and take proper steps according to the owner's directions. If the holder incurs some expense for their custody, both parties will share it. If the samples or goods are lost or damaged, the owner will bear the loss. If they are liable to perish, the holder will inform the owner of the fact and then sell them and keep the money.

Aichi Prefecture

Nakajima *kôri*.

If there are good reasons why the samples or goods cannot be returned, the party holding them should pay the other party for them. If the samples or goods cause him some expense, the holder himself should bear the expense. If they are lost, the holder is responsible for the loss. If they are liable to perish, the holder will sell them off and keep the money.

Nagoya Ward.

If there are good reasons why the samples or goods cannot be returned, the party holding them will pay the owner a reasonable amount of money. If the samples cause the holder any expense, this should be settled between the two. If they are lost, in principle the loss should be paid by the holder, since he is responsible for the loss. In some cases, however, the two parties will discuss the settlement. If they are liable to perish, the two parties will adopt some expedient for example, the holder may sell them and keep the money. There is no established rule.

Chita *kôri*.

If there are good reasons why the goods cannot be returned, it is a matter of course that the holder should inquire of the owner about the steps to be taken. If the samples or goods cause the holder some expense, or if the samples or goods are liable to perish, the holder may sell them off only with the owner's consent. In an emergency, however, if the holder has no time to wait for the owner's consent, he can resort to some expedient, for instance, he may sell off the samples or goods and keep the money. Then the holder bears part of any expense. If they are lost, the loss will be covered by the holder unless the loss is due to unavoidable circumstances.

Minami-shidara *kôri*.

Regarding the first question, the holder should pay a reasonable price. As to the second, the expense will be paid by the owner. If they are lost, the holder will bear the loss. A case such as that described in the third question of the topic occurs from time to time.

Atsumi *kôri*.

When the samples or goods cannot be returned, the holder should take proper steps immediately and inform the owner of what he has done. When the samples cause the holder some expense, or when they are lost, if the owner has sent the samples voluntarily, he bears the loss, but if the holder has ordered them from the owner, the holder is responsible. If they are liable to perish, the holder will sell them off and keep the money.

Kaitô *kôri* and Kaisai *kôri*.

If one party finds that he cannot return the samples, he should ask consent from the other party. If he loses them, he should compensate for the loss at a reasonable price if the owner consents. When the samples are found liable to perish, he cannot freely dispose of them at his own convenience, unless the other party agrees.

Aichi *kôri*.

There is no need for samples to be returned. If one party finds that he cannot return the samples, he should buy them at the current price. Expenses incurred by the holder should be paid by the owner. If they are lost, the holder should compensate for the loss. If the loss is due to unavoidable circumstances, such as a flood, fire, or theft, the owner should make up for the loss. If they are liable to perish, the holder will inform the seller of the fact and will act upon the seller's advice.

Niwa *kôri* and Haguri *kôri*.

It is a matter of course that the samples should be returned. But if there is some reason why they cannot be returned, the matter should be settled between the two parties. If the samples or goods cause the holder some expense, if they are lost, or if they are liable to perish, there should be negotiations between the two parties.

Shizuoka Prefecture

Prefectural Office.

Regarding the first question, if the samples or goods cannot be returned, they should be paid for at reasonable prices by the holder. As to the second, if they cause the holder some expense, or if they are lost, the expense or loss should be for the owner to bear. No such case as described in the third question is known here.

Udo *kôri* and Abe *kôri*.

We have never heard of such a case as described in the first question. If the holder fails to return them without a good reason, the owner will ask him to send them back. As to the second question, if they cause the owner some expense, the owner will pay it himself. If they are lost, the loss also will be upon the owner. Regarding the third question, the holder sometimes finds such action unavoidable.

Inasa *kôri* and Aratama *kôri*.

In our case, samples are always low in price. After keeping them for a short time, the holder will return them to the owner. If they are lost or if they are liable to perish the holder will not return them. If they cause the holder some expense, the owner will pay it.

Kamo *kôri* and Naka *kôri*.

If there is some reason why the samples or goods cannot be returned, the holder will inform the owner of the reason and then he will dispose of them. If they cause the holder some expense while in his hands, the owner will pay it. If they are lost due to carelessness on the part of the holder, he will pay for the loss. If they are liable to perish, the holder will sell them off with the owner's consent. But if the holder has no time to ask for the owner's consent, he will sell them off and inform the owner of the fact. The money will be kept in his hands.

Saya *kôri* and Kitô *kôri*.

Reasons why the samples cannot be returned are as follows: (1) loss, (2) decay, (3) destruction by fire, (4) expense to the holder. In each of these cases, the supplier of the samples must bear the loss. No one asks another to keep perishables in hand, and no one is willing to keep them, without a pre-arranged agreement.

GIFU PREFECTURE

Mugi *kôri*.

Regarding the first question, when the samples or goods cannot be returned, the party keeping them will sell them off, keep the money and discuss the settlement with the other party. As to the second, when the samples, or the goods, cause the holder some expense, the owner will pay the expense. If they are lost, the holder will compensate for the loss. Regarding the third, if they are liable to perish, the holder will occasionally sell them off and keep the money.

Ampachi *kôri*.

Regarding the first question, settlement will be made between the two parties. As to the second, the expense will be paid by the owner. The holder is responsible for the loss. Regarding the third question, if the samples or goods are liable to perish, the holder will sell them off and keep the money in hand.

Fuwa *kôri*.

If they cannot be returned, the holder will keep them longer. If they cause the holder some expense, the owner will pay it. If they are lost, the holder should be blamed for the loss. If they are liable to perish, the holder sells them off and keeps the money.

Atsumi *kôri*, Kagami *kôri* and Katagata *kôri*.

Regarding the first question, after informing the owner of the reasons, the holder will keep them longer. As to the second, if they are lost, the holder will be blamed for the loss. If they cause the holder some expense, it will be paid by either party, depending on the case. Regarding the third, the holder will turn them into money and keep the money for the owner.

Tagi *kôri* and Kami-ishizu *kôri*.

If it is impossible for the holder to return the samples or goods to the owner, the holder will return an amount of money estimated as their worth. If they cause the holder some expense, he will pay it himself. If they are lost, the holder will cover the loss with an estimated amount of money. If they are liable to perish, the holder will inform the owner of the fact and turn them into money, which he will keep for the owner.

Ôno *kôri* and Ikeda *kôri*.

There is no established rule. It is usually settled between the two parties. This also holds true of expenses and loss. If the goods are liable to perish, the holder occasionally sells them off and keeps the money for the owner. This is a duty common to us all.

Haguri *kôri* and Nakajima *kôri*.

Regarding the first question, the holder will pay the prices estimated for the samples or goods. As to the second, the holder will pass the expense on to the owner. If he has lost them through negligence, he will pay the loss. Regarding the third, the holder usually sells them off and keeps the money.

Ena *kôri*.

Regarding the first question, there is no established practice; the steps to be taken are different in each case, depending on the goods and circumstances. As to the second, the expense will be paid by the owner. The loss will be borne, in most cases, by the holder. Regarding the third, the holder will sell them off and keep the money.

Kamo *kôri*.

When the samples or goods cannot be returned due to unavoidable circumstances, the holder will keep them in custody. If the samples or goods are liable to perish, the holder will sell them off and keep the money. If they are lost, or if they cause the holder some expense, he will usually accept the responsibility.

Kani *kôri.*

Regarding the first question, the holder will keep the samples in his hands and inform the owner. As to the second, if they cause the holder some expense, the owner will pay it. If they are lost, the holder will pay for the loss. Regarding the third, if they are liable to perish, the holder will turn them into money and keep the money for the owner.

Atsumi *kôri*, Gifu Township.

If the samples cannot be returned, the holder should inform the owner of the reasons. If they are lost, the holder should compensate for the loss. If they are liable to perish, the holder will keep them as they are or turn them into money for the owner.

Ôgaki.

Regarding the first question, there should be another talk between the two parties. If the goods or samples cause the holder some expense, it should be borne by the owner. If they are lost, the loss should be covered by the holder. Regarding the third question, the holder will sell them off and keep the money for the owner.

Ena *kôri*, Nakatsugawa Village.

When there is some reason why the samples or goods cannot be returned, the holder should inform the owner of the reasons and wait for the latter's directions. If the samples or goods cause the holder some expense, he should pay it. When they are lost, the holder should cover the loss, unless it is caused by natural disaster. When the goods are perishable, the holder may as well sell them at reasonable prices as keep them.

Shimo-ishizu *kôri*, Takasu Township.

When they cannot be returned, the holder can buy them if the prices are reasonable. But, if the prices are unreasonable, he should inform the owner of the fact. If the goods cause the holder some expense, the owner should pay it. As for expenses to the holder while they are in his hands, it should be paid by the holder if he has kept them as part of his job, and it should be paid by the owner if he has kept them as a duty. Sometimes it will be divided between the two, depending on the cause of the loss. If they are liable to perish, the holder usually sells them off, turning them into money for the owner, and informs him of the fact.

Haguri *kôri*, Takegahana Village.

When the samples or goods cannot be returned, the holder has no choice but to keep them in his hands. If they cause the holder some expense, he should pay it himself. If they are lost, the holder should cover the loss, but the owner also should share part of it. If they are liable to perish, it is best for the holder to sell them off and keep the money for the owner.

Yamagata *kôri*, Takatomi Village.

The samples or goods should be returned to the owner without fail, unless there is a good reason acceptable to everyone, such as fire or robbery. If they cause some expense, or if they are lost, the holder should bear the responsibility to the owner at reasonable prices. If perishable goods cannot be returned to the owner within a short time, it is best for the holder to sell them off at reasonable prices.

Mugi *kôri*, Kôzuchi Village.

Regarding the first question, no such case is known here. As to the second, the party keeping them should bear the expense. On the third, even if they are liable to perish, the party keeping them cannot sell them off as he likes. The loss should be covered at a reasonable price.

Haguri *kôri*, Kasamatsu Village.

Regarding the first question, the prices should be paid. As to the second, the expense should be borne by the owner. If they are lost, the prices should be paid, too. On the third, in most cases, they will be turned into money, and the money will be kept in hand.

Fuwa *kôri*, Tarui Village.

Regarding the first question, the party keeping them will inform the owner of the reasons, and they will discuss the proper steps to be taken. As to the second, the expense which they have cost the holder will be paid by the owner. If they are lost, the loss will be borne by the holder himself. On the third, they occasionally will be turned into money, and the money will be kept in hand.

Ôno *kôri*, Miwa Village.

If the holder fails to return the samples or goods to the owner in violation of a prior agreement, the matter will become a legal dispute to be settled in court. If they cause the holder some expense, he will negotiate with the owner. If they are lost, the holder will cover the loss. If they are liable to perish, he will inform the owner of the fact and wait for the owner's reply. After that he will turn them into money and keep the money. Sometimes the holder will return the goods themselves.

Ampachi *kôri*, Gôdo Village.

If the holder fails to return the samples or goods to the owner, he will be regarded as having bought them. If he loses them, he should compensate for the loss. If they are liable to perish, he will wait for the owner's directions and then take proper steps.

Tagi *kôri*, Shimada Village.

No answer is given.

Ena *kôri*, Iwa Village.

Regarding the first question, if there is some reason why they cannot be returned, the loss will be the owner's. As to the second, if they cause some expense, it will be covered by the owner. If they are lost, the loss will be covered by the holder. On the third, they will be turned into money, and the money will be kept in hand.

Kamo *kôri*, Hosome Village.

If there is some reason why the samples or goods cannot be returned, the two parties will make every effort to cover the prices. If they cause some expense, the owner will assume it. If they are lost, the two parties will share the loss as stated above. If they are liable to perish, the party entrusted with them will sell them off and keep the money.

Toki *kôri*, Takayama Village.

Regarding the first question, they will be left with the holder for the time being. As to the second, the expense should be assumed by the owner of the goods. If they are lost due to unavoidable circumstances, the owner will cover the loss. The answer to the third question is yes. The holder will turn them into money and keep it.

Kani *kôri*, Mitake Village.

Regarding the first question, the only possible step is to keep the samples longer and report the fact to the owner by mail or telegram. As to the second, expenses not exceeding the value of the samples will be covered by the owner. If they are lost, the owner of course bears the loss. On the third, they will be turned into money, which will be kept in hand.

Ena *kôri*, Akechi Village.

Regarding the first question, there is no established rule. The steps to be taken are different from case to case, depending on the reason and the goods. As to the second, expenses will be paid by the owner, and a loss, usually by the holder. On the third, they often will be turned into money, and the money kept.

Mugi *kôri*, Seki Village.

Regarding the first question, when they cannot be returned, the samples or goods will be kept in custody for a longer time. As to the second, the expense will be assumed by the owner. When they are lost, the holder will pay for the loss. On the third, when the samples or the goods are liable to perish, the holder should ask the owner for directions. Then he should sell the goods themselves by sample or sell the samples only and keep the money for the owner.

Ôno *kôri*, Takayama Township.

When they cannot be returned, the reason should be reported in writing to the owner. If they cause some expense while being kept in custody, the expense should be paid by the owner. If they are lost, the loss should be covered by the holder. If they are liable to perish, the holder will sell them off and keep the money after obtaining the owner's prior approval either orally or, if he cannot talk with the owner, in writing.

Motosu *kôri*, Kitagata Village.

If one party receives an offer accompanied by samples or goods and finds some reason that they cannot be returned, he should keep them in his custody and inform the owner of the fact. If they cause the holder some expense, or if they are lost for a good reason, the owner should assume responsibility. If they are liable to perish, the holder will sell them off and keep the money.

Kamo *kôri*, Ôta Village.

If one party receives an offer accompanied by samples or goods and finds some reason why they cannot be returned, he should keep them in his custody. If they are liable to perish, he should sell them off and keep the money. If they cause the holder some expense, it is assumed by the owner. If they are lost, the holder usually covers the loss.

Kaisai *kôri* and Shimo-ishizu *kôri*.

When samples or goods cannot be returned, the steps to be taken are as follows: if the price is reasonable, the holder will buy them, and if not, he will keep them in custody. The holder should inform the owner of the reason why the samples or goods cannot be returned. If they cause the holder some expense, the owner should pay it. If they are lost, the loss should be covered by the holder if he has kept them as a commission earner; if he has kept them as an obligation it should be covered by either or both parties after they have discussed the cause of the loss and its proper settlement. If they are liable to perish, the holder will sell them off and keep the money, informing the owner of the fact.

Gujô *kôri*.

If there is a compelling reason why the samples or goods cannot be returned, the holder should negotiate with the owner on the basis of current prices. If they cause the holder some expense, or if they are lost, he should bear the expense or loss himself. Sometimes, the holder will take part of the responsibility by mutual agreement. If they are liable to perish, the holder will sell them off and keep the money for the owner.

Topic 7: After Approval[1] Has Been Given to an Account, or Payment Based on It Has Been Made, Is It Permissible to Raise an Objection[2] If Some Error of Computation or Some Misrepresentation[3] Is Subsequently Found?

TOKYO METROPOLIS

Paper Wholesalers (*Kiu-kumi*).[4]

Yes, it is permissible.

Oil Wholesalers.

It is permissible to raise an objection later.

Stone Wholesalers.

Yes, it is permissible.

Medicine Wholesalers.

Yes, it is.

Sugar Wholesalers.

There cannot be a misrepresentation in computation. In case an unavoidable error in computation is found after an account has been approved, or payment based on it has been made, it is permissible to settle accounts again, even much later, if the original record has been kept.

Dried Bonito Wholesalers.

If an error in computation or a misrepresentation is found later, the account or payment will be corrected even after a long lapse of time.

Soy Wholesalers.

It is permissible to raise an objection.

Timber Wholesalers.

It is permissible to correct the account or payment later, if an error in computation or a misrepresentation is found.

Timber Traders.[5]

It is permissible to raise an objection.

Timber Traders (*Senju*).[6]

[1] *Shôdaku.*

[2] *Koshô-o-môshitateru.*

[3] *Itsuwari.*

[4] *Kiu-kumi kami-donya.*

[5] *Zaimoku tôsei-kumiai.*

[6] *Senju zaimoku-kumiai.*

The account or payment will be corrected at any time if necessary.

Fuel Wholesalers.

The account or payment will be corrected at any time, if an error in computation or a misrepresentation is found, even after the account has been approved, or payment based on it has been made.

Porcelain Wholesalers.

It is permissible to ask for settlement of the accurate account, if an error of computation or a misrepresentation is found later.

Paper Wholesalers (*Shôkai-kumi*).[1]

It is permissible to raise an objection.

Rice Traders.[2]

It is permissible to raise an objection, even after a long lapse of time, in case an error in computation or a misrepresentation is found later. If a dispute occurs owing to the fact that there has been no provision for it beforehand, it will be carried before the court.

Salt Wholesalers.

The account or payment can be corrected later.

Copper and Iron Wholesalers.

It is quite natural that it should be permissible.

Kudari Saké Wholesalers.[3]

If an error of computation is found, it is quite natural to raise an objection to it. We should settle the account or payment once more, and send the other party an accurate account. Of course, there should be a word of apology. We cannot understand at all what the word "misrepresentation" means.

Mosquito Net Wholesalers.

It is quite natural that the account or payment should be settled again if an error in computation or a misrepresentation is found later.

Lime and Shell Wholesalers.

In case an error in computation or a misrepresentation is found later, a serious warning should be given so that the account or

[1] *Shôkai-kumi kami-donya.*

[2] *Beikoku sangyô-kumiai.*

[3] *Kudari sake-donya.*

payment may be corrected. If the warning is flatly rejected, and if no original record is kept, no pressure will be brought upon the wrongdoer. Our only recourse is to break business relations with him forever.

Saké Wholesalers.

If an error in computation is found later, it is natural to correct the account or payment.

Tobacco Wholesalers.

If an error in computation is found later, the account or payment should be resettled. When there is no evidence whatever, there can be no blame, even if it is found to be wrong.

Matting Wholesalers.

Of course it is permissible to settle the account again if an error in computation or a misrepresentation is found later.

Drapery Wholesalers.

Yes, it is. It is permissible to raise an objection to it.

Fuel Wholesalers (*Umite-kumi*).[1]

Yes, it is permissible to settle the account again if an error in computation or a misrepresentation is found later, even after a long lapse of time.

Kôjimachi Ward.

It is permissible to raise an objection to it if an error in computation or a misrepresentation is found later.

Nihombashi Ward.

According to our business practices, it is permissible to settle an error in computation.

Kyôbashi Ward.

Of course it is permissible to raise an objection to it.

Yotsuya Ward and Ushigome Ward.

In case an error in computation or a misrepresentation is found later, it is permissible to raise an objection to it, even if the account has been approved or payment based on it has been made.

Asakusa Ward.

It is permissible to raise an objection to it if an error in computation or some misrepresentation is found later.

Honjo Ward.

It is permissible to raise an objection to an account which has

[1] *Umite-kumi shintan-donya.*

already been approved or paid if an error in computation or some misrepresentation is found later.

Ebara *kôri*.

It is permissible to raise an objection to an account which has already been approved or paid if an error in computation or a misrepresentation is found later.

Higashi-tama *kôri* and Minami-toshima *kôri*.

It is permissible for either party to raise an objection to it to the other party if an error in computation or a misrepresentation is found later.

Kita-toshima *kôri*.

In such a case, all records of the account will be examined closely. If any errors are found in them, we shall settle the account to the satisfaction of both parties.

Minami-adachi *kôri*.

It is permissible to settle the account, or payment, once more if an error in computation or a misrepresentation is found later.

Shitaya Ward.

It is permissible to raise an objection to an account, even after it has been approved or payment based on it has been made, if an error in computation or a misrepresentation is found later.

Kanda Ward.

Yes, it is permissible to raise an objection to it.

Akasaka Ward and Azabu Ward.

Yes, it is.

Hongô Ward.

Yes, it is.

CHIBA PREFECTURE

Awa *kôri*, Hei *kôri*, Asai *kôri* and Nagasa *kôri*.

It is permissible to raise an objection at any time if an error of computation or a misrepresentation is found. However, in the case of a mistake in calculation, the injured party cannot claim a re-settlement, since he had the chance to examine the account. But the parties can ask each other to show their account books.

Katori *kôri*.

It is permissible to raise an objection even after an account has been approved if an error in computation or a misrepresentation is found later.

Yamabe *kôri* and Muza *kôri*.

It is permissible to raise an objection to it at any time if an error in computation or a misrepresentation is found later.

Unakami *kôri* and Sôsa *kôri*.

Even after an account has been approved, it is permissible to raise an objection, if an error in computation or a misrepresentation is found later.

Higashi-katsushika *kôri*.

It is permissible to raise an objection to it.

IBARAKI PREFECTURE

Nishi-katsushika *kôri* and Sashima *kôri*.

In such a case it is permissible to raise an objection to it later.

KANAGAWA PREFECTURE

Miura *kôri*.

Of course it is permissible to raise an objection to it.

Tachibana *kôri*.

Yes, it is. It is permissible to do so.

Kita-tama *kôri*.

After an account has been approved or payment based on it has been made, it is permissible to raise an objection to it if an error in computation or a misrepresentation is found later. There will be no evidence to prove the objection, however, if the two parties have no records of the computation, even when they both agree with each other on moral justice.

Ashigara-shimo *kôri*.

According to our practice, it is permissible for either party to raise an objection to it.

Prefectural Industrial Bureau.

After an account has been approved or payment based on it has been made, it is permissible to raise an objection to it in case an error in computation or a misrepresentation is found later. In that case, however, neither party can break the original contract.

TOCHIGI PREFECTURE

Prefectural Office.

It is permissible to raise an objection to it.

Shimo-tsuga *kôri* and Samukawa *kôri*.

No answer is given.

Ashikaga *kôri* and Yanada *kôri*.

If the party who has suffered the loss raises an objection, showing evidence such as an account book or other things,[1] the other party cannot reject the objection on the ground that the account has already been approved or that payment based on it has been made. If the other party dares to stick to his rejection for his own profit, he will lose very friend and customer forever.

MIE PREFECTURE

Suzuka *kôri.*

Even if an account has been approved or payment based on it has been made, it is permissible to raise an objection to it if an error in computation or a misrepresentation is found later.

Ichishi *kôri.*

If there is no doubt about the error in computation or the misrepresentation, the excess payment should be returned and the accounts resettled.

Nabari *kôri* and Iga *kôri.*

After an account has been approved or payment based on it has been made, it is usually difficult to raise an objection to it. However, if the error or the misrepresentation is beyond question and is recognized by both parties, it is permissible to raise an objection.

Kita-muro *kôri.*

Even after an account has been approved or payment based on it has been made, it is permissible to raise an objection to it immediately if an error in computation or a misrepresentation is found.

AICHI PREFECTURE

Nakajima *kôri.*

Yes, it is.

Nagoya Ward.

Yes, it is permissible.

Chita *kôri.*

If an error in computation is found, it is permissible to raise an objection later.

Minami-shidara *kôri.*

It is permissible to raise an objection.

Atsumi *kôri.*

[1] A record of a business transaction of any kind will be left by one party or the other. Even if one of them has made an error of computation, the other will not. The error can thus be corrected at any time.

It is permissible to raise an objection.

Kaitô *kôri* and Kaisai *kôri*.

If an error in computation or a misrepresentation is found later, it is permissible to raise an objection to it.

Aichi *kôri*.

Even after an account has been approved or payment based on it has been made, it is permissible to raise an objection, if evidence of an error in computation or a misrepresentation is found.

Niwa *kôri* and Haguri *kôri*.

If an error in computation is found later, it is permissible to settle accounts once more, even after the original account has been approved, or payment based on it has been made. If a misrepresentation is found in a contract, it is, of course, permissible to raise an objection.

SHIZUOKA PREFECTURE

Prefectural Office.

Yes.

Udo *kôri* and Abe *kôri*.

Yes, it is permissible. If it occurs after too long a lapse of time, however, it will be regarded as ineffective.

Inasa *kôri* and Aratama *kôri*.

It is permissible to raise an objection.

Kamo *kôri* and Naka *kôri*.

If an error in computation or a misrepresentation is found later it is permissible for either party to raise an objection to it and ask for compensation.

Saya *kôri* and Kitô *kôri*.

Even after an account has been approved or payment based on it has been made, it is permissible to raise an objection to it, if an error in computation or some misrepresentation is found later.

GIFU PREFECTURE

Mugi *kôri*.

If an error in computation is found later, it is permissible to raise an objection to it.

Ampachi *kôri*.

It is permissible to raise an objection without delay and to call on the other party to settle accounts once more.

Fuwa *kôri*.

It is permissible to raise an objection without delay and to ask the other party to settle accounts.

Atsumi *kôri*, Kagami *kôri* and Katagata *kôri*.

Yes.

Tagi *kôri* and Kami-ishizu *kôri*.

Even after an account has been approved or payment based on it has been made, it is permissible to raise an objection to it, if an error in computation or a misrepresentation is found later.

Ôno *kôri* and Ikeda *kôri*.

If an error in computation is found later, it is of course permissible to raise an objection to it.

Haguri *kôri* and Nakajima *kôri*.

Yes, it is.

Ena *kôri*.

Yes.

Kamo *kôri*.

Even after an account has been approved or payment based on it has been made, it is permissible to raise an objection to it if an error in computation or a misrepresentation is found later. However, in such cases the injured party often assumes the loss.

Kani *kôri*.

If an error in computation is found later it is permissible for each party to ask the other to correct the accounts. As for misrepresentation, it appears to be difficult for either party to raise an objection, even if it is permissible to do so.

Atsumi *kôri*, Gifu Township.

It is permissible to raise an objection.

Ôgaki.

According to our practice, it is permissible to raise an objection and to ask the other party to correct the error.

Ena *kôri*, Nakatsugawa Village.

It is permissible to raise an objection.

Shimo-ishizu *kôri*, Takasu Township.

It is permissible to raise an objection later.

Haguri *kôri*, Takegahana Village.

In case an error in computation or a misrepresentation is found later, it is a matter of course to settle accounts once more. The Law of Commerce, however, says that if one party wants to press another for money, he must complete the action within a period of six months. If he fails to finish it within that period, what shall we do? We cannot give a definite answer.

Yamagata *kôri*, Takatomi Village.

If an error in computation or a misrepresentation is found later, the accounts should be settled again accurately.

Mugi *kôri*, Kôzuchi Village.

If an error in computation is found later, it is permissible to raise an objection.

Haguri *kôri*, Kasamatsu Village.

Yes, it is.

Fuwa *kôri*, Tarui Village.

It is permissible to raise an objection.

Ôno *kôri*, Miwa Village.

If an error in computation is found later, it is permissible to settle the accounts once more.

Ampachi *kôri*, Gôdo Village.

An objection cannot be raised in such a case unless the two parties have dealt with each other for a long time.

Tagi *kôri*, Shimada Village.

No answer is given.

Ena *kôri*, Iwa Village.

No answer is given.

Kamo *kôri*, Hosome Village.

It is permissible to raise an objection later.

Toki *kôri*, Takayama Village.

Yes.

Kani *kôri*, Mitake Village.

It is permissible to raise an objection.

Ena *kôri*, Akechi Village.

Yes.

Mugi *kôri*, Seki Village.

It is permissible to raise an objection, and ask the other party to correct the accounts.

Ôno *kôri*, Takayama Township.

If an error in computation or a misrepresentation is found later, close examination should be made once more.

Motosu *kôri*, Kitagata Village.

Even after an account has been approved or payment based on it has been made, it is permissible to raise an objection to it if an error in computation or a misrepresentation is found later.

Kamo *kôri,* Ôta Village.

Even after an account has been approved or payment based on it has been made, it is permissible to raise an objection if an error in computation or a misrepresentation is found later. After correcting it, the payer sometimes bears the loss.

Kaisai *kôri* and Shimo-ishizu *kôri.*

It is permissible to raise an objection.

Gujô *kôri.*

It is permissible to raise an objection.

CHAPTER II
PERFORMANCE OF CONTRACT

Topic 1: It Is a Matter of Course That the Obligor Must Obtain the Permission of the Obligee[1] to Fulfill a Contract by Delivery of Goods Other Than Those Agreed upon in the Contract,—by Fulfilling,[2] for Instance, a Contract for Grain by Delivery of Dry Goods; but Is There Any Situation in Which Permission of This Nature, Though Not Expressed, Is Implied?

Tokyo Metropolis

Paper Wholesalers (*Kiu-kumi*).[3]

The matter will be settled according to the circumstances.

Oil Wholesalers.

We do not have such cases.

Stone Wholesalers.

No, there is not. The obligor must obtain the permission of the obligee.

Dried Bonito Wholesalers.

With the permission of the obligee, we sometimes perform a contract by delivery of other goods.

Sugar Wholesalers.

Such cases cannot be found among us.

Medicine Wholesalers.

Such cases cannot be found among us.

Soy Wholesalers.

Such cases cannot be found among us.

Timber Wholesalers.

With the permission of the obligee, a contract can be performed by delivery of other goods. However, occasionally the permission can be implied though not expressed.

Timber Traders.[4]

With the permission of the obligee, a contract can be performed

1 *Kenrisha.*

2 *Hensai.*

3 *Kiu-kumi kami-donya.*

4 *Zaimoku tôsei-kumiai.*

by delivery of other goods. However, occasionally the permission can be implied though not expressed.

Timber Traders (*Senju*).[1]

Such permission is occasionally implied though not expressed.

Fuel Wholesalers.

Such cases cannot be found among us.

Porcelain Wholesalers.

Such permission must be expressed.

Paper Wholesalers (*Shôkai-kumi*).[2]

Such permission must be expressed by the obligee.

Rice Traders.[3]

Rice is finely graded according to quality for each village or district. So it is impossible for us rice traders to perform a contract by delivery of other goods. Occasionally a certain amount of rice, say 100 bales, is borrowed in one year, as provided in the law, with a promise of returning it in the next year. In such cases, however, it is impossible to perform it by delivery of other goods.

Salt Wholesalers.

No, such a case is impossible.

Copper and Iron Wholesalers.

Such cases cannot be found among us.

Kudari Saké Wholesalers.[4]

Such cases cannot be found among us.

Mosquito Net Wholesalers.

Such cases cannot be found among us.

Lime and Shell Wholesalers.

Unless the permission is definitely expressed by the obligee, a contract cannot be performed by delivery of other goods; the goods we handle fluctuate sharply in value.

Saké Wholesalers.[5]

There are cases in which a contract can be performed by delivery of other goods.

Tobacco Wholesalers.

Such cases cannot be found among us.

[1] *Senju zaimoku-kumiai.*

[2] *Shôkai-kumi kami-donya.*

[3] *Beikoku sangyô-kumiai.*

[4] *Kudari sake-donya.*

[5] *Sake-rui-donya.*

Matting Wholesalers.

Such cases cannot be found among us.

Drapery Wholesalers.

Such a practice cannot be found among us.

Fuel Wholesalers (*Umite-kumi*).[1]

The obligee will not accept delivery of goods different from those agreed upon in a contract. Under unavoidable circumstances, however, such cases occasionally occur.

Kôjimachi Ward.

No, such a case is impossible. Unless the permission is definitely expressed by the obligee, substitution cannot be implied to be permitted.

Nihombashi Ward.

We have no such custom, and no such cases have occurred.

Kyôbashi Ward.

If not expressed, permission cannot be regarded as implied.

Yotsuya Ward and Ushigome Ward.

Only when specific permission is obtained from the obligee can a contract be performed by delivery of other goods.

Asakusa Ward.

No, this is impossible. The only exception is a case where the obligee has consumed the goods himself.

Honjo Ward.

No, this is impossible. It is a matter of course that the obligor must obtain the permission of the obligee if he wants to perform a contract by delivery of other goods.

Ebara *kôri*.

No, this is impossible. The obligor must obtain the permission of the obligee to perform a contract by delivery of other goods.

Higashi-tama *kôri* and Minami-toshima *kôri*.

Such a case cannot be seen in this district.

Kita-toshima *kôri*.

Such a practice cannot be seen here. If substitution is necessary, the two parties should discuss the matter and make a new contract, according to the local practice.

Minami-adachi *kôri*.

No, this is impossible. Permission must be expressed.

[1] *Umite-kumi shintan-donya.*

Shitaya Ward.

Such a case has never been seen here. If not expressed, substitution can never be regarded as permitted.

Kanda Ward.

Only when he gets a definite expression of permission from the obligee can the obligor perform a contract by delivery of other goods.

Azabu Ward and Akasaka Ward.

Substitution cannot be regarded as permitted unless the permission is expressed.

Hongô Ward.

A contract cannot be performed by substitution, if not expressly permitted.

CHIBA PREFECTURE

Awa *kôri*, Hei *kôri*, Asai *kôri* and Nagasa *kôri*.

Unless permission is definitely expressed by the obligee, a contract cannot be performed by delivery of other goods.

Katori *kôri*.

No, this is impossible.

Yamabe *kôri* and Muza *kôri*.

Substitution cannot be regarded as permitted unless the permission is expressed.

Unakami *kôri* and Sôsa *kôri*.

It is a matter of course that the obligor must obtain the permission of the obligee to perform a contract by delivery of other goods. But occasionally, when the two parties are accustomed to dealing with each other, the obligor performs a contract by delivery of other goods. Then the obligor usually regards the obligee as having permitted, for instance, performance of a contract for rice by delivery of barley.

Higashi-katsushika *kôri*.

Substitution cannot be regarded as permitted unless the permission is expressed.

IBARAKI PREFECTURE

Nishi-katsushika *kôri* and Sashima *kôri*.

Unless the sort of goods to be delivered are clearly specified, it cannot be regarded as permitted.

KANAGAWA PREFECTURE

Miura *kôri*.

If not expressed, it cannot be implied as permitted.

Tachibana *kôri*.

If not expressed, it cannot be implied as permitted.

Kita-tama *kôri*.

If it is not expressed, it cannot be regarded as permitted.

Ashigara-shimo *kôri*.

The obligor cannot perform a contract by delivery of other goods without obtaining the permission of the obligee. In case the goods have been lost or destroyed, they will be compensated for in money.

Prefectural Industrial Bureau.

It is a matter of course that obligor must obtain the permission of the obligee, if he is to perform a contract by delivery of other goods than those agreed upon in the contract. If not expressed by the obligee, it will not be regarded as being permitted.

TOCHIGI PREFECTURE

Prefectural Office.

Among the same kind of traders, wholesalers, or brokers, there is a practice here that the obligee is often taken as giving permission even though this has not been expressed, according to the local practice.

Shimo-tsuga *kôri* and Samukawa *kôri*.

If the obligor is to perform a contract by delivery of other goods than those agreed upon in the contract, he should obtain permission from the obligee. But it is possible that the permission may be implied though not expressed.

Ashikaga *kôri* and Yanada *kôri*.

We have no practice here of performing a contract by delivery of other goods.

MIE PREFECTURE

Suzuka *kôri*.

It is a matter of course that the obligor must obtain the permission of the obligee to perform a contract by delivery of other goods. There is no situation in which such permission is implied though not expressed.

Ichishi *kôri*.

Such cases cannot be found here.

Nabari *kôri* and Iga *kôri*.

If not expressed, no permission is implied.

Kita-muro *kôri*.

It is a matter of course that unless he obtains the permission of the obligee, the obligor cannot perform a contract by delivery of other goods. On some occasions, however, when the obligor wishes to perform a contract by delivery of goods[1] that will surely be acceptable to the obligee, it is possible that such permission may be implied though not expressed.

AICHI PREFECTURE

Nakajima *kôri*.

If unavoidable circumstances require it, there may be a situation in which such permission is implied though not expressed.

Nagoya Ward.

When it is not expressed, such permission cannot be taken as implied.

Chita *kôri*.

When it is not expressed, such permission cannot be taken as implied.

Minami-shidara *kôri*.

It can be performed only after full discussion.

Atsumi *kôri*.

When it is not expressed, such permission cannot be taken as implied.

Kaitô *kôri* and Kaisai *kôri*.

Even when it is not expressed, such permission is occasionally taken as implied.

Aichi *kôri*.

When it is not expressed, such permission has never been taken as implied.

Niwa *kôri* and Haguri *kôri*.

If a contract is to be performed by delivery of other goods, there should be deliberations between the two parties. So we have never seen a case of implied permission. If not expressed, such permission cannot be taken as implied.

SHIZUOKA PREFECTURE

Prefectural Office.

If the obligor has failed in an undertaking, though not been ruined, he occasionally performs a contract by delivery of other goods even though permission has not been expressed by the obligee.

[1] Goods equivalent in value to those agreed upon in the contract.

Udo *kôri* and Abe *kôri*.

If not expressed, such permission cannot be taken as implied.

Inasa *kôri* and Aratama *kôri*.

If not expressed, such permission cannot be taken as implied.

Kamo *kôri* and Naka *kôri*.

If the obligor performs a contract by delivery of other goods, it is occasionally considered to be permitted if he performs the contract by delivery to the obligee of necessities.

Saya *kôri* and Kitô *kôri*.

Acceptance of delivery will be considered to constitute permission, even though it has not been expressed as such.

Gifu Prefecture

Mugi *kôri*.

When the obligee has not expressed permission, performance of a contract by delivery of other goods can never be considered permissible.

Ampachi *kôri*.

Though not expressed, substitution is occasionally taken as permitted.

Fuwa *kôri*.

If not expressed, substitution can never be taken as permitted.

Atsumi *kôri*, Katagata *kôri* and Kagami *kôri*.

If not expressed, substitution can never be taken as permitted.

Tagi *kôri* and Kami-ishizu *kôri*.

If the obligor does not specify what sort of goods will be delivered, the obligee can never be judged as giving permission for substitution.

Ôno *kôri* and Ikeda *kôri*.

This is largely a matter of morality among the people concerned. Each district has its own practice.

Haguri *kôri* and Nakajima *kôri*.

If not expressed, substitution cannot be taken as permitted.

Ena *kôri*.

If not expressed, substitution cannot be taken as permitted.

Kamo *kôri*.

It is a matter of course that the obligor must obtain the permission of the obligee to perform a contract by delivery of other goods. Therefore, if not expressed, substitution can never be taken as permitted.

Kani *kôri*.

When it is not expressed by the obligee, substitution can never be taken as permitted.

Atsumi *kôri*, Gifu Township.

It can never be taken as permitted.

Ôgaki.

Though not expressed, substitution is occasionally taken as permitted.

Ena *kôri*, Nakatsugawa Village.

Though not expressed, substitution is occasionally taken as permitted by an implied agreement.

Shimo-ishizu *kôri*, Takasu Township.

If the obligee does not express permission, the obligor cannot perform a contract by delivery of other goods.

Haguri *kôri*, Takegahana Village.

If not expressed, substitution cannot be taken as permitted.

Yamagata *kôri*, Takatomi Village.

Even if the obligor has obtained tentative permission from the obligee without saying what goods will be delivered instead, the contract will become null and void if the obligee does not accept delivery of the goods.

Mugi *kôri*, Kôzuchi Village.

If not expressed, substitution cannot be taken as permitted.

Haguri *kôri*, Kasamatsu Village.

If not expressed, substitution can never be taken as permitted.

Fuwa *kôri*, Tarui Village.

If not expressed, substitution can never be taken as permitted.

Ôno *kôri*, Miwa Village.

Substitution is occasionally taken as permitted.

Ampachi *kôri*, Gôdo Village.

Substitution is occasionally taken as permitted.

Tagi *kôri*, Shimada Village.

No answer is given.

Ena *kôri*, Iwa Village.

If not expressed, substitution cannot be taken as permitted.

Kamo *kôri*, Hosome Village.

It is a matter of course that the obligor must obtain the permission of the obligee to perform a contract by delivery of other goods. Even when the obligee has not expressed it, however, permission for substitution is occasionally taken as having been obtained.

Toki *kôri*, Takayama Village.

Substitution can never be taken as permitted. According to a practice prevailing here, however, a poverty-stricken obligor will occasionally perform a contract by delivering other goods instead. The obligee is then overwhelmed with pity, although he has not expressed permission.

Kani *kôri*, Mitake Village.

If not expressed, substitution cannot be taken as permitted.

Ena *kôri*, Akechi Village.

If not expressed, substitution cannot be taken as permitted.

Mugi *kôri*, Seki Village.

When permission is not expressed by the obligee, the obligor should make every effort to find out whether the substitution is acceptable or not. Without permission, the obligor will not be able to take steps to substitute goods.

Ôno *kôri*, Takayama Township.

Without obtaining permission from the obligee, the obligor cannot perform the contract by delivering other goods. If the contract, however, says in writing that substitution is permitted, it will be accepted even if the obligee keeps silent on the specific case.

Motosu *kôri*, Kitagata Village.

If the obligor wants to perform a contract by delivery of other goods,—by fulfilling, for instance, a contract for grain by delivery of dry goods—he should obtain permission from the obligee without fail. Otherwise, he cannot make the substitution.

Kamo *kôri*, Ôta Village.

It is a matter of course that the obligor must obtain the permission of the obligee to perform a contract by delivery of other goods. However, substitution occasionally is taken as permitted, though the permission is not expressed.

Kaisai *kôri* and Shimo-ishizu *kôri*.

The obligor cannot perform a contract by delivering other goods unless he gets permission from the obligee to perform the contract in such a way.

Gujô *kôri*.

Unless the permission is expressed by the obligee, the obligor cannot regard him as having permitted substitution.

Topic 2: When the Obligee Refuses to Accept without Any Sufficient Reason an Article the Obligor[1] Duly[2] Delivers in Fulfillment of a Contract, How Should the Obligor Dispose of Said Article? If the Article Is Money, How Should the Interest Accruing to It after Its Rejection by the Obligee Be Treated? If It Is Something Other Than Money and Is Impaired by Delay, Whose Loss Is It Deemed to Be?

TOKYO METROPOLIS

Paper Wholesalers (*Kiu-kumi*).[3]

The party who refuses to accept the article must bear the loss if agreement has already been reached over the prices.

Oil Wholesalers.

The case referred to in the first question cannot be found among us. The answer to the second is as stated in the question.

Stone Wholesalers.

The obligee cannot refuse to accept an article delivered in fulfillment of a contract.

Dried Bonito Wholesalers.

Once the obligor has delivered an article in performance of a contract, the obligee cannot refuse to accept it without sufficient reason. The obligor is completely free of responsibility.

Sugar Wholesalers.

This question seems to be closely related to Topic 1 of the present title. We have no practice of lending or borrowing articles, even those of the same kind. In the case of money, we cannot give any answer, since this is not part of our business.

Medicine Wholesalers.

Such cases cannot be found among us.

Soy Wholesalers.

Such cases cannot be found among us.

Timber Wholesalers.

The problem will be settled by deliberations between the two.

[1] *Gimusha.*

[2] *Tôzenni.*

[3] *Kiu-kumi kami-donya.*

Timber Traders.[1]

The same as stated above.

Timber Traders (*Senju*).[2]

Such cases cannot be found here.

Fuel Wholesalers.

Such cases cannot be found among us.

Porcelain Wholesalers.

If the article is undamaged, the obligor should accept it without any condition. If it is damaged, he should discuss the settlement with the obligee and ask him for payment of money equivalent to the loss. If the article is money, the matter should be settled in the same way. If the article is damaged by delayed delivery, the matter will also be settled this way.

Paper Wholesalers (*Shôkai-kumi*).[3]

If the obligee rejects an article without sufficient reason, the obligor will call a witness and discuss the settlement with the obligee. If the article is impaired due to its rejection by the obligee, the obligor will take the same step. Interest accruing to money will also be treated in the same way.

Rice Traders.[4]

This kind of case will be treated as mentioned in the preceding article (Topic 1: Performance of Contract). Whether the obligee has a right to refuse or not depends solely on what is mentioned in the contract.

Copper and Iron Wholesalers.

Such cases are unknown among us.

Kudari Saké Wholesalers.[5]

This practice is unknown among us.

Mosquito Net Wholesalers.

As stated in the topic.

Lime and Shell Wholesalers.

Such cases are unknown among us.

Tobacco Wholesalers.

If the obligee refuses to accept an article which the obligor has

[1] *Zaimoku tôsei-kumiai.*

[2] *Senju zaimoku-kumiai.*

[3] *Shôkai-kumi kami-donya.*

[4] *Beikoku sangyô-kumiai.*

[5] *Kudari sake-donya.*

duly delivered in fulfillment of a contract, the obligor will discuss its disposal with him, showing him the book in which receipt of the order from the obligee has been recorded.

Drapery Wholesalers.

Such cases cannot be found among us.

Matting Wholesalers.

This business practice is unknown among us.

Fuel Wholesalers (*Umite-kumi*).[1]

The obligee does not arbitrarily refuse to receive an article which the obligor duly delivers in fulfillment of a contract in our trade. As for the payment of interest, there is no reason for interest to accrue, according to the practice here. If the article is damaged, there must be some reason. The obligor sometimes rufuses to receive it, depending on the reason.

Saké Wholesalers.

It is impossible for an obligee to reject an article without sufficient reason. If the article is money, it will carry interest. If it is damaged, the loss will be borne by the obligor.

Kôjimachi Ward.

If the obligee arbitrarily refuses to accept an article, the obligor cannot but take it back. The loss, as well as the interest, should be covered by the party who refuses to accept the article or money.

Nihombashi Ward.

Such a business custom and such cases cannot be found among us.

Kyôbashi Ward.

As to the first question, the article should be kept by the obligor. If there is some damage done, the loss should be assumed by the obligee. The interest referred to in the second question should go to the obligor. If the article is damaged, the loss should be covered by the obligee.

Yotsuya Ward and Ushigome Ward.

No answer is given.

Asakusa Ward.

In either case, it is not permissible to refuse to accept an article without reason. If the article should be rejected, the obligor should keep it in custody, together with some pieces of evidence, and re-

[1] *Umite-kumi shintan-donya.*

peatedly ask the obligee to accept it. If the article is money, the interest after the rejection should be paid by the obligor. The responsibility for damage should be taken by the obligor or by the obligee, according to the situation in the particular case.

Honjo Ward.

If the obligee refuses to accept an article duly delivered in performance of a contract without sufficient reason, the obligor should ask a relative of the obligee to keep it in custody. If the obligee has no relative, he should place the case before the court for settlement. If the article is money, the interest after the rejection is beyond the obligor's responsibility. If the article is damaged, the loss will be borne by the obligee. Occasionally, however, the obligor will assume responsibility, according to the nature of the damage.

Ebara *kôri.*

If the obligee arbitrarily refuses to accept an article delivered in fulfillment of a contract, the obligor should take it home and discuss its disposal with the obligee. If the article is money, the interest after the rejection will be a loss on the part of the obligee. If the article is damaged, the loss also will be borne by the obligee.

Higashi-tama *kôri* and Minami-toshima *kôri.*

In theory a case like this seems impossible. If there should be such a case, the two parties should meet and discuss the reasons why it cannot be accepted. According to the situation, the article will be sold to another party, or be taken home by the obligor. If the article is money, the obligor need not pay the interest after the rejection. If the article is damaged, the obligor should cover the loss, since the obligee has not yet accepted it.

Kita-toshima *kôri.*

Such cases are not known among us.

Minami-adachi *kôri.*

It is impermissible for the obligee to refuse it without good reason.

Shitaya Ward.

If the obligee refuses to accept an article delivered in fulfillment of a contract without sufficient reason, the obligor should immediately report the event to the government office concerned and keep the article in his hands. If the article is money, there should be no interest after the obligee has refused to accept it. If the article is damaged, the loss should be upon the obligee, unless the obligor has intentionally caused the damage.

Kanda Ward.

If the obligee refuses to accept the article without sufficient reason, the obligor cannot but bring the matter to trial. If the obligee refuses to pay the interest accruing to money or the loss for damage to the article, the obligor will be taken as having implicitly agreed to this if he does not object. In such a case, the obligor shares the responsibility.

Akasaka Ward and Azabu Ward.

In reference to the first question, the obligor cannot but take the article home. If circumstances require, someone should be asked to witness. As to the second, if the evidence against the obligee is not clear, the interest accruing to the money and the loss for damage to the article are borne by the obligor.

Hongô Ward.

In the case referred to in the first question, when the obligee refuses to accept an article without sufficient reason although the obligor has duly delivered it in performance of a contract, and the two parties fail to reach agreement, the only recourse is to place the matter before the court. However, the obligor, probably appealing to his own moral sense, occasionally turns the article into money, fulfills the contract and pays the money to the obligee. The matter referred to in the second question can only be settled by talks between the two parties.

CHIBA PREFECTURE

Awa *kôri*, Hei *kôri*, Asai *kôri* and Nagasa *kôri*.

It seems improbable that the obligee would refuse to accept an article delivered in fulfillment of a contract for no good reason. However, the obligee may ask the obligor to deliver it a short while later, due to unavoidable circumstances, for instance, lack of storage space. If the article is found to be damaged[1] during this period, the loss will be borne by the obligee. If there is some damage, not caused by such natural disasters as fire or flood, the obligor must bear the loss on some occasions.

Katori *kôri*.

If there is any need to return the article, this should be done within a short period. If it is money, the obligor will make some allowance for down payment. The obligee will usually be ready to

[1] This refers to damage for which the obligor is not responsible.

accept money any time.[1]

Yamabe *kôri* and Muza *kôri*.

There will be no alternative for the obligor but to keep the article if it is rejected by the obligee without any good reason. As for the payment of money, no interest will be added for the period after the rejection. If the article is damaged after the obligee has rejected it, the loss will be borne by the obligee, when it is caused by, for instance, disasters such as fire, flood, storm or earthquake. If the damage is due to recklessness on the part of the obligor, it will be borne by the obligor.

Unakami *kôri* and Sôsa *kôri*.

Such a case has never been heard of here. The obligee never refuses to accept an article delivered in fulfillment of a contract without sufficient reason.

Higashi-katsushika *kôri*.

Such a case has never been heard of here. The obligee never refuses to accept an article delivered in performance of a contract without sufficient reason. Therefore, no answer can be given.

IBARAKI PREFECTURE

Nishi-katsushika *kôri* and Sashima *kôri*.

All we can do is to appeal to the court. The interest accruing to the money after rejection by the obligee is to be paid by the obligee. The loss on an article caused by the obligee's rejection will be borne by the obligee.

KANAGAWA PREFECTURE

Miura *kôri*.

Such a case has not been heard of here.

Tachibana *kôri*.

The matter should be appealed to the court. The interest accruing to the money and damage to the article will be borne by the obligee.

Kita-tama *kôri*.

We have never heard of such a case. An obligee never refuses to accept an article delivered in performance of a contract without sufficient reason. The same is true for money. As for damage to the article, discussion should be held between the two parties, according to the situation.

[1] *Dankô-suru.*

Ashigara-shimo *kôri.*

All we can do is to appeal to the court. As for the second question, we think all responsibilities will be upon the obligee.

Prefectural Industrial Bureau.

If the obligee has refused to accept an article delivered in performance of a contract without sufficient reason, this means that the obligee has broken the contract unilaterally. After receiving evidence from the obligee as to why he has refused to accept it, the obligor should keep the article in his hands together with the evidence. The matter will be placed before the court sooner or later according to custom. If it is money, the obligor need not bear the interest accruing to it from that time on, since it is not the obligor who has failed to fulfill the contract. Possible damage to the article is borne by the obligor. However, this is not acceptable if the damage is due to some unavoidable natural disaster.

TOCHIGI PREFECTURE

Prefectural Office.

If the obligee has refused to accept an article delivered in fulfillment of a contract without sufficient reason, he will be regarded as having violated the contract. The article can then be disposed of by the obligor. If there is some loss of money, it should be paid by the obligee. Such a settlement is not possible in the case of money, though such cases rarely occur. Interest which accrues after the rejection should be paid by the obligor. Possible loss from damage to the article is borne by the obligee.

Shimo-tsuga *kôri* and Samukawa *kôri.*

Regarding the first question, if the obligee refuses to accept an article delivered in fulfillment of a contract without good reason, the obligor will keep it at his own house and wait for a letter requesting its delivery from the obligee. If, as in the second question, the article is money, the obligor need not pay the interest after the rejection. Possible loss from damage to the article should be covered by the obligor.

Ashikaga *kôri* and Yanada *kôri.*

If the obligee stubbornly refuses to accept an article delivered in performance of a contract without good reason, the obligor will take it home and keep it until the obligee asks for it. If the article is money, the obligor will also take it home and keep it at his own house. After the rejection, interest accruing to the money will not be borne by the obligor. Loss from damage to the article is borne by the obligee, judging from the case stated in the preceding topic, though such a case has not occurred here.

MIE PREFECTURE

Suzuka *kôri*.

When the obligee refuses to accept an article delivered in performance of a contract without a sufficient reason, there are various ways of settlement open to the obligor. We have no one established practice.

Ichishi *kôri*.

Such cases cannot be found here, thus no answer can be given. The same holds for the second question.

Nabari *kôri* and Iga *kôri*.

If the obligee refuses to accept an article delivered in performance of a contract without sufficient reason, the obligor will keep it as it is and will discuss the rescission of the contract with the obligee. If the obligee accepts the article later, any loss arising from the matter is borne by the violator[1] of the contract. If the article is money, the interest which may accrue to the money is also borne by the violator.

Kita-muro *kôri*.

The obligee has no reason to refuse to accept an article delivered in fulfillment of a contract. If he does refuse to accept it, he must have good reason. The two parties should discuss disposal of the article. If the article is money and it is refused, the obligor need not pay the interest which accrues on the money after the rejection. If the article is damaged before the obligee accepts it, the loss is borne by the obligor.

AICHI PREFECTURE

Nakajima *kôri*.

If the article is refused, it should be kept as it is in the obligor's custody. If the article is money, no interest will accrue to it. If it is damaged, the loss is borne by the obligee.

Nagoya Ward.

If the article is refused, it should be kept in the obligor's hands. However, if the obligee wants to have it delivered later and the obligor refuses, the obligee should have the obligor pay for it in

[1] *Kusemono*.

current prices. If it is money, the interest after the rejection should be covered by the obligee. If the article is damaged, the loss is borne by the obligee, too.

Chita *kôri*.

It is not permissible for the obligee to refuse to accept an article delivered in performance of a contract without sufficient reason. If the obligee has sufficient reason for refusing to accept it, he should inform the obligor in writing of the reason. If the article is money, the obligee can dispose of it as he likes. Therefore, there is no interest added. Even if there is some damage to the article, it is no concern of the obligor's.

Minami-shidara *kôri*.

We have never heard about such a case here, so we cannot give any answer.

Atsumi *kôri*.

The obligee can never refuse to accept the article if he has no sufficient reason. Therefore, the obligor can ask him to accept it. As for the interest which accrues to the money after the rejection, the obligor need not pay it. If the article is damaged, the loss should rest with the obligee.

Kaitô *kôri* and Kaisai *kôri*.

If the obligee refuses to accept an article without sufficient reason, the obligor will take it home and ask the obligee once more to accept it. If agreement is not reached, he should appeal the matter to the court for final decision. Interest accruing to the money or a loss resulting from damage are not the obligor's responsibility.

Aichi *kôri*.

If the obligee refuses to accept an article delivered in performance of a contract without sufficient reason, the obligor cannot but take it home and keep it in custody. If it is money, the obligor need not pay the interest which accrues to it after the rejection. If the article is damaged, the obligor should bear the loss.

Niwa *kôri* and Haguri *kôri*.

We have never heard of an obligee refusing to accept an article delivered in performance of a contract without sufficient reason. So there is no established rule for such a case. The obligor will have to place the matter before the court, regardless of whether he wants to or not. Even if he has decided not to appeal to the court due to circumstances, the obligee is in duty bound to bear any interest accruing after the rejection. Besides, the obligee cannot ask for repayment as he pleases. If the article is damaged after he has refused to accept it, the loss also should be covered by him.

SHIZUOKA PREFECTURE

Prefectural Office.

Such a case has never been heard of here.

Udo *kôri* and Abe *kôri*.

The obligor will keep the article in custody for the time being and ask the obligee once more to accept it. He need not pay the interest. If it is damaged due to negligence on the part of the obligor, the loss should be borne by the obligor himself, because he is responsible for keeping the article.

Inasa *kôri* and Aratama *kôri*.

If the obligee stubbornly refuses to accept the article even though the obligor asks him many times to accept it, all the obligor can do is place the case before the court. If it is money, it will carry interest. If it is damaged in an accident, the loss will be borne by the obligee.

Kamo *kôri* and Naka *kôri*.

In such a case, the obligor should ask someone to witness and make the obligee explain why he cannot accept the article. If he still goes on refusing, the obligor should make him give directions in writing and then dispose of the article. The interest or loss after the rejection should be borne by the obligee, the party who refuses to accept it.

Saya *kôri* and Kitô *kôri*.

If the obligee refuses to accept the article without sufficient reason, all the obligor has to do is let him go his own way, and wait for the time when he will accept it. Of course the obligor need not pay the interest resulting from the rejection. If it has been damaged in the obligee's hands, the loss will be borne by him, and if it has been damaged in the obligor's hands, he will assume the loss.

GIFU PREFECTURE

Mugi *kôri*.

Such a case is unknown in this district.

Ampachi *kôri*.

This sort of case is unknown here. If this should occur, the obligor should keep the article. If the article is money, even if it carries interest, the obligor need not pay the interest after the rejection.

If the article has been damaged, the loss will be borne by the obligee.

Fuwa *kôri.*

The obligor should let the obligee hold it, and they should discuss its disposal. Sometimes, however, we hear that a person declines to hand it over to the obligee. If it is money, no interest accrues after the rejection by the obligee. If the article has been damaged, the loss should be covered by the obligee.

Atsumi *kôri*, Kagami *kôri* and Katagata *kôri.*

All we have to do is to place it before the court. The interest referred to in the second question should not be paid by the obligor. If the article has been damaged, the loss will be borne by the obligor.

Tagi *kôri* and Kami-ishizu *kôri.*

If the obligee has refused to accept an article delivered in performance of a contract without any sufficient reason, the obligor will take it back and ask a government office how it should be disposed of. If the article is money and interest accrues, the obligor need not pay it after the obligee's rejection. If it has been damaged, a government office will decide how and by whom the loss should be covered.

Ôno *kôri* and Ikeda *kôri.*

There is no established rule; cases vary depending on the people and the place.

Haguri *kôri* and Nakajima *kôri.*

Such a case has never been heard of here.

Ena *kôri.*

The case referred to in the first question is not known here. If such a case should occur, the obligor will be recognized as having fulfilled the contract, and the obligee as having violated it. If, as in the second question, the article is money, the interest which accrues after the obligee's rejection will become a loss for the obligee. If the article has been damaged, the loss will be borne by the obligee.

Kamo *kôri.*

Such cases do not seem to be known here. An obligee never refuses to accept an article delivered in fulfillment of a contract without sufficient reason.

Kani *kôri.*

Such a case has never been heard of in this district. Therefore, this may be mere theory for the sake of theory. If the obligee refuses to accept an article delivered in performance of a contract without sufficient reason, he will be creating a conflict for the distant future, and will thus be forced to perform the contract after all. If the obligee still goes on stoutly rejecting the article, the obligor will be obliged to make a new contract. Therefore, the question asked in the latter half of this section is self-explanatory.

Atsumi *kôri*, Gifu Township.

We have never heard about a case such as that referred to in the first question. Regarding the second question, if the article is money, as a rule the interest accruing to it after rejection by the obligee will be paid by the obligee.

Ôgaki.

A case such as this cannot be found in this district. If such a case should occur, the article would be kept by the obligor. After rejection by the obligee, the obligor would not be held responsible for payment of the interest. If the article is damaged, the obligee should bear the loss.

Ena *kôri*, Nakatsugawa Village.

If the obligee refuses to accept the article without good reason, the obligor cannot but keep it. Of course there will be no interest added to money. If the article is damaged, the loss will be borne by obligee.

Shimo-ishizu *kôri*, Takasu Township.

If the obligee refuses to accept the article without sufficient reason, the obligor will ask him to state the reason. If the obligee declines to do so, the obligor will protest against the rejection. If the article is money, the obligor will refuse to pay interest which accrues to it after the rejection. If it is damaged, the loss will be borne by the obligee.

Haguri *kôri*, Takegahana Village.

If the obligee refuses to accept the article without sufficient reason, all the obligor has to do will be to firmly ask the obligee to fulfill his obligation. After the obligee has refused delivery, responsibility for interest and damage will of course rest solely with him.

Yamagata *kôri*, Takatomi Village.

If the obligee refuses to accept the article without sufficient reason, the obligor need no longer be greatly concerned. Interest and damage should be borne by the obligee.

Mugi *kôri*, Kôzuchi Village.

If it is money, the obligor is not responsible for the interest after the rejection. The loss will go to the obligee.

Haguri *kôri*, Kasamatsu Village.

We have never heard of such a practice here.

Fuwa *kôri*, Tarui Village.

We have not heard of such a business practice here.

Ôno *kôri*, Miwa Village.

It is a matter of course that the obligee has no reason to reject the article. The interest on the money and the loss due to impairment should be borne by the obligee.

Ampachi *kôri*, Gôdo Village.

A case such as this is rarely seen here. The obligee never refuses to accept the article without good reason.

Tagi *kôri*, Shimada Village.

No answer is given.

Ena *kôri*, Iwa Village.

1. The rejected article will be kept in custody by the obligor. 2. Interest after the rejection will be the loss of the obligee. If the article is damaged, the loss will be borne by the obligee.

Kamo *kôri*, Hosome Village.

If it is not accepted, the article will be kept in custody by the obligor. If it is money, the interest after the rejection should be paid by the obligee. If the article is damaged, the loss will be covered by the obligor.

Toki *kôri*, Takayama Village.

A case such as this has never been heard of in this district.

Kani *kôri*, Mitake Village.

It is a matter of course that the obligee has no reason to reject the article without good reason. If such a case should occur, however, the obligor would act as circumstances determine. After rejection, there would be no interest. Loss from damage would rest with the obligee.

Ena *kôri*, Akechi Village.

A case such as this has never been heard of here.

Mugi *kôri*, Seki Village.

The obligee has no good reason to reject the money or article if the obligor duly makes delivery as arranged in the original contract. If the obligee refuses to accept the article at that time, the obligor will be able to persist in the performance of the contract to the last, forcing the obligee to accept it without delay. If the article is damaged, the loss will be borne by the obligor.

Ôno *kôri*, Takayama Township.

The obligee might decline to accept the article for specific reasons, for instance, the poor quality of the article, or falling prices. If it is because of poor quality, the obligor will give a discount, and if it is because of lower prices, he will ask the obligee to pay the balance. If the obligee refuses to accept the proposal, the obligor will call on some one to act as a go-between. If the article is money, the obligor will have some one keep it and inform the obligee of the interest rate. If it is a breakable object, he keeps it himself and informs the obligee that he has no responsibility hereafter to cover possible loss. Only in this way will the obligor be free of responsibility for possible results.

Motosu *kôri*, Kitagata Village.

When the obligee refuses to accept an article delivered in performance of a contract without sufficient reason, the obligor should keep it for the time being or have it kept by some one else. If the article is money, the obligor need not pay the interest which accrues after the rejection. If the article is damaged, the loss will be borne by the obligor, unless he has reasonable evidence that he is not ot blame.

Kamo *kôri*, Ôta Village.

If the obligee refuses to accept an article delivered in performance of a contract without sufficient reason, the obligor should keep it for the time being. If the article is money, the interest accruing to it after the rejection should be paid by the obligee.

Kaisai *kôri* and Shimo-ishizu *kôri*.

It is a matter of course that the obligee cannot be allowed to refuse to accept an article delivered in performance of a contract without good reason. If he has refused it, the obligor should ask him for the reasons. If he declines to explain the reasons, the obligor is not responsible and may dispose of the article as he likes. If the article is money, the obligor need not pay the interest which accrues to it after the rejection. If it is damaged, the loss will be upon the obligee.

Gujô *kôri*.
It is too hard for us to answer the question.

Topic 3: When the Obligor Makes Only Part Payment[1] without Previous Agreement to That Effect, Is the Obligee Allowed to Reject It?

TOKYO METROPOLIS

Paper Wholesalers (*Kiu-kumi*).[2]

He will act as stated in the topic.

Oil Wholesalers.

It is not always easy to predict whether the obligee will reject part payment or not, for it depends on what sort of person he is and how long the two parties have been trading with each other.

Stone Wholesalers.

Of course the obligee can reject it. However, he will accept it if the circumstances warrant.

Medicine Wholesalers.

If the obligor makes part payment before the term of payment is up the obligee sometimes accepts it after the two have conferred together.

Sugar Wholesalers.

If by part payment, you mean payment for an article, our answer is the same as stated in Topics 1 and 2. If you mean payment for the prices, this should be paid in full by the obligor and accepted by the obligee. This is our practice here.

Dried Bonito Wholesalers.

If the obligor makes only part payment without previous agreement to that effect, the obligee may reject it. In some circumstances, he may postpone the payment.

Soy Wholesalers.

The obligee can reject it.

Timber Wholesalers.

Cases vary, depending on what sort of person the obligor is.

Timber Traders.[3]

It is allowable for the obligee to reject it. However, sometimes the obligee accepts part payment, depending on what sort of per-

[1] *Uchibarai.*

[2] *Kiu-kumi kami-donya.*

[3] *Zaimoku tôsei-kumiai.*

son the obligor is.

Timber Traders (*Senju*).[1]

The obligee can decide whether to allow part payment or not.

Porcelain Wholesalers.

When the obligor makes only part payment without previous agreement to that effect, the obligee should be allowed to reject it. But we have not heard about such a rejection.

Paper Wholesalers (*Shôkai-kumi*).[2]

The obligee can reject it.

Rice Traders.[3]

When the obligor makes only part payment without previous agreement to that effect, we do not know whether or not the obligee may reject it, since we have no such business practice here.

Salt Wholesalers.

The obligee can reject it.

Fuel Wholesalers.

Since we do our business in cash, the seller can decide whether to allow part payment or not.

Copper and Iron Wholesalers.

Of course the seller can reject it.

Kudari Saké Wholesalers.[4]

If there is no previous agreement, the obligee can reject it.

Mosquito Net Wholesalers.

If part payment is made before the term closes, the obligee will not reject it.

Lime and Shell Wholesalers.

When the obligor makes part payment, the obligee makes him state when the remainder will be paid.

Saké Wholesalers.

If the obligee has no confidence in the obligor, sometimes he will reject it.

Tobacco Wholesalers.

When the obligor makes part payment, the obligee makes him state in writing when the remainder will be paid.

Drapery Wholesalers.

[1] *Senju zaimoku tôsei-kumiai.*

[2] *Shôkai-kumi kami-donya.*

[3] *Beikoku sangyô-kumiai.*

[4] *Kudari sake-donya.*

The obligee can reject it.

Matting Wholesalers.

If part payment is made before the term closes, the obligee will not reject it.

Fuel Wholesalers (*Umite-kumi*).[1]

The obligee can reject it.

Kôjimachi Ward.

The obligee can reject it.

Nihombashi Ward.

The obligee can reject it.

Kyôbashi Ward.

We have nothing to answer.

Yotsuya Ward and Ushigome Ward.

If the obligor makes part payment without previous agreement to that effect, the obligee can reject it.

Asakusa Ward.

We have no custom of rejecting it.

Honjo Ward.

If the obligor makes part payment without previous agreement to that effect, the obligee can reject it.

Ebara *kôri*.

If the obligor makes part payment without previous agreement to that effect, the obligee can reject it.

Higashi-tama *kôri* and Minami-toshima *kôri*.

When there is no previous agreement indicating whether the payment should be made in part or in full, the obligee can forbid the obligor to make part payment and demand that the payment be made in full.

Kita-toshima *kôri*.

If the partial payment is on the balance and not on the interest, it has always been accepted by all.

Minami-adachi *kôri*.

It can be rejected.

Shitaya Ward.

If there is no previous agreement, the obligee can reject it.

Kanda Ward.

It cannot be rejected.

[1] *Umite-kumi shintan-donya.*

Akasaka Ward and Azabu Ward.

The obligee can reject it.

Hongô Ward.

It can be rejected.

CHIBA PREFECTURE

Awa *kôri*, Hei *kôri*, Asai *kôri* and Nagasa *kôri*.

If the partial payment is on the balance and not on the interest, it has always been accepted by all. If the obligor makes payment little by little at irregular intervals, the obligee may ask him to pay in full when the term comes to a close, because the obligee is inconvenienced by frequent payments. But in general the public here think little of the term of payment. As very few make payments before the term closes, the obligee often finds it convenient to receive the money irregularly from time to time.

Katori *kôri*.

If the obligor makes part payment, the obligee can not reject it.

Yamabe *kôri* and Muza *kôri*.

The obligee usually will not reject it. But he can reject it, saying that it should be paid in full.

Unakami *kôri* and Sôsa *kôri*.

Even if there is no previous agreement, the obligee will not stop the obligor from making part payment.

Higashi-katsushika *kôri*.

It can be rejected.

IBARAKI PREFECTURE

Nishi-katsushika *kôri* and Sashima *kôri*.

The obligee can reject it.

KANAGAWA PREFECTURE

Miura *kôri*.

It can be rejected.

Tachibana *kôri*.

According to our practice, it cannot be rejected.

Kita-tama *kôri*.

If the obligor makes part payment without previous agreement, the obligee will not reject it.

Ashigara-shimo *kôri*.

The obligee has no right to reject it, unless the obligation cannot be divided. According to our experience, in cases of 80 to 90 percent payment, the obligees accept it.

Prefectural Industrial Bureau.

In trading with foreigners, it is our practice to reject it. If the obligor is Japanese, however, it cannot be rejected.

Tochigi Prefecture

Prefectural Office.

It is a practice for the obligee not to reject it.

Shimo-tsuga *kôri* and Samukawa *kôri*.

If the obligor makes part payment without previous agreement, the obligee can reject it.

Ashikaga *kôri* and Yanada *kôri*.

In this district, in principle, business is done not in credit but in cash. If there is no prior agreement on the method of payment, the two parties implicitly understand that the payment should be made in full. The obligor, however, never makes part payment except under unavoidable circumstances. In such a case, the obligee usually seems to accept it.

Mie Prefecture

Suzuka *kôri*.

If the obligor makes part payment without previous agreement to that effect, the obligee will not reject it.

Ichishi *kôri*.

The obligee will accept it.

Nabari *kôri* and Iga *kôri*.

He can reject it.

Kita-muro *kôri*.

If there is no previous agreement to that effect, the obligee can reject it.

Aichi Prefecture

Nakajima *kôri*.

Sometimes it can be rejected, and at others, it cannot.

Nagoya Ward.

Of course it can be rejected, unless prearranged between the two parties.

Chita *kôri*.

The obligor will be forbidden to make part payment without approval by the obligee.

Minami-shidara *kôri*.

It is up to the obligee.

Atsumi *kôri*.

If necessary, the obligee can reject it.

Kaitô *kôri* and Kaisai *kôri*.

If the obligor makes part payment, the obligee will not reject it.

Prefectural Office.

If there is no previous agreement, the obligee can reject it.

Niwa *kôri* and Haguri *kôri*.

If the obligor makes part payment without previous agreement before the term of payment closes, the obligee can reject it.

SHIZUOKA PREFECTURE

Prefectural Office.

No, the obligee will not reject it.

Udo *kôri* and Abe *kôri*.

It cannot be said that the obligee has no right to reject it. But he usually does not. This is because when the obligee receives part of the bill, he can expect the obligee to pay the remainder later.

Inasa *kôri* and Aratama *kôri*.

The obligee can reject it.

Kamo *kôri* and Naka *kôri*.

Sometimes the obligee can reject it.

Saya *kôri* and Kitô *kôri*.

If the obligor makes partial payment without previous agreement, before the term of payment closes, the obligee will not reject it. But here is another case. Suppose a rice broker who receives part payment promises to hand over to a rice dealer a certain amount of rice later. Later, however, the sharply rising price of rice makes it difficult for the broker to buy the amount agreed upon in the contract. In such a case, the broker will not allow the buyer to make another partial payment.

GIFU PREFECTURE

Mugi *kôri*.

When the obligor makes part payment without a previous agreement, the obligee can reject it.

Ampachi *kôri*.

It is possible for the obligee to reject part payment. In most cases, however, he accepts it.

Fuwa *kôri*.

If there is no definite agreement, the obligee can reject it.

Atsumi *kôri*, Kagami *kôri* and Katagata *kôri*.

Yes.

Tagi *kôri* and Kami-ishizu *kôri*.

If the obligor makes partial payment without previous agreement, the practice here is for the obligee not to reject it.

Ôno *kôri* and Ikeda *kôri*.

There is no established rule; the cases vary, depending on what sort of persons the parties are and where the place is situated.

Haguri *kôri* and Nakajima *kôri*.

Yes, that is right.

Ena *kôri*.

Yes.

Kamo *kôri*.

When the obligor makes part payment without previous agreement to that effect, the obligee sometimes rejects it. In most cases, however, he will accept it.

Kani *kôri*.

If there is no previous agreement on part payment, the obligee can reject it.

Atsumi *kôri*, Gifu Township.

The obligee can reject it.

Ôgaki.

It is possible for the obligee to reject part payment. In most cases, however, the obligee accepts it.

Ena *kôri*, Nakatsugawa Village.

It can be rejected.

Shimo-ishizu *kôri*, Takasu Township.

If it is money, sometimes the obligee can reject it until about the end of the same month. If there is no previous agreement, the two parties must discuss the matter.

Haguri *kôri*, Takegahana Village.

If there is no previous agreement, the obligee can reject it.

Yamagata *kôri*, Takatomi Village.

The obligee has a right to reject it.

Mugi *kôri*, Kôzuchi Village.

The obligee can reject it.

Haguri *kôri*, Kasamatsu Village.

Yes, that is right.

Fuwa *kôri*, Tarui Village.

If the obligor makes part payment, the obligee occasionally rejects it. But he sometimes accepts it if necessary.

Ôno *kôri*, Miwa Village.

If the obligor makes part payment, the obligee cannot reject it.

Ampachi *kôri*, Gôdo Village.

The obligee can reject it.

Tagi *kôri*, Shimada Village.

Yes.

Ena *kôri*, Iwa Village.

The obligee cannot reject it.

Kamo *kôri*, Hosome Village.

The obligee can reject it.

Toki *kôri*, Takayama Village.

The obligee has a full right to reject it. But he does not exercise that right according to the practice here.

Kani *kôri*, Mitake Village.

It can be rejected.

Ena *kôri*, Akechi Village.

Yes.

Mugi *kôri*, Seki Village.

Yes, that is right.

Ôno *kôri*, Takayama Township.

When the obligor makes part payment without previous agreement to that effect, the obligee sometimes rejects it if the obligor makes it close to the final day for payment.

Motosu *kôri*, Kitagata Village.

When the obligor makes part payment without previous agreement to that effect, the obligee cannot reject it, unless there are exceptional circumstances.

Kamo *kôri*, Ôta Village.

If the obligor makes part payment without previous agreement to that effect, the obligee can reject it.

Kaisai *kôri* and Shimo-ishizu *kôri*.

If the obligor makes part payment without previous agreement to that effect, the obligee can reject it.

Gujô *kôri*.

Occasionally the obligee can reject it.

Topic 4: If the Time Limit Set in a Contract Is Indicated by Such Expressions as "for a Certain Number of Days,"[1] "for a Certain Number of Months,"[2] or "for a Certain Number of Years,"[3] What Date Should Be Set as the Time for Performing the Contract? If the Time Limit Is Indicated by Such Expressions as "within the Period of a Certain Number of Days," or "within the Period of a Certain Number of Months," or "within the Period of a Certain Number of Years," Can the Contract Be Performed at Any Time within the Period Thus Indicated, and Is the Obligee Entitled to Demand the Performance of the Contract at Any Time within the Period?

TOKYO METROPOLIS

Prefectural Office.

Paper Wholesalers (*Kiu-kumi*).[4]

The time limit for "days" and "months" is the final day of the period, that for "years" is the last month, December. The obligee is not entitled to demand the performance within the period.

Oil Wholesalers.

It is the final day of the stated period. Regarding the matter of the latter half of the topic, the obligor may perform the contract through talks with the obligee. However, the obligee is not entitled to demand the performance.

Stone Wholesalers.

It is the final day of the stated period. The two parties can perform the contract at any time within the period.

Dried Bonito Wholesalers.

The time limit is the final day of the period. The deadline for "months" is the last month of the year.

Sugar Wholesalers.

It is the final day of the period. As to the second question, when the time limit is indicated as "within the period of a certain number of months," the obligor is entitled to perform the contract at

[1] *Nankanichi-kan.*

[2] *Nankagetsu-kan.*

[3] *Nankanen-kan.*

[4] *Kiu-kumi kami-donya.*

any time within the period. The obligee, however, cannot demand performance before the period expires.

Medicine Wholesalers.

The time limit for a monthly contract is the final day of the same month. It is the final day of each period. The time limit for "years" is the final day of the last month.

Fuel Wholesalers.

The time limit is the final day for each period. When the time limit is indicated as "within the period of a certain number of days, months, or years," the obligor is entitled to perform the contract at any time within the period. The obligee is entitled to demand it at any time after about half the period has passed.

Porcelain Wholesalers.

When it is stated as "within the period of a certain number of days, or months," we interpret this to indicate the time when the period comes to a close. If it is stated as "for five months," this means that the final day is the same date of the sixth month, inclusive of the month when the contract is made. It is the same, too, with "years." The obligor is entitled to perform the contract at any time within the period, but the obligee is not entitled to demand performance.

Timber Wholesalers.

The time limit for a contract should be written in the contract. Depending on the contract, the obligor is sometimes entitled to demand performance at any time within the period. But the obligee is not.

Timber Traders.[1]

The time limit for a contract should be written in the contract. If it is indicated as "within the period of a certain number of days, months, or years," the obligor is entitled to perform the contract at any time within the period, but the obligee is not entitled to demand performance.

Timber Traders (*Senju*).[2]

As a general rule, it is the final day of the period. The obligor is entitled to perform the contract at any time within the period, but the obligee is not entitled to demand it.

[1] *Zaimoku-tôsei-kumiai.*

[2] *Senju zaimoku-kumiai.*

Salt Wholesalers.

If the period is indicated as "for ten days," the time limit is the tenth day from the day on which a contract is concluded. If it is indicated as "for three months," it is the final day of that period calculated in days. As to the second question, the obligor is entitled to perform the contract at any time within the period, but the obligee is not entitled to demand performance.

Rice Traders.[1]

We do not conclude contracts for "months" or "years." If the period is indicated as "for a certain number of days," the time limit is the final day of the period.

Paper Wholesalers (*Shôkai-kumi*).[2]

If the period is indicated as "for a certain number of days," the time limit is the final day of the period. The computation begins from the day when a contract is made. If it is indicated as "for a certain number of months," it is the final day (the 30th or 31st day) of the final month, inclusive of the month when the contract is concluded, regardless of the day of the month on which the contract was made. The same is true of "years." The final day, December 31, of the final year is the time limit, regardless of whether the contract is concluded early or late in the first year. When the time limit is indicated as "within the period of a certain number of days, months, or years," this is for the benefit of the obligor. So the obligor is entitled to perform the contract at any time within the period, but the obligee is not entitled to demand performance.

Soy Wholesalers.

When the period is indicated as "for a certain number of days," the time limit we adopt is as shown below. Suppose we have concluded a contract on the first of a month. The time limit is the fourth. In the case of "months," we fix the period not in days but in months. Suppose we have concluded a contract in January for a period of three months. The contract will be performed in April. In the case of "years," we fix the period in years rather than in months. Suppose we have concluded a contract some time this year (the 16th year) for a period of three years. The contract will be performed in the 19th year.

1 *Beikoku sangyô-kumiai.*

2 *Shôkai-kumi kami-donya.*

Copper and Iron Wholesalers.

Cases vary. There is no established practice.

Kudari Saké Wholesalers.[1]

The time limit referred to in the first question is the final day of any of those periods. Regarding the second question, if the contract indicates "within the period of a certain number of days, months, or years," the obligor can perform, and the obligee can demand the performance of, the contract at any time within the period.

Mosquito Net Wholesalers.

If the contract indicates "within the period of a certain number of days," the time limit for performance is the final day of the period. If it indicates "for a certain number of days," the obligor can perform, and the obligee can demand the performance of, the contract at any time within the period.

Lime and Shell Wholesalers.

If the contract indicates "the third day," the time limit is the third day, inclusive of the day on which the contract is concluded. If it indicates "the third month," the time limit is the 30th (or the 31st) of the third month, inclusive of the month in which the contract is concluded. If it indicates "for five years," the time limit is December 31 of the fifth year, inclusive of the year in which the contract is concluded. The obligor can perform the contract at any time within the period of a number of days, months, or years. But the obligee is not entitled to demand performance until the period comes to a close.

Saké Wholesalers.

The time limit for a contract is the final day of the period agreed upon in the contract. Even if the period has not expired, the obligor can perform the contract at any time. The obligee is hardly entitled to demand performance before the end of the period.

Tobacco Wholesalers.

We do not conclude contracts for "months" or "years." If it is "for a certain number of days," the time limit is the final day of the period. Regarding the second question, cases vary. There is no established practice.

Drapery Wholesalers.

It is the final day for each of those periods, for example, the final

[1] *Kudari sake-donya.*

month of a year. If the period is indicated as "for a number of days, or months," the obligor can perform the contract at any time within the period. But the obligee is not entitled to demand performance before the end of the period.

Matting Wholesalers.

If the period is indicated as "within the period of a certain number of days," the time limit is the final day of the period. As for "months," the calculation is made by day, with the final day as the time limit. This is also true of "years." If the contract indicates "within the period of a certain number of months," the obligor can perform, and the obligee can demand the performance of, the contract at any time within the period.

Fuel Wholesalers (*Umite-kumi*).[1]

When the period is indicated as "for a certain number of days," say, a week, the time limit for the performance comes at sunset on the seventh day of the week, regardless of whether the contract was concluded early in the morning, or late in the afternoon of the first day. When the contract indicates "for a certain number of months," the time limit comes on the final day of the last month of the period. The same thing can be said of "years." However, a year is calculated as twelve months. Most worthy of note to you is that the first month of a contract is always taken as a full month with thirty or thirty-one days, regardless of whether the contract is concluded early or late in the month. Therefore, the first of the next month begins the second month of the contract, unless it is otherwise agreed. The obligor can perform the contract at any time and the obligee can demand performance at any time within the period.

Kôjimachi Ward.

The time limit is the final day of the period agreed on. The obligor can perform the contract at any time within the period. The obligee cannot demand the performance before the time limit.

Nihombashi Ward.

According to our past business practice here, the period was agreed on in a very ambiguous expression. People did not think of the time as strictly as we do today. When it was indicated as "the third month," they considered it the final day of the third month, inclusive of the month during which a contract was concluded.

[1] *Umite-kumi shintan-donya.*

The answer to the second question is yes. The obligee may demand performance at any time.

Kyôbashi Ward.

The time limit referred to in the first question is the final day of the period agreed on in the contract. As to the second question, the obligee cannot demand performance unless the period has come to an end.

Yotsuya Ward and Ushigome Ward.

When the period is indicated as "for a certain number of days, months, or years," the time limit is the final day of the period agreed on. When it is indicated as "within the period of a certain number of days, months, or years," the obligor can perform the contract at any time within the period, but the obligee is not entitled to demand performance.

Asakusa Ward.

If the period referred to in the first question is indicated as "for a certain number of days," the time limit is the final day of the period. The same is true of "months." If the period indicated, for example, is "for three months from September 12," the time limit is December 11. If the period is indicated as "for three years from September 12 this year (the 16th year of Meiji), the time limit is September 11 of the 19th year of Meiji. As roughly estimated, the "month" we quote here has only thirty days. The "year" is, of course, a calendar year. As to the second question, when the obligor wants to return money he has borrowed or pay for articles he has already received, he can perform the contract at any time within the period. If the period is indicated as "within the period of a certain number of days, months, or years," the obligee is never entitled to demand the performance unless the period agreed on has passed.

Honjo Ward.

If the period is indicated as "for a certain number of days, months, or years," the time limit is the final day of the period. If it is indicated as "within the period of a certain number of days, months, or years," the obligor can perform the contract at any time within the period. The obligee also is entitled to demand performance.

Ebara *kôri*.

If the period is indicated as "for a certain number of days, or months," the period begins on the day or in the month when the contract is concluded. If the period is indicated as "for a certain number of years," the "year" is calculated as a full year. If it is indicated as "within the period of a certain number of days, months, or years," the obligor can perform the contract at any time within the period. The obligee is also entitled to demand performance at any time within the period.

Higashi-tama *kôri* and Minami-toshima *kôri*.

If the period is indicated as "for a certain number of days, months, or years," the time limit is the final day of the period. If it is indicated as "within the period of a certain number of days, months, or years," the obligor can perform the contract at any time within the period. But the obligee is not entitled to demand performance until the period is about to come to an end.

Kita-tama *kôri*.

We do not indicate the period as "for a certain number of days, months, or years." Usually it is indicated as "for a period ending a certain day of a certain month." If it is indicated as "for a certain number of years," the "year" is calculated as a full year, and the contract indicates "for a period ending a certain month of a certain year." This has been our practice for many years. If the contract involves interest, the obligee cannot demand the performance before the end of the period. Even if the obligor wants to perform the contract, he cannot unless the obligee agrees to it. Even if the obligee wants to demand performance, he cannot unless the obligor agrees to it.

Minami-adachi *kôri*.

The time limit referred to in the first question is the final day of the period agreed on in the contract. As to the second question, the obligor can perform the contract at any time. The obligee cannot demand performance within the period.

Shitaya Ward.

If the period is indicated as "for a certain number of days, months, or years," the two parties will discuss and fix the time limit. When the period is indicated as "within the period of a certain number of days, months, or years," the obligee can demand, and the obligor can deliver, the articles at any time within the period, if the two parties have agreed on this earlier.

Kanda Ward.

If the period is indicated as "for a certain number of days, months, or years," our practice is for the two parties to fix the date of the time limit on some day within the period. If one party fails to perform the contract within the time limit, the other party can appeal to the court to make him perform the contract. Regarding the second question, the obligor can perform the contract at any time within the period, but the obligee cannot demand performance, unless the period has passed.

Akasaka Ward and Azabu Ward.

As to the first question, if the period is indicated as "for a certain number of days, months, or years," it begins on the day the contract is concluded and ends on the final day of the period. As for "months" or "years" the time limit is the final day of a month or a year. As to the second question, the obligor can perform the contract at any time within the period, but the obligee cannot force him to perform it before the time limit.

Hongô Ward.

Regarding the first question, as a general rule, the time limit for the performance is the final day of the period agreed on in the contract. As to the second question, except for payment by monthly installments, we have never seen such a case.

Chiba Prefecture

Awa *kôri*, Hei *kôri*, Asai *kôri* and Nagasa *kôri*.

The final day of the period is the time limit for the performance. The obligor can perform the contract at any time within the period. The obligee can ask the obligor for performance, but he cannot force him to perform it until the period comes to a close.

Katori *kôri*.

Within the period, the obligor can perform the contract at any time. However, the obligee cannot make the obligor perform the contract until the period ends.

Yamabe *kôri* and Muza *kôri*.

If the contract is concluded on the condition that goods should be delivered in full, the final day of the period, as a rule, is the time of performance. The obligor can perform the contract at any time within the period. But the obligee cannot demand the performance unless the period is about to end.

Unakami *kôri* and Sôsa *kôri*.

If the contract indicates "for a certain number of days, months, or years," the final day of the period is the time for performance. If it indicates "within the period of a certain number of days, months, or years," the obligor can perform the contract at any time within the period. The obligee can also demand performance at any time.

Higashi-katsushika *kôri*.

The obligor can perform the contract from the opening day of the period, for instance, on January 1, if the period is indicated as "for twelve months between January and December." The obligor can perform the contract at any time within the period, if the contract indicates "within the period of a certain number of years." But the obligee is not entitled to demand performance.

IBARAKI PREFECTURE

Nishi-katsushika *kôri* and Sashima *kôri*.

The final day of the period is the time of performance. The obligor can perform the contract at any time within the period. But the obligee cannot demand performance except in unavoidable circumstances.

KANAGAWA PREFECTURE

Miura *kôri*.

Regarding the first question, the contract can be performed at any time between the opening day of the contract and the closing day of the period. As to the second question, the obligor can perform, and the obligee can ask performance of, the contract at any time throughout the period. But the obligee cannot force the obligor to perform it before the time limit.

Tachibana *kôri*.

In our practice, the final day of the period is the time of performance. The obligor can perform the contract at any time within the period. But the obligee cannot force the obligor to perform it.

Kita-tama *kôri*.

If the period is indicated as "for a certain number of days, months, or years," the time limit is the final day of the period. The obligor cannot perform the contract within the period unless he gets permission from the obligee. The obligee cannot demand performance unless the period has come to a close.

Ashigara-shimo *kôri*.

Regarding the first question, the final day of the period is the time of performance for the obligor. As to the second question, the obligee obtains the right to demand performance on the final day of the period.

Prefectural Industrial Bureau.

When the period is indicated as "for a certain number of days, months, or years," the time limit is the final day of the period. If the contract indicates "within the period of a certain number of days, months, or years," the obligor can perform the contract at any time within the period, but the obligee cannot demand the performance unless the period has come to a close.

Tochigi Prefecture

Prefectural Office.

If the period is indicated as "for a certain number of days, months, or years," the time limit for the performance is the day after the period comes to a close. When the contract indicates "within the period of a certain number of days, months, or years," the obligor can perform the contract at any time within the period. The obligee is also entitled to demand performance.

Shimo-tsuga *kôri* and Samukawa *kôri*.

Regarding the first question, the contract can be performed at any time within the period, if it is indicated as "for a certain number of days or months." As to the second question, the obligor can perform the contract at any time within the period if it is indicated as "within the period of a certain number of days, or months." In reference to the third question, the obligee can demand the performance only on the final day of the period.

Ashikaga *kôri* and Yanada *kôri*.

The final day of the period is the time limit for performance. Suppose a silk trader has made a contract with a promise to perform it on the 10th of the month. The contract will not be performed earlier than the prearranged day, for instance, on the 3rd or the 7th. If the obligor wants to perform the contract within the period, the obligee, unless he is a pawnbroker, will always permit him to do so. But such a case is quite exceptional. Since the time limit is the final day of the period, the obligee cannot demand performance within the period. However, the obligor occasionally will accept the obligee's demand and perform the contract within the period, for example, if the obligee is severely short of funds because of accidents. Note: Traders here regularly do business on marketing days, the 5th, 10th, 15th, 20th, 25th and 30th of the month. Business is very quiet between these days.

MIE PREFECTURE

Suzuka *kôri*.

When the period is indicated as "for a certain number of days," the time limit is the final day of the period, counting from the day the contract is concluded. When it is indicated as "for a certain number of months," it is the final day of the final month, counting from the month when the contract is concluded. When it is indicated as "for a certain number of years," it is December 31, of the final year, counting from the year the contract is concluded. If it is indicated as "within the period of a certain number of days, months, or years," the obligor can perform the contract at any time within the period. But the obligee cannot demand performance within the period.

Ichishi *kôri*.

The time limit is the final day of the period. The obligor can perform the contract at any time within the period. The obligee cannot demand the performance until the final day of the period.

Nabari *kôri* and Iga *kôri*.

When the period is indicated as "for a certain number of days," the period begins on the day the contract is concluded. As for "months" and "years," the period is counted from the day the contract is concluded. A year is counted as twelve months. If the contract indicates "within the period of a certain number of days, months, or years," the obligor can perform the contract at any time within the period, unless stipulated earlier. The obligee cannot demand the performance before the period comes to an end, except in some unavoidable circumstances.

Kita-muro *kôri*.

When it is indicated as "for a certain number of days, or months," the period counts from the day the contract is concluded. When it is indicated as "for a certain number of years," it counts from the month in which the contract is concluded. The obligor can perform the contract at any time within the period. But the obligee cannot demand performance.

AICHI PREFECTURE

Nakajima *kôri*.

When the period is indicated as "for a certain number of days, months, or years," the time limit for performance is the final day of the period. The obligor can perform the contract at any time within the period, but the obligee cannot demand performance within the period.

Nagoya Ward.

When provided in advance, the obligee can make the obligor perform the contract at any time within the period at his own convenience.

Chita *kôri.*

When it is indicated as "for a certain number of days," the period counts from the day the contract is concluded. As for "months" and "years," the time limit falls on the day preceding the date the contract was concluded in the final year. If a contract for two months is made on July 1 in the 16th year of Meiji, the time limit will be August 31 of the same year. If a contract for a year is made on July 1 of the 16th year of Meiji, it will end on June 30 of the 17th year of Meiji. When the contract indicates "within the period of a certain number of months, or years," the obligor can perform the contract at any time within the period unless otherwise provided. The obligee will not demand performance within the period, though he has the right to do so.

Minami-shidara *kôri.*

The time limit can be fixed only through negotiation.

Atsumi *kôri.*

The time limit is the final day of the period indicated in "days," "months" or "years." Within the period, the obligor cannot perform the contract. The obligee also cannot demand performance.

Kaitô *kôri* and Kaisai *kôri.*

The time limit, as a rule, is the final day of the period. The obligor can perform the contract at any time. The obligee also can demand the performance at any time.

Aichi *kôri.*

The time limit is the final day of the period. The obligor is entitled to perform a contract at any time within the period, though the obligee is not entitled to demand performance by the time limit.

Niwa *kôri* and Haguri *kôri.*

The time limit is always stated in a contract definitely, such as "on a certain day of a certain month of a certain year." When it is indicated by such expressions as "within a certain number of days, months or years," the obligor is entitled to perform his obligation at any time within the period. The obligee, however, is not entitled to demand performance as he pleases within the period.

SHIZUOKA PREFECTURE

Prefectural Office.

Regarding the first question, when the period is indicated as "for a certain number of days, months, or years," the time limit is the final day of the period, either the last day of the final month, or the last day of the last month of the final year, respectively. As to the second question, the obligor can perform the contract at any time, but the obligee does not always demand performance, if the obligor falls into difficult circumstances.

Udo *kôri* and Abe *kôri*.

A period of "three days," for instance, begins on the first day and ends at sunset on the third day. "Three months" is from January to sunset on March 31. A period of "three years" begins the 10th year of Meiji and ends on the December 31 of the 12th year of Meiji. Recently, however, a month or a year sometimes counts as thirty days or twelve months, respectively. The obligor can perform the contract at any time within the period. But the obligee cannot demand performance at any time.

Inasa *kôri* and Aratama *kôri*.

If the period is indicated as "for a certain number of days," the time limit is the final day of the period. As for "months" or "years," it is the last day of the final month or the last day of the last month of the final year. The obligor can perform the contract at any time within the period, but the obligee cannot demand performance.

Kamo *kôri* and Naka *kôri*.

As for "a period of a certain number of days," it is counted from the day the contract is concluded. As for "a period of a certain number of months or years," it is counted from the month or year in which the contract is concluded. The obligor can perform the contract at any time within the period. The obligee also can request performance, but he cannot force the obligor to perform the contract.

Saya *kôri* and Kitô *kôri*.

In the case of a contract at the seller's convenience (*urigachi-no-yaku*), the seller can ask the buyer to accept an article at any time. In the case of a contract at the buyer's convenience (*kaigachi-no-*

yaku), the buyer can ask the seller to deliver the article at any time. If there is no prior agreement, the parties will not perform the contract before the term closes.

GIFU PREFECTURE

Mugi *kôri*.

Regarding the first question, the time limit for "months" is the last day of the final month. For "years," it is the last day of the last month of the final year. As to the second question, the obligor can perform the contract at any time within the period, but the obligee cannot demand performance.

Ampachi *kôri*.

Regarding the first question, the time limit for performance is the final day, the last day of the final month, or the last day of the last month of the final year. As to the second question, the obligor can perform the contract at any time, and the obligee can also demand performance at any time.

Fuwa *kôri*.

The final day of the period is the time limit for performance. The obligor can perform the contract at any time within the period. The obligee can request performance within the period, but he cannot demand it if the obligor refuses his request.

Atsumi *kôri*, Kagami *kôri* and Katagata *kôri*.

Regarding the first question, the final day of the period is the time limit for the performance. As to the second question, the obligor can perform the contract at any time within the period. The obligee can also demand performance at any time.

Tagi *kôri* and Kami-ishizu *kôri*.

If the period is indicated as "for a certain number of days, months, or years," the final day of each period is the time limit for the performance. If the period is indicated as "within the period of a certain number of days, months, or years," the obligor can perform the contract at any time within the period. The obligee can also demand the performance at any time.

Ôno *kôri* and Ikeda *kôri*.

When the period is indicated as "for a certain number of days, months, or years," as a general rule, the final day of the period is the time limit for the performance. When it is indicated as "within the period of a certain number of months or years," either party is possibly entitled to demand performance at any time within the period, but this should be done through negotiation and not without sufficient reason.

Haguri *kôri* and Nakajima *kôri*.

Regarding the first question, the period for the performance counts from the day the contract is concluded. As to the second, yes, the obligor can perform the contract at any time.

Ena *kôri*.

Regarding the first question, "days" are counted from the day the contract is concluded. As for "months" or "years," there are two different ways of calculation, one is to count from the month or year when the contract is concluded, and the other is to count from the day of the month or year for a full period of months or years. As to the second question, the obligor can perform the contract at any time, but the obligee cannot demand performance before the period closes.

Kamo *kôri*.

If the period is indicated as "for a certain number of days, months, or years," according to our practice here the time limit is the final day, the last day of the final month, or the last day of the last month of the final year.

Kani *kôri*.

Regarding the first question, the final day of the period is the time limit for performance. As to the second question, the obligor can perform the contract at any time within the period. But the obligee cannot force him to perform it before the time limit.

Atsumi *kôri*, Gifu Township.

If the period is indicated as "for a certain number of days," it is counted from the day when the contract is concluded. If it is indicated as "for a certain number of months, or years," the time limit for performance is the final day of the period, or the last day of the final month or year. Regarding the second question, the obligor can perform the contract at any time within the period, but the obligee cannot demand performance before the period expires.

Ôgaki.

As to the first question, the time limit for performance is the final day of the period, the last day of the final month, or the last day of the last month of the final year. Regarding the second question, the obligor can perform the contract at any time. The obligee can also demand performance at any time.

Ena *kôri*, Nakatsugawa Village.

The period is counted from the day the contract is concluded. As to the second question, during the period between the day the contract is concluded and the final day of the period, the obligor can perform the contract at any time. The obligee cannot demand performance before the period comes to a close.

Shimo-ishizu *kôri*, Takasu Township.

When the period is indicated as "for a certain number of days," the period begins on the day the loan is made and ends on the day of payment. When it is indicated as "for a certain number of months," each month is counted as a full month. Suppose a contract has been concluded for a period from early January to late March or a period between late January and early March. Then both are counted as three months. This is the prevailing business practice. The obligor is free to perform the contract on any day between March 1 and 31. The same is true of "years." When the period is indicated as "within the period of a certain number of days, months, or years," the obligor can perform the contract at any time within the period. But the obligee cannot demand performance.

Haguri *kôri*, Takegahana Village.

When the period is indicated as "for a certain number of days, months, or years," the obligor and obligee are both at liberty to perform the contract at any time within the period. This is also true when it is indicated as "within the period of a certain number of days, months, or years."

Yamagata *kôri*, Takatomi Village.

Once it is definitely fixed in a contract, the length of a period is not subject to change. If it is indicated as "for a certain number of years," the obligor can perform the contract at any time within the period. But the obligee cannot demand performance. The reason is this. Since it is very difficult for the obligor to return the capital and its interest, the obligee fixes the length of the period in favor of the obligor.

Mugi *kôri*, Kôzuchi Village.

The date agreed upon in the contract is the day of performance. The obligor can perform the contract at any time within the period. The obligee can also demand performance.

Haguri *kôri*, Kasamatsu Village.

Regarding the first question, the period for performance counts from the day, month, or year when the contract is concluded. As to the second question, yes, the obligor can perform the contract at any time within the period.

Fuwa *kôri*, Tarui Village.

When the period is indicated as "for a number of days," say twenty, the time limit for performance of the contract is February 3, if it is concluded on January 15. As for "two months,"[1] or "a year,"[2] it is the final day of the period. The obligor and obligee are able to perform the contract at any time within the period.

Ôno *kôri*, Miwa Village.

The time limit is the final day of the period. The obligor can perform the contract at any time within the period.[3] The obligee also cannot demand the performance.[4]

Ampachi *kôri*, Gôdo Village.

When the period is indicated as "for a certain number of days," the final day of the period is the time limit for performance. When it is indicated as "for a certain number of months, or years," the final month of the period is the time limit for performance.

Tagi *kôri*, Shimada Village.

No answer is given.

Ena *kôri*, Iwa Village.

1) When the period is indicated as "for a certain number of days," the date of performance is counted by day from the day the contract is concluded. When it is indicated as "for a certain number of months, or years," it is counted by month or year from the month when the contract is concluded. Let us suppose a contract has been concluded on July 10 for a period of four months. The time limit for performance is October 31. If the contract is concluded in July, the 12th year of Meiji, for a period of five years, the time limit is December 31, the 16th year of Meiji. 2) The obligor can perform the contract at any time within the period. The obligee cannot demand performance before the period expires.

Kamo *kôri*, Hosome Village.

When the period is indicated as "for a certain number of days,"

[1] When it is concluded on February 15, the time limit is March 31.

[2] When it is concluded on March 27, the time limit is February 28 of the next year.

[3] "Cannot perform?"

[4] "Can demand?"

the time limit for performance is counted by day from the day the contract is concluded. As for "months," the month in which the contract is concluded is counted as one month. As for "years," the year in which the contract is concluded is counted, even if it was concluded in December, as one year, according to our practice here. But recently a new practice has developed, and we use such expressions as "for a certain number of days, months, or years." When the period is indicated as "for a certain number of months or years," each month or year is counted as a full month or year. When it is indicated as "within the period of a certain number of days, months, or years," the obligor can perform the contract at any time within the period. The obligee can also demand performance at any time within the period, but he will usually wait for the final day of the period, if it is impossible for the obligor to perform the contract.

Toki *kôri*, Takayama Village.

The time limit for performance is the last day of the final month. If the period is indicated as "for a period of five months," the time limit will come in the fifth month counting from the month in which the contract was concluded. As for "three years," it comes in the third year counting from the year in which the contract is concluded. If it is indicated as "for a period of fifty days," the time limit is the 50th day. According to our practice here, the obligor can perform the contract at any time within the period. But the obligee cannot demand the performance within the period.

Kani *kôri*, Mitake Village.

Regarding the first question, the final day of the period is the day for performance. As to the second question, the obligor can perform the contract at any time within the period. But the obligee cannot demand the performance within the period.

Ena *kôri*, Akechi Village.

Regarding the first question, when the period is indicated as "for a certain number of days," the time limit is counted from the day the contract is concluded. When it is indicated as "for a certain number of months, or years," it is counted either from the month or year when the contract is concluded, as one month or year, or from the day the contract was concluded for a full period of months or years. As to the second question, the obligor can perform the contract at any time, but the obligee cannot demand performance before the period expires.

Mugi *kôri*, Seki Village.

The date for performance is the time when the contract expires. The obligor can perform the contract within the period. The obligee cannot demand performance within the period.

Ôno *kôri*, Takayama Township.

1) The time limit for performance is the final day of the period. 2) With the consent of the obligee, the obligor can perform the contract within the period. Without it he cannot. Unless it is mentioned in the contract or unless the obligor agrees, the obligee cannot demand performance within the period.

Motosu *kôri*, Kitagata Village.

When the period is indicated as "for a certain number of days, months, or years," the final day of the period is the time limit for performance. When it is indicated as "within the period of a certain number of months or years," the obligor can perform the contract at any time within the period, but the obligee cannot demand performance within the period.

Kamo *kôri*, Ôta Village.

When the period is indicated as "for a certain number of days, months, or years," the final day of the period is the time limit for performance. When it is indicated as "within the period of a certain number of days, months or years," the obligor can perform the contract at any time within the period, but the obligee cannot demand performance within the period.

Kaisai *kôri* and Shimo-ishizu *kôri*.

When it is indicated as "for a certain number of days," the period is counted from the day when the contract is made, putting the time limit on the final day of the period. For instance, if the period is indicated as "for ten days" for a contract made on January 11, the time limit is January 20. When it is indicated as "for a certain number of months," the month when the contract is made is counted as a full month. Suppose a contract of three months is concluded for a period between early January and late March. The period is three months. Let us take another example. When a contract is made for a period between late January and early March, the period is also three months. According to our practice, the obligor can perform the contract at any time within the period. Suppose an obligor has made a contract on January 5 for a period of one month. He can perform it at any time between January 5 and 31. As for "years," the same rule holds good here.

Gujô *kôri.*

When the period is indicated as "for a certain number of days, months, or years," the period counts from the day when the contract is made, putting the time limit on the final day of the period. As for "months," the time limit is the last day of the final month. As for "years," there are two ways of calculation. The one is to count from the month when the contract was made for a full period of years, putting the time limit on the last day of the month after a certain number of full years. The other time limit is the last day of the last month of the final year. It is irrelevant whether the contract is made early or late in the month. It is counted as a full month. When the period is indicated as "within the period of a certain number of days, months, or years," the obligor can perform the contract at any time within the period, unless the trade is of special kind, if the obligee consents. Even before the period comes to a close, the obligee can demand performance, if he has sufficient reason and the obligor understands the reason.

Topic 5: Is the Time Limit Set in a Contract Computable from the Day When the Contract Is Made, or from the Day Following the Day When the Contract Is Made?

TOKYO METROPOLIS

Prefectural Office.

Paper Wholesalers (*Kiu-kumi*).[1]

It is computable from the day when the contract is made.

Oil Wholesalers.

It is computable from the day when the contract is made.

Stone Wholesalers.

It is computable from the day when the contract is made.

Medicine Wholesalers.

It is computable from the day when the contract is made.

Sugar Wholesalers.

The time limit for performance is counted from the day when the contract is concluded.

Dried Bonito Wholesalers.

It is counted from the day when the contract is made.

Soy Wholesalers.

It is computable from the day when the article is handed over.

Paper Wholesalers (*Shôkai-kumi*).[2]

It is computable from the day when the contract is made.

Rice Traders.[3]

It is our practice to compute it from the day when the contract is made.

Salt Wholesalers.

It is computed from the day when the contract is concluded.

Timber Wholesalers.

As stated above.

Timber Traders.[4]

As stated above.

Timber Traders (*Senju*).[5]

1 *Kiu-kumi kami-donya.*
2 *Shôkai-kumi kami-donya.*
3 *Beikoku sangyô-kumiai.*
4 *Zaimoku tôsei-kumiai.*
5 *Senju zaimoku-kumiai.*

As stated above.

Porcelain Wholesalers.

As stated above.

Fuel Wholesalers.

As stated above.

Copper and Iron Wholesalers.

As stated above.

Kudari Saké Wholesalers.[1]

As stated above.

Mosquito Net Wholesalers.

As stated above.

Lime and Shell Wholesalers.

As stated above.

Saké Wholesalers.

As stated above.

Tobacco Wholesalers.

There is no established practice; cases vary.

Drapery Wholesalers.

It is computable from the day when the contract is concluded.

Matting Wholesalers.

Our answer is the same as stated above by the drapery wholesalers. The same holds true for the second question.

Fuel Wholesalers (*Umite-kumi*).[2]

As stated above.

Kôjimachi Ward.

In cases of normal business, it is computable from the day when the contract is made.

Nihombashi Ward.

There is no established practice; cases vary.

Kyôbashi Ward.

It is computable from the day when the contract is made.

Yotsuya Ward and Ushigome Ward.

The time limit for business is computed from the day when the contract is concluded.

Asakusa Ward.

It is computable from the day when the contract is made.

[1] *Kudari sake-donya.*

[2] *Umite-kumi shintan-donya.*

Honjo Ward.

The time limit for business is computed from the day when the contract is made.

Ebara *kôri*.

The time limit for business is computed from the day when the contract is made.

Higashi-tama *kôri* and Minami-toshima *kôri*.

The time limit for business is usually computable from the day when the contract is concluded.

Kita-toshima *kôri*.

The time limit for business is computable from the day when the contract is made. This is because interest is counted from that day. But the period for performance is the same as stated in Topic 2. So it is rare that such a case is seen.

Minami-adachi *kôri*.

The time limit for business is computed from the day when the contract is made.

Shitaya Ward.

According to our practice the time limit for business is computed from the day when the contract is made.

Kanda Ward.

The time limit for business is computed from the day when the contract is made.

Akasaka Ward and Azabu Ward.

It is computable from the day when the contract is made.

Hongô Ward.

According to our practice, it is computed from the day when the contract is concluded.

Chiba Prefecture

Awa *kôri*, Hei *kôri*, Asai *kôri* and Nagasa *kôri*.

It is computable from the day when the contract is made.

Katori *kôri*.

It is usually computed from the day when the contract is made.

Yamabe *kôri* and Muza *kôri*.

It is our practice to compute it from the day when the contract is made.

Unakami *kôri* and Sôsa *kôri*.

It is our practice to compute it from the day when the contract is made.

Higashi-katsushika *kôri.*

In general, it is computable from the day when the contract is made.

IBARAKI PREFECTURE

Nishi-katsushika *kôri* and Sashima *kôri.*

It is computed from the day when the contract is made.

KANAGAWA PREFECTURE

Miura *kôri.*

It is computable from the day when the contract is concluded.

Tachibana *kôri.*

It is computable from the day when the contract is made.

Kita-tama *kôri.*

The time limit for business is computed from the day when the contract is made.

Ashigara-shimo *kôri.*

It is a matter of course that it is computable from the day when the contract is made.

Prefectural Industrial Bureau.

According to our practice, the time limit for business is computed from the day when the contract is made. In trade with foreigners, however, it is usually computed from the day following the day when the contract is concluded.

TOCHIGI PREFECTURE

Prefectural Office.

According to our practice it is computable from the day when the contract is made.

Shimo-tsuga *kôri* and Samukawa *kôri.*

The time limit for business is computable from the day when the contract is made.

Ashikaga *kôri* and Yanada *kôri.*

As for silk and twilled threads,[1] it is computable from the day when the contract is made. As for other articles,[2] it is computable from the day following the day when the contract is made.

MIE PREFECTURE

Suzuka *kôri.*

The time limit for business is computed from the day when the

[1] *Kara-ito.*

[2] Fabrics.

contract is made.

Ichishi *kôri.*

It is computable from the day when the contract is made, unless otherwise provided.

Nabari *kôri* and Iga *kôri.*

It is computable from the day when the contract is made.

Kita-muro *kôri.*

It is computable from the day when the contract is made.

AICHI PREFECTURE

Nakajima *kôri.*

The time limit for business is computed from the day when the contract is made.

Nagoya Ward.

The method of computation varies with each contract.

Chita *kôri.*

The time limit for business is computed from the day when the contract is made.

Minami-shidara *kôri.*

It is computable from the day when the contract is made.

Atsumi *kôri.*

The time limit for business is computed from the day when the contract is made.

Kaitô *kôri* and Kaisai *kôri.*

It is usually computable from the day when the contract is made.

Aichi *kôri.*

It is computable from the day when the contract is made.

Niwa *kôri* and Haguri *kôri.*

It is usually computable from the day when the contract is made. But there are some cases in which it is computed from the day following the day when the contract is made, depending on the contract.

SHIZUOKA PREFECTURE

Prefectural Office.

It is computable from the day when the contract is made.

Udo *kôri* and Abe *kôri.*

It is computable from the day when the contract is made.

Inasa *kôri* and Aratama *kôri.*

It is computable from the day when the contract is made.

Kamo *kôri* and Naka *kôri.*

It is computable from the day when the contract is made.

Saya *kôri* and Kitô *kôri*.

When we speak of the time limit for trade, we mention the final day rather than the opening day. We say, for example, " It expires on a certain day of a certain month."

Gifu Prefecture

Mugi *kôri*.

According to our practice here, it is computable from the day when the contract is made.

Ampachi *kôri*.

It is computable from the day when the contract is made.

Fuwa *kôri*.

It is computable from the day when the contract is made.

Atsumi *kôri*, Kagami *kôri* and Katagata *kôri*.

It is computed from the day when the contract is made.

Tagi *kôri* and Kami-ishizu *kôri*.

The time limit for business is computed from the day when the contract is made.

Ôno *kôri* and Ikeda *kôri*.

The time limit for business is computed from the day when the contract is made.

Haguri *kôri* and Nakajima *kôri*.

It is computed from the day when the contract is made.

Ena *kôri*.

It is computed from the day when the contract is made.

Kamo *kôri*.

The time limit for business is computed from the day when the contract is made.

Kani *kôri*.

It is usually computed from the day when the contract is made.

Atsumi *kôri*, Gifu Township.

The time limit is computed from the day when the contract is made.

Ôgaki.

It is computed from the day when the contract is made.

Ena *kôri*, Nakatsugawa Village.

It is computed from the day when the contract is made.

Shimo-ishizu *kôri*, Takasu Township.

It is usually computed from the day when the contract is made.

Haguri *kôri*, Takegahana Village.

There is no established practice. In some cases it is computed from the day when the contract is made. In other cases it is computed from the day following the day when the contract is made.

Yamagata *kôri*, Takatomi Village.

It is computable from the day when the contract is made.

Mugi *kôri*, Kôzuchi Village.

The time limit for business is computable from the day when the contract is made.

Haguri *kôri*, Kasamatsu Village.

It is computable from the day when the contract is made.

Fuwa *kôri*, Tarui Village.

It is computed from the day when the contract is made.

Ôno *kôri*, Miwa Village.

It is computed from the day when the contract is made.

Ampachi *kôri*, Gôdo Village.

It is computed from the day when the contract is made.

Tagi *kôri*, Shimada Village.

The time limit for business is computable from the day when the contract is made.

Ena *kôri*, Iwa Village.

It is computed from the day when the contract is made.

Kamo *kôri*, Hosome Village.

It is computed from the day when the contract is made.

Toki *kôri*, Takayama Village.

It is computed from the day when the contract is made.

Kani *kôri*, Mitake Village.

It is computed from the day when the contract is made.

Ena *kôri*, Akechi Village.

It is computed from the day when the contract is made.

Mugi *kôri*, Seki Village.

It is computed in either way according to what article is handled and what contract is made.

Ôno *kôri*, Takayama Township.

It is computed from the day when the contract is made.

Motosu *kôri*, Kitagata Village.

The time limit for business is computed from the day when the contract is made.

Kamo *kôri*, Ôta Village.

The time limit for business is computed from the day when the contract is made.

Kaisai *kôri* and Shimo-ishizu *kôri*.

According to our business practice here, it is computed from the day when the contract is made.

Gujô *kôri*.

The time limit for business is computed from the day when the contract is made.

Topic 6: In Commercial Transactions, Is the Period of One Month or Half a Month Computable in Days? Or Is There Any Other Method for Its Computation?

TOKYO METROPOLIS

Prefectural Office.

Paper Wholesalers (*Kiu-kumi*).[1]

It is computed in days.

Oil Wholesalers.

This practice is unknown here.

Stone Wholesalers.

The computation is made not in months but in days.

Dried Bonito Wholesalers.

The day of payment in commercial transactions is fixed in the contract between the two parties in advance.

Sugar Wholesalers.

Our practice has already been stated in Topic 4, "Performance of Contract." The period between delivery and payment was once computed in days. But now all business is done in cash.

Medicine Wholesalers.

It is computed in months, not in days.

Porcelain Wholesalers.

It is computed in days. For instance, a month has thirty days, and half a month, fifteen days.

Salt Wholesalers.

It is computed by the number of days.

Soy Wholesalers.

A month is not computed in days. Half a month is a period ending or beginning with the 15th of the month.

Paper Wholesalers (*Shôkai-kumi*).[2]

If a contract for a month is made today, it should be performed on the same day next month. Let us suppose a contract has been made on January 1. The time limit will be February 1. A contract for half a month should be performed on the 15th day from the day when the contract is made.

[1] *Kiu-kumi kami-donya.*

[2] *Shôkai-kumi kami-donya.*

Timber Wholesalers.

It is computed in days.

Timber Traders.[1]

As stated above.

Timber Wholesalers (*Senju-kumi*).[2]

As stated above.

Fuel Wholesalers.

It usually is computed in days. A month is counted as thirty days. If the scheduled time limit falls on a regular monthly payment day, the 14th or the 30th, delivery and payment are sometimes made a few days earlier or later than scheduled.

Rice Traders.[3]

If the period is simply indicated as "for a month," it is computed in days.

Copper and Iron Wholesalers.

It is always computed in days.

Kudari Saké Wholesalers.[4]

It is computed in days.

Mosquito Net Wholesalers.

When the period is indicated as "for a month" or "for half a month," it is computed in days.

Lime and Shell Wholesalers.

It is computed in days.

Saké Wholesalers.

It is often permissible for the obligor to compute it in days.

Tobacco Wholesalers.

There is no established practice; cases vary.

Drapery Wholesalers.

It is computed in days.

Matting Wholesalers.

As stated above.

Fuel Wholesalers (*Umite-kumi*).[5]

Regardless of whether the contract is made early or late in the month, the period until the last day of that month is counted as

[1] *Zaimoku tôsei-kumiai.*

[2] *Senju-kumi zaimoku-donya.*

[3] *Beikoku sangyô-kumiai.*

[4] *Kudari sake-donya.*

[5] *Umite-kumi shintan-donya.*

one month. In the same way, half a month is the period from the day the contract is made to the 14th of that month.

Kôjimachi Ward.

When the period is indicated as "a month," or "half a month," it is not permissible for us to compute it in days. In our ward, however, it is a prevailing practice to indicate "a certain day of a certain month."

Nihombashi Ward.

It is usually computed in days.

Kyôbashi Ward.

It is computed in days.

Yotsuya Ward and Ushigome Ward.

According to our business practice, a period such as a month or half a month is computed in days.

Asakusa Ward.

Except when it is indicated as "computable in months,"[1] it is usually computed in days.

Honjo Ward.

When the period is indicated as "a month" or "half a month," the time limt is the final day of, or about the 15th of, respectively, the month in which the contract is made. The computation of the number of days is made in "a full number of days."

Ebara *kôri*.

In commercial transactions, a month and half a month are composed of thirty days and fifteen days, respectively.

Higashi-tama *kôri* and Minami-toshima *kôri*.

A month is composed of thirty days and half a month, fifteen days.

Kita-toshima *kôri*.

It is rare that it is computed in days.[2] Usually the day of payment is fixed as the 14th or the last day of a month. It is our practice that the article is delivered in advance and the payment is made later on the above-mentioned days. Sometimes a partial payment is made in advance on condition that the delivery be made on a prescribed later date. In this method of payment, called

[1] *Tsuki-shibari.*

[2] This is not true of "*hibu-gashi*" or "*hizumi-gashi*," cases in which a loan is made at daily interest. "*Hibu*" means daily interest rate.

"*maekin-watashi*," the price is a little lower than on the market. In another method of payment, called "*nobe-gane*," delivery is made in advance on condition that the money be paid later "on a certain day of a certain month." Due to the length of the period, of course, there is some price difference. Suppose the price of 13 *shô* (23.4 liters) rice is ¥1 in September when the contract is made. When the date of payment comes on the last day of October, the buyer may have only 12 *shô* (21.6 liters), that is, one *shô* (1.8 liters) less.

Minami-adachi *kôri*.

In our business, "a month" and "half a month" are computed as thirty days and fifteen days, respectively.

Shitaya Ward.

In our business, when the period is indicated as "for a month or half a month," it is usually computed in days.

Kanda Ward.

When the period is indicated as "one month," this means the month when the contract is made. "Half a month" is a period up to the 14th of that month.

Akasaka Ward and Azabu Ward.

In our business transactions, "one month" is a period ending on the last day of the month, and "half a month," a period ending on the 14th of the month.

Hongô Ward.

In our business the period is always computed in days.

Chiba Prefecture

Awa *kôri*, Hei *kôri*, Asai *kôri* and Nagasa *kôri*.

If the contract is for less than a month, the time limit is computed in days. "Half a month" is rarely used. When the period is indicated as "one month," it runs to the last day of that month, regardless of whether the contract is made early or late in the month.

Katori *kôri*.

According to our practice, a month is counted as thirty days, and half a month as fifteen days.

Yamabe *kôri* and Muza *kôri*.

In the past, a period indicated as "a month" meant a calendar month, not the number of days involved. "Half a month" was a period ending or beginning at the 15th of the month. Since the new commercial law came into effect, a month and half a month have sometimes been counted as thirty days and fifteen days, respectively.

Unakami *kôri* and Sôsa *kôri.*

" One month" means a full month, or thirty days, and "half a month," a period of fifteen days.

Higashi-katsushika *kôri.*

If the contract is for more than one month, it is computed in months. If it is for less than one month, it usually is computed in days.

IBARAKI PREFECTURE

Nishi-katsushika *kôri* and Sashima *kôri.*

The period is computed in months, not in days. "Half a month" is a period ending or beginning at the 15th of the month.

KANAGAWA PREFECTURE

Miura *kôri.*

"Half a month" is a period ending on the 15th of the month. If the period is longer than fifteen days, it is computed as "one month."

Tachibana *kôri.*

It is always computed in days.

Kita-tama *kôri.*

In our business, "one month" is computed as follows. Suppose that on the 25th of a certain month an obligor asks an obligee to wait for another month for payment. He will be allowed to make his payment on the last day of the next month. When the period is indicated as "half a month," it probably means a period ending on the 15th of the next month. There are no other methods.

Ashigara-shimo *kôri.*

It is computed in days.

Prefectural Industrial Bureau.

In business "a month" and "half a month" are computed in days. "A month" means a period between the 1st and the last day of the month. "Half a month" is a period ending or beginning at the 15th of the month, regardless of whether the month is odd or even.

TOCHIGI PREFECTURE

Prefectural Office.

It is a common practice here to compute the period in days. Sometimes, however, "half a month" means a period ending or beginning at the 15th of the month, or a period ending before the 10th, or beginning after the 20th. "A month" also sometimes means a period ending on the final day of the month.

Shimo-tsuga *kôri* and Samukawa *kôri.*

In business, "a month" means a period ending on the final day of the next month. "Half a month" is computed in days.

Ashikaga *kôri* and Yanada *kôri.*

"Half a month" is computed as fifteen days. As for "a month," it may be either a calendar month or thirty days. Suppose a contract has been made on January 31. The time limit will be February 28. If it is made on May 10, the time limit will be June 10.

Mie Prefecture

Suzuka *kôri.*

In business a "month" means a period ending on the last day of the month in which a contract is made, regardless of whether it is made early or late in the month. The period of "half a month" is usually computed in days.

Ichishi *kôri.*

It is not computed in days. The time limit is the last day of, or the 15th of, the month.

Nabari *kôri* and Iga *kôri.*

The period indicated in expressions such as "for a month," is the period up to the final day of the month. A period of "half a month" is also within the month in which the contract is made. It is a period ending or beginning at the 15th. We do not use the number of months in place of the number of days.

Kita-muro *kôri.*

The period is computed by the number of days from the day when a contract is made. A month is counted as thirty days, and half a month as fifteen days. If the time limit is indicated as "within the month," the contract should be performed by the last day of the month.

Aichi Prefecture

Nakajima *kôri.*

In business a month is a period of more than fifteen days. Half a month is a period of about fifteen days.

Nagoya Ward.

The period of a month or half a month applies only to the month when the contract is made. It thus cannot be counted in days. If it is computed in days, it is indicated by expressions such as "within several days," or "within several ten-day periods."

Chita *kôri*.

When the period is indicated in expressions such as "for a month," it is computed either in months or in days. Cases vary. The period "half a month" is usually computed in days.

Minami-shidara *kôri*.

A month is the period ending on the last day of the month, regardless of whether it is odd or even. Half a month is a period of fifteen days.

Atsumi *kôri*.

The period is computed in days. There are no other methods.

Kaitô *kôri* and Kaisai *kôri*.

It is computed in days. There are no other methods.

Aichi *kôri*.

A month applies only to the month when the contract is made. It is irrelevant whether it is made early or late in the month.

Niwa *kôri* and Haguri *kôri*.

In commercial transactions, a month, or half a month, is computed in days. But there are other methods of computation, according to the district. Suppose a person has borrowed some money before the 15th of the month with the promise that he will repay it at the end of the month. This is "one month." If he has borrowed it after the 16th, and has promised to return it at the end of the month, the loan is for "half a month."

SHIZUOKA PREFECTURE

Prefectural Office.

Regarding the first question, it is computed in months. As to the second, in most cases the time limit is given by a prescribed date, such as "until a certain day of a certain month," or "until a certain month of a certain year."

Udo *kôri* and Abe *kôri*.

There are no other methods. The word "half a month" is not popular. Such a period is indicated by expressions such as "until a certain day of a certain month." An example might be "until the 15th of this month."

Inasa *kôri* and Aratama *kôri*.

It is computed in days.

Kamo *kôri* and Naka *kôri*.

It is computed in days.

Saya *kôri* and Kitô *kôri*.

According to our practice, a month, or half a month, applies only to the month when the contract is made. If the period is to be computed in days, it is referred to with expressions such as "for a certain number of days from today," or "for a certain number of days from tomorrow."

GIFU PREFECTURE

Mugi *kôri*.

It is our practice to compute the period in months, not in days.

Ampachi *kôri*.

In place of "half a month," the number of days, fifteen days, is generally used. When the period is indicated in expressions such as "for a month," it always means a period which ends on the final day of the month.

Fuwa *kôri*.

We compute the period in days. For instance, we count a month as thirty days, and half a month as fifteen days.

Atsumi *kôri*, Kagami *kôri* and Katagata *kôri*.

Half a month is computed in days. A month is a calendar month, ending on the last day of that month.

Tagi *kôri* and Kami-ishizu *kôri*.

According to the practice prevailing here, a period of a month or half a month is computed in days. In some districts, however, a month is interpreted as meaning "within the month," and half a month as "the second half of the month." Let us suppose that early in the month an obligee has asked an obligor to pay a bill early in the month, and has given him permission to pay it a month later. The obligee will then implicitly expect the payment to be made at the end of the same month.

Ôno *kôri* and Ikeda *kôri*.

In business, a month is a calendar month. Half a month is counted as fifteen days.

Haguri *kôri* and Nakajima *kôri*.

The period is not computed in days. There are no other methods.

Ena *kôri*.

There are two methods of computation. Some people use the number of days, but others use the period of a month, or half a month.

Kamo *kôri*.

In business, the period of a month, or half a month, is not counted by the number of days. When the period is indicated as "half a month," the time limit is the 15th of that month, if a contract is made during the first half of the month. In the same way, the time limit is the 30th, that is, the final day of the month, if the contract is made during the second half of the month. When the period is indicated as "a month," the time limit is the 30th of the next month. However, there are some cases where it is computed in days.

Kani *kôri*.

It is computed in days. As for a month, the time limit usually is the day in the following month preceding the same day of the current month the contract is made. If the contract has been made on July 10, the time limit is August 9.

Atsumi *kôri*, Gifu Township.

A month is not related to the number of days. The time limit is the final day of the month. In some cases, however, the period is computed in days.

Ôgaki.

The period of "half a month" is usually computed in days. "A month" is usually until the final day of the month.

Ena *kôri*, Nakatsugawa Village.

It is computed in days.

Shimo-ishizu *kôri*, Takasu Township.

According to a business practice prevailing here, regardless of the number of days, the period ending on the final day of the month when the contract is made is taken as a month. In the same way, the period ending about the middle of the month is half a month. This has long been a practice among us. When the period is indicated as "for a month, or half a month from today," the period is computed by the full number of days.[1]

Haguri *kôri*, Takegahana Village.

Taking a month as thirty days, we have long computed it in days.

Yamagata *kôri*, Takatomi Village.

When the period is indicated early in the month, or before the

[1] *Man-no-nissû*.

15th, the time limit "for a month" is the 31st of the month. Half a month means a period between the 15th and the last day of the month. In some cases, it is computed in days.

Mugi *kôri*, Kôzuchi Village.

In business, the periods of "a month" or "half a month" are computed in days. If the period is indicated as "within this month," or "within next month," it is not related to the number of days.

Haguri *kôri*, Kasamatsu Village.

It is computed in days. There are no other methods.

Fuwa *kôri*, Tarui Village.

A month is computed as thirty days, and half a month as fifteen days.

Ôno *kôri*, Miwa Village.

It is computed in days.

Ampachi *kôri*, Gôdo Village.

The method of computation is usually agreed on in a contract.

Tagi *kôri*, Shimada Village.

In business, the periods of "a month" and "half a month" are computed in days. But there are some other cases where the period is shown as "until a certain day of a certain month."

Ena *kôri*, Iwa Village.

It is computed in days.

Kamo *kôri*, Hosome Village.

In business, the periods of "a month" and "half a month" are computed in days.

Toki *kôri*, Takayama Village.

If the contract is for a month, the period is regarded as the remainder of that month, even when this is short of a calendar month. "Half a month" is computed in days.

Kani *kôri*, Mitake Village.

"Half a month" is computed in days. When the period is indicated in expressions such as "for a month, two months, or three months," the month when the contract is made will be regarded as a full month, even if it is short of thirty days, as, for instance, when the contract is concluded on the 10th.

Ena *kôri*, Akechi Village.

There are two methods of computation. Some people use the number of days, but others use the period of a month, or half a month.

Mugi *kôri*, Seki Village.

It is computed in days.

Ôno *kôri*, Takayama Township.

Independently of the number of days involved, the "month" is taken as a full month. "Half a month" means the period preceding the 15th or following the 16th. There are no other methods.

Motosu *kôri*, Kitagata Village.

In business, the periods of "a month" and "half a month" are computed in days.

Kamo *kôri*, Ôta Village.

In business, the periods of "a month" or "half a month" have no connection with the number of days involved. For example, if a contract is for "half a month," the time limit is accepted as the 15th if the contract is made before that day. The time limit will be the 30th of the month if the contract is made after the 15th. When the period is indicated with an expression such as "for a month," the time limit is taken as the 30th of the next month.

Kaisai *kôri* and Shimo-ishizu *kôri*.

According to our business practice, a "month" means a full month. "Half a month" is the first or second half of the month. If, however, the period is indicated in a contract with an expression such as "for a month, or half a month," it is computed by the full number of days.[1]

Gujô *kôri*.

In business, the periods of "a month" and "half a month" are computed in days.

[1] *Man-nissû.*

Topic 7: If the Time Limit Set in a Contract Is Due on a General Holiday, or a Local Holiday, or the Holiday of the Store (That Is, One of the Parties to the Contract), How Should the Transaction Be Handled?

TOKYO METROPOLIS

Paper Wholesalers (*Kiu-kumi*).[1]

No business is conducted on a holiday.

Oil Wholesalers.

Holiday or no holiday, business must go on.

Stone Wholesalers.

Having no holidays, we are always ready to do business.

Medicine Wholesalers.

Even on general holidays contracts shall be fulfilled.

Sugar Wholesalers.

If the last day for fulfilling the contract falls on a generally accepted holiday, the parties will talk it over. However, when it falls on a local holiday or on a business holiday set by the store, business will be conducted as usual.

Dried Bonito Wholesalers.

If it falls on a holiday, business will be put off until the following day.

Timber Wholesalers.

We have no holidays.

Timber Traders.[2]

As stated above.

Timber Traders (*Senju*).[3]

As stated above.

Fuel Wholesalers.

When the time limit falls on a holiday, the party closing its doors will ask the other party to name another day.

Paper Wholesalers (*Shôkai-kumi*).[4]

If a contract becomes due on a generally accepted holiday, business will be put off until the following day.

[1] *Kiu-kumi kami-donya.*

[2] *Zaimoku-kumiai.*

[3] *Senju zaimoku-kumiai.*

[4] *Shôkai-kumi kami-donya.*

Soy Wholesalers.

We take no holidays.

Porcelain Wholesalers.

When a contract becomes due on any kind of holiday, business will be put off until the following day.

Salt Wholesalers.

The parties will discuss the matter and take care of the business either before or after the holiday.

Rice Traders.[1]

When a contract becomes due on a generally accepted holiday, a local holiday or a special holiday designated by the store, business usually will be done on the following day, provided such holidays are known in advance.

Copper and Iron Wholesalers.

Regardless of whether or not a contract becomes due on a holiday, the provisions of the contract must be fulfilled.

Kudari Saké Wholesalers.[2]

The contract will be fulfilled in accordance with the wishes of each party, regardless of any holidays.

Mosquito Net Wholesalers.

If a contract falls due on a holiday, business will be postponed until the following day.

Lime and Shell Wholesalers.

If a contract falls due on either a public or a private holiday, business will be put off until the following day.

Saké Wholesalers.

For those with an obligation, there are no holidays. Business must be conducted as usual.

Tobacco Wholesalers.

We have no holidays.

Drapery Wholesalers.

Even if a contract falls due on a holiday, business will be conducted as usual.

Matting Wholesalers.

In such cases, the obligation will be postponed until the following day.

[1] *Beikoku sangyô-kumiai.*

[2] *Kudari sake-donya.*

Fuel Wholesalers (*Umite-kumi*).[1]

We have no holidays.

Kôjimachi Ward.

In the case of either a generally accepted holiday or a local holiday, business will be postponed until the following day. This is not always the case with a holiday set aside by only one of the two parties.

Nihombashi Ward.

Except for a few banks and other companies, our stores have no holidays. Although many close their doors on New Year's Day, the Day of the Lantern Festival and the other five annual festivals, they do not always stop doing business entirely.

Kyôbashi Ward.

The obligation will be put off until the following day.

Yotsuya Ward and Ushigome Ward.

No answer is given.

Asakusa Ward.

The obligation will be put off until the following day.

Honjo Ward.

In the case of a generally accepted holiday, a holiday according to local custom or a holiday of one of the stores, the transaction will be moved up to the previous day or postponed until the following day. Sometimes, however, the parties may agree to do business on a holiday.

Ebara *kôri*.

In the case of a general holiday, a local holiday or a store holiday, business will be postponed until the following day.

Higashi-tama *kôri* and Minami-toshima *kôri*.

In the case of a holiday, business will be put off until the following day.

Kita-toshima *kôri*.

A few companies close their doors on a holiday. But, with the exception of New Year's Day and the Day of the Lantern Festival (July 16), we traders have no holidays. Even on the two days just mentioned, we will not refuse to do business if someone comes. We have no practice of closing our doors just because it is a holiday.

Minami-adachi *kôri*.

[1] *Umite-kumi shintan-donya.*

In case of a holiday, obligations will be put off until the following day.

Shitaya Ward.

In the case of a holiday as stated in the question, business usually will be put off until the following day.

Kanda Ward.

If a contract falls due on a holiday, business will be conducted.

Akasaka Ward and Azabu Ward.

We shall never refuse or postpone business simply becaues it is a holiday.

Hongô Ward.

In the case of a general holiday or a local holiday, business will be postponed until the following day. In the case of a store holiday, business will usually, but not always, be postponed.

Chiba Prefecture

Awa *kôri*, Hei *kôri*, Asai *kôri* and Nagasa *kôri*.

The traders here have no practice of closing their doors on a holiday. Some traders take holidays for New Year's Day and the Lantern Festival (July 15). Transactions arising on such days will be put off until the following day.

Katori *kôri*.

Unless we are in mourning for a dead person, we will do business even on holidays.

Yamabe *kôri* and Muza *kôri*.

Most traders will postpone business until the following day.

Unakami *kôri* and Sôsa *kôri*.

There are few who close their doors. Even on holidays, every trader will do as much business as possible with a customer of long standing.

Higashi-katsushika *kôri*.

Even though it be a holiday, business will usually be done on the prescribed day. If there is some unavoidable circumstance, the two parties concerned will discuss the possibility of a postponement.

Ibaraki Prefecture

Nishi-katsushika *kôri* and Sashima *kôri*.

Business will be done on the following day.

Kanagawa Prefecture

Miura *kôri*.

Most traders in this port here are engaged in shipping. They thus have no practice of closing their doors for a holiday.

Tachibana *kôri*.

Business will be put off until the following day, according to the practice here.

Kita-tama *kôri*.

We have never heard of traders here closing their doors on a holiday, except for a wedding or a funeral. In some cases, however, the two parties concerned may talk over the possibility of postponing business.

Ashigara-shimo *kôri*.

Traders here close their doors on a holiday. But they are not at liberty on a privately designated holiday to refuse to do business with the other party.

Prefectural Industrial Bureau.

In the case of a general holiday, a local holiday or a store holiday, the transaction will be made on the day preceding or following the holiday. If the transaction must be made strictly within the period prescribed in the contract, it will be made on the day preceding the holiday.

TOCHIGI PREFECTURE

Prefectural Office.

Business will be conducted as usual even on a holiday. Some banks and firms, however, have private regulations to close their doors on holidays, thereby putting off their business until the following day.

Shimo-tsuga *kôri* and Samukawa *kôri*.

Business will not be postponed or moved up even for a holiday.

Ashikaga *kôri* and Yanada *kôri*.

In business, there are no holidays.

MIE PREFECTURE

Suzuka *kôri*.

Even on a holiday, business will never be put off.

Ichishi *kôri*.

Even on a holiday, business will be conducted as usual.

Nabari *kôri* and Iga *kôri*.

With the exception of New Year's Day and the Day of the Lantern Festival, commercial transactions are conducted even on holidays.

Kita-muro *kôri*.

Even on public or private holidays, a contract is performed when it is due.

AICHI PREFECTURE

Nakajima *kôri.*

Even if the date of performance falls on a national holiday, the contract is fulfilled.

Nagoya Ward.

If it falls on a general or local holiday, the date of execution is postponed until the following day.

Chita *kôri.*

When the time limit falls on a general holiday, it is sometimes put off until the following day. When it falls on the holiday of a district or a firm, however, commercial transactions are carried out on that day, unless the other party agrees to a postponement.

Minami-shidara *kôri.*

There are no commercial transactions on holidays, even on store holidays.

Atsumi *kôri.*

Even on holidays, the obligor ought to perform his obligations, unless the obligee allows him to postpone their execution.

Kaitô *kôri* and Kaisai *kôri.*

In business, there are no holidays.

Aichi *kôri.*

When the date of performance falls on holidays, it is put off until the following day.

Niwa *kôri* and Haguri *kôri.*

Even when the time limit falls on a holiday, it is unusual to change it, unless there are unavoidable circumstances.

SHIZUOKA PREFECTURE

Prefectural Office.

The contract is performed even on a holiday.

Udo *kôri* and Abe *kôri.*

Trading will be advanced to the day preceeding, or postponed to the day following, the holiday. In case of a store holiday, business cannot be postponed or moved up unless the other party has been informed of the suspension in advance.

Inasa *kôri* and Aratama *kôri.*

Business will be conducted on the following day.

Kamo *kôri* and Naka *kôri.*

If a deadline has been set beforehand and it is necessary to meet that deadline, business should be conducted as usual even on a holiday.

Saya *kôri* and Kitô *kôri*.

In case of a holiday, trading will be postponed until the following day. However, business will be taken care of on the day originally prescribed if the matter is urgent. With the exception of some banks and a few other firms, however, stores do not close their doors on a holiday.

Gifu Prefecture

Mugi *kôri*.

Traders usually take no holidays.

Ampachi *kôri*.

If agreed upon in the contract, business will be conducted as usual, even on a holiday.

Fuwa *kôri*.

Even on a holiday, business should continue.

Atsumi *kôri*, Kagami *kôri* and Katagata *kôri*.

Trading sometimes will be postponed until the following day, depending upon discussions between the two. However, most traders make it a rule to do business even on holidays.

Tagi *kôri* and Kami-ishizu *kôri*.

Even in the case of general holidays or local holidays, business will be conducted as usual. On a store holiday, however, no business will be conducted.

Ôno *kôri* and Ikeda *kôri*.

There is no established practice.

Haguri *kôri* and Nakajima *kôri*.

Generally speaking, trading will be put off until the following day.

Ena *kôri*.

Business will be conducted as usual even on a holiday.

Kamo *kôri*.

In the case of a generally recognized holiday, New Year's Day, the five annual festivals, and other similar days on the old calendar, business will be put off until the following day. In the case of a local holiday or a store holiday, traders will conduct business.

Kani *kôri*.

In most cases, traders will carry out the contract as required.

Atsumi *kôri,* Gifu Township.

Business will be postponed until the following day.

Ôgaki.

Since it has been agreed by both parties to the contract, business should be carried out on the prescribed day.

Ena *kôri,* Nakatsugawa Village.

In the case of a general holiday, business will not be conducted. On a local holiday or a store holiday, business will be performed according to the contract.

Shimo-ishizu *kôri,* Takasu Township.

Trading will not be conducted on holidays, unless it becomes necessary to do so due to unavoidable circumstances. There are many different cases.

Haguri *kôri,* Takegahana Village.

Business will be postponed until the following day only if so required by unavoidable circumstances.

Yamagata *kôri,* Takatomi Village.

Business should be carried on even on holidays of whatever kind. This is because the parties agreed to do so by making such a contract.

Mugi *kôri,* Kôzuchi Village.

Business can be conducted regardless of whether it is a holiday or not.

Haguri *kôri,* Kasamatsu Village.

Business usually will be put off until the following day.

Fuwa *kôri,* Tarui Village.

Even in the case of a holiday, business will be conducted as usual.

Ôno *kôri,* Miwa Village.

Business is conducted on all holidays with the one exception of New Year's Day.

Ampachi *kôri,* Gôdo Village.

According to the practice here, business will be conducted at any time.

Tagi *kôri,* Shimada Village.

Since the deadline has been agreed upon by both parties in the contract, business should be conducted on all holidays and festivals.

Ena *kôri,* Iwa Village.

Even on a holiday, business will go on.

Kamo *kôri,* Hosome Village.

Even if a time limit is set so as to cause an obligation to come due on a general holiday or a local holiday, business will be postponed until the following day. In our village, traders have no private holidays of their own.

Toki *kôri*, Takayama Village.

In this area there are no regular holidays. On the occasion of an extraordinary holiday, proper measures will be taken as thought fit.

Kani *kôri*, Mitake Village.

In such cases, we shall immediately inform the other party of the holiday, adding that the contract cannot be fulfilled on the prescribed day. Business will be conducted on the day preceding or following the holiday.

Ena *kôri*, Akechi Village.

Business will be conducted regardless of the holiday.

Mugi *kôri*, Seki Village.

Business will be conducted even on a general holiday.

Ôno *kôri*, Takayama Township.

Whether a holiday or not, business will occur. The obligee, however, occasionally will agree with the obligor to put off the business until a later date.

Motosu *kôri*, Kitagata Village.

If a contract falls due on a general holiday, a local holiday or a store holiday, business will be postponed until the following day, unless other provisions have been made.

Kamo *kôri*, Ôta Village.

In the case of a general holiday, the transaction will be put off until the following day. In the case of a local holiday, or a store holiday, the transaction will be made earlier than scheduled.

Kaisai *kôri* and Shimo-ishizu *kôri*.

If a contract falls due, as stated here, on a holiday, the obligation will be put off until the following day. However, there may be unavoidable circumstances which require one to fulfill the conditions of the contract even on a holiday. Practices are different from one place to another.

Gujô *kôri*.

In the case of a holiday, business will sometimes be conducted as scheduled, depending on the circumstances. Generally speaking, the business will be postponed until the day following the holiday.

Topic 8: In Commercial Transactions, Is the Period of One Day Computable by the Number of Hours? Or Is There Any Other Method for Its Computation?

Tokyo Metropolis

Paper Wholesalers (*Kiu-kumi*).[1]

The period is from dawn until sunset of the same day.

Oil Wholesalers.

It is from dawn until sunset of the same day.

Stone Wholesalers.

According to the practice here, it is from dawn until sunset of the same day.

Dried Bonito Wholesalers.

From dawn until sunset of the same day.

Sugar Wholesalers.

In our business, it is a period not extending to the following day. There is no other method.

Medicine Wholesalers.

It is not computed by the number of hours, but by the full day.

Rice Traders.[2]

The period of one day is from dawn until sunset. As for things that can be delivered at night, such as money, the day ends at 12 p.m.

Porcelain Wholesalers.

In business, the day is a full day, from morning until evening. It cannot be thought of as a specific number of hours.

Paper Wholesalers (*Shôkai-kumi*).[3]

The period of one day ends at 10 p.m. There is no other criterion.

Soy Wholesalers.

The period is from dawn till sunset.

Fuel Wholesalers.

So far as conventional transactions are concerned, the day begins at dawn and ends at sunset. However, trading can be carried on at night under certain circumstances if either of the two parties, or

[1] *Kiu-kumi kami-donya.*

[2] *Beikoku sangyô-kumiai.*

[3] *Shôkai-kumi kami-donya.*

both, cannot wait until the following day. If it is necessary to count the number of days within which some act must be performed, the period of a full day (twenty-four hours) should be used.

Timber Wholesalers.

The period of one day is computed by the number of hours.

Timber Traders.[1]

The same as the preceding answer.

Timber Wholesalers (*Senju*).[2]

The same as the preceding answer.

Salt Wholesalers.

From dawn until sunset.

Copper and Iron Wholesalers.

Business hours include the period between morning and evening.

Kudari Saké Wholesalers.[3]

In business, the period of one day is generally from dawn until sunset.

Mosquito Net Wholesalers.

Regardless of the number of hours, the period of one day is from dawn until sunset.

Lime and Shell Wholesalers.

The day is from dawn until sunset,[4] according to our practice. The number of hours is not important.

Saké Wholesalers.

The business day lies between morning and evening.

Tobacco Wholesalers.

From dawn until sunset.

Drapery Wholesalers.

From dawn until sunset.

Matting Wholesalers.

From dawn until sunset.

Fuel Wholesalers (*Umite-kumi*).[5]

From dawn until sunset. It is the length of time in a day, regardless of the number of hours.

Kôjimachi Ward.

[1] *Zaimoku tôsei-kumiai.*

[2] *Senju zaimoku-donya.*

[3] *Kudari sake-donya.*

[4] *Nichi-gen-no-sadame.*

[5] *Umite-kumi shintan-donya.*

According to the practice here, the day is from dawn until sunset.

Nihombashi Ward.

According to our practice, the period of one day is from sunrise until the time we go to bed at 10 p.m.

Kyôbashi Ward.

When a contract is made, it may be fulfilled up to 12 p.m. of the day on which it is due.

Yotsuya Ward and Ushigome Ward.

In business, the day is usually a full day, from morning until evening. However, some stores open their doors everyday for a certain number of hours.

Asakusa Ward.

The day is a full day, from dawn until sunset. There is no other specific method for setting the length of the day.

Honjo Ward.

In business, the day begins at dawn, and ends at sunset.

Ebara *kôri*.

In commercial transactions, the day is a full day from morning until evening, not extending to the following day.

Higashi-tama *kôri* and Minami-toshima *kôri*.

The day is a full day, from morning until evening.

Kita-toshima *kôri*.

Traders here rather think of the day only in the most general terms, simply saying, "this morning," or "until tomorrow noon."

Minami-adachi *kôri*.

When a contract is made for one day, it refers only to the remainder of the day.

Shitaya Ward.

In business, the period of one day is thought of in terms of the number of hours.

Kanda Ward.

Traders here do not think too much about it. In most cases, it is from morning until evening.

Akasaka Ward and Azabu Ward.

The number of hours is not important. A period of one day in a contract would refer only to the day on which the contract is made.

Hongô Ward.

For traders here, the period of one day is from dawn until sunset.

Few of them think of it in terms of the number of hours.

CHIBA PREFECTURE

Awa *kôri*, Hei *kôri*, Asai *kôri* and Nagasa *kôri*.

Independently of the number of hours, it is the period remaining in the day.

Katori *kôri*.

In business, the period of one day is a full day from morning until evening and does not involve counting the number of hours. There are no other methods.

Yamabe *kôri* and Muza *kôri*.

The day is not based upon the number of hours. It only means a full day.

Unakami *kôri* and Sôsa *kôri*.

According to our business practice, the period of one day is a full day from morning until evening. The number of hours is not important.

Higashi-katsushika *kôri*.

In contracts, the number of days refers to the number of calendar days, not some precise number of hours.

IBARAKI PREFECTURE

Nishi-katsushika *kôri* and Sashima *kôri*.

The number of hours is not important. Rather, a full day is from dawn until sunset.

KANAGAWA PREFECTURE

Miura *kôri*.

In a contract the number of days refers only to calendar days. In a contract the day of signing is considered the first day.

Tachibana *kôri*.

According to the practice here, the period of one day is from dawn until sunset.

Kita-tama *kôri*.

The day is a period ending at sunset, unless a provision otherwise about the number of hours is made in the contract.

Ashigara-shimo *kôri*.

The business day is counted as one day, regardless of the number of hours.

Prefectural Industrial Bureau.

There are various interpretations. However, a day usually refers to one's business hours.

TOCHIGI PREFECTURE

Prefectural Office.

According to the business practice prevailing here, the day is from dawn until 10 p.m.

Shimo-tsuga *kôri* and Samukawa *kôri*.

In business, the business day is a period ending at sunset.

Ashikaga *kôri* and Yanada *kôri*.

Neither a period of one day, nor a number of hours is much used here. When used, however, the obligee will ask the obligor if it means the day itself, or the following day.

MIE PREFECTURE

Suzuka *kôri*.

In business, it means only the day.

Ichishi *kôri*.

A day is a period marked off by nights. It is independent of the number of hours.

Nabari *kôri* and Iga *kôri*.

Independent of the number of hours, the period of one day is from dawn until sunset, or from midnight to midnight.

Kita-muro *kôri*.

According to our practice, it is from dawn until sunset.

AICHI PREFECTURE

Nakajima *kôri*.

The period of one day is from dawn until sunset.

Nagoya Ward.

It is the daytime. No business is done at night.

Chita *kôri*.

In business, it means the full length of the day, independent of the number of hours. Usually it is a period ending at sunset.

Minami-shidara *kôri*.

It is independent of the number of hours, only being from dawn until after sunset, or about 12 p.m.

Atsumi *kôri*.

We do not use the "number of hours" but a "day."

Kaitô *kôri* and Kaisai *kôri*.

Usually it is from dawn until night, or 12 p.m.

Aichi *kôri*.

It means the full length of the day, independent of the number of hours.

Niwa *kôri* and Haguri *kôri*.

In business, the period of one day is from dawn until sunset, or sometimes until 12 p.m.

SHIZUOKA PREFECTURE

Prefectural Office.

Regarding the first question, it is computed by the day. We have no such practice as referred to in the second question.

Udo *kôri* and Abe *kôri*.

It is from dawn until sunset.

Inasa *kôri* and Aratama *kôri*.

According to our practice, the period is from sunrise today until sunrise tomorrow.

Kamo *kôri* and Naka *kôri*.

In business, the period of one day is from sunrise until sunset, or until the time to go to bed.

Saya *kôri* and Kitô *kôri*.

It is computed by the day, not by the number of hours.

GIFU PREFECTURE

Mugi *kôri*.

According to our business practice, it is computed by the day, not by the number of hours.

Ampachi *kôri*.

We make it a rule to compute it by the day, not by the number of hours.

Fuwa *kôri*.

In business, the period of one day is the daytime, during which time people are working.

Atsumi *kôri*, Kagami *kôri* and Katagata *kôri*.

It is a business practice common to banks and firms to compute it by the number of hours. Most traders, however, do not always have a practice established.

Tagi *kôri* and Kami-ishizu *kôri*.

In business, the period of one day means only that day, and none other.

Ôno *kôri* and Ikeda *kôri*.

For some traders, the market is a place where not a moment is to be lost. Most traders, however, think only of the day when a contract is made, regardless of what time in the day it may be made.

Haguri *kôri* and Nakajima *kôri*.

Traders here do not use the number of hours.

Ena *kôri*.

It is taken as a day, not as the number of hours.

Kamo *kôri*.

In business, the period of one day means only the day when a contract is made. No business is done by the hour.

Kani *kôri*.

According to our practice, it is a whole day and night.

Atsumi *kôri*, Gifu Township.

We have no established practice.

Ôgaki.

Not by the number of hours, but by the day.

Ena *kôri*, Nakatsugawa Village.

A day begins at 1 a.m. and ends at 12 p.m. Even when a contract is made at 1 p.m. for a period of one day, the day comes to an end at 12 p.m.

Shimo-ishizu *kôri*, Takasu Township.

It is from dawn until sunset. No business is done at night.

Haguri *kôri*, Takegahana Village.

According to a practice long prevailing here, it only means the day when a contract is made.

Yamagata *kôri*, Takatomi Village.

When a contract is made for a period of one day, the period comes to an end about sunset of that day, according to our practice.

Mugi *kôri*, Kôzuchi Village.

The word "day" does not convey any meaning such as the "number of hours."

Haguri *kôri*, Kasamatsu Village.

We do not use the number of hours.

Fuwa *kôri*, Tarui Village.

In business, it usually means the daytime.

Ôno *kôri*, Miwa Village.

In business, we do not use the number of hours. It is from dawn until sunset.

Ampachi *kôri*, Gôdo Village.

Not by the number of hours, but by the day.

Tagi *kôri*, Shimada Village.

In business, it is computed by the day, not by the number of hours.

Ena *kôri*, Iwa Village.

By the number of hours.

Kamo *kôri*, Hosome Village.

It may be a matter of course that a day should be computed by the number of hours. According to our practice here, however, it only means the day when a contract is made.

Toki *kôri*, Takayama Village.

Whenever a contract may be made, whether early or late in the day, we compute it as a full day, not referring to the remaining hours.

Kani *kôri*, Mitake Village.

In case of necessity, traders use the number of hours. If a three-day contract is made at noon today, the time limit comes at 6 p.m. on the third day, today being counted as the first day.

Ena *kôri*, Akechi Village.

It is computed as a full day, independent of the number of hours.

Mugi *kôri*, Seki Village.

A day is a period beginning at dawn and ending at the time when we go to bed.

Ôno *kôri*, Takayama Township.

A day is from dawn until midnight.

Motosu *kôri*, Kitagata Village.

Traders sometimes compute it by the number of hours. In that case a day is a period of twenty-four hours.

Kamo *kôri*, Ôta Village.

It may be a matter of course that a day should be computed by the number of hours. According to our practice here, however, it only means the day when a contract is made.

Kaisai *kôri* and Shimo-ishizu *kôri*.

In business, a day means a period between 6 a.m. and 6 p.m. No business is done at night.

Gujô *kôri*.

In business, a day is a period ending at midnight.

Topic 9: If an Extension of the Time Limit for a Contract Is Agreed upon but There Is No Stipulation as to The Time When the Computation of the Extended Period Should Start, Is It Computable from the Day When the New Contract about the Extension[1] Is Made, or from the Day When the Time Limit Set in the Original Contract Expires?

TOKYO METROPOLIS

Paper Wholesalers (*Kiu-kumi*).[2]

We have no practice of making a new contract for such extensions.

Oil Wholesalers.

The period of day begins from the day following the date of expiration set in the original contract.

Stone Wholesalers.

From the day following the date of expiration set in the original contract.

Medicine Wholesalers.

It begins on the day following the date of expiration set in the original contract.

Sugar Wholesalers.

If an extension of the time limit in a contract is agreed upon, there must also be a stipulation as to the time when the newly agreed upon period should be considered to have started.

Dried Bonito Wholesalers.

From the day following the date of expiration set in the original contract.

Salt Wholesalers.

From the day following the date of expiration set in the original contract.

Timber Wholesalers.

From the day following the date of expiration set in the original contract.

Timber Traders.[3]

[1] *Enki.*

[2] *Kiu-kumi kami-donya.*

[3] *Zaimoku tôsei-kumiai.*

The same as in the preceding answer.

Timber Wholesalers (*Senju*).[1]

The same as in the preceding answer.

Soy Wholesalers.

It is computed from the day when the contract for the extension is made.

Porcelain Wholesalers.

From the day following the date of expiration set in the original contract.

Paper Wholesalers (*Shôkai-kumi*).[2]

From the day following the date of expiration set in the original contract.

Fuel Wholesalers.

From the day when the new contract for the extension is made.

Rice Traders.[3]

From the day of expiration set in the original contract.

Copper and Iron Wholesalers.

From the day of expiration set in the original contract.

Kudari Saké Wholesalers.[4]

From the day following the date of expiration on which the new contract is made.

Lime and Shell Wholesalers.

From the day of expiration set in the original contract.

Saké Wholesalers.

From the day following the date of expiration set in the original contract.

Tobacco Wholesalers.

From the day on which the new contract is made.

Drapery Wholesalers.

From the day on which the new contract for the extension is made.

Matting Wholesalers.

From the day following the date of expiration set in the original contract.

[1] *Senju zaimoku-donya.*

[2] *Shôkai-kumi kami-donya.*

[3] *Beikoku sangyô-kumiai.*

[4] *Kudari sake-donya.*

Fuel Wholesalers (*Umite-kumi*).[1]

The same as in the preceding answer.

Kôjimachi Ward.

From the day following the date of expiration set in the original contract.

Nihombashi Ward.

Usually from the day on which the new contract for the extension is made.

Kyôbashi Ward.

From the day following the date of expiration set in the original contract.

Yotsuya Ward and Ushigome Ward.

Usually from the day following the date of expiration set in the original contract.

Asakusa Ward.

From the day following the date of expiration set in the original contract.

Honjo Ward.

If an extension of the time limit for a contract is agreed upon, but there is no stipulation as to when the new period should start, it will begin from the day on which the new contract is made.

Ebara *kôri*.

If an extension of the time limit for a contract is agreed upon, but there is no stipulation as to when the new period should start, it will begin from the day following the date of expiration set in the original contract.

Higashi-tama *kôri* and Minami-toshima *kôri*.

From the day following the date of expiration set in the original contract.

Kita-toshima *kôri*.

Matters about the extension of the time limit have already been discussed in Topic 4. The examples stated in this topic are seldom seen in these parts.

Minami-adachi *kôri*.

From the day following the date of expiration set in the original contract.

Shitaya Ward.

[1] *Umite-kumi shintan-donya.*

If an extension of the deadline in a contract is agreed upon, the new time period will begin from the day on which the new contract is made.

Kanda Ward.

If there is no stipulation as to when the new period should begin, it will begin on the day following the date of expiration set in the original contract.

Akasaka Ward and Azabu Ward.

If there is no stipulation as to when the new period should start, it will usually begin on the day following the date of expiration set in the original contract.

Hongô Ward.

From the day following the date of expiration set in the original contract.

CHIBA PREFECTURE

Awa *kôri*, Hei *kôri*, Asai *kôri* and Nagasa *kôri*.

If an extension of the deadline for a contract is agreed upon, but there is no stipulation as to when the new period should start, it will start on the day on which the new contract is made.

Katori *kôri*.

From the day following the date of expiration set in the original contract.

Yamabe *kôri* and Muza *kôri*.

From the day on which the new contract is made.

Unakami *kôri* and Sôsa *kôri*.

If an extension of the deadline for fulfilling a contract is agreed upon, but there is no stipulation as to when the new period should start, it will begin on the day following the date of expiration set in the original contract.

Higashi-katsushika *kôri*.

From the day following the date of expiration set in the original contract.

IBARAKI PREFECTURE

Nishi-katsushika *kôri* and Sashima *kôri*.

From the day following the date of expiration set in the original contract.

KANAGAWA PREFECTURE

Miura *kôri*.

From the day on which the new contract is made.

Tachibana *kôri.*

According to the practice here, from the day following the date of expiration set in the original contract.

Kita-tama *kôri.*

When an extension of the deadline is agreed upon, it will begin on the day on which the new contract is made, since the deadline set in the original contract is no longer of importance.

Ashigara-shimo *kôri.*

The time when the newly agreed upon period should start will be stipulated in the new contract. Even if further extensions are made, each subsequently agreed upon time period will be stipulated in each new contract.

Prefectural Industrial Bureau.

If an extension of the deadline for a contract is agreed upon, but there is no stipulation as to when the new period should start, it will begin on the day following the date of expiration set in the original contract.

TOCHIGI PREFECTURE

Prefectural Office.

According to our practice, it will begin on the day following the date of expiration set in the original contract.

Shimo-tsuga *kôri* and Samukawa *kôri.*

From the day following the date of expiration set in the original contract.

Ashikaga *kôri* and Yanada *kôri.*

In the silk trade, it will begin on the day which was to have been the deadline in the original contract. Whether that deadline has expired or not is not important.

MIE PREFECTURE

Suzuka *kôri.*

If an extension of the time period set forth in a contract is agreed upon, but there is no stipulation as to when the newly agreed upon period should start, it will begin on the day following the date of expiration set in the original contract.

Ichishi *kôri.*

Usually from the day following the date of expiration set in the original contract.

Nabari *kôri* and Iga *kôri.*

From the day the new contract is made. If another new contract is not made, and only the extension is agreed upon, it will start from the day following the deadline set in the original contract.

Kita-muro *kôri*.

From the day following the date of expiration set in the original contract.

Aichi Prefecture

Nakajima *kôri*.

From the day following the date of expiration set in the original contract.

Nagoya Ward.

From the day following the date of expiration set in the original contract.

Chita *kôri*.

From the day following the date of expiration set in the original contract.

Minami-shidara *kôri*.

From the day following the date of expiration set in the original contract.

Atsumi *kôri*.

From the day following the date of expiration set in the original contract.

Kaitô *kôri* and Kaisai *kôri*.

From the day following the date of expiration set in the original contract.

Aichi *kôri*.

If an extension of a deadline in a contract is agreed upon, but there is no stipulation as to when the new period should start, it will begin on the day following the date of expiration set in the original contract.

Niwa *kôri* and Haguri *kôri*.

Whenever a contract, whether for goods or for a loan, is made, the time limit for performance of the contract will be clearly expressed. This is true of the original contract or one replacing it. If an extension of the time period for a contract is agreed upon, but there is no stipulation as to when the new period should start, it will begin on the day following the date of expiration set in the original contract.

Shizuoka Prefecture

Prefectural Office.

It will be computed from the day following the date of expiration set in the original contract. In most cases, however, the date of the new deadline will be clearly stated as a given day of a certain month.

Udo *kôri* and Abe *kôri*.

From the day following the date of expiration set in the original contract.

Inasa *kôri* and Aratama *kôri*.

From the day on which the new contract is made.

Kamo *kôri* and Naka *kôri*.

From the day following the date of expiration set in the original contract.

Saya *kôri* and Kitô *kôri*.

The time limit will be clearly written as a given day of a certain month. As for a given period of time, the first day of that period will be clearly stipulated.

GIFU PREFECTURE

Mugi *kôri*.

If an extension of the time period for a contract is agreed upon, the new period will begin on the day following the end of the period agreed upon in the original contract.

Ampachi *kôri*.

From the day following the date of expiration set in the original contract.

Fuwa *kôri*.

From the day following the date of expiration set in the original contract.

Atsumi *kôri*, Kagami *kôri* and Katagata *kôri*.

From the day when the new contract is made.

Tagi *kôri* and Kami-ishizu *kôri*.

If an extension of the period for a contract is agreed upon, but there is no stipulation as to when the new period should start, it will begin on the day following the date of expiration set in the original contract.

Ôno *kôri* and Ikeda *kôri*.

From the day following the date of expiration set in the original contract.

Haguri *kôri* and Nakajima *kôri*.

From the day following the date of expiration set in the original contract.

Ena *kôri*.

From the day following the date of expiration set in the original contract.

Kamo *kôri*.

If an extension of the period for a contract is agreed upon, but there is no stipulation as to when the new period should start, it will begin on the day following the date of expiration set in the original contract.

Kani *kôri*.

From the day when the new contract is made.

Atsumi *kôri*, Gifu Township.

From the day when the new contract is made.

Ôgaki.

From the day following the date of expiration set in the original contract.

Ena *kôri*, Nakatsugawa Village.

From the day following the date of expiration set in the original contract.

Shimo-ishizu *kôri*, Takasu Township.

From the day following the date of expiration set in the original contract.

Haguri *kôri*, Takegahana Village.

From the day following the date of expiration set in the original contract.

Yamagata *kôri*, Takatomi Village.

From the day following the date of expiration set in the original contract.

Mugi *kôri*, Kôzuchi Village.

From the day on which the period set in the original contract expires.

Haguri *kôri*, Kasamatsu Village.

Usually from the day following the date of expiration set in the original contract.

Fuwa *kôri*, Tarui Village.

From the day following the date of expiration set in the original contract.

Ôno *kôri*, Miwa Village.

From the day following the date of expiration set in the original contract.

Ampachi *kôri*, Gôdo Village.

From the day when the new contract is made.

Tagi *kôri*, Shimada Village.

If an extension of the period in the contract is agreed upon, the new period will begin on the day following the date of expiration set in the original contract.

Ena *kôri*, Iwa Village.

From the day following the date of expiration set in the original contract.

Kamo *kôri*, Hosome Village.

From the day following the date of expiration set in the original contract.

Toki *kôri*, Takayama Village.

From the day on which the new contract is made.

Kani *kôri*, Mitake Village.

From the day on which the new contract is made.

Ena *kôri*, Akechi Village.

From the day following the period set in the original contract.

Mugi *kôri*, Seki Village.

From the day following the period set in the original contract.

Ôno *kôri*, Takayama Township.

From the day on which the new contract is made. If an agreement is reached over the extension some time after the time period set in the original contract has expired, it will begin on the day following the original expiration date.

Motosu *kôri*, Kitagata Village.

If an extension of the time period in a contract is agreed upon, but there is no stipulation as to when the new period should start, it will begin on the day following the date of expiration set in the original contract.

Kamo *kôri*, Ôta Village.

If an extension of the time period for a contract is agreed upon, but there is no stipulation as to when the new period should start, it will begin on the day following the date of expiration set in the original contract.

Kaisai *kôri* and Shimo-ishizu *kôri*.

From the day following the date of expiration set in the original contract.

Gujô *kôri*.

If an extension of the time period for a contract is agreed upon, but there is no stipulation as to when the new period should start, it will begin on the day, or the month, following the date of expiration set in the original contract.

Topic 10: If No Stipulations Have Been Made in the Contract as to the Place Where Payment Should Be Made and Received, or Where the Goods Should Be Delivered or Taken Delivery of, Where Should the Payment or the Delivery Take Place?

TOKYO METROPOLIS

Soy Wholesalers.[1]

There is no fixed practice about the place.

Sugar Wholesalers.

If the contract does not specify the place where payment should be made or goods delivered, another agreement will be drawn up between the two.

Dried Bonito Wholesalers.

At the store of either of the two.

Medicine Wholesalers.

It is our practice to make the payment and delivery ex store.[2]

Paper Wholesalers (*Kiu-kumi*).[3]

At any place agreed to by either party.

Oil Wholesalers.

It takes place ex store[4] usually on the third day from the day when the contract is made.

Stone Wholesalers.

The payment will be made at the debtor's house, and the delivery at our warehouse.[5]

Fuel Wholesalers.

Payment will be made at the buyer's store. The goods are to be delivered to the same place.

Porcelain Wholesalers.

Unless there is some special agreement, both the payment and the delivery will be made at the buyer's store.

Paper Wholesalers (*Shôkai-kumi*).[6]

[1] *Shôyu donya-kumiai.*

[2] *Niwa-chaku, niwa-barai.*

[3] *Kiu-kumi kami-donya.*

[4] *Niwa-barai, niwa-uke-watashi.*

[5] *Okiba.*

[6] *Shôkai-kumi kami-donya.*

If there is no stipulation as to where payment and delivery should be made, the place will be decided by the buyer only when both parties are in the same business in this prefecture. Otherwise, business will be conducted ex store[1] or ex farm.[2]

Rice Traders.[3]

Money is usually paid at the buyer's store. However, the deliverer will receive the money at his store, or at any place else, if it is brought by the deliveree. Goods are usually delivered at our warehouse.[4]

Salt Wholesalers.

At the seller's store.

Timber Wholesalers.

Another agreement should be reached between the two about these matters.

Timber Traders.[5]

The place will be decided upon after further consultation between the two parties.

Timber Traders (*Senju*).[6]

The place will be decided upon by the two parties.

Tobacco Wholesalers.

If payment is made in cash, the buyer will receive the goods at the seller's warehouse.[7] If goods are received on credit, the buyer will have the seller sign a contract and later on receive the goods, on the day agreed upon, either at the seller's or at the buyer's.

Matting Wholesalers.

Payment and delivery can be made only at a place previously agreed upon by both parties.

Saké Wholesalers.

No contract can be concluded until the place of payment and delivery are decided upon.

Drapery Wholesalers.

If no place is provided for in the contract, payment and delivery

[1] *Ibarai.*

[2] *Niwa-chaku.*

[3] *Beikoku sangyô-kumiai.*

[4] *Kuradokoro.*

[5] *Zaimoku tôsei-kumiai.*

[6] *Senju zaimoku-kumiai.*

[7] *Kuramae-barai.*

should be made at the seller's store.

Saké Wholesalers.

As for the payment, it may be made at the store of either of the two parties. The delivery will be made at the seller's store.

Lime and Shell Wholesalers.

We make it a rule to receive payment at our store in exchange for the goods. However we sometimes will be paid at the buyer's store.

Mosquito Net Wholesalers.

The payment and delivery will be made only at a place agreed upon in the contract.

Copper and Iron Wholesalers.

If the place has not been specified in the contract, payment and delivery may be made at an appropriate place.

Fuel Wholesalers (*Umite-kumi*).[1]

Any place will do: the store of either of the parties, on a ship or a cart.

Kôjimachi Ward.

At the store of either party, depending upon the kinds of goods being handled.

Nihombashi Ward.

Each case is different. However, payment and delivery are usually made at the buyer's store.

Kyôbashi Ward.

Answer missing.

Yotsuya Ward and Ushigome Ward.

Both will be made at the buyer's store.

Asakusa Ward.

At the seller's store.

Honjo Ward.

If the places for payment and delivery are not clearly specified, the two will decide the matter through further talks.

Ebara *kôri*.

If the places for payment and delivery are not clearly specified, both will take place at the seller's store.

Higashi-tama *kôri* and Minami-toshima *kôri*.

If the places for payment and delivery are not specified, both

[1] *Umite-kumi shintan-donya.*

will be made at the buyer's house.

Kita-toshima *kôri.*

The place to which the goods should be delivered ought always to be the first topic in business negotiations. This is particularly true when the costs of delivery are great, as with large or heavy merchandise. The terms of delivery, such as *ibarai*[1] or *mochi-komi*[2] or on a certain day or to a certain warehouse, therefore, will constitute the first article in the contract. Then they talk about the price, according to the practice. Thus, no case of trouble arising in this fashion has ever been heard of.

Minami-adachi *kôri.*

There are many different cases. As for goods themselves, the craftsman or farmer usually takes them to the trader's store. If the transaction is between merchants, or between a merchant and an independent individual, the seller usually takes the goods to the buyer's house. As for the payment for the goods, a craftsman or a farmer will call at the buyer's house and receive it there. If the business is between merchants or between a merchant and an individual, the buyer will call at the seller's store and receive the payment there. Of course, there are many exceptions.

Shitaya Ward.

It is a very rare case when the place of payment and delivery are not specified in the contract. If such a provision should be omitted, however, the two parties should immediately decide upon the place.

Kanda Ward.

There are no established rules.

Akasaka Ward and Azabu Ward.

Accounts are settled at the buyer's house. As for cash payments, on receipt of the goods, no definite rule is established. As for a loan, or something borrowed, the debtor or borrower will always return the item in question to the house of the creditor or lender. The delivery of goods is always made at the place where they are kept by the seller.

Hongô Ward.

Generally speaking, payment is made at the seller's store and

[1] *Ibarai* refers to the seller's intention to turn over the goods at his warehouse or wherever he happens to hold the goods in stock.

[2] *Mochi-komi* refers to the seller's intention to deliver the goods to the buyer's house, warehouse, or other place for storing.

delivery at the buyer's store. For some goods, however, delivery is made at the place where the seller keeps the goods.

CHIBA PREFECTURE

Awa *kôri*, Hei *kôri*, Asahi *kôri* and Nagasa *kôri*.

If the place of delivery is not specified in the contract, delivery is made at the seller's store. This method is called *ibarai*.

Katori *kôri*.

All contracts specify the place of delivery.

Yamabe *kôri* and Muza *kôri*.

The delivery of the goods is usually made at the place where they are kept by the seller.

Unakami *kôri* and Sôsa *kôri*.

If the place of delivery is not specified in the contract, the seller and the buyer will hold further discussions and agree upon a convenient place. According to the kind of goods involved, they often agree to *kawagishi-watashi*[1] or *niwa-barai*.[2]

Higashi-katsushika *kôri*.

If the places for payment and delivery are not specified in the contract, these will usually take place at the seller's store.

IBARAKI PREFECTURE

Nishi-katsushika *kôri* and Sashima *kôri*.

Payment and delivery are made at the place where the buyer is.

KANAGAWA PREFECTURE

Miura *kôri*.

At the place where the contract is made.

Tachibana *kôri*.

According to our practice, payment and delivery are made at wherever the money and goods happen to be at the time.

Kita-tama *kôri*.

If the place of payment and delivery is not clearly specified, the two parties should correspond to agree on a convenient place.

Ashigara-shimo *kôri*.

According to the practice here, it should be made at the seller's store.

Prefectural Industrial Bureau.

[1] *Kawagishi-watashi* means ex wharf.

[2] *Niwa-barai* means ex store.

If the place for delivery is not specified in the contract, the seller should take the goods to the buyer, and the buyer should receive them at the place where the goods lie. As for the payment, the choice of a place lies with the seller.

TOCHIGI PREFECTURE

Prefectural Office.

If the places for payment and delivery are not specified in the contract, the two will hold further discussions to reach an agreement upon a convenient place. In such cases, as a general rule, the seller acts to please the buyer and the debtor acts to please the creditor.

Shimo-tsuga *kôri* and Samukawa *kôri*.

If the places for payment and delivery are not specified in the contract, the seller will take the trouble to deliver the goods to and collect his bill at the buyer's store.

Ashikaga *kôri* and Yanada *kôri*.

The payment and delivery will be made at the buyer's store, if it is in the neighborhood of the seller. However, if it is far away from the seller's store, business will be done at the seller's store.

MIE PREFECTURE

Suzuka *kôri*.

If the places for payment and delivery are not specified in the contract, no rule exists to indicate the place where either act should occur.

Ichishi *kôri*.

At the seller's place.

Nabari *kôri* and Iga *kôri*.

If the places for payment and delivery are not specified in the contract, the seller and the buyer will discuss the matter and agree upon a convenient place. If business is done in cash, the payment and the delivery are made at the seller's store. In the case of a credit sale, they may be made at in half of the cases, the seller's store or, in the other half of the cases, the buyer's store. If business is done by a wholesaler and if the goods are to be carried to the buyer's store, payment and delivery will be made, in most cases, at the buyer's store.

Kita-muro *kôri*.

Payment will be made at the seller's store. The matter will be discussed and a suitable place agreed upon. As for goods like timber and fuel which are stocked at a specific place, delivery will be made at that place.

Aichi Prefecture

Nakajima *kôri*.

At the seller's store.

Nagoya Ward.

Payment will be made at the creditor's store. Delivery will be made at the seller's store.

Chita *kôri*.

If the places for payment and delivery are not specified, the matter will be discussed and a convenient place agreed upon.

Minami-shidara *kôri*.

Payment will be made at place agreed upon. Delivery is at the place where the goods are kept by the seller.

Atsumi *kôri*.

The matter will be discussed and a convenient place agreed upon.

Kaitô *kôri* and Kaisai *kôri*.

A convenient place will be agreed upon.

Aichi *kôri*.

Payment will be made at the creditor's place of business. Delivery will be made at the seller's store.

Niwa *kôri* and Haguri *kôri*.

It is a general practice here to specify the place of delivery in the contract. There are various ways in which payment is made, according to the convenience of the two parties.

Shizuoka Prefecture

Prefectural Office.

There is no established practice. Generally, these acts occur at the place of the offeree.

Udo *kôri* and Abe *kôri*.

Generally speaking, it is made at the place of business of the buyer.

Inasa *kôri* and Aratama *kôri*.

Money will be paid at the creditor's store. As for the goods, they will be delivered to an office of a transport company or forwarding agent.

Kamo *kôri* and Naka *kôri*.

At the place where the party with the greater right is.

Saya *kôri* and Kitô *kôri*.

Payments are made at a place convenient for both parties. No trouble has ever been heard of. Delivery will be made at the place where the goods are kept by the seller.

GIFU PREFECTURE

Mugi *kôri.*

No established practice is known. They will be settled according to circumstances.

Ampachi *kôri.*

Generally speaking, it is made at the seller's place of business.

Fuwa *kôri.*

It is made at the seller's place of business.

Atsumi *kôri,* Kagami *kôri* and Katagata *kôri.*

There are no established rules.

Tagi *kôri* and Kami-ishizu *kôri.*

They will be made at the buyer's place of business.

Ôno *kôri* and Ikeda *kôri.*

The places where the payment and the delivery are to be made should be stipulated in the contract. If they are not, these matters will be decided upon in talks between the two.

Haguri *kôri* and Nakajima *kôri.*

They are made at the buyer's store.

Ena *kôri.*

In most cases, the payment and the delivery are made at the buyer's store.

Kamo *kôri.*

When no stipulation has been made in the contract as to the place of delivery and payment, they are performed at the place where the contract is made.

Kani *kôri.*

Payment and delivery are carried out at the shop front where the contract is formed.

Atsumi *kôri,* Gifu township.

There has been no settled practice about the matter.

Ôgaki.

In most cases, the payment and the delivery are made at the seller's store, according to local practice.

Ena *kôri,* Nakatsugawa Village.

In such cases, payment or delivery is performed at the seller's house.

Shimo-ishizu *kôri*, Takasu Township.

Regarding the present matter, the party who is in charge of the delivery will deliver the goods.

Haguri *kôri*, Takegahana Village.

They are performed where the contract for sale is closed.

Yamagata *kôri*, Takatomi Village.

If the place of the delivery or the payment is not specified in the contract, the buyer visits the seller's house, according to local usage.

Mugi *kôri*, Kôzuchi Village.

A place will be agreed upon by the seller and the buyer.

Haguri *kôri*, Kasamatsu Village.

They will be made at the place where the debtor is.

Fuwa *kôri*, Tarui Village.

There are no established practices.

Ôno *kôri*, Miwa Village.

They will be made at the buyer's store.

Ampachi *kôri*, Gôdo Village.

They will be made at the place where the contract is signed.

Tagi *kôri*, Shimada Village.

No answer.

Ena *kôri*, Iwa Village.

They will be made at the place where the contract is made.

Kamo *kôri*, Hosome Village.

At the place where the contract is made.

Toki *kôri*, Takayama Village.

There are no established practices.

Kani *kôri*, Mitake Village.

Payment will be made at the place where the creditor is. Delivery will be made at the place where the goods are kept in stock by the seller.

Ena *kôri*, Akechi Village.

Generally speaking, it will be made at the place where the obligee is.

Mugi *kôri*, Seki Village.

At the place of business of either the seller or the buyer. Occasionally it will be made at the place where the wholesaler, owner of the goods, is.

Ôno *kôri*, Takayama Township.

At the place where the obligee is.

Motosu *kôri*, Kitagata Village.

At the place where the seller is.

Kamo *kôri*, Ôta Village.

At the place where the contract is made.

Kaisai *kôri* and Shimo-ishizu *kôri*.

In such cases, the obligee will make the obligor perform the contract at the place where the obligor is, according to our business practice here.

Gujô *kôri*.

In such cases, they are made at the place of business of the seller. In some cases, however, payment and delivery occur at the place of business of the buyer.

Topic 11: If There Is No Specific Stipulation in the Contract Regarding the Obligation on the Part of an Obligor to Forward Goods, Should the Goods Be Forwarded to the Dwelling[1] of the Obligee, or to the Ordinary Unloading Place[2] in the Locality of His Abode?[3] Or Is It Regarded as Adequate for the Obligor to Deliver the Goods to the Obligee at the Ordinary Unloading Place of the Locality of the Former's Abode?

TOKYO METROPOLIS

Soy Wholesalers.

Such a case is unknown in these parts.

Sugar Wholesalers.

According to the practice here, the goods should be forwarded to the buyer's store with the cost of land and sea transport being borne by the buyer. If they are to be forwarded to any other place at the convenience of the consignee, the seller should inform the buyer of that place.

Dried Bonito Wholesalers.

The place where the goods should be delivered will be decided upon as the situation may require through discussions between the two parties.

Medicine Wholesalers.

As stated in Performance of Contract, Topic 10.

Paper Wholesalers (*Kiu-kumi*).[4]

The place of delivery will be agreed upon to the satisfaction of both parties.

Oil Wholesalers.

The goods will be delivered as far as the buyer's warehouse.

Stone Wholesalers.

The delivery will be made at the place where the buyer dwells, or a convenient unloading place nearby.

Fuel Wholesalers.

We wholesalers made delivery ex store (*niwa-barai*). Suppose we

[1] *Jûsho.*

[2] *Nioroshiba.*

[3] *Jûchi.*

[4] *Kiu-kumi kami-donya.*

have a certain number of goods, for example, tens of thousands of packs of charcoal, in stock. When we enter into a definite contract for sale, we wholesalers assume no responsibility for damage to goods already sold but still in our warehouse (*uri-oki*), due to force majeure including flood, fire, and robbery, even if we have not yet received the total price. However, suppose a buyer orders goods from us in such term as "a certain quantity of goods" or "goods corresponding to a certain price," knowing we do not have the goods in stock. In such cases, our obligation with respect to delivery differs according to the way of delivery. For example, if the transporting agent is under the charge of the buyer, the delivery and the receipt are made at our warehouse. If, however, the carrier is under our charge, they are made at the buyer's unloading place, yet the cost for delivery is borne by the buyer.

Porcelain Wholesalers.

If such matters are not specified in the contract, the parties will follow the same measures as outlined above in Topic 10. Then the seller will have no more obligations with respect to delivery.

Paper Wholesalers (*Shôkai-kumi*).[1]

The goods should be forwarded to the place where the buyer[2] is. If the buyer is out of the prefecture, they should be forwarded to a nearby loading place of a forwarding agent.[3]

Rice Traders.[4]

Unless otherwise agreed, we deliver the goods to the ordinary unloading place.

Salt Wholesalers.

The delivery of the goods is made at the seller's warehouse.

Timber Wholesalers.

The matter will be negotiated each time.

Timber Traders.[5]

It will be agreed upon by the two.

Timber Wholesalers (*Senju-kumi*).[6]

It will be agreed upon for each transaction.

[1] *Shôkai-kumi kami-donya.*

[2] *Saishu.*

[3] *Nizumi-donya.*

[4] *Beikoku sangyô-kumiai.*

[5] *Zaimoku tôsei-kumiai.*

[6] *Senju-kumi zaimoku-donya.*

Tobacco Wholesalers.

We have had no such cases here.

Matting Wholesalers.

If there is no stipulation in advance, the delivery will be made at the dwelling[1] of the seller.

Saké Wholesalers.[2]

The goods will be forwarded to the dwelling[3] of the obligor[4] or to the ordinary loading place.[5]

Drapery Wholesalers.

The delivery will be made at the dwelling of the obligee, or at the ordinary loading place, unless otherwise provided.

Saké Wholesalers.

At the dwelling of the seller.

Lime and Shell Wholesalers.

Our business practice is to turn over the goods at the warehouse of the seller. The delivery, however, is sometimes made at a more convenient place if the buyer so requests.

Mosquito Net Wholesalers.

At the dwelling of the obligor.[6]

Copper and Iron Wholesalers.

If the place is not specified in the contract, the goods will be forwarded to the place which is ordinarily used, accompanied with a paper giving the buyer's name and address.

Fuel Wholesalers (*Umite-kumi*).[7]

The goods should be handed over at the dwelling[7] of the seller, or at the place where his goods are kept in stock. However, if requested by the buyer,[8] the goods should be delivered to a more convenient place.

Kôjimachi Ward.

There are no established rules.

[1] *Jûchi.*

[2] *Sake-rui-donya.*

[3] *Jûkyo.*

[4] *Gimusha.*

[5] *Nizumi-ba.*

[6] *Gimusha.*

[7] *Umite-kumi shintan-donya.*

[8] *Saishu.*

Nihombashi Ward.

Our business with wholesalers is usually done ex farmhouse, a system called *niwa-barai*. As soon as the goods leave his store, the seller is completely free of responsibility. But if he deals with a retail dealer, he is never free.

Kyôbashi Ward.

The delivery will be made at the dwelling[1] of the seller,[2] or at the ordinary place of delivery in the vicinity of his abode.[3]

Yotsuya Ward and Ushigome Ward.

In principle, the place for delivery should be specified in the contract. If it is not, the delivery will be made to the store of the buyer.

Asakusa Ward.

As stated in the second half of the present topic.

Honjo Ward.

The goods should be forwarded to the dwelling of the buyer, unless otherwise provided.

Ebara *kôri*.

Unless otherwise provided for, the goods should be forwarded to the dwelling of the buyer, or to the ordinary loading place[4] in the vicinity of his abode.[5]

Higashi-tama *kôri* and Minami-toshima *kôri*.

Unless otherwise provided for, the goods will be forwarded to the dwelling of the buyer, or to the ordinary unloading place[6] in the vicinity of his abode.

Kita-toshima *kôri*.

As answered in Topic 10.

Minami-adachi *kôri*.

To a place satisfactory to the obligee.

Shitaya Ward.

The goods should always be forwarded to the dwelling of the buyer, even if there are no stipulations about it, according to com-

[1] *Jûsho*.
[2] *Gimusha*.
[3] *Nizumi-ba*.
[4] *Nizumi-ba*.
[5] *Jûchi*.
[6] *Nioroshi-ba*.

mon practice.

Kanda Ward.

It is our practice that they should be forwarded to the dwelling of the buyer, or to the place where he usually receives such shipments. However, delivery occasionally is made to the yard of a forwarding agent[1] in the locality of the seller, if the contract has been agreed to at his home.

Akasaka Ward and Azabu Ward.

The goods will be turned over at the dwelling of the seller, or at the ordinary loading place in the nearby vicinity.

Hongô Ward.

The seller has a duty to forward the goods to the address of the buyer.

CHIBA PREFECTURE

Awa *kôri*, Hei *kôri*, Asai *kôri* and Nagasa *kôri*.

If a contract is made with a provision for *chaku-sôba*,[2] the seller has a duty to forward the goods to the buyer. Probably this cannot take place in a case where no stipulation about the place for delivery is made in the contract. However, if it should take place, the seller should immediately send the goods to the buyer. If he does not know where the buyer dwells, he will hold the goods in storage, while waiting for word from the buyer. If the goods should suffer any damage while in transit, or because of bad packing or traffic trouble, the loss should be borne by the seller.

Katori *kôri*.

As a general rule, the place of delivery is to be written clearly in the contract. If not, the goods will be forwarded to a forwarding agent of long standing. The goods, prior to their shipment, will be packaged and sealed by the seller. On arrival at their destination, the forwarding agent will check them for damage. If any damage is found at that time, the loss will be covered by the agent. If any of the seals are broken, or, although the seal is not broken, some damage is done inside, the loss will be shared by the obligor and obligee.

Yamabe *kôri* and Muza *kôri*.

All contracts will specify the place for delivery. However, if only

1 *Tsumi-donya*.

2 Delivery price.

the name of the town or village is written, the seller will forward the goods to the dwelling of the buyer. There are no established rules about damage in transit. But it is often borne by the buyer, unless otherwise agreed.

Unakami *kôri* and Sôsa *kôri*.

All contracts will specify the place of delivery. Otherwise, the seller will immediately contact the buyer to inquire about the place for delivery. If some damage occurs because of bad packaging, the seller will cover the loss. If damage occurs due to transportation trouble, the two parties will share the loss.

Higashi-katsushika *kôri*.

The goods will be forwarded to whatever place the buyer happens to think convenient. Usually such a place is the dwelling of the buyer, or the ordinary unloading place in the vicinity of his abode.

IBARAKI PREFECTURE

Nishi-katsushika *kôri* and Sashima *kôri*.

If the contract does not specify the place, the goods will be forwarded to the dwelling of the buyer, or to the ordinary unloading place in the vicinity of his abode.

KANAGAWA PREFECTURE

Miura *kôri*.

The delivery will be made at the ordinary loading place in the locality of the seller's abode.

Tachibana *kôri*.

If the contract does not specify the place, the goods will be forwarded to the dwelling of the buyer, or to the ordinary unloading place in the vicinity of his abode.

Kita-tama *kôri*.

Unless otherwise provided for, the goods will be forwarded with an invoice by land or sea to the ordinary unloading place in the vicinity of the buyer's abode. However, occasionally the goods will be forwarded directly to the place where the buyer dwells. The destination will be agreed upon prior to shipment.

Ashigara-shimo *kôri*.

The general practice here calls for the goods to be handed over at the place where the seller dwells. As for the goods sold to a retail dealer living in the same district, they often will be sent directly to his abode. Needless to add, they will not be so forwarded if the dealer lives outside the same district.

Prefectural Industrial Bureau.

Unless otherwise provided for in the contract, the goods will be forwarded to the dwelling of the buyer, or to the ordinary loading place (wharf or railway station) in the vicinity of his abode. If the means of transport have not been specified by the buyer, the seller will decide upon a forwarding agent or boat for shipping the goods.

TOCHIGI PREFECTURE

Prefectural Office.

The goods will be forwarded to the dwelling of the buyer, or to the ordinary unloading place in the vicinity of his abode.

Shimo-tsuga *kôri* and Samukawa *kôri*.

To the dwelling of a buyer, unless otherwise provided for in the contract.

Ashikaga *kôri* and Yanada *kôri*.

Even if not otherwise provided, the delivery should be made at the dwelling of an obligor (for instance, of textile fabrics), or at the ordinary loading place.

MIE PREFECTURE

Suzuka *kôri*.

Unless otherwise provided for, the goods will be forwarded to the dwelling of the buyer, or to the ordinary unloading place in the vicinity of his abode.

Ichishi *kôri*.

All contracts specify the place of delivery. If somehow such a condition were forgotten, the goods would be turned over at the place where the goods are.

Nabari *kôri* and Iga *kôri*.

There is no established practice.

Kita-muro *kôri*.

The goods should be forwarded to a place in accord with the wishes of the creditor.

AICHI PREFECTURE

Nakajima *kôri*.

The delivery should be made at the dwelling of the obligor, unless otherwise provided.

Nagoya Ward.

The delivery will be made, according to our practice, at the dwelling of the obligor. This form of delivery is called *niwa-barai*.

Chita *kôri.*

As a general rule here, the seller is obliged to forward them to the dwelling of the creditor, or to the ordinary unloading place in the locality of his abode. However, if circumstances require, the delivery may be made at the obligor's abode.[1]

Minami-shidara *kôri.*

In general, the delivery is made at the dwelling of the creditor.

Atsumi *kôri.*

It is a matter of course that the goods should be forwarded to the dwelling of the creditor. The general practice, however, is that the delivery is made at the ordinary place convenient for shipment by land and sea.

Kaitô *kôri* and Kaisai *kôri.*

As a general rule, the delivery will be made, unless otherwise provided, at the dwelling of an obligor, or at the ordinary loading place in the locality of his abode.

Aichi *kôri.*

The goods should be forwarded to the dwelling of a creditor, or to the ordinary unloading place in the locality of his abode. The obligor[2] cannot be allowed to deliver the goods at his own abode.

Niwa *kôri* and Haguri *kôri.*

The contract should specify the point where the goods will be handed over. One way is to hand over the goods at the seller's store (*urinushi-niwa*). Another way is to deliver them to the buyer's store (*kainushi-niwa*). In the former case, the total expenses for transport should be covered by the buyer. In the latter case, the cost should be borne by the seller.

SHIZUOKA PREFECTURE

Prefectural Office.

The goods should be forwarded to the dwelling of the buyer, or to the ordinary unloading place in the locality of his abode.

Udo *kôri* and Abe *kôri.*

They should be forwarded to the dwelling of an obligee, according to a practice prevailing here.

Inasa *kôri* and Aratama *kôri.*

The delivery will be made at the ordinary loading place in the

1 *Gimusha-no-jûchi.*

2 *Gimusha.*

locality of the obligor's abode.

Kamo *kôri* and Naka *kôri*.

The obligor has no responsibility to forward the goods to the dwelling of an obligee, or to the ordinary unloading place in the locality of his abode, unless so provided. The obligor should deliver them at his dwelling, or at the ordinary loading place in the locality of his abode.

Saya *kôri* and Kitô *kôri*.

There are two ways to dispose of the goods, *ibarai* and *todoke*. *Ibarai* refers to the handing over of the goods at the place where they are kept by the seller. *Todoke* refers to the delivery of the goods to the dwelling of the buyer, or at some agreed upon place.

GIFU PREFECTURE

Mugi *kôri*.

As a rule, the goods should be forwarded to the dwelling of a creditor.

Ampachi *kôri*.

As answered in Topic 10.

Fuwa *kôri*.

The delivery should be made at the dwelling of the obligor, or to the ordinary loading place in the locality of his abode.

Atsumi *kôri*, Kagami *kôri* and Katagata *kôri*.

The goods should be forwarded to the dwelling of the creditor.

Tagi *kôri* and Kami-ishizu *kôri*.

Unless otherwise provided, the goods will be forwarded to the dwelling of the creditor, or to the ordinary unloading place of his abode.

Ôno *kôri* and Ikeda *kôri*.

The delivery will be made at the dwelling of an obligor, or at the ordinary loading place in the locality of his abode.

Haguri *kôri* and Nakajima *kôri*.

As stated in the second half of this topic, the goods will be delivered to the obligee at the ordinary unloading place in the locality of the obligor's abode.

Ena *kôri*.

The delivery will be made at the dwelling of the obligor.

Kamo *kôri*.

Unless otherwise agreed upon, the delivery will be made at the ordinary loading place in the locality of the obligee's abode, according to our practice.

Kani *kôri*.

They will be forwarded, as a general rule, to the dwelling of the creditor.

Atsumi *kôri*, Gifu Township.

There is no established rule.

Ôgaki.

As answered in Topic 10.

Ena *kôri*, Nakatsugawa Village.

The delivery will be made at the dwelling of the obligor, or at the ordinary loading place in the locality of his abode.

Shimo-ishizu *kôri*, Takasu Township.

The goods will be forwarded to the dwelling of the creditor.

Haguri *kôri*, Takegahana Village.

Unless agreement is reached between the obligor and obligee, the delivery will be made at the place where the contract is made.

Yamagata *kôri*, Takatomi Village.

Even if there are no stipulations in the contract, the goods, needless to say, should be forwarded to the dwelling of the creditor, or to the ordinary unloading place in the locality of his abode.

Mugi *kôri*, Kôzuchi Village.

The delivery is made at the dwelling of the obligor, or at the ordinary loading place in the locality of his abode.

Haguri *kôri*, Kasamatsu Village.

As stated in the second half of this topic, the goods will be delivered to the obligee at the ordinary unloading place in the locality of the obligor's abode.

Fuwa *kôri*, Tarui Village.

Our practice is that the way of delivery should be stipulated in the contract. Therefore, we have no such cases here.

Ôno *kôri*, Miwa Village.

In some cases, the delivery will be made at the dwelling of the obligor,[1] but in other case it will be made at the dwelling of the obligee.[2]

Ampachi *kôri*, Gôdo Village.

They should be forwarded to the dwelling of the creditor, or the

[1] *Gimusha.*

[2] *Saishu.*

ordinary unloading place near his abode.

Tagi *kôri*, Shimada Village.

No answer is given.

Ena *kôri*, Iwa Village.

The delivery will be made at the dwelling of the creditor unless otherwise agreed upon.

Kamo *kôri*, Hosome Village.

Even if there is no stipulations in the contract, the goods should be forwarded to the dwelling of the creditor, or to the ordinary unloading place in the locality of his abode.

Toki *kôri*, Takayama Village.

Acting as the obligee wishes, the obligor will forward the goods to any unloading place convenient to the obligee.

Kani *kôri*, Mitake Village.

The goods should be forwarded to the dwelling of the obligee, or to the ordinary unloading place in the vicinity of his abode. However, the distance is limited to three '*ri*' (about twelve kilometers).

Ena *kôri*, Akechi Village.

The delivery should be made at the dwelling of the obligor.

Mugi *kôri*, Seki Village.

The goods will be forwarded from the dwelling of the obligee, or from a forwarding agent[1] in the locality of the obligee's abode. In some cases, the delivery will be made at the dwelling of the obligee, or at the ordinary unloading place in the locality of his abode.

Ôno *kôri*, Takayama Township.

The contract should specify the place for delivery. If it does not, the goods will be handed over to a forwarding agent. If the buyer dwells near by, the seller will forward them directly to the buyer's residence.

Motosu *kôri*, Kitagata Village.

The delivery should be made at the dwelling of the obligor, or at the ordinary loading place in the locality of his abode, unless otherwise agreed upon.

Kamo *kôri*, Ôta Village.

The goods should be forwarded to the dwelling of the obligee,

[1] *Ni-donya.*

or to the ordinary unloading place in the locality of his abode.

Kaisai *kôri* and Shimo-ishizu *kôri*.

They should be forwarded to the dwelling of the creditor.

Gujô *kôri*.

No answer can be given.

Topic 12: If There Is No Stipulation in the Contract as to the Details of the Method of the Delivery, such as Weights,[1] Measures,[2] Tares,[3] and the Like, Should the Customs[4] of the Place of Delivery[5] Be Followed; or Should the Usual Practices of the Forwarder,[6] or the Practices Usually Observed in Connection with Goods to Be Delivered, Be Followed?

TOKYO METROPOLIS

Prefectural Office.

Soy Wholesalers.

The customs of the place of delivery are followed.

Sugar Wholesalers.

The customs of the place of delivery should be practiced.

Dried Bonito Wholesalers.

The method of delivery follows the customs of the place of delivery.

Medicine Wholesalers.

The customs of the place of delivery are followed.

Paper Wholesalers (*Kiu-kumi*).

There is no settled custom about it.

Oil Wholesalers.

The customs of the place of delivery are followed.

Stone Wholesalers.

The method of delivery follows customs and practices.

Fuel Wholesalers.

Regarding the present matter, the method of delivery of goods follows the practices of their place of production.

Porcelain Wholesalers.

The method of delivery follows the customs of the place of delivery of goods.

Paper Wholesalers (*Shôkai-kumi*).

[1] *Ryômoku.*

[2] *Masume.*

[3] *Fūtai.*

[4] *Shikitari.*

[5] *Hikiwatashi-chi.*

[6] *Hikiwatashi-nin.*

The customs of the place of delivery or the practices usually observed in connection with goods to be delivered are followed.

Rice Traders.

Regarding goods for which the contract of sale and the delivery is made at the seller's dwelling, the method of delivery follows the practices, including weights, measures, tares and the like, of the place. When the seller visits the buyer to make a contract and delivers the goods to the latter's dwelling, the practices of the latter's dwelling should be followed.

Salt Wholesalers.

The practices of the place of delivery are followed.

Timber Wholesalers.

The customs are followed.

Timber Wholesalers (*Zaimoku-tôsei*).

All is done following customs.

Timber Wholesalers (*Senju*).

We have never heard of this case.

Tobacco Wholesalers.

In the trading of tobacco, unfinished goods are delivered in amounts measured by weight, while finished goods are delivered in amounts designated by the number of cases in which they are packaged.

Matting Wholesalers.

Unless otherwise agreed, the customs of the place of delivery are followed.

Saké Wholesalers.

The practices usually observed in connection with goods are followed.

Drapery Wholesalers.

We have never heard of this case.

Saké Wholesalers.

The method of delivery follows the practices observed in connection with the goods.

Lime and Shell Wholesalers.

The method of delivery, including weights, measures and tares, follows the customs of the place of delivery or the practices in connection with the goods to be delivered.

Mosquito Net Wholesalers.

Unless otherwise provided for in the contract, the practices of the place of delivery are followed.

Copper and Iron Wholesalers.

In the case of goods sold by measures,[1] their delivery is made after close examination of the weight, by balance. However, some articles are sold by numbers. Hence, the method of delivery is decided according to the sort of goods.

Fuel Wholesalers (*Umite-kumi*).

A mixture of the practices of the place of delivery, those of the forwarder, and those in connection with the goods is followed.

Kôjimachi Ward.

The customs of the place of delivery are followed.

Nihombashi Ward.

Generally speaking, the practices observed in connection with the goods to be delivered are followed.

Kyôbashi Ward.

The method of delivery of the goods follows the usual practices of the forwarder.

Yotsuya Ward and Ushigome Ward.

Unless otherwise agreed, the method of delivery observes the practices of the forwarder or those in connection with the goods.

Asakusa Ward.

It follows the customs of the place of delivery.

Honjo Ward.

If there is no detailed stipulation about the method of delivery, including weights, measures, tares, and the like, it follows the customs of the place of delivery or the practices in connection with the goods.

Ebara *kôri.*

Unless otherwise provided for, the method of delivery, including weights, measures, tares, and the like, observes the customs of the place of delivery. Sometimes it follows the practices in connection with the goods to be delivered.

Higashi-tama *kôri* and Minami-toshima *kôri.*

Regarding weights, measures, tares and the like, the customs of the place of delivery are, in most cases, followed.

Kita-toshima *kôri.*

With regard to the present topic on method of delivery, each

[1] *Ryômoku-kae.*

article and each place has its own customs and practices. Both seller and buyer enter into a contract after consideration of them. Hence we have never heard of disputes.

Minami-adachi *kôri*.

Regarding the present topic, the customs of the place of delivery are, in most cases, followed. However, the practices in connection with the goods sometimes obtain.

Shitaya Ward.

If no stipulation has been made as to the detailed method of delivery, including weights, measures, tares, and the like, the practices of the forwarder are followed.

Kanda Ward.

In most cases, the practices of the place of delivery are followed.

Akasaka Ward and Azabu Ward.

It is taken for granted that the practices in connection with the goods are followed. In case there are no such practices, the customs of the forwarder are followed.

CHIBA PREFECTURE

Awa *kôri*, Hei *kôri*, Asai *kôri* and Muza *kôri*.

Answer missing.

Katori *kôri*.

Answer missing.

Yamabe *kôri* and Muza *kôri*.

Answer missing.

Unakami *kôri* and Sôsa *kôri*.

Answer missing.

Higashi-katsushika *kôri*.

Though each place has its own customs, the method of delivery follows the practices observed in connection with the goods.

IBARAKI PREFECTURE

Nishi-katsushika *kôri* and Sashima *kôri*.

The practices observed in connection with the goods to be delivered are followed.

KANAGAWA PREFECTURE

Miura *kôri*.

The customs of the place of delivery are followed.

Tachibana *kôri*.

The customs of the place of delivery are followed.

Kita-tama *kôri*.

When there is no stipulation as to the method of delivery, it follows the customs of the place of delivery and the practices of the forwarder.

Ashigara-shimo *kôri*.

Regarding the present topic, the measures usually observed in connection with the goods to be delivered or those of the forwarder are followed, according to local practice.

Prefectural Industrial Bureau.

When there is no stipulation in the contract as to the details of the method of delivery and receipt in international trading, the goods to be delivered follow the customs of the place of delivery, for instance, in this port silk is sold by the package[1] and tea by units of a hundred *kin*.[2] Goods to be received, meanwhile, follow the practices usually observed in connection with the goods, for example, the American method is followed for oil, the English method is followed for twilled threads (*kara-ito*) and fabrics (*kin-kin*).

TOCHIGI PREFECTURE

Prefectural Office.

The practices in connection with the goods to be delivered are followed.

Shimo-tsuga *kôri* and Samukawa *kôri*.

When there is no stipulation as to the method of delivery, the customs in the place of delivery and the practices in connection with the goods are followed.

Ashikaga *kôri* and Yanada *kôri*.

The customs of the place of delivery are followed.

MIE PREFECTURE

Suzuka *kôri*.

When there is no stipulation about the method of delivery, including weights, measures, tares, and the like, the customs of the place of delivery, the practices of the forwarder or those in connection with the goods to be delivered are followed.

Ichishi *kôri*.

The practices in connection with the goods to be delivered are followed.

1 *Kon*.

2 One *kin* is about 600 grams.

Nabari *kôri* and Iga *kôri*.

If there is no detailed stipulation about the method of delivery, the measure of goods to be delivered is determined in keeping with the customs of the place of delivery. For instance, rice is delivered in a rice bag, whose measure is four *to*, five *gô*,[1] containing a leakage (*komemai*) of five *gô*. A horse carries a pair of bags on its back. This is called one *da* and is the measure of eight *to*, one *shô*. Rice is sold by the *da*. After the Meiji Restoration, leakage per rice bag became as much as one *shô*. Hence one *da* has recently become a measure of eight *to* two *shô*. However, when it is sold in the Yamato (neighboring) district, a commission of one *shô* per rice bag is charged. Hence, one *da* delivered to Yamato amounts to no more than eight *to*. However, other grains are sold by the *koku*.

Kita-muro *kôri*.

The seller and the buyer will talk about the matter, taking the customs of the place of delivery and the practices in connection with the goods into consideration.

AICHI PREFECTURE

Nakajima *kôri*.

The method of delivery, including weights, measures, tares, and the like, follows the customs of the place of delivery.

Nagoya Ward.

The customs of the place of delivery are followed.

Chita *kôri*.

Unless otherwise agreed, the customs of the place of delivery are followed.

Minami-shidara *kôri*.

Usually the customs of the place of delivery are followed.

Atsumi *kôri*.

The customs of the place of delivery are followed.

Kaitô *kôri* and Kaisai *kôri*.

The customs of the place of delivery are followed, according to the usual practice.

Aichi *kôri*.

The customs of the place of delivery or the practices in connection with the goods to be delivered are followed.

[1] 1 *koku* = 10 *to*; 1 *to* = 10 *shô*; 1 *shô* = 10 *gô*.

Niwa *kôri* and Haguri *kôri*.

Even when there is no stipulation about the method of delivery, including weights, measures, tares, and the like, the local practice of delivery obtains.

SHIZUOKA PREFECTURE

Prefectural Office.

As stated in the first half of the topic, the customs of the place of delivery, that is, the customs of the receiver, are followed.

Udo *kôri* and Abe *kôri*.

Usually the customs of the place of delivery are followed.

Inasa *kôri* and Aratama *kôri*.

The customs of the place of delivery are followed.

Kamo *kôri* and Naka *kôri*.

The customs of the place of delivery are followed.

Saya *kôri* and Kitô *kôri*.

The method of delivery, including weights, measures, tares, and the like, follows the practices in connection with the goods in the place of delivery. For instance, rice is delivered at the tare of 4 *to* 2 *shô*, weighing 17 *kan*, 400 *momme*.

GIFU PREFECTURE

Mugi *kôri*.

When there is no stipulation about the method of delivery, usually the customs of the place of delivery are followed. However, this is not a settled practice, but depends on the goods.

Ampachi *kôri*.

Usually the customs of the place of delivery are followed.

Fuwa *kôri*.

When there is no agreement, the customs of the place of delivery and the practices in connection with the goods are followed.

Atsumi *kôri*, Kagami *kôri* and Katagata *kôri*.

The customs in connection with the trade are followed.

Tagi *kôri* and Kami-ishizu *kôri*.

Unless agreed in the contract, the method of delivery follows the customs of the place of delivery.

Ôno *kôri* and Ikeda *kôri*.

Regarding the present topic, the customs of the place of delivery and the practices in connection with the goods to be delivered are followed.

Haguri *kôri* and Nakajima *kôri*.

The practices in connection with the goods to be delivered are followed.

Ena *kôri*.

The practices observed in connection with the goods to be delivered are followed.

Kamo *kôri*.

When there is no stipulation about the method of delivery, the customs of the place of delivery are followed.

Kani *kôri*.

The practices usually observed in connection with the goods to be delivered are followed.

Atsumi *kôri*, Gifu Township.

The practices observed among merchants of the same trade are followed.

Ôgaki.

Usually the customs of the place of delivery are followed.

Ena *kôri*, Nakatsugawa Village.

The customs of the dwelling of the other party are followed.

Shimo-ishizu *kôri*, Takasu Village.

The practices of the place of delivery are followed.

Haguri *kôri*, Takegahana Village.

The practices of the place where the contract was concluded are followed.

Yamagata *kôri*, Takatomi Village.

The customs of the place of delivery shall be followed.

Mugi *kôri*, Kôzuchi Village.

The practices observed in connection with the goods to be delivered are followed.

Haguri *kôri*, Kasamatsu Village.

Usually the practice is as stated in the latter half of the topic.

Fuwa *kôri*, Tarui Village.

Unless otherwise provided in the contract, the customs of the place of delivery are followed.

Ôno *kôri*, Miwa Village.

When there is no agreement, the practices of the place of delivery are followed.

Ampachi *kôri*, Gôdo Village.

The method of delivery, including weights, measures, tares, and the like, sometimes follows the customs of the place of delivery and sometimes the practices observed in connection with the goods.

Ena *kôri*, Iwa Village.

The practices observed in connection with the goods are followed.

Kamo *kôri*, Hosome Village.

When there is no stipulation, the method of delivery follows the customs of the place of delivery.

Toki *kôri*, Takayama Village.

The customs of the place of delivery are followed, depending upon the goods.

Kani *kôri*, Mitake Village.

The practices observed in connection with the goods are followed.

Ena *kôri*, Akechi Village.

The practices observed in connection with the goods to be delivered are followed.

Mugi *kôri*, Seki Village.

The customs of the place of delivery or the practices observed in connection with the goods are followed, depending upon the case.

Ôno *kôri*, Takayama Township.

When there is no agreement and no custom of the place of delivery, the practices observed in connection with the goods are followed.

Motosu *kôri*, Kitagata Village.

When there is no stipulation about the method of delivery, including weights, measures, tares and the like, the practices observed in connection with the goods in the place of delivery are followed.

Kamo *kôri*, Ôta Village.

When there is no agreement about the method of delivery, sometimes the customs of the place of delivery are followed.

Kaisai *kôri* and Shimo-ishizu *kôri*.

Regarding the present matter, the practices observed in connection with the goods are followed.

Gujô *kôri*.

When there is no agreement about the method of delivery, including weights, measures, tares and the like, the customs of the place of delivery or the practices observed in connection with the goods are followed, depending upon the case.

Topic 13: If One Party (the First Party) Should Happen to Incur a Debt to Another Party (the Second Party), and There Has Been No Specific Agreement as to How the Debt Should Be Repaid, Is the First Party Free to Repay the Debt with Any Kind of Goods He Prefers? Or May the Second Party Dictate the Commodity for Repayment to the First Party?

Moreover, If There Is a Contract Which Specifies Two Articles, Either of Which Would Satisfy the Terms for Repayment, and Both Articles Have Been Lost by the First Party, How Should a Substitute Article Be Decided Upon?

TOKYO METROPOLIS

Soy Wholesalers.[1]

We have no examples to refer to.

Sugar Wholesalers.

We have nothing to refer to in this case.

Dried Bonito Wholesalers.

The case referred to in the first question cannot be found among us. With regard to the second question, the debt will be paid in money or with some other articles after talks on the matter.

Medicine Wholesalers.

The case referred to in the first question cannot be found among us. With regard to the second question, if the article for repayment has been lost by the first party, the debt should be paid with another article equivalent in value to the one which was lost.

Paper Wholesalers (*Kiu-kumi*).[2]

The debt will be repaid so as to satisfy the second party. The second party can decide for himself on the type of commodity to be used. In most cases, settlement can be arrived at through direct negotiations between the two parties.

Oil Wholesalers.

Another article can never be substituted for the one which was lost. A settlement can be reached by discussing the matter together.

[1] *Shôyu-donya-kumiai.*

[2] *Kiu-kumi kami-donya.*

Stone Wholesalers.

Repayment should be made so as to satisfy the second party. However, the obligor sometimes can decide for himself on the article to be substituted.

Fuel Wholesalers.

We have never had such a case.

Porcelain Wholesalers.

The second party will decide on the commodity for repayment. Even if both of the articles have been lost, he will name another.

Paper Wholesalers (*Shôkai-kumi*).[1]

If there is no specific agreement on the kind of goods to be used for repayment, the first party may choose whatever kind of goods he wants. This is because the contract should be made in behalf of the obligor. Suppose the second party has agreed with the first party that either of two articles, A or B, should be returned. If both are lost by the first party, a substitute will be decided upon with the consent of the second party.

Rice Traders.[2]

If there is no specific agreement as to what kind of goods should be used for repayment, the second party[3] will inform the first as to which goods would be acceptable. However, the obligor will never fail to stipulate what kind of goods should be delivered. If both of the articles have been lost, the substitute will be decided on by the obligee.

Salt Wholesalers.

We know of no such case.

Timber Wholesalers.

An agreement will be reached through talks between the two.

Timber Traders.[4]

An agreement will be found through talks between the two.

Timber Traders (*Senju*).[5]

We know of no such case.

Matting Wholesalers.

We have never heard of such a business practice.

[1] *Shôkai-kumi kami-donya.*

[2] *Beikoku sangyô-kumiai.*

[3] *Uketori-nin.*

[4] *Zaimoku tôsei-kumiai.*

[5] *Senju zaimoku-kumiai.*

Saké Wholesalers.[1]

We have no custom of lending or borrowing another's goods.

Tobacco Wholesalers.

There is no established practice, since settlement is reached through talks between the two, depending upon the circumstances.

Saké Wholesalers.

We have not heard of such a case.

Lime and Shell Wholesalers.

We have no custom of lending or borrowing another's article.

Mosquito Net Wholesalers.

We have no such business practice.

Copper and Iron Wholesalers.

We have no established rules.

Fuel Wholesalers (*Umite-kumi*).[2]

The first party should repay the second with the original goods. If certain articles have been lost by mistake, other articles should be used to repay the debt.

Drapery Wholesalers.

We do not have such a practice.

Kôjimachi Ward.

We do not have such a practice in this district.

Nihombashi Ward.

If no specific agreement has been made as to what kind of commodities should be used, the same kind of article should be used for repayment. If the article has been lost, a replacement should be decided upon by the second party.

Kyôbashi Ward.

As for the first question, the first party should seek to satisfy the second. The answer to the second question is as you have stated above.

Yotsuya Ward and Ushigome Ward.

No answer.

Asakusa Ward.

As for the first question, the kind of goods to be used in repaying one's debt is always specified.

Honjo Ward.

[1] *Sake-rui-donya.*

[2] *Umite-kumi shintan-donya.*

If no agreement exists as to what kind of goods should be delivered in repayment, the first party should immediately discuss the matter with the second party. If the contract specifies that repayment should be made with one of two articles, and both of the articles have been lost by the first party, the decision as to what article should replace the lost ones will be mutually arrived at.

Ebara *kôri.*

If there is no specific arrangement for the kind of goods to be used for repayment, the second party will ask the first for repayment in a particular article. If the contract specifies that repayment should be made with one of two articles, and both of the articles have been lost by the first party, the second party may decide the article that will be substituted for the lost ones.

Higashi-tama *kôri* and Minami-toshima *kôri.*

If there is no specific arrangement on the kind of goods to be used for repayment, the second party will ask the first for repayment in a particular article. If the contract specifies that repayment should be made with one of two articles, and both of the articles have been lost by the first party, the decision as to what article should replace the lost ones will be mutually arrived at.

Kita-toshima *kôri.*

If there is no specific arrangement for the kind of goods to be used for repayment, the second party will ask the first for repayment in a particular article. Prior to that, however, the obligor should first choose an article and ask the obligee to accept it. When the first party loses the articles for repayment, the above procedure is followed to decide upon another article. In this case, however, the second party occasionally will ask the first for an apology. Then the obligee will allow the obligor some reduction in the repayment of the goods, or allow him to resort to monetary payment in monthly or yearly installments.

Minami-adachi *kôri.*

As for the first question, the same kind of goods should be repaid. As for the second question, the debt should be repaid in money.

Shitaya Ward.

If there is no specific arrangement for the kind of goods to be used for repayment, the second party will ask the first for repayment in a particular article. If the contract specifies that repayment should be made with one of two articles, and both of the articles have been lost by the first party, the decision as to what article should replace the lost ones will be mutually arrived at.

Kanda Ward.

If there is no specific arrangement for the kind of goods to be used for repayment, the second party will ask the first for repayment in a particular article. If the contract specifies that repayment should be made with one of two articles, and both of the articles have been lost by the first party, the decision as to what article should replace the lost ones will be mutually arrived at.

Akasaka Ward and Azabu Ward.

We have no established practice regarding the matter referred to in the first question. In each case, there will be a dialogue between the two. As for the second question, the answer is as stated above.

Hongô Ward.

If one trader in District A and a second trader in District B draw up a bill, the first party occasionally will repay the second with some article of his own choosing. In most cases, however, the second party will dictate the article to the first. If both of the articles have been lost, the first party will ask the second to accept another kind of article.

Chiba Prefecture

Awa *kôri*, Hei *kôri*, Asai *kôri* and Nagasa *kôri*.

Although there are some exceptions, the articles for repayment must be approved by the second party. If both articles have been lost, the article to be substituted will be chosen by the second party or, if possible, through mutual agreement. However, there is no absolute rule, as each case is different.

Katori *kôri*.

Even if no stipulation has been made as to what kind of goods should be delivered, the obligor, consulting the obligee, can dictate to him goods he chooses.

Yamabe *kôri* and Muza *kôri*.

The article for repayment must be decided by the second party. If the contract specifies that repayment should be made with one of two articles, and both of the articles have been lost by the first party, the second party may decide the article that will be substituted for the lost ones.

Unakami *kôri* and Sôsa *kôri*.

All contracts state the kind of goods to be used for repayment.

But if otherwise, the second party will decide the matter. In some cases, however, mutual agreement is reached through talks. If both of the articles have been lost, the second party will name another.

Higashi-katsushika *kôri.*

In both cases the second party will decide upon the article or articles to be used in repayment.

IBARAKI PREFECTURE

Nishi-katsushika *kôri* and Sashima *kôri.*

The second party must accept any kind of goods. In the second case, the second party should decide upon a substitute item.

KANAGAWA PREFECTURE

Miura *kôri.*

In both cases the second party will decide upon the article or articles to be used in repayment.

Tachibana *kôri.*

In both cases the second party will decide upon the article or articles to be used in repayment.

Kita-tama *kôri.*

The second party must be satisfied. When both of the articles are lost, the first party will probably ask the second party to make a new contract. However, no such case has been heard of.

Ashigara-shimo *kôri.*

Regarding the first question, as a general rule the obligor is probably free to repay the obligee with any sort of goods the former chooses. In many cases, however, the matter will be decided upon mutually by the two. As for the second question, since the articles have been lost through the carelessness of the first party, it is only natural that the second party name a substitute article for repayment.

Prefectural Industrial Bureau.

If there is no specific arrangement for the kind of goods to be used for repayment, the second party will ask the first for repayment in a particular article. If the contract specifies that repayment should be made with one of two articles, and both of the articles have been lost by the first party, the second party may decide the article that will be substituted for the lost ones. In reality, however, such cases have not been heard of in these parts.

TOCHIGI PREFECTURE

Prefectural Office.

As for the first question, the first party repays the second with goods of his own choosing. If the first party has borrowed money in advance from the second party, however, the former usually will be asked to repay the loan by delivering goods of the latter's choosing. As for the second question, if the two articles have been lost by the first party, articles for substitution will be mutually decided upon.

Shimo-tsuga *kôri* and Samukawa *kôri*.

If no previous arrangement has been made as to what kind of goods should be used for repayment, the matter will be decided by the second party. As for the second matter, it is as you have suggested: the matter will be decided upon by the second party.

Ashikaga *kôri* and Yanada *kôri*.

Such business practices do not exist in these parts.

MIE PREFECTURE

Suzuka *kôri*.

If there is no specific agreements for the kind of goods to be used for repayment, the first party should act to satisfy the second party. If the contract specifies that repayment should be made with one of two articles, and both of the articles have been lost by the first party, the second party may decide the article that will be substituted for the lost ones.

Ichishi *kôri*.

As for the first question, the goods for repayment should be mutually decided upon. As for the second question, the second party will decide the article for substitution.

Nabari *kôri* and Iga *kôri*.

In general it seems that the second party will decide these matters.

Kita-muro *kôri*.

In both cases, there should be some mutual agreement.

AICHI PREFECTURE

Nakajima *kôri*.

If there is no specific agreement for the kind of goods to be used for repayment, the obligor may repay his debt with any kind of goods. In the second case regarding the goods to be substituted, the second party may decide the matter.

Nagoya Ward.

In general it seems that the second party will decide these matters.

Chita *kôri*.

If there is no specific agreement as to what kind of goods should be delivered, the matter will be settled mutually. If the contract specifies that repayment should be made with one of two articles, and both of the articles have been lost by the first party, the decision as to what article should replace the lost ones will be mutually arrived at, with special attention given to the needs of the second party.

Minami-shidara *kôri*.

In the first instance, the goods for repayment will be specified by the second party. In the second instance, the goods will be mutually agreed upon.

Atsumi *kôri*.

If there is no specific agreement as to what kind of goods should be delivered, the first party is free to decide the matter. If both articles have been lost, the second party will specify the substitute goods.

Kaitô *kôri* and Kaisai *kôri*.

The debt should be repaid with goods similar to the kind originally borrowed. If the contract specifies that repayment should be made with one of two articles, and both of the articles have been lost by the first party, the decision as to what article should replace the lost ones will be mutually arrived at.

Aichi *kôri*.

The debt should be repaid with goods acceptable to both parties. If the goods have been lost, the second party, needless to say, should specify the kinds of goods acceptable as substitute. The goods should be the same in price and quality as the original ones.

Niwa *kôri* and Haguri *kôri*.

All contracts for loans and sales specify the kinds of goods to be used for repayment. If there is no specific agreement as to the goods to be used for repayment, and there are no goods on hand at the time the agreed upon delivery should occur, some mutual agreement should be reached.

Shizuoka Prefecture

Prefectural Office.

As for the first question, a mutual agreement should be reached. There is, however, no established practice. As for the second question, the first party will specify the goods to be used.

Udo *kôri* and Abe *kôri*.

Debts should be repayed with goods which are the same as those borrowed. If the first party wants to repay with other goods, he should ask for the second party's approval. If interest is involved, it must also be taken into consideration.

Inasa *kôri* and Aratama *kôri*.

We have no such lending practice here.

Kamo *kôri* and Naka *kôri*.

If the goods are not of a kind similar to those originally borrowed, the second party will dictate the goods. As for the second question, the second party will dictate the goods.

Saya *kôri* and Kitô *kôri*.

As circumstances require, there will be talks between the two parties. If an agreement cannot be reached, compensation should be made with money.

Gifu Prefecture

Mugi *kôri*.

As for the first question, there is no established practice. In the second case, the second party will specify the goods to be used for repayment.

Ampachi *kôri*.

As for the first question, the deliveree will dictate what the goods should be. In the second case, the first party should ask the approval of the second party.

Fuwa *kôri*.

All contracts specify the goods to be used for repayment. Substitutes for lost goods will be mutually decided upon.

Atsumi *kôri*, Kagami *kôri* and Katagata *kôri*.

These matters will be mutually decided.

Tagi *kôri* and Kami-ishizu *kôri*.

No answer can be given since there is no such practice. The matter will no doubt be mutually settled.

Ôno *kôri* and Ikeda *kôri*.

These matters will be mutually settled. There are no established rules.

Haguri *kôri* and Nakajima *kôri*.

As for the first question, the second party usually decides. In the second case, the second party often decides.

Ena *kôri*.

In both cases, the second party will decide the matter.

Kamo *kôri*.

If there is no specific agreement as to what kind of goods should be delivered, neither the obligor nor the obligee can decide it, since the matter will be settled mutually. But we have no established practice. If the contract specifies that repayment should be made with one of two articles, and both of the articles have been lost by the first party, the decision as to what article should replace the lost ones will be mutually arrived at. Here again, however, there is no established practice.

Kani *kôri*.

As for the first question, repayment obviously should be made with goods similar to those which were borrowed. If no specific agreement exists as to what kind of goods should be used for repayment, therefore, goods similar to those borrowed should be used. As for the second question, the first party will decide upon the goods to be used.

Atsumi *kôri*, Gifu Township.

There is no established custom in either case.

Ôgaki.

As for the first question, it should be decided upon by the second party. In the second case, the second party should ask for the approval of the first.

Ena *kôri*, Nakatsugawa Village.

If no agreement exists, goods similar to those borrowed should be repaid. If there are no such goods available, the second party should ask the first for instructions. In the second case, the first will specify the goods for substitution.

Shimo-ishizu *kôri*, Takasu Township.

As for the first question, the first party should try to conform with the expectations of the second party as much as possible. If the contract specifies that repayment should be made with one of two articles, and both of the articles have been lost by the first party, the second party may decide the article that will be substituted for the lost ones.

Haguri *kôri*, Takegahana Village.

The duty of repayment presupposes that some articles were borrowed. If no stipulation has been made as to how the debt should be repaid, the original articles themselves should be returned. If the contract specifies that repayment should be made with one of two articles, and both of the articles have been lost by the first party, the decision as to what article should replace the lost ones will be mutually arrived at.

Yamagata *kôri*, Takatomi Village.

If the article borrowed no longer exists, there is nothing for the deliverer to do but to follow the deliveree's instructions. If both of the articles have been lost, the first party should inform the second of the fact and follow the wishes of the latter.

Mugi *kôri*, Kôzuchi Village.

The first party is never free to repay the second with just any kind of goods. Rather, he should seek to satisfy the latter. Neither of the two can decide upon the goods to be substituted.

Haguri *kôri*, Kasamatsu Village.

As for the first question, the first party generally should follow the advice of the second party. In the second instance, the first party will generally specify the articles to be used as substitutes.

Fuwa *kôri*, Tarui Village.

As for the first question, there is no established practice. As for the second, the first party may decide upon the matter with the consent of the second party.

Ôno *kôri*, Miwa Village.

In both cases, these matters should be mutually settled.

Ampachi *kôri*, Gôdo Village.

The second party has the right to specify the goods for repayment. If both of the articles have been lost, the first party should repay the second with money.

Tagi *kôri*, Shimada Village.

No answer is given.

Ena *kôri*, Iwa Village.

As for the first question, we have no answer. In the second case, the second party will decide the matter.

Kamo *kôri*, Hosome Village.

If there is no specific agreement as to what kind of goods to be used for repayment, the first party should talk things over with the second party through an arbitrator. If the first party feels some particular difficulty in repaying the debt, he is sometimes free to repay the second party with any sort of goods he chooses. In the second case, goods similar to those lost should be obtained from any of the first party's fellow traders and repaid to the second party.

Toki *kôri*, Takayama Village.

The first party is free to repay the debt with any sort of goods he happens to choose. In the second case, the second party will decide upon the matter.

Kani *kôri*, Mitake Village.

The first party is free to repay the debt with any sort of goods he happens to choose. In the second case, the second party will decide upon the matter.

Ena *kôri*, Akechi Village.

In both cases the second party will decide upon the article or articles to be used in repayment.

Mugi *kôri*, Seki Village.

The second party will generally indicate the goods to be used in substitution, but will often confer with the first party in these matters. In many cases, however, there will be talks between the two parties.

Ôno *kôri*, Takayama Township.

If there is no specific agreement as to what kind of goods should be used for repayment, the first party will act after consulting the second party. If the articles agreed to have been lost, the first party will inform the second of his wish to repay the debt with another article. With the consent of the second party, he will repay him with different goods. If the goods differ in quality, the first party will take account of the difference in price and hand over a little more or less in terms of quantity. If several kinds of goods are involved, and there is no difference in price, the first party will let the second party make a free choice. If there are no goods suitable for substitution, the first party will repay the second with money.

Motosu *kôri*, Kitagata Village.

If there is no specific arrangement for the kind of goods to be used for repayment, the second party will ask the first for repayment in a particular article. If the contract specifies that repayment should be made with one of two articles, and both of the articles have been lost by the first party, the second party may decide the article that will be substituted for the lost ones.

Kamo *kôri*, Ôta Village.

If there is no specific agreement as to what kind of goods should be delivered, neither the obligor nor the obligee can decide upon the goods to be used in substitution, since the matter will be settled mutually. In general, however, there is no established practice. If the contract specifies that repayment should be made with one of two articles, and both of the articles have been lost by the first party, the decision as to what article should replace the lost ones will be mutually arrived at. Here, too, there is no established practice.

Kaisai *kôri* and Shimo-ishizu *kôri*.

As for the first question, it is generally the first party that decides upon the goods to be used for repayment. In the second case, the first party should let the second party make a free choice.

Gujô *kôri*.

In the first case, the first party is free to repay the second party with any sort of goods. If the second party does not feel like accepting them, however, the first party should act in accordance with the wishes of the second party. In the second case, the first party can repay the second party with other articles after having conferred with the latter. In some cases, he can repay the debt with money.

CHAPTER III
RESTITUTION OF PRICE,[1] DAMAGES,[2] AND DISCOUNT[3]

Topic 1: If the Obligor Does Not Fulfill His Obligations within the Prescribed Time,[4] Is the Obligee Free to Rescind the Contract or Demand Restitution of Price from the Obligor? If Any Loss Results, Is He Entitled to Demand Damages for It?

TOKYO METROPOLIS

Prefectural Office.

Soy Wholesalers.

The obligee is entitled to cancel the contract, though he is not entitled to recover the price and damages.

Sugar Wholesalers.

Regarding the present topic, the obligee may, at his discretion, resort to any reasonable remedy, which the party in default is not entitled to reject. If any loss is incurred owing to the delay, the injured party may demand compensation.

Dried Bonito Wholesalers.

The injured party may demand damages.

Medicine Wholesalers.

(The practice is) as stated in the topic.

Paper Wholesalers (*Kiu-kumi*).

The injured party is entitled to sue for damages from the defaulting party.

Oil Wholesalers.

The matter is settled through talks between the two.

Stone Wholesalers.

When the obligor breaks the contract, the obligee may sue for damages.

Fuel Wholesalers.

Regarding the present matter, the obligee may cancel the con-

[1] *Kagaku-hoshô.*

[2] *Songai-baishô.*

[3] *Waribiki.*

[4] *Teiki.*

tract or sue for damages after talks with the obligor.

Porcelain Wholesalers.

The injured party may, at his discretion, resort to any remedy, including damages.

Paper Wholesalers (*Shôkai-kumi*).

When the obligor fails to perform his obligations within the prescribed time, the injured party is entitled to cancel the contract, but not entitled to recover the price. The obligee may demand that the obligor return the goods delivered but may not demand payment of the price.

Rice Traders.

When the obligor does not perform his obligations within the prescribed time, the obligee is free to resort to any remedy. However, if the contract is not in writing, the obligee may cancel the contract from the moral sense (*tokugi*), according to the practice here. It is rather difficult to give a definite answer.

Salt Wholesalers.

The matter is settled through talks between the two parties.

Timber Wholesalers.

Unless clearly stipulated in the contract beforehand, the matter is settled through talks.

Timber Traders.

Same as above.

Timber Wholesalers.

The two parties will have talks in a case where there is no stipulation about the matter in the contract.

Matting Wholesalers.

In a case of the obligee canceling the contract owing to the obligor's nonperformance within the prescribed time, the former may, at his discretion, recover the price or sue for damages.

Saké Wholesalers.

When the obligor fails to perform his obligations, the obligee has no other course but to cancel the contract.

Tobacco Wholesalers.

In our trade, the relation between seller and buyer is, like that of fish and water, so close that the obligee does not resort to suing for damages, even if the obligor does not perform his obligations within the prescribed time.

Mosquito Net Wholesalers.

When the obligee cancels the contract, he may, at his discretion, recover the price or damages.

Copper and Iron Wholesalers.

In commercial transactions a contract, once concluded, is to be performed. However in case of breach, the party in default should pay some amount of money to compensate the injured party for his loss and hold talks.

Drapery Wholesalers.

We have never heard of such a case.

Fuel Wholesalers.

The recovery of the price depends upon the circumstances under which the obligor fails to perform his obligations and the obligee cancels the contract. If the obligor's nonperformance is due to unreasonable negligence, the obligee is entitled to cancel the contract, recover the price or sue for damages.

Kôjimachi Ward.

The obligee may, at his discretion, recover the price, sue for damages or discount.

Nihombashi Ward.

The obligee may sue for damages, according to both the old usage and recent practice.

Kyôbashi Ward.

The obligee is free to act.

Yotsuya Ward and Ushigome Ward.

In a case where the obligor fails to perform his obligations within the prescribed time, the obligee is entitled to cancel the contract. However, whether or not the obligee may sue for damages depends upon the contract.

Asakusa Ward.

The obligee may cancel the contract or recover the price. If he suffers any loss, he may also sue for damages.

Honjo Ward.

When the obligor fails to perform his obligations within the prescribed time, the obligee may, at his discretion, resort to cancellation of the contract or recovery of the price. He is also entitled to sue for damages for the inflicted loss. However, this is seldom resorted to.

Ebara *kôri*.

In the case of the obligor's nonperformance within the prescribed time, the obligee is entitled to cancel the contract, but neither to recover the price nor to sue for damages.

Higashi-tama *kôri* and Minami-toshima *kôri*.

In a case of the obligor not performing his obligations within the prescribed time, the obligee may cancel the contract or recover the price. He is also entitled to sue for damages. However, in most cases the party in default cannot afford to pay the damages.

Kita-toshima *kôri*.

In the case of the obligor's nonperformance within the prescribed time, the obligee may demand performance. If the former asks the latter to permit his nonperformance, it often occurs among merchants of the same trade that the latter cancels the original contract in exchange for a new contract profitable for him. A step of novation like this is called *iriawase*. In some cases, the matter is settled through talks between the two, the former paying interest on the price.

Minami-adachi *kôri*.

Regarding the present matter, the obligee is entitled to cancel the contract, but not to recover the price or damages.

Shitaya Ward.

In a case of the obligor not performing his obligations within the prescribed time, the obligee is entitled, at his discretion, to cancel the contract or to recover the price of the goods. If any loss is incurred owing to the fluctuations of the market price, the obligee may recover the difference from the obligor.

Kanda Ward.

In a case of the obligor's nonperformance within the prescribed time, the obligee may, at his discretion, resort to cancellation of the contract, recovery of the price or suing for damages.

Akasaka Ward and Azabu Ward.

The obligee is entitled to cancel the contract, but not to recover the price or damages from the obligor, unless agreed upon beforehand.

Hongô Ward.

The obligee is free to cancel the contract or recover the price. If he suffers any loss, he sometimes sues for damages.

Chiba Prefecture

Awa *kôri*, Hei *kôri*, Asai *kôri* and Nagasa *kôri*.

The obligee is entitled to cancel the contract or recover the price, and to sue for damages for the loss inflicted by the obligor's default as well. However, the matter is settled in most cases through talks between the two, for default occurs when the obligor does not observe the merchants' moral sense (*tsûgi*), or falls into financial difficulties or when the two parties dispute due to a defect in the contract.

Katori *kôri*.

The obligee is entitled to cancel the contract or recover the price, but not to sue for damages.

Yamabe *kôri* and Muza *kôri*.

The obligee may cancel the contract but may not recover the price or damages, unless stipulated in the contract.

Unakami *kôri* and Sôsa *kôri*.

The obligee may resort to any remedy in the case of nonperformance. He sometimes sues for damages.

Higashi-katsushika *kôri*.

The obligee is entitled to cancel the contract or to sue for damages, but not to recover the price.

Ibaraki Prefecture

Nishi-katsushika *kôri* and Sashima *kôri*.

The obligee may resort to any remedy, including cancellation, recovery of the price and recovery of damages, if any loss is inflicted.

Kanagawa Prefecture

Miura *kôri*.

The obligee may resort to any remedy.

Tachibana *kôri*.

The obligee is entitled to cancel the contract or recover the price. If any loss is incurred, he sometimes sues for damages.

Kita-tama *kôri*.

In the case of the obligor's nonperformance within the prescribed time, the obligee may cancel the contract, but may not recover the price at his discretion. If any loss is inflicted, he may recover a reasonable amount of damages from the obligor.

Ashigara-shimo *kôri*.

Regarding the present matter, the obligee is entitled to cancel the contract or recover damages. However, in commercial practice today, the obligee does not resort to any remedy, since commercial transactions are made by oral agreement based on mutual trust, not under written contract.

Prefectural Industrial Bureau.

In the case of the obligor's nonperformance, the obligee may, at his discretion, cancel the contract or recover the price. If any loss is inflicted, he may also sue for damages.

TOCHIGI PREFECTURE

Prefectural Office.

When the obligor does not perform his obligations, the obligee is free to act as he pleases, according to custom. He may also sue for damages, if any.

Shimo-tsuga *kôri* and Samukawa *kôri*.

In a case of the obligor failing to perform his obligations, the obligee is entitled to cancel the contract or recover the prices at his discretion.

Ashikaga *kôri* and Yanada *kôri*.

In the case of textile fabrics, when the obligor does not perform his obligations within the prescribed time, the obligee is entitled to cancel the contract or demand performance at his discretion. But he may not recover the price, according to the custom here. In the case of the silk trade, the obligee may not cancel the contract without performing his own obligations. He may recover the price depending upon the circumstances under which the nonperformance has taken place. However, we have never heard of a case where the obligor recovered damages or lost profits.[1]

MIE PREFECTURE

Suzuka *kôri*.

When the obligor fails to perform his obligations within the prescribed time, the obligee may, at his discretion, cancel the contract or recover the price. If any loss is inflicted, he is entitled to sue for damages. As for the recovery of the price, the total amount or a respectable amount of the price is paid; while, as for damages, the total amount is not paid, only a trifling amount or no amount at all.

Ichishi *kôri*.

The obligee is free to cancel the contract, but he may not recover the price or damages, unless agreed upon beforehand.

Nabari *kôri* and Iga *kôri*.

[1] See also the answer to Topic 6 below.

Regarding the present matter, the obligee is free to act at his discretion. If he suffers any loss, he may sue for damages, although in most cases the matter is settled through talks.

Kita-muro *kôri*.

When the obligor fails to perform his obligations without any sufficient reason, the obligee may, at his discretion, cancel the contract or recover the price. If the obligor suffers any loss owing to the fluctuations of the market price, the obligee also shares a part of the loss. When the default is intentional on the part of the obligor, the obligee is, at his discretion, entitled to cancel the contract or recover the price. Any loss that he suffers should be covered by the obligor.

Aichi Prefecture

Nakajima *kôri*.

As stated in the topic.

Nagoya Ward.

In such cases, the obligee is entitled, at his discretion, to recover the price or damages.

Chita *kôri*.

The obligee may, at his discretion, cancel the contract or recover the price and sue the obligor for damages.

Minami-shidara *kôri*.

The obligee may cancel the contract. As for the recovery of the price or damages, it is difficult to realize in practice.

Atsumi *kôri*.

In the case of the obligor's nonperformance within the prescribed time, the obligee is, at his discretion, entitled to cancel the contract, recover the price or sue for damages.

Kaitô *kôri* and Kaisai *kôri*.

The obligee may cancel the contract. Recovery of the price or damages is seldom resorted to.

Aichi *kôri*.

When the obligor fails to perform his obligations within the prescribed time, the obligee asks the reason and resorts to cancellation of the contract or recovery of the price, depending upon the case. He may recover from the obligor any loss suffered, since such loss was caused by the obligor's negligence.

Niwa *kôri* and Haguri *kôri*.

In the case of the obligor's nonperformance within the prescribed time, the obligee may of course cancel the contract. He is also entitled to recover the price or damages, although in most cases he makes some allowance, taking the circumstances into consideration.

SHIZUOKA PREFECTURE

Prefectural Office.

Yes, the obligee is entitled to act as he pleases and, furthermore, to recover damages from the obligor.

Udo *kôri* and Abe *kôri*.

The obligee may cancel the contract and sue for damages, although he may not recover the price.

Inasa *kôri* and Aratama *kôri*.

The obligee may, at his discretion, cancel the contract or recover the price. He sometimes obtains damages for the loss which he has suffered.

Kamo *kôri* and Naka *kôri*.

The obligee is entitled to resort to cancellation of the contract or recovery of the price. He may recover any loss suffered.

Saya *kôri* and Kitô *kôri*.

As long as the two parties continue transactions, the obligor never fails to perform his obligations. If he did, it would be because of insolvency. In some cases the obligee cancels the contract and, in other cases, he recovers the damages, but there is no established rule. The matter is often settled through an arbitrator (*chûnin*) or, if he fails, by a judge.

GIFU PREFECTURE

Mugi *kôri*.

The obligee may resort to any remedy.

Ampachi *kôri*.

In such cases, the obligee is entitled, at his discretion, to cancel the contract, to recover the price or to recover damages.

Fuwa *kôri*.

The obligee may act as he pleases and may recover damages too.

Atsumi *kôri*, Kagami *kôri* and Katagata *kôri*.

The obligee may cancel the contract or recover damages as he pleases.

Tagi *kôri* and Kami-ishizu *kôri*.

When the obligor fails to perform his obligations within the prescribed time, the obligee is entitled to cancel the contract. He may not sue for damages though, according to the practice here.

Ôno *kôri* and Ikeda *kôri*.

In the case of the obligor's nonperformance within the prescribed time, the obligee may cancel the contract or recover the price, depending upon the agreement.

Haguri *kôri* and Nakajima *kôri*.

The obligee is entitled to recover the price or damages if so stipulated in the contract.

Ena *kôri*.

Yes.

Kamo *kôri*.

When the obligor does not perform his obligations within the prescribed time, the obligee may cancel the contract, but may not recover the price. If he suffers any loss, he may sue for damages.

Kani *kôri*.

The obligee may cancel the contract or recover the price, but we have never heard of a case of obtaining damages.

Atsumi *kôri*, Gifu Township.

The obligee may, at his discretion, cancel the contract or recover the price. If he suffers any loss, he may or may not sue for damages, depending upon the case.

Ôgaki.

In such cases, the obligee may cancel the contract, recover the price or sue for damages.

Ena *kôri*, Nakatsugawa Village.

The obligee may act at his discretion. He may also recover any damages.

Shimo-ishizu *kôri*, Takasu Township.

Regarding the present topic, the obligee may cancel the contract or recover the price. If he suffers any loss, and it is caused by the handling of the goods, he may sue for damages. Otherwise, he may not.

Haguri *kôri*, Takegahana Village.

The obligee may, at his discretion, cancel the contract, recover the price or sue for damages.

Yamagata *kôri*, Takatomi Village.

If the obligor fails to perform his obligations within the prescribed time, the obligee may, at his discretion, resort to cancellation of the contract or recovery of the price. If any damages are inflicted, he may sue for compensation.

Haguri *kôri*, Kasamatsu Village.

Regarding the present topic, the obligor shall pay compensation when it is stipulated for in the contract beforehand.

Fuwa *kôri*, Tarui Village.

When the obligor does not perform his obligations after the expiration of the term, the obligee may act as he pleases.

Ôno *kôri*, Miwa Village.

When the obligor does not perform his obligations within the prescribed time, the obligee may cancel the contract or recover the price. If he suffers any loss, he may sue for damages after talks with the obligor.

Ampachi *kôri*, Gôdo Village.

When the obligor does not perform his obligations, the obligee may resort to any remedy, including recovery of damages.

Tagi *kôri*, Shimada Village.

Answer missing.

Ena *kôri*, Iwa Village.

The obligor may cancel the contract, recover the price or sue for damages.

Kamo *kôri*, Hosome Village.

When the obligor fails to perform his obligations within the prescribed time, the obligee may cancel the contract or recover the price. If he suffers any loss, he may sue for damages.

Kani *kôri*, Mitake Village.

The obligee may do as he likes, including recovering the price.

Ena *kôri*, Akechi Village.

Yes.

Mugi *kôri*, Seki Village.

The obligee is entitled to cancel the contract or recover the price. If any damages are inflicted, he may also sue for compensation.

Ôno *kôri*, Takayama Township.

When the obligor fails to perform his obligations within the prescribed time, the obligee may, at his discretion, cancel the contract or recover the price. If he suffers any loss, he is entitled to sue for damages.

Motosu *kôri*, Kitagata Village.

In the case of the obligor's nonperformance within the prescribed time, the obligee is entitled to cancel the contract or recover damages. If any loss is inflicted, the obligee may also recover damages.

Kamo *kôri*, Ôta Village.

When the obligor fails to perform his obligations within the prescribed time, the obligee may cancel the contract or recover the price. He is also entitled to sue for damages.

Kaisai *kôri* and Shimo-ishizu *kôri*.

Regarding the present matter, when the obligor does not perform his obligations after expiration of the term, the obligee may, and in most cases does, cancel the contract or recover the price. However, if he suffers any loss caused by the handling of the goods, he may recover such loss. Otherwise, he may not.

Gujô *kôri*.

When the obligor fails to perform his obligations within the prescribed time, the obligee may cancel the contract. As for recovery of the price, he may resort to this after talks with the obligor.

Topic 2: Is Any Interest Supposed to Accrue on the Recovery of the Price Referred to in Topic 1? If It Does, from What Date Should the Computation of Interest Commence?

TOKYO METROPOLIS

Prefectural Office.

Soy Wholesalers.

We have never heard of instances of the two cases referred to in the present topic.

Sugar Wholesalers.

Regarding the recovery of the price, when a part of the price is paid in advance, it may or may not yield interest depending upon the circumstances. The amount of damages, which is fixed through talks between the two, is the difference between the contract price and the market price at the time of the breach of contract.

Dried Bonito Wholesalers.

In the case of recovery of the price, interest accrues on the unpaid price according to the circumstances.

Medicine Wholesalers.

We have never heard of a case where interest accrued on the unpaid price. We have never heard of an instance of the case referred to in the latter half of the topic either.

Paper Wholesalers (*Kiu-kumi*).

The matter is settled depending on the case.

Oil Wholesalers.

The matter is settled through talks between the two.

Stone Wholesalers.

Regarding the present topic, interest does not accrue unless agreed beforehand. And we never fail to fix the price.

Fuel Wholesalers.

With regard to the present topic, if interest is allowed, it is calculated for every calendar month. For instance, if the prescribed date of performance is January 30 and the date of actual performance is June 1, six months' interest is charged unless otherwise provided in the contract. When the price has not been fixed beforehand, it is decided by taking into consideration the place of production and the market price at the time of actual performance, according to the practice here.

Porcelain Wholesalers.

Whether interest accrues or not depends upon the original agreement. When it is allowed, it is computed from the day the money was handed over.

Paper Wholesalers (*Shôkai-kumi*).

Interest does not accrue unless specially provided for in the contract.

Rice Traders.

With regard to the recovery of the price, if interest accrues from the unpaid price, it is computed from the day when the contract was concluded. Theoretically the price of the goods is fixed beforehand. But when it is not fixed, interest or resale profit often accrues on the unpaid price, by way of compensation.

Salt Wholesalers.

Interest is not allowed. As for the second case, the two parties will have talks, and decide according to the circumstances.

Timber Wholesalers.

Same as the preceding topic.

Timber Traders.

Same as the above.

Timber Wholesalers (*Senju*).

Same as the above.

Matting Wholesalers.

The obligee may act at will, as stated in the answer to Topic 1.

Saké Wholesalers.

Since the obligee is entitled to unilaterally cancel the contract, we have never heard of such a case.

Saké Wholesalers.

The answer is already stated in Topic 1.

Lime and Shell Wholesalers.

The two parties will have talks, as stated in Topic 1.

Mosquito Net Wholesalers.

The obligee may act at his discretion.

Copper and Iron Wholesalers.

The answer is as stated in the preceding topic.

Tobacco Wholesalers.

There is no fixed practice.

Fuel Wholesalers.

There is no fixed practice, since every case is different. Interest accrues depending on the case. The price is decided on the basis of the current price at the time of the execution of the contract.

Drapery Wholesalers.

We have never heard of such a case.

Kôjimachi Ward.

We have never heard of a case of interest accruing on the unpaid price. The price is set based on the current price.

Nihombashi Ward.

We have never heard of a case where interest was allowed on the unpaid price. As for the second question, there is no fixed practice.

Kyôbashi Ward.

Interest is charged on the unpaid price from the day following the breach. As for the second case, an arbitrator will be selected to fix the price.

Yotsuya Ward and Ushigome Ward.

Whether interest accrues or not depends upon the contract.

Asakusa Ward.

As for the first case, no interest is allowed. With regard to the second case, the matter is settled before the court.

Honjo Ward.

With regard to the first half of the topic, interest is sometimes charged on the price to be recovered. In such cases, it is computed from the day when part of the price was handed over to the obligee. If the price has not been fixed, there is no recovery of the price.

Ebara *kôri*.

As stated in the preceding topic, interest does not accrue.

Higashi-tama *kôri* and Minami-toshima *kôri*.

As for the recovery of the price, interest is not allowed on the unpaid price, according to the practice here. If the price has not been fixed beforehand, the two parties will have talks to set the price, taking into consideration the grade of the goods and the current price.

Kita-toshima *kôri*.

The answer has already been stated in the preceding topic.

Minami-adachi *kôri*.

It would seem that no interest is charged. But this is not a definite answer, for no such case has been heard of. This is also the case with the second half of the topic.

Shitaya Ward.

With regard to the recovery of the price, interest is computed from the execution of the agreement, according to the practice here. We cannot say anything about the settlement of the price, since it is invariably fixed beforehand.

Kanda Ward.

Interest is not always charged on the unpaid price to be recovered. If it is, it is computed from the day when part of the price is paid or from the day of breach. If the price has not been fixed, it is set by taking the current price into consideration.

Akasaka Ward and Azabu Ward.

As stated in the preceding topic, no such cases have been heard of.

Hongô Ward.

No interest is charged on the unpaid price. It accrues, however, when the obligor falls into insolvency and is unable to pay the price.

CHIBA PREFECTURE

Awa *kôri*, Hei *kôri*, Asai *kôri* and Nagasa *kôri*.

When the obligee recovers the price from the obligor owing to the default of the latter, the former may of course charge interest on the unpaid price, interest which is computed from the day when the first payment of the price was made. No interest accrues on the damages. If the price has not been fixed beforehand, it is set with reference to goods of the same grade.

Katori *kôri*.

Interest is not charged. If the price has not been fixed, the current price is taken into consideration.

Yamabe *kôri* and Muza *kôri*.

No interest is allowed on the unpaid price, unless otherwise stipulated in the contract. As for goods whose price has not been fixed, the current price is taken into consideration.

Unakami *kôri* and Sôsa *kôri*.

Interest is not borne. When the price has not been fixed beforehand, it is determined by the current price.

Higashi-katsushika *kôri*.

Answer missing.

IBARAKI PREFECTURE

Nishi-katsushika *kôri* and Sashima *kôri*.

No interest accrues from the unpaid price. The current price is taken into consideration if the price has not been fixed beforehand.

KANAGAWA PREFECTURE

Miura *kôri*.

As for the first case, interest is computed from the day following the date of performance. As for the second case, the price to be recovered is determined by the market price.

Tachibana *kôri*.

No interest accrues.

Kita-tama *kôri*.

We cannot give any definite answer, since, as stated in the preceding topic, there are no such cases here. If such a case should occur, interest would not accrue from the unpaid price. As for the determination of the price, again, we have never heard of such a case.

Ashigara-shimo *kôri*.

Regarding the present matter, no interest is charged. As for the second case, a matter like this has never actually taken place here.

Prefectural Industrial Bureau.

Interest is not allowed on the unpaid price. If the price has not been fixed beforehand, it will be estimated by an arbitrator.

TOCHIGI PREFECTURE

Prefectural Office.

As for the recovery of the price, interest is charged and is computed from the day following the date of performance. If the price has not been fixed beforehand, the market price is taken into consideration.

Shimo-tsuga *kôri* and Samukawa *kôri*.

As for the first case of the recovery of the price, interest accrues from the day following the date of performance. As for the second case, the answer is missing.

Ashikaga *kôri* and Yanada *kôri*.

In the silk trades, no interest is charged on the unpaid price. As for the determination of the price, there are two methods used. One is to determine it by the market price at the time of the execution of the contract, the other is to determine it by the market price at the time of recovery.

MIE PREFECTURE

Suzuka *kôri*.

Regarding the recovery of the price, no interest accrues. The two parties will have talks regarding the price.

Ichishi *kôri*.

With regard to the latter half of the present topic, there is no fixed practice, since the matter is settled through talks between the two.

Nabari *kôri* and Iga *kôri*.

There is no definite practice, since the matter is, in most cases, settled through negotiations between the two parties. If interest accrues from the unpaid price, it is computed from the day after the prescribed date. As for the price, no fixed practice is known, except in the case of goods whose market price is well known.

Kita-muro *kôri*.

With regard to the first half of the topic, interest is not usually allowed. If it is, it is computed from the month of the prescribed time. If the price has not been fixed beforehand, the two parties will talk the matter over, taking the market price into consideration.

Aichi Prefecture

Nakajima *kôri*.

No interest accrues.

Nagoya Ward.

Interest is charged from the day after the prescribed date. The price is set by the market price at the prescribed date.

Chita *kôri*.

Interest is allowed, according to local practice.

Minami-shidara *kôri*.

Interest accrues. It is computed from the day following the date of performance. However, the matter is settled, like the preceding topic, through talks between the two parties.

Atsumi *kôri*.

In a case when interest accrues from the price, it is computed from the day following the prescribed date of payment. Otherwise, it is not charged. If the price has not been fixed beforehand, it is determined by the current price.

Kaitô *kôri* and Kaisai *kôri*.

As stated in Topic 1.

Aichi *kôri*.

As for the recovery of the price, interest is not allowed in most cases. If the price has not been fixed, it is fixed by the market price at the time of recovery.

Niwa *kôri* and Haguri *kôri*.

Though recovery of the price is allowed, interest is not charged on the unpaid price. If the price has not been fixed beforehand, an estimator (*kantei-nin*) is selected to fix it.

Shizuoka Prefecture

Prefectural Office.

As for the first half of the topic, interest is allowed. With regard to the latter half, we have never heard of such a case.

Udo *kôri* and Abe *kôri*.

Answer missing.

Inasa *kôri* and Aratama *kôri*.

Interest accrues from the prescribed date of payment. If the price has not been fixed beforehand, the two parties will have talks and determine it by the market price at the time of the execution of the contract or at the time of the payment.

Kamo *kôri* and Ikeda *kôri*.

Interest is not charged in most cases. An estimator will be selected to fix the price.

Saya *kôri* and Ikeda *kôri*.

There is no set practice regarding this.

Gifu Prefecture

Mugi *kôri*.

As for the first half of the topic, interest is charged from the day following the prescribed date of payment. As for the second half, the two parties will hold talks, there being no fixed practice.

Ampachi *kôri*.

Interest does not accrue in most cases. If it does, it is computed from the day after the prescribed date of performance. The price is settled by the market price.

Fuwa *kôri*.

No interest is allowed. The price is fixed by merchants of the same trade, according to the practice here.

Atsumi *kôri*, Kagami *kôri* and Katagata *kôri*.

When interest accrues from the unpaid price, it is computed from the prescribed date of performance. If the price has not been fixed beforehand, it is decided by an arbitrator or fixed with reference to the current price.

Tagi *kôri* and Kami-ishizu *kôri*.

There is no fixed practice.

Ôno *kôri* and Ikeda *kôri*.

Interest may accrue depending upon the contract, although there is no fixed practice.

Haguri *kôri* and Nakajima *kôri*.

There are no fixed rules regarding interest. As for the price, an estimator will be selected.

Ena *kôri*.

Whether interest is charged or not depends upon the contract. If it is, computation commences from the day following the prescribed date of payment. As for the price, an arbitrator will be selected.

Kamo *kôri*.

Interest is not allowed, since no case of the recovery of the price has been heard of.

Kani *kôri*.

With regard to the first half of the topic, interest is not charged, according to the local practice. As for the second half, the price to be recovered is determined by the current price.

Atsumi *kôri*, Gifu Township.

Interest accrues depending upon the circumstances. If it does, it is computed from the day after the prescribed date of performance. As for the price, it is settled by an arbitrator or according to the market price.

Ôgaki.

Interest does not accrue on the unpaid price in most cases. If it does, computation commences from the day following the prescribed date of payment. The price to be recovered is determined by the current price.

Ena *kôri*, Nakatsugawa Village.

Interest is to be charged from the prescribed date of performance. The price is settled by other merchants' estimation, if it is not the cost price.

Shimo-ishizu *kôri*, Takasu Township.

Regarding the present topic, interest is allowed, though it is difficult to charge it in practice.

Haguri *kôri*, Takegahana Village.

It is difficult, in practice, to charge interest on the unpaid price.

Yamagata *kôri*, Takatomi Village.

Interest is charged from the day following the prescribed date. The two parties will hold talks regarding the price.

Mugi *kôri*, Kôzuchi Village.

No interest accrues from the unpaid price. If the price has not been fixed beforehand, it will not be recovered.

Haguri *kôri*, Kasamatsu Village.

No fixed practice is known regarding the first half of the topic. As for the latter half, an arbitrator is selected.

Fuwa *kôri*, Tarui Village.

With regard to the first half of the topic, interest does not accrue. With regard to the second, merchants of the same trade will settle the matter.

Ôno *kôri*, Miwa Village.

As for the first case, interest is not charged on the unpaid price. As for the second, the two parties will hold talks.

Ampachi *kôri*, Gôdo Village.

If the price has not been paid within the prescribed time, it bears interest from the month of the prescribed time. If the price has not been fixed beforehand, it is determined by the market price.

Tagi *kôri*, Shimada Village.

Answer missing.

Ena *kôri*, Iwa Village.

Interest computation commences from the day after the prescribed date. As for the price, it is fixed by merchants of the same trade.

Kamo *kôri*, Hosome Village.

Interest is charged on the unpaid price from the day following the prescribed date. With regard to the price, other merchants will fix it.

Toki *kôri*, Takayama Village.

The unpaid price bears interest from the day after the prescribed date of payment. If the price has not been fixed beforehand, an approximate estimate is made.

Kani *kôri*, Mitake Village.

In most cases, interest does not accrue. However, if the obligor fails to pay the price within the prescribed date, the unpaid price yields interest from the following day. When the price is not fixed, the two parties will hold talks.

Ena *kôri*, Akechi Village.

As for the first half of the topic, it depends on the contract. When interest accrues, computation commences from the day after the prescribed date. As for the second half, an estimator is selected to fix the price.

Mugi *kôri*, Seki Village.

The compensation money bears no interest. If the amount of the compensation has not been fixed, an arbitrator will decide it.

Ôno *kôri*, Takayama Township.

Whether interest is charged or not depends upon the contract. If it is, computation commences from the day following the prescribed date. If the price has not been fixed beforehand, other merchants will decide it, and it is on this that interest is computed.

Motosu *kôri*, Kitagata Village.

The unpaid price does not bear interest. If the price has not been fixed beforehand, it is decided by comparison with the prices of other goods of ordinary grade.

Kamo *kôri*, Ôta Village.

No interest is charged on the unpaid price, according to the local practice.

Kaisai *kôri* and Shimo-ishizu *kôri*.

It is difficult to charge interest on the unpaid price, although it is allowed in theory. If the price has not been fixed beforehand, the two parties will have talks and select an estimator.

Gujô *kôri*.

No interest accrues from the unpaid price.

Topic 3: Is Any Interest Supposed to Accrue to the Money One Has Paid on Behalf of Another or the Money Advanced on Behalf of Another?

TOKYO METROPOLIS

Prefectural Office.

Soy Wholesalers.[1]

No.

Sugar Wholesalers.

One does not pay money on behalf of someone about whom one does not know. Whether interest accrues or not depends upon the degree of acquittance and the amount of money paid, so no definite answer can be given.

Dried Bonito Wholesalers.

The payment of interest usually will be agreed upon in a contract. However, interest sometimes does not accure, according to the circumstances.

Medicine Wholesalers.

When one pays or advances money on behalf of another, one is free to receive the interest to the money.

Paper Wholesalers (*Kiu-kumi*).[2]

Interest will not accrue.

Oil Wholesalers.

We have no practice of paying interest.

Stone Wholesalers.

Interest is not paid by acquaintances.

Fuel Wholesalers.

We have no practice of paying interest.

Porcelain Wholesalers.

Unless otherwise provided, interest will accrue.

Paper Wholesalers (*Shôkai-kumi*).[3]

Interest will not be paid.

Rice Traders.[4]

If the money he has paid on behalf of another is for freight, for

[1] *Shôyu-donya-kumiai.*

[2] *Kiu-kumi kami-donya.*

[3] *Shôkai-kumi kami-donya.*

[4] *Beikoku sangyô-kumiai.*

example, it will not bear interest. If it is in the form of a documentary bill, it will.

Salt Wholesalers.

Interest will accrue if more than fifty yen is involved. In the case of expenses, it will not.

Timber Wholesalers.

In some cases, it will accrue, while in others it will not.

Timber Traders.[1]

The same as in the preceding answer.

Timber Traders (*Senju*).[2]

The same as in the preceding answer.

Matting Wholesalers.

When a small sum of money is paid or advanced on behalf of another, interest will not accrue.

Saké Wholesalers.[3]

Unless otherwise provided, interest will not accrue.

Drapery Wholesalers.

Interest will not accrue.

Tobacco Wholesalers.

There is no established rule. Each case will be talked over between the two.

Saké Wholesalers.

As for expenses, interest will not accrue. When money is advanced on behalf of another, the matter of interest will be detailed in a contract.

Lime and Shell Wholesalers.

We have no custom of paying interest.

Mosquito Net Wholesalers.

When a small sum of money is paid or advanced on behalf of another, interest will not accrue.

Copper and Iron Wholesalers.

The payment or non-payment of interest will be decided in each case according to the circumstances.

Fuel Wholesalers (*Umite-kumi*).[4]

Cases differ. There is no established practice.

[1] *Zaimoku tôsei-kumiai.*

[2] *Senju zaimoku-kumiai.*

[3] *Sake-rui-donya.*

[4] *Umite-kumi shintan-donya.*

Kôjimachi Ward.

We have no practice of paying or receiving interest.

Nihombashi Ward.

Unless otherwise provided, interest will not accrue.

Kyôbashi Ward.

We have no established practice.

Yotsuya Ward and Ushigome Ward.

Please refer to our answer in Topic 2.

Asakusa Ward.

When money is paid or advanced on behalf of another for temporary use, interest does not accrue.

Honjo Ward.

When money is paid or advanced on behalf of another, interest will accrue only if a large amount of money is involved, or the money is lent for a long period of time.

Ebara *kôri*.

Money paid or advanced on behalf of another will not bear interest.

Higashi-tama *kôri* and Minami-toshima *kôri*.

Money paid on behalf of another will bear no interest. Money advanced on behalf of another will not bear interest if only a small sum is involved.

Kita-toshima *kôri*.

Money paid on behalf of another will bear no interest. As for money which has been advanced, large amounts will usually be treated as debts. If any damage occurs due to the intention of the other party, compensation can be claimed.[1] If it occurs due to negligence, the two parties will talk about the matter, depending on the circumstances.

Minami-adachi *kôri*.

In such cases, interest will not accrue.

Shitaya Ward.

The matter is wholly dependent upon the contract. Money paid on behalf of another has never borne interest unless provided for in the contract. However, money advanced on behalf of another often yields interest.

Kanda Ward.

[1] This is the answer to Topic 4. See page 269.

Interest usually accrues, on money paid or advanced on behalf of another.

Akasaka Ward and Azabu Ward.

Interest will not accrue.

Hongô Ward.

Interest will only rarely be paid.

CHIBA PREFECTURE

Awa *kôri*, Hei *kôri*, Asai *kôri* and Nagasa *kôri*.

Money advanced by another will usually be repaid with an expression of thanks and a reasonable amount of interest. In day-to-day transactions, however, the payment of interest will only rarely be asked for. Two parties should help each other. If a long period of time is involved, however, interest will be paid.

Katori *kôri*.

In business transactions, money paid or advanced on behalf of another usually will bear no interest.

Yamabe *kôri* and Muza *kôri*.

One usually expects a debt to be repaid with interest.

Unakami *kôri* and Sôsa *kôri*.

Money paid or advanced on behalf of another will bear no interest.

Higashi-katsushika *kôri*.

There are no established rules. However, if a large amount of money is involved, interest will be paid.

IBARAKI PREFECTURE

Nishi-katsushika *kôri* and Sashima *kôri*.

In either case, the money will bear no interest.

KANAGAWA PREFECTURE

Miura *kôri*.

Interest will not be paid.

Tachibana *kôri*.

Interest will not be paid.

Kita-tama *kôri*.

Money paid or advanced on behalf of another is but a token of friendship. Therefore, the money usually will bear no interest.

Ashigara-shimo *kôri*.

The computation of interest begins on the day when the money is paid or advanced. Through talks, however, the money usually will bear no interest.

Prefectural Industrial Bureau.

Money paid or advanced on behalf of another usually will involve interest.

TOCHIGI PREFECTURE

Prefectural Office.

Wholesalers and brokers expect interest to be paid. Among commission earners, however, interest will not be paid.

Shimo-tsuga *kôri* and Samukawa *kôri*.

Money paid or advanced on behalf of another will bear no interest.

Ashikaga *kôri* and Yanada *kôri*.

Money paid on behalf of another will bear no interest. In textile trading, money advanced on behalf of another will bear interest, according to the rate prevailing at financial institutions. In silk trading, money advanced on behalf of another sometimes will bear interest. In most cases, however, interest accrues to even a small amount of money.

MIE PREFECTURE

Suzuka *kôri*.

Interest does not accrue to money paid or advanced on behalf of another.

Ichishi *kôri*.

Interest will accrue.

Nabari *kôri* and Iga *kôri*.

Money paid will bear no interest. Money advanced will bear interest.

Kita-muro *kôri*.

Money paid or advanced on behalf of another for business purposes is supposed to bear interest. The obligor cannot refuse to pay it, if the obligee requires it.

AICHI PREFECTURE

Nakajima *kôri*.

Yes.

Nagoya Ward.

Interest will obviously accrue. However, if money is advanced only for actual expenses incurred, and is paid on behalf of a close customer or the like, no interest will be paid.

Chita *kôri*.

Unless otherwise provided for, no interest will accrue.

Minami-shidara *kôri*.

Money paid on behalf of another will bear no interest. However, money advanced will bear interest.

Atsumi *kôri*.

Money advanced will bear no interest.

Kaitô *kôri* and Kaisai *kôri*.

As a rule interest will be paid.

Aichi *kôri*.

Interest will be paid.

Niwa *kôri* and Haguri *kôri*.

Money paid or advanced on behalf of another will bear no interest.

SHIZUOKA PREFECTURE

Prefectural Office.

Money paid will not bear interest, but money advanced will.

Udo *kôri* and Abe *kôri*.

Unless money is paid or advanced on request, it will bear no interest.

Inasa *kôri* and Aratama *kôri*.

Money will bear interest.

Kamo *kôri* and Naka *kôri*.

Money paid on behalf of another usually will bear no interest. However, money advanced will involve interest.

Saya *kôri* and Kitô *kôri*.

We have no established practice in this matter.

GIFU PREFECTURE

Mugi *kôri*.

If large amounts are involved, money paid on behalf of another will bear interest. Money of any amount which is advanced will carry interest.

Ampachi *kôri*.

Interest will usually be paid.

Fuwa *kôri*.

According to practices in these parts, such sums will usually bear no interest.

Atsumi *kôri*, Kagami *kôri* and Katagata *kôri*.

In both cases, interest will occasionally accrue.

Tagi *kôri* and Kami-ishizu *kôri*.

Money paid or advanced on behalf of another will bear no

interest. If money advanced is to be taken as a debt, it will carry interest.

Ôno *kôri* and Ikeda *kôri*.

Money advanced usually will bear interest.

Haguri *kôri* and Nakajima *kôri*.

The question of interest will be decided according to the nature of the money involved, the length of time until repayment and other similar matters.

Ena *kôri*.

Unless otherwise provided, interest will not accrue.

Kamo *kôri*.

Money paid or advanced on behalf of another usually will bear no interest. However, if money is advanced by wholesalers or the like, interest usually will be paid.

Kani *kôri*.

According to business practices here, interest will accrue.

Atsumi *kôri*, Gifu Township.

Sometimes interest will accrue, and at other times it will not.

Ôgaki.

As a rule interest will be paid.

Ena *kôri*, Nakatsugawa Village.

A considerable sum of interest should be paid.

Shimo-ishizu *kôri*, Takasu Township.

In both cases the matter should be discussed.

Haguri *kôri*, Takegahana Village.

In some cases interest will accrue, while in others it will not. No brief answer will suffice.

Yamagata *kôri*, Takatomi Village.

Money paid or advanced on behalf of another will bear interest.

Mugi *kôri*, Kôzuchi Village.

Interest will accrue.

Haguri *kôri*, Kasamatsu Village.

The matter will be determined by the nature of the money, the length of time involved and other similar matters.

Fuwa *kôri*, Tarui Village.

According to practices here, interest will not accrue in most cases.

Ôno *kôri*, Miwa Village.

Money paid or advanced on behalf of another will bear interest.

Ampachi *kôri*, Gôdo Village.

Money paid or advanced will bear interest.

Tagi *kôri*, Shimada Village.

No answer.

Ena *kôri*, Iwa Village.

Interest will not be paid.

Kamo *kôri*, Hosome Village.

Interest will accrue.

Toki *kôri*, Takayama Village.

Money paid will bear no interest but money advanced will.

Kani *kôri*, Mitake Village.

Interest will not accrue.

Ena *kôri*, Akechi Village.

Unless otherwise provided, interest will not accrue.

Mugi *kôri*, Seki Village.

A number of factors will determine whether or not any interest will be paid.

Ôno *kôri*, Takayama Township.

Interest will accrue.

Motosu *kôri*, Kitagata Village.

Money paid or advanced on behalf of another will bear interest.

Kamo *kôri*, Ôta Village.

Money paid or advanced on behalf of another will usually bear no interest. However, wholesalers and similar merchants usually charge interest.

Kaisai *kôri* and Shimo-ishizu *kôri*.

Money paid or advanced on behalf of another should bear interest through talks.

Gujô *kôri*.

In both cases interest will accrue.

Topic 4: Whenever Damage Has Been Done, Whether Intentionally[1] or Not, May Compensation Be Claimed for It?

TOKYO METROPOLIS

Soy Wholesalers.

Compensation can be claimed whether the damage is intentional or not.

Sugar Wholesalers.

If some damage is done, it is a matter of course that one should receive compensation.

Dried Bonito Wholesalers.

It can be claimed.

Medicine Wholesalers.

It can be claimed.

Oil Wholesalers.

Whether intentional or not, it is a matter of course that damage should be compensated.

Fuel Wholesalers.

Whether intentional or not, compensation can be claimed.

Porcelain Wholesalers.

If the damage is intentional, full compensation can be claimed. However, if the damage is accidental, only partial compensation can be claimed.

Paper Wholesalers (*Shôkai-kumi*).[2]

We have no practice of claiming compensation.

Rice Traders.[3]

When any damage is done, whether intentionally or not, compensation can be claimed.

Salt Wholesalers.

It can be claimed.

Timber Wholesalers.

It can be claimed.

Timber Traders.[4]

As stated above.

[1] *Koi.*

[2] *Shôkai-kumi kami-donya.*

[3] *Beikoku sangyô-kumiai.*

[4] *Zaimoku tosei-kumiai.*

Timber Traders (*Senju*).[1]

As stated above.

Matting Wholesalers.

When any damage is done, whether intentionally or not, compensation can be claimed.

Saké Wholesalers.[2]

Even if it can be claimed by the obligor, it seems to be difficult to settle through talks only.

Drapery Wholesalers.

Whether intentional or not, a reasonable amount of compensation can be claimed.

Tobacco Wholesalers.

The payment of compensation will be mutually discussed each time as circumstances require. Therefore, we have no established practice.

Saké Wholesalers.

We have never heard of such a case.

Lime and Shell Wholesalers.

The payment of compensation will be mutually discussed and decided upon.

Mosquito Net Wholesalers.

Whether intentional or not, compensation can be claimed.

Copper and Iron Wholesalers.

Whether intentional or not, it is a matter of course that compensation can be claimed.

Fuel Wholesalers (*Umite-kumi*).[3]

Even a verbal agreement can bind one to pay compensation if the fact of intentional damage is clear.

Kôjimachi Ward.

It is a matter of course that compensation can be claimed.

Nihombashi Ward.

If any damage occurs intentionally, a reasonable amount of compensation can be claimed. In the case of accidental damage, however, it is usually impossible to claim compensation. However, in the latter case few traders will place the dispute before the court

[1] *Senju zaimoku-kumiai.*

[2] *Sake-rui-donya.*

[3] *Umite-kumi shintan-donya.*

since they want to maintain their good relations in the future.

Kyôbashi Ward.

Whether intentional or not, compensation can be claimed.

Yotsuya Ward and Ushigome Ward.

Compensation can be claimed.

Asakusa Ward.

It can be claimed.

Honjo Ward.

Whether intentional or not, compensation can be claimed.

Ebara *kôri.*

Whether intentional or not, compensation can be claimed.

Higashi-tama *kôri* and Minami-toshima *kôri.*

Whether intentional or not, compensation can be claimed.

Kita-toshima *kôri.*

See our answer in Topic 3.

Minami-adachi *kôri.*

If damage occurs intentionally, compensation can be claimed. If it occurs unintentionally, compensation cannot be claimed.

Shitaya Ward.

Whether intentional or not, it is a matter of course that compensation be paid. In most cases, however, it is not actually claimed.

Kanda Ward.

Whether intentional or not, compensation can be claimed.

Akasaka Ward and Azabu Ward.

If damage occurs intentionally, it is a matter of course that compensation be paid. Even if it occurs unintentionally, compensation can be claimed if no reasonable explanation can be given.

Hongô Ward.

When unintentional damage occurs, no compensation can be claimed, according to the practice here.

CHIBA PREFECTURE

Awa *kôri,* Hei *kôri,* Asai *kôri* and Nagasa *kôri.*

No answer.

Katori *kôri.*

No answer.

Yamabe *kôri* and Muza *kôri.*

No answer.

Unakami *kôri* and Sôsa *kôri.*

No answer.

Higashi-katsushika *kôri*.

If the damage occurs intentionally, compensation can usually be claimed.

IBARAKI PREFECTURE

Nishi-katsushika *kôri* and Sashima *kôri*.

Whether intentional or not, compensation can be claimed.

KANAGAWA PREFECTURE

Miura *kôri*.

Whether intentional or not, compensation can be claimed.

Tachibana *kôri*.

If the damage is done intentionally, compensation can be claimed. If not, compensation cannot be claimed.

Kita-tama *kôri*.

If the damage is done intentionally, compensation can be claimed. If one refuses to pay compensation, a settlement must be reached through talks before the court. Otherwise, a reasonable amount of compensation will be paid according to the circumstances.

Ashigara-shimo *kôri*.

If any damage occurs, it is a matter of course that compensation be paid.

Prefectural Industrial Bureau.

Whether intentional or not, one party's failure to fulfill his obligations is grounds for having to pay compensation. However, damage due to unavoidable circumstances need not be compensated.

TOCHIGI PREFECTURE

Prefectural Office.

Whether intentional or not, compensation can be claimed. If the damage is due to unavoidable circumstances, however, the loss will be shared by both parties.

Shimo-tsuga *kôri* and Samukawa *kôri*.

Compensation can be claimed only when damage is done intentionally.

Ashikaga *kôri* and Yanada *kôri*.

When damage occurs, compensation is rarely claimed. Even if one claims it, he rarely gets it. Thus one will not often accuse another of failure. The one party does sometimes compensate for part of the loss and extends some expression of sympathy. If the damage is done by default or mistake, few claim compensation.

Mie Prefecture

Suzuka *kôri.*

Whether intentional or not, compensation can obviously be claimed. If the loss is small, however, one usually does not claim it.

Ichishi *kôri.*

There are no established rules. A settlement should be reached through mutual agreement.

Nabari-*kôri* and Iga *kôri.*

If the damage is unintentional, and involves only a small sum, compensation will not be claimed. If the loss is large, it will sometimes be claimed.

Kita-muro *kôri.*

Whether intentional or not, compensation will be claimed.

Aichi Prefecture

Nakajima *kôri.*

Compensation can obviously be claimed. For some kinds of articles, however, no compensation will be claimed.

Nagoya Ward.

Compensation can be claimed. If the damage is unintentional, a settlement occasionally will be reached through mutual discussion.

Chita *kôri.*

If the damage is intentional, compensation obviously should be claimed. If the damage is done unintentionally and under unavoidable circumstances, few will claim compensation.

Minami-shidara *kôri.*

Compensation can be claimed only if the damage is intentional.

Atsumi *kôri.*

Whether intentional or not, compensation should be claimed.

Kaitô *kôri* and Kaisai *kôri.*

If the damage is intentional, compensation will be claimed. If it is unintentional, it would not be moral to collect compensation.

Aichi *kôri.*

Whether intentional or not, compensation can be claimed.

Niwa *kôri* and Haguri *kôri.*

Whether intentional or not, compensation can be claimed. If it is unintentional, however, some allowance will be made for extenuating circumstances.

Shizuoka Prefecture

Prefectural Office.

Yes, that is right. However, compensation will not always be requested if the damage is unintentional.

Udo *kôri* and Abe *kôri*.

Yes, compensation can be claimed.

Inasa *kôri* and Aratama *kôri*.

If the damage is intentional, full compensation will be claimed. If it is unintentional, the loss will be shared evenly by both parties.

Kamo *kôri* and Naka *kôri*.

One can claim compensation if he thinks the loss is too great.

Saya *kôri* and Kitô *kôri*.

There are no established practices.

GIFU PREFECTURE

Mugi *kôri*.

Compensation can be claimed.

Ampachi *kôri*.

If the damage is intentional, compensation can obviously be claimed. If it is unintentional, some allowance will be made for extenuating circumstances.

Fuwa *kôri*.

If the damage is intentional, compensation can obviously be claimed. Even if it is unintentional, compensation sometimes will be claimed.

Atsumi *kôri*, Kagami *kôri* and Katagata *kôri*.

Unless it is intentional, no compensation will be claimed.

Tagi *kôri* and Kami-ishizu *kôri*.

Even if the damage is intentional, no compensation can be claimed unless otherwise provided.

Ôno *kôri* and Ikeda *kôri*.

If the damage is intentional, compensation should obviously be claimed. If it is accidental, a variety of possibilities exists.

Haguri *kôri* and Nakajima *kôri*.

Yes, that is right.

Ena *kôri*.

Yes, that is right.

Kamo *kôri*.

Whether intentional or not, compensation should be claimed.

Kani *kôri*.

Compensation can be claimed. If the damage is done unintentionally, the injured party may sometimes not claim.

Atsumi *kôri*, Gifu Township.

If any damage occurs, compensation will sometimes be claimed.

Ôgaki.

If the damage is intentional, compensation can obviously be claimed. If it is unintentional, some allowance will be made for extenuating circumstances.

Ena *kôri*, Nakatsugawa Village.

Compensation can be claimed.

Shimo-ishizu *kôri*, Takasu Township.

Whether intentional or not, compensation can be claimed.

Haguri *kôri*, Takegahana Village.

If any damage at all occurs, whether unintentional or intentional, compensation can be claimed.

Yamagata *kôri*, Takatomi Village.

Unless it is intentional, compensation cannot be claimed.

Mugi *kôri*, Kôzuchi Village.

Whether intentional or not, compensation can be claimed.

Haguri *kôri*, Kasamatsu Village.

Yes, that is right.

Fuwa *kôri*, Tarui Village.

If the damage is intentional, compensation can obviously be claimed. If it is unintentional, some allowance will be made for extenuating circumstances.

Ôno *kôri*, Miwa Village.

Whether compensation will be paid or not will be decided upon in talks.

Ampachi *kôri*, Gôdo Village.

If any damage occurs, compensation will be claimed.

Tagi *kôri*, Shimada Village.

No answer.

Ena *kôri*, Iwa Village.

Compensation occasionally will be claimed.

Kamo *kôri*, Hosome Village.

If any damage is done, as stated here, compensation should be claimed.

Toki *kôri*, Takayama Village.

Yes, that is right.

Kani *kôri*, Mitake Village.

Compensation can be claimed. However, in reality, some allowance for extenuating circumstances is often made.

Ena *kôri*, Akechi Village.

Yes, that is right.

Mugi *kôri*, Seki Village.

Yes, that is right.

Ôno *kôri*, Takayama Village.

Compensation can be claimed at any time.

Motosu *kôri*, Kitagata Village.

Whether intentional or not, compensation can be claimed.

Kamo *kôri*, Ôta Village.

Whether intentional or not, compensation can be claimed.

Kaisai *kôri* and Shimo-ishizu *kôri*.

Whether intentional or not, compensation can be claimed.

Gujô *kôri*.

We cannot give a definite answer.

Topic 5: Is Compensation Limited to the Amount of Damage Actually Done, or Does It Include the Probable Profit That Would Have Accrued Were It Not for the Damage?
In the Latter Case, How Is the Amount of Damage to Be Estimated?

TOKYO METROPOLIS

Soy Wholesalers.

Compensation is to be limited to the amount of damage actually done.

Sugar Wholesalers.

Compensation is to be limited to the actual damage.

Dried Bonito Wholesalers.

Compensation is to be limited to the amount of damage actually done.

Medicine Wholesalers.

Compensation is to be limited to the actual damage.

Paper Wholesalers (*Kiu-kumi*).[1]

In business, there is a considerable amount of profit expected to accrue in the future.

Oil Wholesalers.

Compensation is to be limited to the actual damage.

Stone Wholesalers.

Unless otherwise provided, compensation is to be limited to the amount of damage actually done.

Fuel Wholesalers.

Unless otherwise provided, compensation is to be limited to the actual damage. The answer to the second question is as stated above.

Porcelain Wholesalers.

Compensation is to be limited to the actual damage.

Paper Wholesalers (*Shôkai-kumi*).[2]

Such a practice is not known.

Rice Traders.[3]

[1] *Kiu-kumi kami-donya.*

[2] *Shôkai-kumi kami-donya.*

[3] *Beikoku sangyô-kumiai.*

Usually, compensation is to be limited to the amount of damage actually done. However, sometimes the profit which would have accrued in the future is also paid. The amount of such profit should obviously be prorated according to the extent of the damage. Therefore, it can be decided upon only after the damage has been done.

Salt Wholesalers.

Compensation will include the profit which probably would have accrued in the future. Depending upon the circumstances, however, there will be a compromise. Generally speaking, the probable profit is calculated at 2.5 percent of the actual damage.

Timber Wholesalers.

Compensation is to be limited to the actual damage.

Timber Traders.[1]

Yes, same as the above answer.

Timber Traders (*Senju*).[2]

Yes, same as above.

Matting Wholesalers.

Compensation is to be limited to the actual damage. It never includes any of the future profit which might have accrued.

Saké Wholesalers.[3]

Compensation is to be limited to the amount of the damage actually done.

Drapery Wholesalers.

Compensation is to be limited to the actual damage.

Saké Wholesalers.

Compensation is to be limited to the amount of damage actually done.

Lime and Shell Wholesalers.

There is no established practice. In consideration of the existing circumstances, there will be some compromise.

Mosquito Net Wholesalers.

Compensation is to be limited to the actual damage. It never includes any of the future profit which might have accrued.

Copper and Iron Wholesalers.

1 *Zaimoku tôsei-kumiai.*

2 *Senju zaimoku-kumiai.*

3 *Sake-rui-donya.*

In general, compensation is to be limited to the contracted value of the goods actually damaged.

Tobacco Wholesalers.

We have no established practice.

Fuel Wholesalers (*Umite-kumi*).[1]

Compensation is to be limited to the actual damage. We have never heard of including any future profit which might have accrued.

Kôjimachi Ward.

Compensation is to be limited to the actual damage. It never includes any of the future profit which might have accrued.

Nihombashi Ward.

Compensation is to be limited to the amount of damage actually done.

Kyôbashi Ward.

Compensation is to be limited to the actual damage.

Yotsuya Ward and Ushigome Ward.

No answer.

Asakusa Ward.

In general, compensation is to be limited to the actual damage.

Honjo Ward.

Compensation is to be limited to the actual damage. It never includes any of the future profit which might have accrued.

Ebara *kôri*.

Compensation is to be limited to the amount of damage actually suffered.

Higashi-tama *kôri* and Minami-toshima *kôri*.

Generally speaking, compensation is to be limited to the amount of actual damage. It never includes any of the future profit which might have accrued.

Kita-toshima *kôri*.

Compensation is to be limited to the contracted value of the goods actually damaged. It never includes any of the future profit which might have accrued. Prior to the conclusion of a contract (the contract does not specify about compensation.), no agreement will be made on the probable compensation in future.

Minami-adachi *kôri*.

[1] *Umite-kumi shintan-donya.*

Compensation is to be limited to the amount of damage actually incurred.

Shitaya Ward.

According to our business practice, compensation will include the probable future profit which would have accrued. If the amount of profit is fixed prior to the business transaction, the difference between the two prices, that at the beginning and that at the time of performance, is taken into consideration. The obligee, however, as stated in the answer to the preceding topic, is free to pass it over for his obligor.

Kanda Ward.

Compensation is limited to the amount of actual damage. Even if future profit is claimed, it will not be obtained.

Akasaka Ward and Azabu Ward.

Compensation is to be limited to the amount of damage actually suffered. It never includes any of the future profit which might have accrued.

Hongô Ward.

Compensation is to be limited to the actual damage. It never includes any of the future profit which might have accrued.

CHIBA PREFECTURE

Awa *kôri*, Hei *kôri*, Asai *kôri* and Nagasa *kôri*.

Compensation is to be limited to the actual damage. It seldom includes any future profit which might have accrued.

Katori *kôri*.

Compensation is to be limited to the amount of damage actually done. It never includes any of the future profit which might have accrued.

Yamabe *kôri* and Muza *kôri*.

Compensation is to be limited to the actual damage.

Unakami *kôri* and Sôsa *kôri*.

Compensation is to be limited to the actual damage. It never includes any of the future profit which might have accrued.

Higashi-katsushika *kôri*.

Compensation is to be limited to the actual damage. It never includes any of the future profit which might have accrued.

IBARAKI PREFECTURE

Nishi-katsushika *kôri* and Sashima *kôri*.

Compensation is to be limited to the actual damage. It never includes any of the future profit which might have accrued. The answer to the second question has already been given above.

KANAGAWA PREFECTURE

Miura *kôri*.

Compensation is to be limited to the amount of damage actually done.

Tachibana *kôri*.

Compensation is to be limited to the actual damage.

Kita-tama *kôri*.

According to our practice, compensation is to be limited to the amount of damage actually incurred. In general, however, a business transaction covers a period of several years. So it is settled by compromise between the two concerned. With respect to civil affairs, if a contract has been concluded, compensation is limited to the amount of damage actually done. Sometimes it will include the future profit which might have accrued.

Ashigara-shimo *kôri*.

It will not always be limited to the actual damage. As for the second question, total damages of direct consequence can be claimed.

Prefectural Industrial Bureau.

Compensation will include the amount of damage actually done and the probable profit which might accrue at the time of the compensation. It will not include the probable profit to accrue in the future.

TOCHIGI PREFECTURE

Prefectural Office.

According to the practice here, compensation is to be limited to the actual damage.

Shimo-tsuga *kôri* and Samukawa *kôri*.

Compensation is to be limited to the actual damage.

Ashikaga *kôri* and Yanada *kôri*.

Compensation is to be limited to the amount of damage actually suffered. It never includes any of the future profit which might have accrued.

MIE PREFECTURE

Suzuka *kôri*.

Compensation is to be limited to the actual damage. It never includes any of the future profit which might have accrued.

Ichishi *kôri.*

Compensation is to be limited to the amount of damage actually done. The kind of case referred to in the second question cannot be found here.

Nabari *kôri* and Iga *kôri.*

Compensation is to be limited to the actual damage.

Kita-muro *kôri.*

Compensation is to be limited to the actual damage. In the case of some articles, however, if it is feared that some damage will accrue in future, the contract will be cancelled, or a new contract made. The amount of the probable profit that might accrue in the future will be decided upon by the two at the time the new contract is made.

AICHI PREFECTURE

Nakajima *kôri.*

Compensation is to be limited to the amount of damage actually done.

Nagoya Ward.

Compensation is to be limited to the actual damage. It never includes any of the future profit which might have accrued.

Chita *kôri.*

Compensation is to be limited to the actual damage.

Minami-shidara *kôri.*

Compensation is to be limited to the amount of damage actually done.

Atsumi *kôri.*

Compensation is to be limited to the actual damage.

Kaitô *kôri* and Kaisai *kôri.*

According to the practice here, compensation is to be limited to the actual damage.

Aichi *kôri.*

Compensation is to be limited to the actual damage. It never includes any of the future profit which might have accrued.

Niwa *kôri* and Haguri *kôri.*

Compensation is to be limited to the amount of damage actually done. It never includes any of the future profit which might have accrued.

SHIZUOKA PREFECTURE

Prefectural Office.

Our answer is the same as given in the first half of the first question in the present topic.

Udo *kôri* and Abe *kôri*.

Compensation is to be limited to the actual damage.

Inasa *kôri* and Aratama *kôri*.

Compensation is to be limited to the actual damage.

Kamo *kôri* and Naka *kôri*.

Compensation is to be limited to the actual damage. It never includes any of the future profit which might have accrued.

Saya *kôri* and Kitô *kôri*.

There is no established practice here.

Gifu Prefecture

Mugi *kôri*.

Compensation is to be limited to the actual damage. The answer to the second question is as given above.

Ampachi *kôri*.

In general, compensation is to be limited to the actual damage.

Fuwa *kôri*.

Compensation is to be limited to the amount of damage actually done.

Atsumi *kôri*, Kagami *kôri* and Katagata *kôri*.

Compensation is to be limited to the actual damage.

Tagi *kôri* and Kami-ishizu *kôri*.

There is no established practice. No answer can be given.

Ôno *kôri* and Ikeda *kôri*.

According to the practice here, compensation is to be limited to the actual damage.

Haguri *kôri* and Nakajima *kôri*.

Regarding the first question, if the damage is intentional, compensation will include the probable profit which would have accrued in the future. As for the second question, an assessor should be selected.

Ena *kôri*.

Compensation is to be limited to the actual damage.

Kamo *kôri*.

Compensation is to be limited to the actual damage. It never includes any of the future profit which might have accrued.

Kani *kôri*.

Compensation is to be limited to the actual damage.

Atsumi *kôri*, Gifu Township.

Compensation is to be limited to the amount of damage actually incurred. It never includes any of the future profit which might have accrued.

Ôgaki.

According to the practice here, compensation is to be limited to the actual damage.

Ena *kôri*, Nakatsugawa Village.

Compensation should include not only the actual damage but also the probable profit in the future, if it can be definitely expected at present. Regarding the second question, the future profit is limited to the amount which can be expected and estimated clearly at the time when the damage is inflicted.

Kami-ishizu *kôri*, Takasu Township.

There are many situations, each different from the other depending upon the kind of article and the time at which the damage occurred. Nevertheless, compensation is in most cases, to be limited to the contracted value of the goods actually damaged. It seldom includes any of the future profit which might have accrued.

Haguri *kôri*, Takegahana Village.

Compensation is to be limited to the actual damage. Only rarely will compensation include the probable profit which might have accrued in the future.

Yamagata *kôri*, Takatomi Village.

Compensation is to be limited to the actual damage.

Mugi *kôri*, Kôzuchi Village.

Compensation is to be limited to the actual damage. It never includes any of the future profit which might have accrued.

Haguri *kôri*, Kasamatsu Village.

As for the first question, the practice here is as stated in the first half of the question. If the damage is intentional, the probable profit which might have accrued in the future will also be paid. As for the second question, an assessor should be chosen.

Fuwa *kôri*, Tarui Village.

As for the first question, compensation is to be limited to the actual damage. Regarding the second, no established practice can be found here.

Ôno *kôri*, Miwa Village.

Compensation is to be limited to the amount of damage actually done.

Ampachi *kôri*, Gôdo Village.

Compensation is to be limited to the actual damage.

Tagi *kôri*, Shimada Village.

No answer.

Ena *kôri*, Iwa Village.

Compensation is to be limited to the actual damage.

Kamo *kôri*, Hosome Village.

Compensation is to be limited to the amount of damage actually done.

Toki *kôri*, Takayama Village.

Compensation is to be limited to the actual damage.

Kani *kôri*, Mitake Village.

Compensation should include not only the amount of the actual damage but the lost profit at present. It does not include the probable profit in the future.

Ena *kôri*, Akechi Village.

Compensation is to be limited to the actual damage.

Mugi *kôri*, Seki Village.

Compensation is to be limited to the amount of actual damage. It never includes any of the future profit which might have accrued.

Ôno *kôri*, Takayama Township.

The amount of actual damage will be compensated. Only when one thinks it necessary, will any compensation be paid for future profit. Therefore, the amount of damage will be decided upon in proportion to the importance of the accident. In the Takayama district, however, such a case has never been found.

Motosu *kôri*, Kitagata Village.

Compensation is to be limited to the amount of actual damage.

Kamo *kôri*, Ôta Village.

Compensation is to be limited to the amount of damage actually done.

Kaisai *kôri* and Shimo-ishizu *kôri*.

The damage will be compensated. It will not include any compensation for probable future profits. The amount of profit, as has been stated in the first half of the first question, cannot be fixed in advance. Therefore it will not include the profit.

Gujô *kôri.*

Compensation is to be limited to the amount of damage actually done.

Topic 6: When It Is Found That the Amount of the Price or of the Damages to Be Recovered, an Amount Which Has Been Agreed upon Beforehand, Does Not Conform to the Current Prices, What Should Be Done?

Tokyo Metropolis

Prefectural Office.

Soy Wholesalers.

We have never heard of such a case.

Sugar Wholesalers.

Regarding the present topic, the sum originally agreed upon is to be paid, regardless of the current prices, since it has been stipulated in the contract.

Medicine Wholesalers.

The amount agreed upon cannot be changed.

Paper Wholesalers (*Kiu-kumi*).

The injured party may recover a reasonable amount of the price or damages from the party in breach.

Oil Wholesalers.

The amount originally agreed upon is to be in effect.

Stone Wholesalers.

The amount originally agreed upon is to be paid, regardless of fluctuations of the market price.

Porcelain Wholesalers.

The sum originally agreed upon is not subject to change.

Fuel Wholesalers.

Regarding the present topic, the amount originally stipulated in the contract is to be recovered.

Paper Wholesalers (*Shôkai-kumi*).

Once the amount of price or damages has been agreed upon, that amount is to be paid, no matter how great the fluctuations of the market price are.

Rice Traders.

When the amount of the price or the amount of damages has been agreed upon beforehand, this amount may not be changed if the agreement is to the effect that the agreed amount should not be subject to change regardless of fluctuations of the market price. Otherwise, the injured party may sue for the additional sum, if the agreed sum does not cover his loss.

Salt Wholesalers.

The two parties will have talks.

Timber Wholesalers.

The matter is settled through talks between the two.

Timber Traders.

Same as the above.

Timber Wholesalers (*Senju*).

The damages agreed upon are to be paid.

Matting Wholesalers.

The defaulting party is obliged to pay the difference if the agreed price falls short of the actual price.

Saké Wholesalers.

After exact calculation, if the stipulated sum is larger than the amount required to compensate the injured party for his loss, the difference is returned to the defaulting party. If the agreed sum falls short of the actual loss, the defaulting party should pay the additional damages.

Dry Goods Wholesalers.

There is no set practice.

Saké Wholesalers.

We have no practice regarding this.

Lime and Shell Wholesalers.

There is no settled practice, since the matter is determined according to the case.

Mosquito Net Wholesalers.

If the agreed sum is less than the amount required to compensate the injured party for his loss, the defaulting party should pay the additional damages.

Tobacco Wholesalers.

There is no fixed practice, since the matter is settled through talks between the two.

Copper and Iron Wholesalers.

We do not know of this practice.

Fuel Wholesalers (*Umite-kumi*).

It is difficult to give a definite statement about the matter, since the contract itself differs with the place.

Kôjimachi Ward.

The agreed sum is recovered, regardless of the fluctuations of the market price.

Nihombashi Ward.

The stipulated amount is not subject to change.

Kyôbashi Ward.

The sum stipulated in advance is to be recovered.

Yotsuya Ward and Ushigome Ward.

If the two parties agreed upon a sum of money payable for breach, the agreed sum is not subject to change, regardless of the fluctuations of the market price.

Asakusa Ward.

The amount to be recovered for compensating the injured party does not excede the sum agreed upon. If the actual damages of the injured party are less than the agreed sum, in most cases the sum required to compensate the injured party for his actual loss is paid.

Ebara *kôri.*

If the two parties have stipulated the amount of the price or the damages, the sum agreed upon is paid, regardless of the market price.

Higashi-tama *kôri* and Minami-toshima *kôri.*

Once the amount of the price or the damages has been agreed upon, the stipulated sum is to be recovered.

Kita-toshima *kôri.*

As stated in Topic 5.

Minami-adachi *kôri.*

Regarding the present topic, the sum agreed upon shall be paid.

Shitaya Ward.

When the two parties have stipulated the amount of the price or the damages to be recovered, according to the local practice the sum agreed upon is recovered, regardless of the current price.

Kanda Ward.

Once agreed upon, the stipulated sum shall be paid regardless of the current price.

Akasaka Ward and Azabu Ward.

The stipulated amount is recovered, irrespective of fluctuations of the market price.

Hongô Ward.

The matter is settled through talks between the two.

Chiba Prefecture

Awa *kôri*, Hei *kôri*, Asai *kôri* and Nagasa *kôri*.

With the exception of some special cases, the sum agreed upon is paid, whether the market price of the goods rises or falls.

Katori *kôri*.

The sum agreed upon is subject to change depending upon the current price, according to the practice here.

Yamabe *kôri* and Muza *kôri*.

The agreement regarding the amount of money payable for a breach is executed, irrespective of the market price.

Unakami *kôri* and Sôsa *kôri*.

The stipulated sum of money is paid, regardless of the fluctuation of the market price.

Higashi-katsushika *kôri*.

The sum of money stipulated in the contract is recovered.

Ibaraki Prefecture

Nishi-katsushika *kôri* and Sashima *kôri*.

The sum of money agreed upon is recovered, regardless of the current price.

Kanagawa Prefecture

Miura *kôri*.

The sum stipulated for in the contract is paid.

Tachibana *kôri*.

The amount of money agreed upon is not subject to change. This amount is recovered from the defaulting party.

Kita-tama *kôri*.

The sum stipulated in the contract is to be paid to the injured party, regardless of the fluctuations of the market price. However, in commercial transactions the two parties will have talks.

Ashigara-shimo *kôri*.

With regard to the present topic, the amount of money agreed upon is paid by the defaulting party.

Prefectural Industrial Bureau.

If the amount of the price or the damages agreed upon does not conform to the current price, the agreed amount may be subject to change.

Tochigi Prefecture

Prefectural Office.

If the two parties have agreed upon a sum of money payable for breach, the stipulated amount is to be paid, regardless of whether it conforms to the current price or not.

Shimo-tsuga *kôri* and Samukawa *kôri*.

The sum agreed upon is to be paid by the defaulting party, irrespective of the current price, when the amount of price or damages to be recovered for a breach is stipulated in the contract.

Ashikaga *kôri* and Yanada *kôri*.

We have never heard of such a case in the textile trade. In the silk trade, one-tenth of the contract price is recovered from the defaulting party. For instance, in the case of goods whose contract price is ¥100, ¥10 is awarded to the injured party, even though the current price rises to ¥110 or falls to ¥90.

Mie Prefecture

Suzuka *kôri*.

The sum agreed upon is not subject to change, regardless of whether or not it conforms to the current price, if the two parties have agreed upon the amount payable for breach.

Ichishi *kôri*.

The amount of money stipulated in the contract is recovered, without fail.

Nabari *kôri* and Iga *kôri*.

If the injured party does not suffer any loss owing to the fluctuations of the market price, the defaulting party is not required to pay the damages. However, when the agreed sum does not compensate the injured party for his actual loss, additional damages need to be paid.

Kita-muro *kôri*.

The sum stipulated for in the contract is subject to change, depending upon the fluctuations of the market price.

Aichi Prefecture

Nakajima *kôri*.

The sum agreed upon is recovered from the defaulting party.

Nagoya Ward.

At the time of recovery, the two parties will meet and calculate the amount of the actual loss which is to be paid by the defaulting party.

Chita *kôri*.

The two parties will have talks in the case of fluctuations of the market price.

Minami-shidara *kôri*.

The sum agreed upon is paid, regardless of the market price.

Atsumi *kôri*.

The two will talk about the matter.

Kaitô *kôri* and Kaisai *kôri*.

No definite answer can be given, since such a case has never been heard of.

Aichi *kôri*.

If the amount of money payable for breach is agreed upon in the contract, the sum is not subject to change, irrespective of the current price.

Niwa *kôri* and Haguri *kôri*.

The amount agreed upon is to be recovered, regardless of the actual loss, when the sum of money payable by the defaulting party for breach is agreed upon in the contract.

SHIZUOKA PREFECTURE

Prefectural Office.

The two parties will estimate the actual loss which is to be recovered, depending upon the circumstances.

Udo *kôri* and Abe *kôri*.

If the fluctuations of the market price are reasonable and unavoidable, the amount agreed upon is subject to change.

Inasa *kôri* and Aratama *kôri*.

It depends upon the contract.

Kamo *kôri* and Naka *kôri*.

The sum of money agreed upon in the contract is recovered from the party in default.

GIFU PREFECTURE

Mugi *kôri*.

The sum agreed upon in the contract is recovered from the defaulting party in most cases. However, the two parties sometimes have talks in the case of a great fluctuation of the market price.

Ampachi *kôri*.

The amount stipulated in the contract is to be paid to the injured party, according to the practice here.

Fuwa *kôri*.

The amount agreed upon is not subject to change.

Atsumi *kôri*, Kagami *kôri* and Katagata *kôri*.

If the amount of damages or price has been fixed in the contract, the sum agreed upon is to be paid, regardless of the current price.

Tagi *kôri* and Kami-ishizu *kôri*.

The amount provided for in the contract is subject to change.

Ôno *kôri* and Ikeda *kôri*.

Answer missing.

Haguri *kôri* and Nakajima *kôri*.

The two parties will have talks in most cases if the market price fluctuates.

Ena *kôri*.

The sum originally agreed upon in the contract is not subject to change, regardless of the current price.

Kamo *kôri*.

The sum agreed upon may not be changed, if the amount of price or damages payable in the case of breach is stipulated for in the contract.

Kani *kôri*.

The agreed amount is recovered without exceptions.

Atsumi *kôri*, Gifu Twonship.

The sum provided for in the contract is to be awarded to the injured party, irrespective of the current price.

Ôgaki.

The sum originally agreed upon is to be recovered from the defaulting party, according to the practice here.

Ena *kôri*, Nakatsugawa Village.

The agreement regarding the sum is executed.

Shimo-ishizu *kôri*, Takasu Township.

When the one party asks the other party to change the amount owing to fluctuations of the market price, but is rejected, the sum agreed upon is paid.

Haguri *kôri*, Takegahana Village.

The two parties will estimate the actual loss by the current price, if the amount of price or damages agreed upon does not conform to the current price.

Yamagata *kôri*, Takatomi Village.

The sum originally agreed upon may not be changed.

Mugi *kôri*, Kôzuchi Village.

The sum of money to compensate the injured party for his loss agreed upon in the contract is paid.

Haguri *kôri*, Kasamatsu Village.

Regarding the present matter, the two parties will have talks.

Fuwa *kôri*, Tarui Village.

The sum agreed upon in the contract is recovered from the defaulting party, according to the practice here.

Ôno *kôri*, Miwa Village.

The two parties will have talks.

Ampachi *kôri*, Gôdo Village.

The amount of money agreed upon is to be recovered, regardless of the current price.

Tagi *kôri*, Shimada Village.

Answer missing.

Ena *kôri*, Iwa Village.

When the amount agreed upon does not conform to the amount required to compensate the injured party for his actual loss, the lesser sum of the two is paid.

Toki *kôri*, Takayama Village.

The sum agreed upon is to be paid, regardless of the fluctuations of the market price, according to the practice here.

Kani *kôri*, Mitake Village.

The amount agreed upon is to be recovered from the defaulting party.

Ena *kôri*, Akechi Village.

The amount stipulated for in the contract is not subject to change, irrespective of the fluctuations of the market price.

Mugi *kôri*, Seki Village.

The two will talk about the matter, if the agreed amount does not conform to the sum required by the injured party to compensate for his loss.

Ôno *kôri*, Takayama Township.

The two parties will have talks to estimate the actual loss, which amount is paid, regardless of the sum agreed upon.

Motosu *kôri*, Kitagata Village.

The amount agreed upon is paid, regardless of the fluctuations of the market price.

Kamo *kôri*, Ôta Village.

If the amount agreed upon does not conform to the actual loss, the lesser amount of the two is to be awarded to the injured party.

Kaisai *kôri* and Shimo-ishizu *kôri*.

Regarding the present topic, the two parties will have talks depending upon the current price.

Gujô *kôri.*

No definite answer is to be given.

Topic 7: If an Obligor Repays His Debt before It Falls Due, Is He Still Supposed to Pay the Interest That Would Accrue between the Date of the Repayment and the Original Date of Maturity? Or, Is the Obligation of the Payment of the Interest Supposed to Extend No Further Than the Day When the Repayment Is Made?

TOKYO METROPOLIS

Soy Wholesalers.[1]

We know of no such example.

Sugar Wholesalers.

Such a business contract supposedly is concluded on the condition that the money should be paid back with interest. In such cases, the obligation of repayment extends no further than the day when repayment of the principal is made.

Dried Bonito Wholesalers.

A settlement will be reached by mutual agreement.

Medicine Wholesalers.

A reasonable amount of interest should be paid.

Paper Wholesalers (*Kiu-kumi*).[2]

As circumstances require, a suitable settlement will be found.

Oil Wholesalers.

The obligation to pay interest will not extend beyond the day repayment of the principal is made.

Stone Wholesalers.

As far as our practice is concerned, loans are not made against interest.

Porcelain Wholesalers.

Unless other arrangements are made in the contract, the obligation to pay interest will not extend beyond the day repayment of the principal is made.

Fuel Wholesalers.

Unless other arrangements are made in the contract, the obligation to pay interest will not extend beyond the day repayment of

[1] *Shôyu donya-kumiai.*

[2] *Kiu-kumi kami-donya.*

the principal is made.

Paper Wholesalers (*Shôkai-kumi*).[1]

The obligation to pay interest will not extend beyond the day repayment of the principal is made.

Rice Traders.[2]

When money is lent or borrowed, interest is calculated by the day. When repayment is made before it is due, the obligation to pay interest ends. When money is loaned by the month, interest for the agreed upon period is due. As for the lending of goods, there is a variety of cases and the terms of repayment should be provided for in the contract.

Salt Wholesalers.

The obligation to pay interest will not extend beyond the day repayment of the principal is made.

Timber Wholesalers.

It will be left to the creditor's discretion.

Timber Traders.[3]

The same as in the preceding answer.

Timber Traders (*Senju*).[4]

It will be left to the creditor's discretion.

Matting Wholesalers.

Regarding the principal in the present topic, an agreement will be made between the two.

Saké Wholesalers.[5]

The obligation to pay interest will not extend beyond the day repayment of the principal is made.

Drapery Wholesalers.

There are no established practices.

Saké Wholesalers.

The obligation to pay interest expires on the day or in the month when the repayment of the principal is made.

Lime and Shell Wholesalers.

There will be a mutual consultation as the occasion demands. In other words, there is no established practice.

[1] *Shôkai-kumi kami-donya.*

[2] *Beikoku sangyô-kumiai.*

[3] *Zaimoku tôsei-kumiai.*

[4] *Senju zaimoku-kumiai.*

[5] *Sake-rui-donya.*

Mosquito Net Wholesalers.

Regarding the obligation to pay interest, the two will have a talk to make an agreement.

Copper and Iron Wholesalers.

There will be a mutual consultation as the occasion demands. In other words, there is no established practice.

Fuel Wholesalers (*Umite-kumi*).[1]

The obligation to pay interest will not extend beyond the day repayment of the principal is made.

Kôjimachi Ward.

According to our practice, the obligation to pay interest will not extend beyond the day repayment of the principal is made.

Nihombashi Ward.

When credit is granted for a certain number of months, the obligation to pay interest expires on the last day of the month in which repayment of principal is made. When credit is granted in terms of days, the obligation expires on the day when that repayment is made. Sometimes, however, the obligor pays interest for the whole period when such an agreement has been made beforehand.

Kyôbashi Ward.

There is an obligation to pay interest on the period up until the original due date.

Yotsuya Ward and Ushigome Ward.

Unless the debtor obtains the lender's consent, there is an obligation to pay interest on the period up until the original due date.

Asakusa Ward.

The credit usually is granted for a certain number of days. Unless it is granted for a certain number of months, the obligation to pay interest expires on the day the payment of the principal is made.

Honjo Ward.

The obligation to pay interest will not extend beyond the day repayment of the principal is made.

Ebara *kôri*.

The obligation to pay interest will not extend beyond the day repayment of the principal is made.

Higashi-tama *kôri* and Minami-toshima *kôri*.

[1] *Umite-kumi shintan-donya.*

When a debt is repaid before it is due, the obligation to pay further interest is usually waived.

Kita-toshima *kôri*.

When a debt is repaid before it is due, with the consent of the lender, interest for the remaining period is usually waived.

Minami-adachi *kôri*.

There is an obligation to pay interest on the period up until the original due date.

Shitaya Ward.

The obligation to pay interest will not extend beyond the day repayment of the principal is made.

Kanda Ward.

Unless interest is calculated daily, interest must be paid for the remainder of the month; that is, even if the debt is repaid in the middle of the month, interest must be paid for the whole of the month. In some cases, the lender may ask for all of the interest and deduct it from the principal beforehand. This practice is called *tenri*. Once the matter has been agreed to by contract, the debtor can never expect his prepaid interest to be returned, even if he repays the loan before the agreed upon date.

Akasaka Ward and Azabu Ward.

If the lender agrees to receive the principal before it is due, he usually cannot ask for interest for the period after repayment.

Hongô Ward.

Usually, there is an obligation to pay interest on the period up until the original due date.

CHIBA PREFECTURE

Awa *kôri*, Hei *kôri*, Asai *kôri* and Nagasa *kôri*.

No answer.

Katori *kôri*.

No answer.

Yamabe *kôri* and Muza *kôri*.

No answer.

Unakami *kôri* and Sôsa *kôri*.

No answer.

Higashi-katsushika *kôri*.

The obligation to pay interest will not extend beyond the day repayment of the principal is made.

IBARAKI PREFECTURE

Nishi-katsushika *kôri* and Sashima *kôri.*

The obligation to pay interest will not extend beyond the day repayment of the principal is made.

KANAGAWA PREFECTURE

Miura *kôri.*

In our town of Uraga, there has never been such a business practice.

Tachibana *kôri.*

The payment of interest usually ends when the repayment of principal is made.

Kita-tama *kôri.*

The obligation to pay interest will not extend beyond the day repayment of the principal is made.

Ashigara-shimo *kôri.*

The obligation to pay interest ends when the principal is repaid.

Prefectural Industrial Bureau.

The obligation to pay interest will not extend beyond the day the repayment of the principal is made. However, if the contract specifies that interest be against the whole period agreed upon beforehand, then that amount of interest must be paid.

TOCHIGI PREFECTURE

Prefectural Office.

The obligation to pay interest will not extend beyond the day the repayment of the principal is made.

Shimo-tsuga *kôri* and Samukawa *kôri.*

The obligation to pay interest will not extend beyond the day the repayment of the principal is made.

Ashikaga *kôri* and Yanada *kôri.*

Usually, the obligation to pay interest will not extend beyond the day the repayment of the principal is made.

MIE PREFECTURE

Suzuka *kôri.*

The obligation to pay interest will not extend beyond the day the repayment of the principal is made.

Ichishi *kôri.*

The obligation to pay interest will not extend beyond the day the repayment of the principal is made.

Nabari *kôri* and Iga *kôri.*

The obligation to pay interest will not extend beyond the day the repayment of the principal is made.

Kita-muro *kôri*.

If the lender agrees to receive the principal, he cannot expect interest for the remainder of the period.

AICHI PREFECTURE

Nakajima *kôri*.

The obligation to pay interest will not extend beyond the day repayment of the principal is made.

Nagoya Ward.

The obligation to pay interest will not extend beyond the day repayment of the principal is made.

Chita *kôri*.

There will be a mutual consultation as the occasion demands. In other words, there is no established practice.

Minami-shidara *kôri*.

The obligation to pay interest will not extend beyond the day repayment of the principal is made.

Atsumi *kôri*.

There is an obligation to pay interest on the period up until the original due date.

Kaitô *kôri* and Kaisai *kôri*.

It is seldom that the obligation to pay interest does not extend beyond the day repayment of the principal is made.

Aichi *kôri*.

The obligation to pay interest will not extend beyond the day repayment of the principal is made.

Niwa *kôri* and Haguri *kôri*.

There is an obligation to pay interest on the period up until the original due date. The reason is that an obligor, if the interest rate is high, will leave it unrepaid to his obligee, and he, if the rate is low, will repay him with money borrowed from another person.

SHIZUOKA PREFECTURE

Prefectural Office.

The obligation to pay interest will not extend beyond the day repayment of the principal is made.

Udo *kôri* and Abe *kôri*.

The obligation to pay interest will not extend beyond the day repayment of the principal is made.

Inasa *kôri* and Aratama *kôri*.

These matters should be specified in the contract.

Kamo *kôri* and Naka *kôri*.

The obligation to pay interest will not extend beyond the day repayment of the principal is made.

Saya *kôri* and Kitô *kôri*.

No answer.

GIFU PREFECTURE

Mugi *kôri*.

The obligation to pay interest will not extend beyond the day repayment of the principal is made.

Ampachi *kôri*.

According to our business practice, the obligation to pay interest will not extend beyond the day repayment of the principal is made.

Fuwa *kôri*.

The obligation to pay interest will not extend beyond the day repayment of the principal is made.

Atsumi *kôri*, Kagami *kôri* and Katagata *kôri*.

There is an obligation to pay interest on the period up until the original due date. But sometimes, with the lender's consent, the obligation to pay interest does not extend beyond the day repayment of the principal is made.

Tagi *kôri* and Kami-ishizu *kôri*.

The obligation to pay interest will not extend beyond the day repayment of the principal is made.

Ôno *kôri* and Ikeda *kôri*.

There is a variety of cases.

Haguri *kôri* and Nakajima *kôri*.

The obligation to pay interest will not extend beyond the day repayment of the principal is made.

Ena *kôri*.

The obligation to pay interest will not extend beyond the day repayment of the principal is made.

Kamo *kôri*.

The obligation to pay interest will not extend beyond the day repayment of the principal is made.

Kani *kôri*.

If the lender receives the principal before it is due, the obligation to pay interest will not extend beyond the day repayment of the principal is made.

Atsumi *kôri*, Gifu Township.

There is an obligation to pay interest on the period up until the original due date. By agreement, however, sometimes the obligation to pay interest will not extend beyond the day repayment of the principal is made.

Ôgaki.

According to our business practice, the obligation to pay interest will not extend beyond the day repayment of the principal is made.

Ena *kôri*, Nakatsugawa Village.

The lender is free to accept or reject repayment before it is due. Whether interest should be paid for the whole period agreed upon beforehand, or whether it should be paid only up until the day of the repayment, is a matter to be decided by the lender.

Shimo-ishizu *kôri*, Takasu Township.

Usually, there is an obligation to pay interest on the period up until the original due date. With business in the money market being slow, however, the lender may sometimes agree to receive repayment before it is due without asking for interest against the remaining period.

Haguri *kôri*, Takegahana Village.

There will be mutual consultation as the occasion demands. In other words, there is no established practice.

Haguri *kôri*, Takatomi Village.

The obligation to pay interest will not extend beyond the day repayment of the principal is made.

Mugi *kôri*, Kôzuchi Village.

The obligation to pay interest will not extend beyond the day repayment of the principal is made.

Haguri *kôri*, Kasamatsu Village.

Our answer usually is as given in the second half of the topic.

Fuwa *kôri*, Tarui Village.

The obligation to pay interest will not extend beyond the day repayment of the principal is made.

Ôno *kôri*, Miwa Village.

The obligation to pay interest will not extend beyond the day repayment of the principal is made.

Ampachi *kôri*, Gôdo Village.

The obligation to pay interest will not extend beyond the day repayment of the principal is made.

Tagi *kôri*, Shimada Village.

No answer.

Ena *kôri*, Iwa Village.

The obligation to pay interest will not extend beyond the day repayment of the principal is made.

Kamo *kôri*, Hosome Village.

As a rule, there is an obligation to pay interest on the period up until the original due date. However, the lender usually will return some part of the paid interest.

Toki *kôri*, Takayama Village.

The obligation to pay interest will not extend beyond the day repayment of the principal is made.

Kani *kôri*, Mitake Village.

The obligation to pay interest will not extend beyond the day repayment of the principal is made.

Ena *kôri*, Akechi Village.

The obligation to pay interest will not extend beyond the day repayment of the principal is made.

Mugi *kôri*, Seki Village.

The obligation to pay interest will not extend beyond the day repayment of the principal is made.

Ôno *kôri*, Takayama Village.

When repayment is made before it is due, the lender asks that interest be paid for the remainder of the period as provided by the contract.

Motosu *kôri*, Kitagata Village.

The obligation to pay interest will not extend beyond the day repayment of the principal is made.

Kamo *kôri*, Ôta Village.

The obligation to pay interest will not extend beyond the day repayment of the principal is made.

Kaisai *kôri* and Shimo-ishizu *kôri*.

Usually, there is an obligation to pay interest on the period up until the original due date. With business in the money market being slow, however, the lender may sometimes agree to receive repayment before it is due without asking for interest against the remaining period.

Gujô *kôri*.

The obligation to pay interest will not extend beyond the day repayment of the principal is made.

Topic 8: When a Contract Is Rescinded Due to Negligence[1] on the Part of an Obligor, and Goods Which Have Already Been Delivered to the Obligee Are Returned to the Obligor, Is He Bound to Accept the Goods, as They Are Returned, If They Are Fewer Than the Amount Delivered or If They Are Impaired through No Fault of the Obligee; or May Compensation Be Claimed for the Damage?

If the Goods Are to Be Returned to the Obligee by the Obligor, Are Goods Which Are Reduced in Quantity or Damaged to Be Returned as They Are; or Should Compensation Be Paid for the Damage?

TOKYO METROPOLIS

Soy Wholesalers.[2]

When a contract is rescinded due to negligence on the part of an obligor, the goods are to be returned to him. He must accept them as they are and cannot claim compensation for damage. The situation described in the latter half of the topic is not known among us.

Sugar Wholesalers.

In the case when a contract is rescinded due to negligence on the part of an obligor and goods which have already been delivered to the obligee are returned, any reduction in quantity or damage to the goods is solely due to negligence on the part of the obligee. This also applies to goods to be returned to the obligee. In any case, there should be a good deal of compensation. If the goods decrease in weight while they are stored, and if the two parties foresee the decrease in weight in advance, our answer will go beyond the scope of your question.

Dried Bonito Wholesalers.

If the goods are reduced in quantity or damaged through no act of the obligee, compensation should be made by the seller.

Medicine Wholesalers.

The obligor must accept the goods as they are returned.

Paper Wholesalers (*Kiu-kumi*).[3]

[1] *Okotari.*

[2] *Shôyu donya-kumiai.*

[3] *Kiu-kumi kami-donya.*

If the obligor breaks a contract, he should pay a sizeable amount of compensation.

Oil Wholesalers.

Such a case is unknown among us.

Stone Wholesalers.

If the goods have already been delivered to the obligee, he should pay a considerable amount of compensation even if the loss is not his fault. As for the second situation, some compensation should be paid.

Porcelain Wholesalers.

If only a small quantity of goods is missing or damaged, the obligor will accept the loss. If the quantity is large, he will ask the obligee to pay part of it. The same practice applies to goods to be returned to the obligee.

Fuel Wholesalers.

With regard to goods to be returned to the obligor as described here, each producing district has its own business standard. Take the example of the large-sized charcoal sack, *ôtaba*, in Mitsukaidô.[1] A special standard is set at such and such *shaku*[2] for measuring the circumference of the sack, excepting knots. But in Hitachi,[3] there is another standard, since a sack from a certain district measures such and such *kan*[4] in weight, or such and such *shaku* in length. If the goods to be returned have become very different from the general standard, the obligor, taking into consideration the prices at the time when he delivered the goods, will decide on the amount of compensation and make the obligee pay it.

Paper Wholesalers (*Shôkai-kumi*).[5]

The obligee must pay compensation. When the goods are returned to him, compensation should be paid by the obligor in the same way.

Rice Traders.[6]

If the goods have been reduced in quantity or damaged through no fault of the obligee, the obligor shall accept the loss. This is

[1] Mitsukaidô, name of a place in Ibaraki Prefecture.

[2] *Shaku*, length of 30.3 centimeters.

[3] Hitachi, name of an area in northern Ibaraki Prefecture.

[4] *Kan*, weight of 3.759 kilograms.

[5] *Shôkai-kumi kami-donya.*

[6] *Beikoku sangyô-kumiai.*

just the same as the case seen in the private rules for pawnbrokers about losses caused by rats, fire or robbery. The same applies to the second question.

Salt Wholesalers.

The obligee must pay compensation. The same applies to the second question.

Timber Wholesalers.

Final settlement will be arranged in talks between the two parties.

Timber Traders.[1]

When a contract is rescinded due to negligence on the part of obligor, and goods delivered to him have been reduced in quantity or damaged, the settlement will be arranged in talks between the two parties. As for the second question, the matter will be settled through talks.

Timber Traders (*Senju*).[2]

Final settlement can be arranged only through negotiation between the two parties.

Matting Wholesalers.

When a contract is rescinded due to negligence on the part of an obligor, he cannot claim compensation even if the goods have been reduced in quantity or damaged. The same applies to the second question.

Saké Wholesalers.[3]

If the goods have been reduced in quantity or damaged, the obligee must pay compensation.

Drapery Wholesalers.

Such practices as these are unknown.

Tobacco Wholesalers.

The case will be settled by talks between the two parties. Therefore, there is no established practice.

Saké Wholesalers.

No such business practice is known among us.

Lime and Shell Wholesalers.

There will be negotiations between the two parties. There is no

1 *Zaimoku tôsei-kumiai.*

2 *Senju zaimoku-kumiai.*

3 *Sake-rui donya.*

established practice.

Mosquito Net Wholesalers.

When a contract is rescinded due to negligence on the part of a seller, he cannot claim compensation, even if the goods have been reduced in quantity or damaged. The same applies to the second question.

Copper and Iron Wholesalers.

If such a case as this occurs, it should be settled by friendly talks between the two parties because it has been caused by the negligence of both parties.

Fuel Wholesalers (*Umite-kumi*).[1]

When the goods have been slightly reduced in quantity or damaged due to negligence on the part of an obligor, he cannot make the obligee pay compensation, although there may be special circumstances to be considered. This is quite natural, because the situation was caused by negligence on the part of the obligor himself. The same applies to the second question if the loss is due to negligence on the part of the obligee. If the reduction or impairment is not the fault of the buyer, it is quite another question.

Kôjimachi Ward.

When a contract is rescinded due to negligence on the part of an obligor, he cannot claim compensation immediately. Compensation should be paid in the case of goods to be returned to an obligee.

Nihombashi Ward.

There is no need to pay compensation. If the reduction or damage has occurred because of his own negligence, the seller has no right to claim compensation. Of course this rule does not apply to traders who have dealt with each other for a long time.

Kyôbashi Ward.

Regarding the first question, the obligor is responsible for the loss. No answer can be given to the second.

Yotsuya Ward and Ushigome Ward.

No answer is given.

Asakusa Ward.

Regarding the first question, according to our practice, the return of goods which have already been delivered will never be demanded. A case such as that in the second question is unknown among us.

[1] *Umite-kumi shintan-donya.*

Honjo Ward.

When a contract is rescinded due to negligence on the part of an obligor, and goods which have already been delivered to the obligee are returned, the goods cannot be immediately accepted and compensation cannot be claimed if they have been reduced in quantity or damaged through no fault of the obligee. In contrast, compensation should be claimed as long as the goods remain in the obligor's hands.

Ebara *kôri*.

When a contract is rescinded due to negligence on the part of an obligor, and goods which have already been delivered to the buyer are returned, the seller will not immediately accept the goods or claim compensation. If goods to be returned to the obligee have been reduced in quantity or impaired, the obligor should pay compensation.

Higashi-tama *kôri* and Minami-toshima *kôri*.

When a contract is rescinded due to negligence on the part of an obligor and goods which have already been delivered to the obligee are returned, the obligor will not immediately accept them regardless of whether or not the damage is the fault of the obligee. The obligee must pay full or partial compensation. If goods returned to the obligee have been reduced in quantity or damaged, the obligor should pay compensation.

Kita-toshima *kôri*.

Not knowing of a case such as this, we cannot give an answer.

Minami-adachi *kôri*.

As regards the first question, the obligee must pay compensation. The answer to the second question is as stated above.

Shitaya Ward.

When a contract is rescinded due to negligence on the part of an obligor, and goods which have already been delivered to the obligee are returned, the obligor should pay compensation if the goods have been reduced in quantity or damaged through no fault of the obligee. If goods to be returned to the obligee have been reduced in quantity or damaged, the obligor must also pay compensation, according to our practice.

Kanda Ward.

When examination shows goods delivered and received to be reduced in quantity or damaged, compensation should be paid whether or not the loss is due to negligence on the part of the keeper of the goods.

Akasaka Ward and Azabu Ward.

When the reduction or damage has occurred because of negligence on the part of the obligor, he cannot demand compensation. As for goods to be returned to the obligee, the obligor must pay compensation even if the damage is due to negligence on the part of the obligee.

Hongô Ward.

In the case of the first question, the obligee should pay compensation. In the second, the obligor should pay.

CHIBA PREFECTURE

Awa *kôri*, Hei *kôri*, Asai *kôri* and Nagasa *kôri*.

Unless the reduction or impairment is the fault of the obligee, he cannot be made to pay compensation. This is because it was the obligor's failure to deliver the remaining goods that caused the obligee to rescind the contract. If the goods have been lost for an acceptable reason, for example, due to fire or flood, the obligor must pay the compensation himself.

Katori *kôri*.

When a contract is rescinded due to negligence on the part of an obligor and the goods have been reduced in quantity or damaged, it is quite clear that the obligee is completely free of responsibility and need not pay compensation. Only when there is something doubtful and unclear about his conduct must he pay compensation.

Yamabe *kôri* and Muza *kôri*.

The obligee must pay compensation.

Unakami *kôri* and Sôsa *kôri*.

When the goods are reduced in quantity or damaged through no fault of an obligee, the obligor must accept the goods as they are.

Higashi-katsushika *kôri*.

If a contract is rescinded by an obligee, the obligor will have no choice but to accept the goods. If goods to be returned to an obligee have been reduced in quantity or damaged, the obligor will have to pay the compensation.

IBARAKI PREFECTURE

Nishi-katsushika *kôri* and Sashima *kôri*.

When the goods are reduced in quantity or impaired through no fault of an obligee, he cannot evade paying compensation for the damage. The obligor must pay compensation in the case referred to in the second question.

KANAGAWA PREFECTURE

Miura *kôri.*

Regarding the first question, even if there has been some reduction or damage, no compensation will be claimed. As to the second, when goods are returned to the obligee, compensation will be claimed for any damage, according to the amount of loss.

Tachibana *kôri.*

Regarding the first question, the goods will be accepted as they are. As to the second, when goods are returned to the obligee, some compensation will be claimed for any loss.

Kita-tama *kôri.*

When a contract is rescinded due to negligence on the part of an obligor and goods which have already been delivered to an obligee are reduced in quantity or damaged, the obligor cannot make the obligee pay compensation if the loss is not caused by the obligee's act. If goods returned to the obligee have been reduced in quantity or damaged, the obligor, needless to say, should pay compensation. In many cases, however, the obligor has to inform his obligee of what reduction or damage has been caused by his careless mistake and pay him a sizable amount of compensation.

Ashigara-shimo *kôri.*

With regard to the first and second questions, the obligor is responsible in either case.

Prefectural Industrial Bureau.

Even if the reduction or damage is not the fault of an obligee, compensation should be paid to an obligor. The goods should not be returned as they are.

TOCHIGI PREFECTURE

Prefectural Office.

If a contract is rescinded due to negligence on the part of an obligor, he should accept the goods as they are. If goods are to be returned to the obligee, a good deal of compensation should be paid.

Shimo-tsuga *kôri* and Samukawa *kôri.*

Regarding the first question, when a contract is rescinded due to negligence on the part of an obligor, and goods which have already been delivered to an obligee are reduced in quantity or damaged through no fault of the obligee, our practice is to accept the goods as they are. As to the second, if goods to be returned to the obligee are reduced in quantity or damaged, the obligor should pay compensation.

Ashikaga *kôri* and Yanada *kôri.*

Regarding the first question, suppose an obligor has received an order from a buyer for 100 rolls of cloth and has delivered 50 of them, promising the remainder by such and such day. After that he fails to deliver the remainder by the promised date, and the obligee (buyer) returns 40 rolls, not 50. This is not the fault of the obligee, but nevertheless, he must pay compensation. If the reduction or damage is small in amount, however, the seller cannot make the buyer pay compensation. Cases such as that referred to in the second question are unknown in textiles. (Tiny cloth samples are used in negotiating transactions.) Even if the cancellation is due to negligence on the part of an obligor, the same thing applies, if the particular local practice is not much different from that in most places.

MIE PREFECTURE

Suzuka *kôri.*

When a contract is rescinded due to negligence on the part of an obligor, and goods which have already been delivered to an obligee are reduced in quantity or damaged through no fault of the obligee, the obligor will either accept them as they are or make the obligee pay compensation. When goods to be returned to the obligee are reduced in quantity or damaged, the same applies.

Ichishi *kôri.*

The goods will be accepted as they are. As for the second case, compensation should be claimed.

Nabari *kôri* and Iga *kôri.*

Since the reduction in quantity or damage is due to the obligor's negligence, the obligee need not pay compensation unless he has caused the loss intentionally. If goods returned to the obligee are reduced in quantity or damaged, compensation should be claimed for the loss.

Kita-muro *kôri.*

When the reduction in quantity or damage is not the fault of an obligee, an obligor can demand compensation if the damage occurred while the goods were in the obligee's hands. If goods are to be returned to an obligee, the obligor should pay compensation.

AICHI PREFECTURE

Nakajima *kôri.*

It is the obligor's loss.

Nagoya Ward.

Regarding the first question, after investigating the situation, the obligor should reach a decision which takes consideration of the obligee's views. As to the second, if the damage has occurred due to his own negligence, he should pay compensation. If the damage is due to unavoidable circumstances, the two parties should discuss the matter.

Chita *kôri.*

In either case, if the goods are reduced in quantity or damaged, compensation should be claimed. With regard to goods to be returned to the obligee, compensation should be paid, according to our practice here. In some special cases, however, no compensation will be claimed.

Minami-shidara *kôri.*

When the goods are reduced in quantity or damaged, the obligee must pay compensation even if he did not cause the damage. The second question is answered as above.

Atsumi *kôri.*

When the damage is done due to the obligor's negligence, all the loss should be accepted by him. If the goods to be returned are reduced in quantity or damaged, compensation should also be paid by him.

Kaitô *kôri* and Kaisai *kôri.*

The goods should be accepted unconditionally. No compensation will be claimed. As for the second question, the goods should be accepted without reserve. There is no compensation for the damage.

Aichi *kôri.*

When the goods are reduced in quantity or damaged, an obligor will not make the obligee pay compensation, unless the obligee has caused the damage. When goods to be returned to the obligee are reduced in quantity or damaged, the obligor is bound to pay compensation.

Niwa *kôri* and Haguri *kôri.*

When a contract is rescinded due to negligence on the part of an obligor and goods which have already been delivered to the obligee are returned, the obligor must accept the goods as they are, if they are reduced in quantity or damaged through no fault of the obligee. As for goods to be returned to the obligee, if they are reduced in quantity or damaged, they will not be returned without conditions. Compensation should be paid for the damage.

SHIZUOKA PREFECTURE

Prefectural Office.

The answer to the first question is as stated in the first half of the present topic, and that to the second, as stated in the second half.

Udo *kôri* and Abe *kôri*.

If the reduction in quantity or damage is solely due to the obligor's negligence, he must pay for the damage, since he is responsible for the cancellation of the contract. If cancellation resulted from other causes and if the reduction in quantity or damage is due to a willful mistake by either party, it is quite natural that the party responsible for the damage should pay compensation. The answer to the second question is almost the same as above.

Inasa *kôri* and Aratama *kôri*.

In the first case, the goods will be accepted as they are. In the second case, they will be returned to the obligee.

Kamo *kôri* and Naka *kôri*.

When a contract is rescinded due to negligence on the part of an obligor, and goods which have already been delivered to an obligee are returned, the obligor can demand compensation, even if the reduction in quantity or damage is not the fault of the obligee. If goods to be returned to the obligee are reduced in quantity or damaged, the obligor must pay compensation.

Saya *kôri* and Kitô *kôri*.

No answer is given.

GIFU PREFECTURE

Mugi *kôri*.

When a contract is rescinded due to negligence on the part of an obligor, and the goods are reduced in quantity or damaged through no fault of the obligee, the latter has no obligation to pay compensation. If goods to be returned to an obligee are reduced in quantity, the obligor must pay compensation.

Ampachi *kôri*.

In such a case the obligor will have to accept the goods unconditionally, because the damage is due to his own negligence. With regard to the second question, the obligor can make the compensation for the loss.

Fuwa *kôri*.

Regarding the first question, there is no compensation for the damage. Compensation should be paid in the case referred to in the second question.

Atsumi *kôri*, Kagami *kôri* and Katagata *kôri*.

Regarding the first question, the loss is the obligor's. As to the second, if the goods are reduced in quantity or damaged, compensation should be paid by the obligor.

Tagi *kôri* and Kami-ishizu *kôri*.

Even if the goods are reduced in quantity or damaged through no fault of the obligee, the obligor cannot make the obligee pay compensation. As for goods to be returned to the obligee, the obligee will demand partial compensation if they are reduced in quantity or damaged. In all the four situations described above, appropriate steps will be taken as circumstances require.

Ôno *kôri* and Ikeda *kôri*.

There is no established practice in this locality. When the goods are reduced in quantity or damaged through no fault of an obligee, it is quite natural that the obligor cannot demand compensation. As for goods to be returned to an obligee, it is a matter of course that the obligor should pay compensation for the damage.

Haguri *kôri* and Nakajima *kôri*.

Regarding the first question, compensation cannot be claimed. In the case referred to in the second, it can be.

Ena *kôri*.

Regarding the first question, the goods should be accepted unconditionally. As for the second, if goods to be returned to an obligee are reduced in quantity or damaged, compensation should be paid.

Kamo *kôri*.

When a contract is rescinded due to negligence on the part of an obligor, and goods which have already been delivered to an obligee are returned, the obligee need not pay compensation if they have been reduced in quantity or damaged through no fault of his own. As to goods to be returned to the obligee, the obligor should pay compensation if they have been reduced in quantity or damaged.

Kani *kôri*.

The kind of case referred to in the first question is unknown here. However, there would be no choice but to accept the goods unconditionally. As for the second question, compensation should be paid.

Atsumi *kôri*, Gifu Township.

Regarding the first question, the goods should be accepted without any compensation. As to the second, if the reduction in quantity or damage was caused intentionally by the obligor, he should pay compensation. If not, he should return the goods to the obligee without paying any compensation.

Ôgaki.

The reduction in quantity or damage is due to the obligor's own negligence, so he must accept the goods unconditionally. As regards the second question, the obligor must compensate.

Ena *kôri*, Nakatsugawa Village.

The damage is due solely to the obligor's negligence. He cannot make his innocent obligee pay compensation. In the second question, the damage is due to the obligor's negligence. He should pay compensation.

Shimo-ishizu *kôri*, Takasu Township.

In such a case, the goods should be accepted without reserve. If goods to be returned to the obligee have been reduced in quantity or damaged, they should be repaired and returned just as they have been delivered.

Haguri *kôri*, Takegahana Village.

In these cases, neither of them will be able to demand compensation.

Yamagata *kôri*, Takatomi Village.

Even if the goods have been reduced in quantity or damaged, no compensation will be paid. As for goods to be returned to the obligee, compensation should be paid if they are reduced in quantity or damaged.

Mugi *kôri*, Kôzuchi Village.

When a contract is rescinded due to negligence on the part of an obligor and goods which have already been delivered to an obligee are reduced in quantity or damaged through no fault of an obligee, they should be accepted unconditionally. When a contract is rescinded due to negligence by either party and the goods to be returned are reduced in quantity or damaged, neither of them will demand compensation.

Haguri *kôri*, Kasamatsu Village.

As for the first question, no compensation can be claimed. It can be, however, in the case of the second.

Fuwa *kôri*, Tarui Village.

In the case of the first question, no compensation should be paid. Compensation should be paid in the case of the second.

Ôno *kôri*, Miwa Village.

If the goods have been reduced in quantity or damaged through no fault of the obligee, they will not be accepted unconditionally. As for the second case, compensation should be paid.

Ampachi *kôri*, Gôdo Village.

The goods will be accepted without reserve. The obligee will return them as they are.

Tagi *kôri*, Shimada Village.

No answer is given.

Ena *kôri*, Iwa Village.

Regarding the first question, even if the goods are reduced in quantity or damaged, they will be accepted unconditionally. As to the second, if goods to be returned to the obligee are reduced in quantity or damaged, the obligor should pay compensation.

Kamo *kôri*, Hosome Village.

When a contract is rescinded due to negligence on the part of an obligor, and goods which have already been delivered to an obligee are reduced in quantity or damaged through no fault of the obligee, the obligor should accept them without reserve. As for goods to be returned to an obligee, if they are reduced in quantity or damaged, the obligor should pay compensation.

Toki *kôri*, Takayama Village.

Our answer to the first question is that he must compensate for it. As for the second, compensation should be paid.

Kani *kôri*, Mitake Village.

In this case, the obligee need not compensate. When goods are to be returned to the obligee, compensation should be paid.

Ena *kôri*, Akechi Village.

Regarding the first question, the goods should be accepted without reserve. With respect to the second, as for goods to be returned to the obligee, compensation should be paid if they are reduced in quantity or damaged.

Mugi *kôri*, Seki Village.

When the goods are reduced in quantity or damaged through no fault of the obligee, the obligor will pay compensation. When the goods are reduced in quantity or damaged through no fault of the obligor, the obligee will pay compensation.

Ôno *kôri*, Takayama Township.

When the goods are reduced in quantity due to negligence on the part of the obligee, it is the obligor's loss. Even if the damage is not his fault, the obligee must pay for part of the damage if the goods are kept sealed or locked. As for the damage, since it is due to the carelessness of the obligee, he must compensate for part of it. As for goods to be returned to the obligee, the same thing applies.

Motosu *kôri*, Kitagata Village.

When a contract is rescinded due to negligence on the part of an obligor and goods which have already been delivered to the obligee are returned, the obligor should accept them without reserve even if they have been reduced in quantity or damaged through no fault of the obligee. As for goods to be returned to the obligee, the obligor must pay compensation if they are reduced in quantity or damaged.

Kamo *kôri*, Ôta Village.

When a contract is rescinded due to negligence on the part of an obligor and goods which have already been delivered to an obligee are reduced in quantity or damaged through no fault of the obligee, the obligor will not demand compensation. As for goods to be returned to the obligee, the obligor will sometimes pay compensation if they are reduced in quantity or damaged.

Kaisai *kôri* and Shimo-ishizu *kôri*.

In this case, the loss is due to the obligor's negligence, so he should accept them unconditionally. As for goods to be returned to the obligee, he should pay compensation as described above if they are reduced in quantity or damaged due to his own negligence.

Gujô *kôri*.

The questions cannot be answered.

Appendix: If Any Expense Is Incurred through Negligence[1] on the Part of the Obligor, Should the Amount Be Added to the Price as Provided in Topic 2? Or Should a Separate Claim Be Made?

CHIBA PREFECTURE

Awa *kôri*, Hei *kôri*, Asai *kôri* and Nagasa *kôri*.

No claim will be made for any expense incurred for this reason. However, in some cases the obligor may fix the price anticipating that some expense will arise later. If there is any expense for employment of a messenger because he is doing business with a person in a distant place, he may at any rate ask the other party for the wages separately.

Katori *kôri*.

The expense will not be added to the price as provided in Topic 2, nor will a claim for the payment be made separately.

Yamabe *kôri* and Muza *kôri*.

Payment of the expense will be claimed separately.

Unakami *kôri* and Sôsa *kôri*.

If any expense is incurred through negligence on the part of the obligor, a separate claim will be made for its payment.

[1] *Okotari*.

CHAPTER IV
PENALTY FOR BREACH OF CONTRACT

Topic 1: May Payment of Penalty for Breach of Contract Be Demanded Only When It Has Been Stipulated Beforehand in the Contract? When There Is No Previous Agreement to the Effect, May Such Penalty Be Demanded When an Occasion Therefor Occurs? May It Happen That Penalty for Breach of Contract[1] and Compensation for Damage in General[2] Are Cumulative and the Use of One Remedy Is Not Taken to Exclude or Waive the Use of Another?

TOKYO METROPOLIS

Soy Wholesalers.[3]

Unless provided beforehand, penalty will not be demanded. As for the second question, penalty for breach of contract and compensation for damage in general will be demanded cumulatively.

Sugar Wholesalers.

When payment of penalty for breach of contract is stipulated beforehand in the contract, and it is demanded, the claim should be accepted. If not stipulated in the contract, the two parties should discuss the matter each time such an occasion occurs.

Dried Bonito Wholesalers.

Such a practice is unknown.

Medicine Wholesalers.

It should be done as the party not in breach of contract pleases.

Paper Wholesalers (*Kiu-kumi*).[4]

Payment of penalty should be made just as stipulated beforehand in the contract.

Oil Wholesalers.

Such a practice is unknown.

Stone Wholesalers.

Unless stipulated in the contract, payment of penalty for breach

[1] *Iyaku-kin.*

[2] *Songai-baishô.*

[3] *Shôyu donya-kumiai.*

[4] *Kiu-kumi kami-donya.*

of contract cannot be demanded. It is our practice that either penalty or compensation for damage in general is demanded exclusively.

Fuel Wholesalers.

Unless stipulated in the contract beforehand, payment of penalty for default will not be demanded. As for compensation for damages in general, however, this will be demanded on the basis of the situation, regardless of whether or not it is stipulated beforehand in the contract.

Porcelain Wholesalers.

Unless provided beforehand in the contract, payment of penalty for breach of contract cannot be demanded. It cannot be demanded separately.

Paper Wholesalers (*Shôkai-kumi*).[1]

Only when it is stipulated beforehand in the contract, can it be demanded. When not so stipulated, it can never be demanded. As for the second question, payment will not be demanded.

Rice Traders.[2]

Unless stipulated beforehand in the contract, payment of penalty for default cannot be demanded. Compensation for damanges in general also cannot be demanded, unless there is a firm agreement.

Salt Wholesalers.

Penalty for default is unknown among us. If the breach of contract has caused damages, however, payment should be demanded.

Timber Wholesalers.

Unless stipulated beforehand in the contract, penalty cannot usually be demanded. But there may be a variety of cases. As for the second question, compensation will not be demanded.

Timber Traders.[3]

Just as answered above.

Timber Traders (*Senju*).[4]

Just as answered above.

Matting Wholesalers.

Unless stipulated beforehand in the contract, penalty cannot be demanded. Penalty and damages in general shall not be demanded

[1] *Shôkai-kumi kami-donya.*

[2] *Beikoku sangyô-kumiai.*

[3] *Zaimoku tôsei-kumiai.*

[4] *Senju zaimoku-kumiai.*

separately.

Saké Wholesalers.[1]

Unless stipulated beforehand in the contract, penalty cannot be demanded. As for the second question, compensation will not be demanded.

Drapery Wholesalers.

There is no established practice.

Tobacco Wholesalers.

There will be consultation between the two parties when necessary. There is no established practice.

Saké Wholesalers.

There is no established business practice.

Lime and Shell Wholesalers.

Consultation will be held between the two parties when necessary. No practice is established.

Mosquito Net Wholesalers.

Penalty for breach of contract can be demanded only when it is stipulated beforehand in the contract. It includes the damages in general.

Copper and Iron Wholesalers.

Penalty for default, as well as the compensation for damages in general, can be demanded only when it is stipulated beforehand in the contract. When it is not stipulated beforehand, it cannot be demanded even when an occasion therefor occurs.

Fuel Wholesalers (*Umite-kumi*).[2]

Only when it is stipulated beforehand in the contract, can penalty be demanded. If not so stipulated, it will be demanded when such an occasion occurs. In some cases, penalty for default and damages in general are demanded separately, but this is unusual.

Kôjimachi Ward.

Unless stipulated beforehand in the contract, only actual damages may be demanded. Penalties for breach of contract and compensation for damages in general should never be demanded separately.

Nihombashi Ward.

Even if penalty is not stipulated beforehand in the contract, it can often be demanded, depending on the damage. According to

[1] *Sake-rui-donya.*

[2] *Umite-kumi shintan-donya.*

our business practice, there seems to be no difference between penalty for breach of contract and compensation for damages in general.

Kyôbashi Ward.

Regarding the first question, only when penalty is stipulated beforehand in the contract can it be demanded. As for the second, only payment of penalty for breach of contract can be demanded.

Yotsuya Ward and Ushigome Ward.

Unless stipulated beforehand in the contract, penalty cannot be demanded when such an occasion occurs.

Asakusa Ward.

Regarding the first question, such a case as that described in the second half cannot be permitted. As for the second question, upon payment of penalty for breach of contract, the defaulting party shall be released from the responsibility for the damages.

Honjo Ward.

If payment of penalty for breach of contract is stipulated beforehand in the contract, of course it can be demanded. If not stipulated beforehand, it can be demanded if necessary. Payment of penalty for breach of contract and compensation for damages in general can never be demanded separately. In most cases, either of them will do.

Ebara *kôri*.

If penalty for breach of contract is stipulated beforehand in the contract, it can be demanded. If it is not, the party not in default may request the defaulting party to pay it, if circumstances require, but cannot force him to pay. Payment of penalty and compensation for damages in general can be demanded separately.

Higashi-tama *kôri* and Minami-toshima *kôri*.

No payment of penalty for breach of contract can be demanded when it is not stipulated beforehand in the contract. Penalty for default is one thing, and compensation for damages in general is another. The two can be demanded cumulatively.

Kita-toshima *kôri*.

If payment of penalty for breach of contract is stipulated beforehand, it should be demanded. If not, it will be requested, each time such an occasion occurs. Payment of penalty for breach of contract and compensation for damages in general will be demanded separately, according to the particular case. There is no established practice.

Minami-adachi *kôri.*

Regarding the first question, only when it is stipulated beforehand, shall penalty be demanded. As for the second, only penalty for default shall be demanded.

Shitaya Ward.

As for our business transactions, penalty for breach of contract can be demanded, whether or not it is stipulated beforehand. Once penalty for breach of contract is made, compensation for other damages cannot be demanded, according to the practice here.

Kanda Ward.

If it is not stipulated beforehand in the contract, penalty cannot be demanded. When payment of penalty for breach of contract is made, compensation for damages in general will not be demanded separately, unless provided beforehand in the contract.

Akasaka Ward and Azabu Ward.

Only when it is stipulated beforehand can penalty be demanded. When it is not, proper steps will be taken according to the situation. There is no established practice. Penalty for breach of contract and damages will sometimes be demanded separately.

Hongô Ward.

Penalty for breach of contract can be demanded only when it is stipulated beforehand in the contract. In the domestic trade, however, it is a good commercial custom for us traders to respect each other's credit and honor. Even if one party has paid penalty for breach of contract as required in the original contract, the other one will rarely accept them. Of course, this is not the case with a speculative trader[1] or a wicked trader.[2] Penalty and damages in general may be demanded separately. Such a case, however, has never been heard of.

CHIBA PREFECTURE

Awa *kôri*, Hei *kôri*, Asai *kôri* and Nagasa *kôri.*

If payment of penalty for breach of contract is not stipulated beforehand in the contract, it can not be demanded. Even if it is demanded when not stipulated, probably payment of the interest will be all that can be expected. Penalty is included in compensa-

[1] *Tôki-shô.*

[2] *Kan-shô.*

tion for damages in general. Therefore, the two cannot be demanded separately.

Katori *kôri.*

Payment of penalty for breach of contract can be demanded when an occasion therefor occurs, even if it is not stipulated beforehand in the contract. Penalty for breach of contract and compensation for damages in general cannot be demanded separately.

Yamabe *kôri* and Muza *kôri.*

Payment of penalty for breach of contract can be demanded only when stipulated beforehand in the contract. Compensation for damages in general can be demanded when penalty is not stipulated beforehand. Penalty for breach of contract and compensation for damages in general cannot be demanded separately.

Unakami *kôri* and Sôsa *kôri.*

Payment of penalty for breach of contract can be demanded only when it is stipulated beforehand in the contract. Penalty for breach of contract and compensation for damages in general can be demanded separately.

Higashi-katsushika *kôri.*

Even when payment of penalty for breach of contract is not stipulated beforehand in the contract, it can be demanded. In a few cases, however, payment of penalty for breach of contract and compensation for damages in general can be demanded separately.

IBARAKI PREFECTURE

Nishi-katsushika *kôri* and Sashima *kôri.*

When payment of penalty for breach of contract is stipulated beforehand in the contract, it can be demanded. Payment of penalty for breach of contract and compensation for damages in general can be demanded separately.

KANAGAWA PREFECTURE

Miura *kôri.*

Regarding the first question, when it is agreed beforehand, penalty can be demanded. As for the second, when it is not stipulated beforehand, it cannot be demanded.

Tachibana *kôri.*

When it is provided for beforehand, penalty can be demanded. When it is not stipulated beforehand, it can be demanded if such an occasion occurs. When penalty for breach of contract is demanded, compensation for damages in general cannot be demanded.

Kita-tama *kôri.*

Only when it is stipulated beforehand in the contract can penalty be demanded; otherwise it cannot be demanded. Whether penalty for breach of contract and compensation for damages should be demanded separately or not depends on the original contract. Since there is no established practice, we do not know how it is done.

Ashigara-shimo *kôri.*

This depends on the original contract. If it has not been stipulated beforehand, penalty cannot be demanded. As for the second question, it seems to be quite natural that the defaulting party should compensate for any damages.

Prefectural Industrial Bureau.

As to payment of penalty for breach of contract, even if it is not stipulated beforehand, it can still be demanded when such an occasion occurs. Damages can sometimes be demanded in addition.

TOCHIGI PREFECTURE

Prefectural Office.

Only when penalty for breach of contract is stipulated beforehand can it be demanded, according to our business practice here. Compensation for damages can be demanded separately whether or not penalty for breach of contract is claimed. According to our prevailing practice, however, compensation for damages is usually included in the penalty for breach of contract.

Shimo-tsuga *kôri* and Samukawa *kôri.*

Regarding the first question, penalty for breach of contract can be demanded only when it is agreed beforehand in the contract. As for the second, penalty for breach of contract and compensation for damages are not cumulative. Only one of the two can be demanded.

Ashikaga *kôri* and Yanada *kôri.*

No answer is given.

MIE PREFECTURE

Suzuka *kôri.*

When payment of penalty for breach of contract is stipulated beforehand in the contract, it can be demanded. Penalty for breach of contract and compensation for damages cannot be cumulative.

Ichishi *kôri.*

Only when it is agreed beforehand can it be demanded. If the penalty for breach of contract is demanded, compensation for damages will not be demanded.

Nabari *kôri* and Iga *kôri*.

Only when it is stipulated beforehand can it be demanded. According to our business practice, the penalty for breach of contract is taken as liquidated damages. Penalty and damages cannot be demanded cumulatively.

Kita-muro *kôri*.

If it is stipulated beforehand, naturally penalty can be demanded. If not, it can be demanded at the amount of about 10 percent of the contracted price. Penalty for breach of contract and compensation for damages can be demanded cumulatively.

Aichi Prefecture

Nakajima *kôri*.

Only when it is stipulated beforehand can it be demanded. If not, it cannot be.

Nagoya Ward.

Only when it is stipulated beforehand can it be demanded. Otherwise, it cannot be. Penalty for breach of contract and compensation for damages can be demanded cumulatively.

Chita *kôri*.

Only when it is stipulated beforehand can it be demanded. However, the amount will be reduced if circumstances warrant. We have no established business practice as to whether or not payment of damages for breach of contract and compensation for damages should be demanded cumulatively. It seems that either one of the two is enough.

Minami-shidara *kôri*.

It can be demanded whether or not it is stipulated beforehand. Only payment of penalty for breach of contract seems to be demanded. Sometimes, however, compensation for damages is demanded in addition.

Atsumi *kôri*.

If payment of damages for breach of contract is not stipulated beforehand in the contract, it will be demanded in proportion to the amount of money involved. If such payment is demanded, compensation for damages will not be.

Kaitô *kôri* and Kaisai *kôri*.

If payment of damages for breach of contract is not stipulated beforehand, it cannot be demanded. As to the second question, the two can be demanded separately.

Aichi *kôri.*

When penalty for breach of contract is not stipulated beforehand, it cannot be demanded. Penalty and damages in general can be demanded separately.

Niwa *kôri* and Haguri *kôri.*

Only when payment of penalty for breach of contract is stipulated beforehand can it be demanded. When not, it cannot be. If such payment is demanded, compensation for damages will not be.

SHIZUOKA PREFECTURE

Prefectural Office.

Regarding the first question, it can be demanded, whether or not it is stipulated beforehand. As for the second, penalty for breach of contract is accepted as including compensation for damages.

Udo *kôri* and Abe *kôri.*

Even if it is not stipulated beforehand, it can be demanded when such an occasion occurs. As for the second question, the two can be demanded cumulatively.

Inasa *kôri* and Aratama *kôri.*

Payment of penalty for breach of contract can be demanded only when it is stipulated beforehand in the contract. In addition to such payment, compensation for damages can be demanded.

Kamo *kôri* and Naka *kôri.*

Penalty for default can be demanded only when it is stipulated beforehand in the contract. No separate compensation for damages due to breach of contract will be demanded if the penalty for breach of contract is demanded.

Saya *kôri* and Kitô *kôri.*

When penalty for breach of contract is not stipulated beforehand, it cannot be demanded. But compensation for damages can be demanded.

GIFU PREFECTURE

Mugi *kôri*

Regarding the first question, it is our practice that penalty for breach of contract can be demanded only when it is stipulated beforehand in the contract. As for the second, cumulative compensation for damages can be demanded.

Ampachi *kôri.*

Penalty for breach of contract can be demanded only when it is stipulated beforehand in the contract. When such payment is demanded, compensation for damages cannot be demanded.

Fuwa *kôri*.

Penalty for breach of contract sometimes can be demanded whether or not it is stipulated beforehand in the contract. Regarding the second question, it is our practice that only one of them can be demanded.

Atsumi *kôri*, Kagami *kôri* and Katagata *kôri*.

Regarding the first question, if it is not stipulated beforehand, penalty cannot be demanded. As for the second, both can sometimes be demanded.

Tagi *kôri* and Kami-ishizu *kôri*.

Penalty for breach of contract can be demanded only when it is stipulated beforehand. If it is not stipulated beforehand, it can never be demanded when such an occasion occurs. Penalty and compensation for damages will not be demanded separately.

Ôno *kôri* and Ikeda *kôri*.

We have no established practice about penalty for default, since it depends upon the nature of the contract. Neither is there an established practice as to whether payment of damages and compensation for damages can be demanded cumulatively.

Haguri *kôri* and Nakajima *kôri*.

Both cases are exactly as described here.

Ena *kôri*.

Regarding the first question, both cases described here can be seen. The answer to the second question is as stated above.

Kamo *kôri*.

Penalty for breach of contract can be demanded only when it is stipulated beforehand. When penalty is demanded, compensation for damages cannot be.

Kani *kôri*.

Regarding the first question, penalty shall be paid only when it is stipulated beforehand; otherwise, in practice, it is impossible to get it, even if it is demanded. As for the second, though the nature of the penalty differs as stated above, from that of damages, we have never heard of a case where both of the two are paid cumulatively.

Atsumi *kôri*, Gifu Township.

As for the first question, it can be demanded. Regarding the second, they cannot be demanded separately.

Ôgaki.

Penalty for breach of contract can be demanded only when it is stipulated beforehand. Compensation for damages cannot be demanded in addition to the penalty.

Ena *kôri*, Nakatsugawa Village.

Only when it is stipulated beforehand can penalty for breach of contract be demanded. If it is not, only compensation for damages can be. As for the second question, neither can be demanded separately.

Shimo-ishizu *kôri*, Takasu Township.

Whether or not it is stipulated beforehand, penalty can sometimes be demanded, depending on the case. If compensation for damages is stipulated beforehand in the contract, a decision regarding a penalty for breach of contract will be reached in talks between the two parties.

Haguri *kôri*, Takegahana Village.

If it is stipulated beforehand, payment can sometimes be demanded. Even if not, it may be demanded when such an occasion occurs. It seems to be difficult to demand both compensation for damages and payment of damages.

Yamagata *kôri*, Takatomi Village.

Penalty can be demanded only when it is stipulated beforehand. Penalty for breach of contract and compensation for demages can be demanded cumulatively.

Mugi *kôri*, Kôzuchi Village.

Penalty can be demanded only when it is stipulated beforehand. Although in some cases it is demanded when it is not so stipulated, this is a question of morality. Penalty for breach of contract and compensation for damages cannot be demanded cumulatively.

Haguri *kôri*, Kasamatsu Village.

Yes, that is right.

Fuwa *kôri*, Tarui Village.

Whether or not it is stipulated beforehand, penalty can sometimes be demanded, depending on the case. As for the second question, only one of them can be demanded.

Ôno *kôri*, Miwa Village.

Penalty can be demanded only when it is stipulated beforehand.

Penalty for breach of contract and compensation for damages are sometimes demanded separately.

Ampachi *kôri*, Gôdo Village.

Penalty can normally be demanded only when it is stipulated beforehand. However, it can be demanded when such an occasion occurs even if it is not stipulated beforehand. Penalty for breach of contract and compensation for damages can never be demanded cumulatively.

Tagi *kôri*, Shimada Village.

No answer is given.

Ena *kôri*, Iwa Village.

Regarding the first question, penalty for breach of contract can be demanded only when it is stipulated beforehand in the contract. As for the second, if penalty is demanded, compensation of damages cannot be.

Kamo *kôri*, Hosome Village.

If penalty for breach of contract is stipulated beforehand in the contract, it will be demanded without fail. If it is not, it cannot be demanded. When penalty is demanded, compensation for damages cannot be demanded.

Toki *kôri*, Takayama Village.

The answer to the first question is that it can be demanded. In the case of the second question, it cannot be.

Kani *kôri*, Mitake Village.

Penalty for breach of contract can be demanded only when it is stipulated beforehand. Compensation for damages cannot be demanded in addition to the penalty.

Ena *kôri*, Akechi Village.

Both cases are exactly as described.

Mugi *kôri*, Seki Village.

If it is not stipulated beforehand, a decision will be reached each time circumstances require. A case such as that referred to in the second question has never been seen.

Ôno *kôri*, Takayama Township.

Whether or not it is stipulated beforehand, penalty for breach of contract can sometimes be demanded. Penalty is one thing, and compensation for damages is another. The two, therefore, can be demanded separately.

Motosu *kôri*, Kitagata Village.

Only when penalty for breach of contract is stipulated beforehand in the contract can it be demanded. Penalty and compensation for damages can sometimes be demanded separately.

Kamo *kôri*, Ôta Village.

Only when the penalty for breach of contract is stipulated beforehand can it be demanded. Otherwise, it cannot be.

Kaisai *kôri* and Shimo-ishizu *kôri*.

Not only when it is stipulated beforehand, but even when penalty for breach of contract is not stipulated beforehand in the contract, it can often be demanded. When penalty and compensation for damages are demanded separately, the amount of penalty will be decided upon in talks between the two parties.

Gujô *kôri*.

Yes, that is right.

Topic 2: When the Obligee Receives Penalty for Breach of Contract, Does He Still Have the Right to Demand Performance of the Contract, or Is This Right Nullified?[1]

TOKYO METROPOLIS

Soy Wholesalers.[2]

He still has the right to demand fulfillment of the contract.

Sugar Wholesalers.

When the obligee receives penalty for breach of contract, his right is nullified.

Dried Bonito Wholesalers.

When the obligee receives penalty for breach of contract, his right is nullified.

Medicine Wholesalers.

When the obligee receives penalty for breach of contract, his right is nullified.

Paper Wholesalers (*Kiu-kumi*).[3]

The two parties will handle the matter as they think fit.

Oil Wholesalers.

Cases such as this cannot be found among us.

Stone Wholesalers.

When the obligee receives payment of damages for breach of contract, his right is nullified unless otherwise provided.

Fuel Wholesalers.

Such a case will usually go to trial. The right to demand fulfillment of the contract, however, is usually nullified when the obligee receives penalty for breach of contract.

Porcelain Wholesalers.

This sort of case cannot be found among us.

Paper Wholesalers (*Shôkai-kumi*).[4]

When the obligee receives penalty for breach of contract, his right to demand fulfillment of the contract is nullified.

Rice Traders.[5]

[1] *Shômetsu.*

[2] *Shôyu-donya-kumiai.*

[3] *Kiu-kumi kami-donya.*

[4] *Shôkai-kumi kami-donya.*

[5] *Beikoku sangyô-kumiai.*

Even after the obligee has received penalty for breach of contract, his right to demand fulfillment of the contract is not nullified as long as the contract remains effective.

Salt Wholesalers.

His right is nullified.

Timber Wholesalers.

He still has the right.

Timber Traders.[1]

As stated above.

Timber Traders (*Senju*).[2]

As stated above.

Matting Wholesalers.

When the obligee receives penalty for breach of contract, his right to demand fulfillment of the contract is nullified.

Saké Wholesalers.[3]

Even after the obligee has received penalty for breach of contract, he sometimes retains the right to demand fulfillment of the contract.

Drapery Wholesalers.

Such a practice cannot be seen among us.

Tobacco Wholesalers.

The matter is settled as circumstances require. There is no established practice.

Saké Wholesalers.

Such a business practice cannot be seen among us.

Lime and Shell Wholesalers.

As circumstances require. There is no established practice.

Mosquito Net Wholesalers.

When the obligee receives penalty for breach of contract, his right to demand performance of the contract is nullified.

Copper and Iron Wholesalers.

If the obligee receives penalty for default, his right to demand fulfillment of the contract is nullified, whatever breach of contract there may have been.

Fuel Wholesalers (*Umite-kumi*).[4]

We have never heard that he still has the right.

[1] *Zaimoku tôsei-kumiai.*

[2] *Senju zaimoku-kumiai.*

[3] *Sake-rui-donya.*

[4] *Umite-kumi shintan-donya.*

Kôjimachi Ward.

When the obligee receives penalty for breach of contract, he can no longer demand fulfillment of the contract.

Nihombashi Ward.

According to our business practice, his right to demand fulfillment of the contract is nullified if he receives penalty for breach of contract.

Kyôbashi Ward.

When the obligee receives penalty for breach of contract, his right to demand performance of the contract is nullified.

Yotsuya Ward and Ushigome Ward.

When the obligee receives penalty for breach of contract, whether he still has the right to demand fulfillment of the contract depends on its original provisions.

Asakusa Ward.

When the obligee receives penalty for breach of contract, his right to demand fulfillment of the contract is nullified.

Honjo Ward.

When the obligee receives penalty for default, he retains the right to demand fulfillment of the contract.

Ebara *kôri*.

When the obligee receives penalty for breach of contract, he retains the right to demand fulfillment of the contract.

Higashi-tama *kôri* and Minami-toshima *kôri*.

When the obligee receives penalty for breach of contract, his right to demand fulfillment of the contract is nullified.

Kita-toshima *kôri*.

We have already answered this in Topic 1.

Minami-adachi *kôri*.

In this case his right to demand fulfillment of the contract is nullified.

Shitaya Ward.

When the obligee receives penalty for breach of contract, it is quite natural that his right to demand fulfillment of the contract should be nullified.

Kanda Ward.

When the obligee receives penalty for breach of contract, his right to demand fulfillment of the contract is nullified.

Akasaka Ward and Azabu Ward.

The provisions of the original contract determine whether the right to demand fulfillment of the contract remains in effect or is nullified.

Hongô Ward.

He retains the right to demand fulfillment of the contract.

CHIBA PREFECTURE

Awa *kôri*, Hei *kôri*, Asai *kôri* and Nagasa *kôri*.

If the buyer breaks a contract, his deposit will go to the seller. When the seller receives the deposit, he can no longer demand compensation for damages.

Katori *kôri*.

Penalty can never be demanded for breach of contract. Whether or not there is a deposit will be decided in talks between an obligor and an obligee.

Yamabe *kôri* and Muza *kôri*.

Even when not specially provided, the deposit will go to the seller. The deposit is not returned, nor will compensation for damages be demanded.

Unakami *kôri* and Sôsa *kôri*.

If a buyer breaks a contract after delivering a deposit to a seller, the deposit will go to the seller even if this has not been specially provided beforehand. The deposit shall not be returned to the buyer, nor will the seller demand payment of damages for breach of contract.

Higashi-katsushika *kôri*.

The right to demand fulfillment of the contract is nullified.

IBARAKI PREFECTURE

Nishi-katsushika *kôri* and Sashima *kôri*.

When the obligee receives penalty for breach of contract, his right to demand fulfillment of the contract is nullified.

KANAGAWA PREFECTURE

Miura *kôri*.

There is no established practice.

Tachibana *kôri*.

The right to demand fulfillment of the contract is nullified.

Kita-tama *kôri*.

No answer is given.

Ashigara-shimo *kôri*.

It is our business practice that the contract becomes ineffective when payment of penalty for breach of contract is made. However, the obligee may sometimes ask his obligor for fulfillment of the contract in addition.

Prefectural Industrial Bureau.

When the obligee receives payment of penalty for breach of contract, his right to demand fulfillment of the contract is nullified, according to the practice prevailing here.

TOCHIGI PREFECTURE

Prefectural Office.

When the obligee receives payment of penalty for breach of contract, the contract itself is nullified, according to our practice.

Shimo-tsuga *kôri* and Samukawa *kôri*.

When the obligee receives payment of penalty for breach of contract, the remainder of the contract is nullified.

Ashikaga *kôri* and Yanada *kôri*.

The practice of paying penalty for breach of contract is not known in this area. Recently some people, for instance, those at the Ashikaga Chamber of Commerce and Industry, have been discussing the necessity of such a system. However, few people seem to be for the system, because they find it too rigorous.

MIE PREFECTURE

Suzuka *kôri*.

When the obligee receives payment of penalty for breach of contract, he can no longer demand fulfillment of contract.

Ichishi *kôri*.

When the obligee receives penalty for default, his right to demand fulfillment of the contract is nullified.

Nabari *kôri* and Iga *kôri*.

Penalty in contract is regarded as an unusual matter. A sudden rise or fall in the prices of the goods, a possible loss of good sales opportunities, or an urgent need to lay in a stock of the goods would lead us to agree on payment of penalty for breach of contract. Even after payment of penalty has been made, therefore, the right to demand fulfillment remains in effect. In some cases, however, there are still some exceptions to the rule.

Kita-muro *kôri*.

Even after payment of penalty for breach of contract has been made, the right to demand payment seems to continue.

AICHI PREFECTURE

Nakajima *kôri*.

When the obligee receives penalty for breach of contract, his right to demand fulfillment of the contract is nullified.

Nagoya Ward.

In such a case the right to demand fulfillment of the contract is nullified.

Chita *kôri*.

When the obligee receives penalty for breach of contract, his right to demand fulfillment of the contract is nullified.

Minami-shidara *kôri*.

Even after the obligee has received penalty for breach of contract, his right to demand fulfillment of the contract still remains in effect.

Atsumi *kôri*.

When the obligee receives penalty for default, his right to demand fulfillment of the contract is nullified.

Kaitô *kôri* and Kaisai *kôri*.

When the obligee receives penalty for breach of contract, his right to demand fulfillment of the contract is usually nullified.

Aichi *kôri*.

When the obligee receives penalty for breach of contract, he can no longer demand fulfillment of the contract.

Niwa *kôri* and Haguri *kôri*.

When the obligee receives penalty for breach of contract, his right to demand fulfillment of the contract is nullified.

SHIZUOKA PREFECTURE

Prefectural Office.

As stated in the second half.

Udo *kôri* and Abe *kôri*.

The right is nullified.

Inasa *kôri* and Aratama *kôri*.

No answer is given.

Kamo *kôri* and Naka *kôri*.

When the obligee receives penalty for breach of contract, his right to demand fulfillment of the contract is nullified.

Saya *kôri* and Kitô *kôri*.

A contract is still to be fulfilled after an obligee has received penalty for breach of contract, when stipulated in the contract.

In business, however, such a case has never been heard of.

GIFU PREFECTURE

Mugi *kôri.*

When the obligee receives penalty for breach of contract, his right to demand fulfillment of the contract is nullified.

Ampachi *kôri.*

When the obligee receives payment of penalty for default, his right to demand fulfillment of the contract is no longer in effect.

Fuwa *kôri.*

When the obligee receives penalty for breach of contract, according to our practice his right to demand fulfillment of the contract is nullified.

Atsumi *kôri,* Kagami *kôri* and Katagata *kôri.*

In theory, the right to demand fulfillment of the contract should continue in effect. However, since most traders do not like to cause trouble, in most cases the right seems to be nullified.

Tagi *kôri* and Kami-ishizu *kôri.*

When the obligee receives penalty for breach of contract, his right to demand fulfillment of the contract is nullified.

Ôno *kôri* and Ikeda *kôri.*

If specially provided in the original contract, the right to demand fulfillment of the contract will remain in effect even after the obligee has received penalty for breach of contract.

Haguri *kôri* and Nakajima *kôri.*

The right is nullified.

Ena *kôri.*

The right to demand fulfillment of the contract is nullified.

Kamo *kôri.*

When the obligee receives penalty for breach of contract, his right to demand fulfillment of the contract is usually nullified.

Kani *kôri.*

The right is nullified.

Atsumi *kôri,* Gifu Township.

The right to demand fulfillment of the contract is nullified.

Ôgaki.

When the obligee receives penalty for breach of contract, his right to demand fulfillment of the contract no longer remains in effect.

Ena *kôri,* Nakatsugawa Village.

When the obligee receives penalty for breach of contract, his right to demand fulfillment of the contract is no longer in effect.

Shimo-ishizu *kôri*, Takasu Township.

When the obligee receives penalty for breach of contract, his right to demand fulfillment of the contract is nullified.

Haguri *kôri*, Takegahana Village.

When the obligee receives penalty for breach of contract, it will be difficult for him to continue to demand fulfillment of the contract.

Yamagata *kôri*, Takatomi Village.

When the obligee receives penalty for default, his right to demand fulfillment of the contract is nullified.

Mugi *kôri*, Kôzuchi Village.

When the obligee receives penalty for breach of contract, his right to demand fulfillment of the contract is nullified.

Haguri *kôri*, Kasamatsu Village.

The right is nullified.

Fuwa *kôri*, Tarui Village.

When the obligee receives penalty for breach of contract, according to our practice, his right to demand fulfillment of the contract is nullified.

Ôno *kôri*, Miwa Village.

Whether or not the right is nullified depends solely on the original contract.

Ampachi *kôri*, Gôdo Village.

The right to demand performance of contract becomes extinguished.

Tagi *kôri*, Shimada Village.

No answer is given.

Ena *kôri*, Iwa Village.

When the obligee receives penalty for breach of contract, his right to demand fulfillment of the contract is nullified.

Kamo *kôri*, Hosome Village.

When the obligee receives penalty for breach of contract, his right to demand fulfillment of the contract is nullified.

Toki *kôri*, Takayama Village.

The right is nullified.

Kani *kôri*, Mitake Village.

When the obligee receives penalty for default, his right to demand fulfillment of the contract is nullified.

Ena *kôri*, Akechi Village.

The right to demand fulfillment of the contract is nullified.

Mugi *kôri*, Seki Village.

The right is nullified.

Ôno *kôri*, Takayama Township.

When the obligee receives penalty for breach of contract, his right to demand fulfillment of the contract is nullified. However, if the original contract so stipulates, he will retain his right.

Motosu *kôri*, Kitagata Village.

When the obligee receives penalty for breach of contract, naturally his right to demand fulfillment of the contract is nullified.

Kamo *kôri*, Ôta Village.

When the obligee receives penalty for default for breach of contract, the right to demand fulfillment of the contract is nullified.

Kaisai *kôri* and Shimo-ishizu *kôri*.

When the obligee receives payment of penalty for breach of contract, his right to demand fulfillment of the contract is nullified.

Gujô *kôri*.

When the obligee receives payment of penalty for breach of contract, his right to demand fulfillment of the contract is nullified.

CHAPTER V
AGENCY[1]

Topic 1: Is There Any Situation in Which Agency in a Commercial Transaction May Be Assumed by One to Whom No Letter of Attorney[2] Has Been Issued?

TOKYO METROPOLIS

Soy Wholesalers.[3]

A person to whom no letter of attorney has been issued may assume agency in a commercial transaction.

Sugar Wholesalers.

In the case of appointment of an agent in commercial transactions, the power of attorney is not always required, as the case may be. There is no settled practice.

Dried Bonito Wholesalers.

For the convenience of business, one may act as an agent without securing the power of attorney.

Sugar Wholealers.

In some cases, a person to whom no letter of attorney has been issued may assume agency if he is an employee of either of the two parties concerned.

Paper Wholesalers (*Kiu-kumi*).[4]

In a commercial transaction, a person to whom no letter of attorney has been issued may sometimes assume agency.

Oil Wholesalers.

Agency may be assumed.

Stone Wholesalers.

A person to whom no letter of attorney has been issued may assume agency.

Fuel Wholesalers.

In a commercial transaction, a person to whom no letter of attorney has been issued may assume agency. In such a case the agent does not sign his own name or use his own seal, but signs the princi-

[1] *Dairi.*

[2] *Ininjô.*

[3] *Shôyu donya-kumiai.*

[4] *Kiu-kumi kami-donya.*

pal's name and uses his seal.

Porcelain Wholesalers.

A person to whom no letter of attorney has been issued may sometimes assume agency.

Paper Wholesalers (*Shôkai-kumi*).[1]

A person to whom no letter of attorney has been issued may sometimes assume agency.

Rice Traders.[2]

In theory, agency cannot be assumed in such a case. However, a person to whom no letter of attorney has been issued can sometimes assume agency if he is a long-time employee of a store and is trusted by the other store. The provisions on agency so far have not been established; it is not clear who are members of our circles.

Salt Wholesalers.

A person to whom no letter of attorney has been issued may sometimes assume agency.

Timber Wholesalers.

A person to whom no letter of attorney has been issued may sometimes assume agency.

Timber Traders.[3]

A person to whom no letter of attorney has been issued may sometimes assume agency.

Timber Traders (*Senju*).[4]

As stated above.

Matting Wholesalers.

In a commercial transaction a person to whom no letter of attorney has been issued may often assume agency.

Saké Wholesalers.[5]

Such a person may sometimes assume agency.

Drapery Wholesalers.

A person to whom no letter of attorney has been issued may sometimes assume agency. Of course the agent should be a person acceptable to the other party.

Tobacco Wholesalers.

[1] *Shôkai-kumi kami-donya.*

[2] *Beikoku sangyô-kumiai.*

[3] *Zaimoku tôsei-kumiai.*

[4] *Senju zaimoku-kumiai.*

[5] *Sake-rui-donya.*

The two parties will agree on this question as circumstances require. There is no established practice.

Saké Wholesalers.

In a commercial transaction, a trader's credit is an important asset. Anyone whose credit is good will be allowed to assume agency even when he is not carrying a letter of attorney.

Lime and Shell Wholesalers.

No letter of attorney is necessary for commercial transaction and bill-collecting. The agent carries the principal's official business seal[1] or principal's private seal for receipt.[2]

Mosquito Net Wholesalers.

In a commercial transaction, agency is often assumed by a person to whom no letter of attorney has been issued.

Copper and Iron Wholesalers.

In a commercial transaction, a contractor sometimes makes his employee assume agency without issuing a letter of attorney for him.

Fuel Wholesalers (*Umite-kumi*).[3]

A person to whom no letter of attorney has been issued may assume agency if he is an employee or clerk[4] of the contractor.

Kôjimachi Ward.

A person to whom no letter of attorney has been issued may assume agency if he is the chief clerk[5] or an employee[6] of the contractor.

Nihombashi Ward.

According to our usual practice a person to whom no letter of attorney has been issued may assume agency.

Kyôbashi Ward.

A person to whom no letter of attorney has been issued may sometimes assume agency if he is an employee who has been previously introduced to the other party or officially announced to the general public.

Yotsuya Ward and Ushigome Ward.

In a commercial transaction, only a person to whom a letter of

[1] *Shôhô-inkan,* popularly called *Shikiri-in.*

[2] *Kaketori-dai-in.*

[3] *Umite-kumi shintan-donya.*

[4] *Tedai.*

[5] *Bantô.*

[6] *Tedai.*

attorney or a letter of confidence has been issued can assume agency unless he is a contractor's employee always acting as agent in place of the contractor himself.

Asakusa Ward.

A person to whom no letter of attorney has been issued may assume agency.

Honjo Ward.

In a commercial transaction, a person to whom no letter of attorney has been issued can assume agency.

Ebara *kôri*.

Agency in a commercial transaction may sometimes be assumed by a person to whom no letter of attorney has been issued.

Higashi-tama *kôri* and Minami-toshima *kôri*.

In a commercial transaction, a person to whom no letter of attorney has been issued may usually assume agency.

Kita-toshima *kôri*.

In a commercial transaction, agency can be assumed only by a person trusted by his employer. Therefore no letter of attorney is necessary. The employee[1] is to his employer what an official is to his government, and the employer should be liable for any damages done by his employee to himself or to a third party, whether the damage was caused by mistake or intention. How to deal with the employee is a private problem for the employer.

Minami-adachi *kôri*.

A person to whom no letter of attorney has been issued may sometimes assume agency.

Shitaya Ward.

In a commercial transaction, a person such as a manager,[2] chief clerk[3] or employee may usually assume agency without a letter of attorney. It is natural according to the Civil Law that a letter of attorney should be issued if agency is assumed by another person.

Kanda Ward.

In a commercial transaction, a person to whom no letter of attorney has been issued may usually assume agency. Since the beginning of the new era, people began issuing letters of attorney and leaving their transactions to an agent in accordance with the laws and

[1] *Tedai.*

[2] *Shihai-nin.*

[3] *Bantô.*

regulations. For the present, however, such people are very few in number.

Akasaka Ward and Azabu Ward.

A person to whom no letter of attorney has been issued may sometimes assume agency. In some cases, a letter of confidence may be used in place of a letter of attorney.

Hongô Ward.

The wholesaler often sends his chief clerk or another employee to collect bills or purchase goods. If this is called agency, a person to whom no letter of attorney has been issued may usually assume it.

CHIBA PREFECTURE

Awa *kôri*, Hei *kôri*, Asai *kôri* and Nagasa *kôri*.

A person to whom no letter of attorney has been issued may usually assume agency. When a trader sends his employee to collect a large sum of money or to meet the other party's agent, whom his employee has never seen before, the trader will sometimes use a letter of confidence to inform the other party that the agent is acting on his behalf.

Katori *kôri*.

A person to whom no letter of attorney has been issued can assume agency.

Yamabe *kôri* and Muza *kôri*.

A person to whom no letter of attorney has been issued may usually assume agency.

Unakami *kôri* and Sôsa *kôri*.

In a commercial transaction, a person to whom no letter of attorney has been issued may assume agency.

Higashi-katsushika *kôri*.

A person to whom no letter of attorney has been issued may assume agency.

IBARAKI PREFECTURE

Nishi-katsushika *kôri* and Sashima *kôri*.

A person to whom no letter of attorney has been issued may never assume agency.

KANAGAWA PREFECTURE

Miura *kôri*.

A person to whom no letter of attorney has been issued may assume agency.

Tachibana *kôri*.

In a commercial transaction, a person to whom no letter of attorney has been issued can usually assume agency.

Kita-tama *kôri.*

No answer is given.

Ashigara-shimo *kôri.*

An employee to whom no letter of attorney has been issued may sometimes assume ageney.

Prefectural Industrial Bureau.

The business practice here for a commercial transaction is that the authority to assume agency comes not from a letter of attorney but from a written or oral statement. Unless specially provided in laws or regulations, no letters of attorney are necessary.

TOCHIGI PREFECTURE

Prefectural Office.

In a commercial transaction, a person to whom no letter of attorney has been issued can usually assume agency. If the agent is not chief clerk[1] or employee,[2] he should have a letter of attorney.

Shimo-tsuga *kôri* and Samukawa *kôri.*

In a commercial transaction, a person to whom no letter of attorney has been issued cannot assume agency.

Ashikaga *kôri* and Yanada *kôri.*

Here in this district, a letter of attorney is used only for a manager[3] representing a branch office. In addition to the manager, some other employee may be sent to collect bills and purchase goods. They will be selected from reliable longtime employees of the branch office, and no letter of attorney will be issued. An official seal[4] is enough attorney for acting as agent.

MIE PREFECTURE

Suzuka *kôri.*

In a commercial transaction, a person to whom no letter of attorney has been issued may assume agency. In some cases, however, a letter of attorney is necessary.

Ichishi *kôri.*

A person to whom no letter of attorney has been issued may assume agency.

[1] *Bantô.*

[2] *Tedai.*

[3] *Shihai-nin.*

[4] *Shôhô-in.*

Nabari *kôri* and Iga *kôri*.

A person to whom no letter of attorney has been issued may assume agency.

Kita-muro *kôri*.

A person to whom no letter of attorney has been issued may sometimes assume agency.

AICHI PREFECTURE

Nakajima *kôri*.

A person to whom no letter of attorney has been issued may assume agency.

Nagoya Ward.

A person to whom no letter of attorney has been issued may assume agency.

Chita *kôri*.

According to our practice, a person to whom no letter of attorney has been issued may sometimes assume agency.

Minami-shidara *kôri*.

A person to whom no letter of attorney has been issued may sometimes assume agency.

Atsumi *kôri*.

Agency sometimes may be assumed by one to whom no letter of attorney has been issued.

Kaitô *kôri* and Kaisai *kôri*.

A person to whom no letter of attorney has been issued may usually assume agency.

Aichi *kôri*.

In a commercial transaction, a person to whom no letter of attorney has been issued may usually assume agency.

Niwa *kôri* and Haguri *kôri*.

In a commercial transaction, a person to whom no letter of attorney has been issued can usually assume agency. But the agent should be a reliable person of good credit.

SHIZUOKA PREFECTURE

Prefectural Office.

In a commercial transaction, a person to whom no letter of attorney has been issued may assume agency.

Udo *kôri* and Abe *kôri*.

Agency in a commercial transaction is different from that provided in the Civil Law. The agent is usually selected from among persons with close connections who can be trusted. Therefore no letter of attorney is necessary.

Inasa *kôri* and Aratama *kôri*.

No answer is given.

Kamo *kôri* and Naka *kôri*.

If the agent is the principal's chief clerk[1] or employee,[2] or his father or brother, often no letter of attorney is necessary.

Saya *kôri* and Kitô *kôri*.

Agency can be assumed by one to whom no letter of attorney has been issued. However, if the other party wants to have it, it will be issued.

GIFU PREFECTURE

Mugi *kôri*.

According to our practice, a person to whom no letter of attorney has been issued can assume agency.

Ampachi *kôri*.

According to our practice, a person to whom no letter of attorney has been issued can usually assume agency.

Fuwa *kôri*.

A person to whom no letter of attorney has been issued may sometimes assume agency.

Atsumi *kôri*, Kagami *kôri* and Katagata *kôri*.

A person to whom no letter of attorney has been issued may sometimes assume agency.

Tagi *kôri* and Kami-ishizu *kôri*.

In a commercial transaction, a person to whom no letter of attorney has been issued may assume agency. This can be done only through a talk between the two agents representing the principals.

Ôno *kôri* and Ikeda *kôri*.

In a commercial transaction, a person to whom no letter of attorney has been issued may sometimes assume agency.

Haguri *kôri* and Nakajima *kôri*.

A person to whom no letter of attorney has been issued may usually assume agency.

Ena *kôri*.

[1] *Bantô*.

[2] *Tedai*.

Sometimes agency can be assumed.

Kamo *kôri*.

In a commercial transaction, a person to whom no letter of attorney has been issued can assume agency.

Kani *kôri*.

According to our practice, a letter of attorney is often unnecessary.

Atsumi *kôri*, Gifu Township.

Usually no letter of attorney is necessary.

Ôgaki.

According to our practice, a person to whom no letter of attorney has been issued may usually assume agency.

Ena *kôri*, Nakatsugawa Village.

A letter of attorney is seldom necessary. It is subject to the old practice.

Shimo-ishizu *kôri*, Takasu Township.

A person to whom no letter of attorney has been issued may usually assume agency. In such a case, however, some people may have doubts about the transaction if they are not shown some authorization. Then something will be offered as evidence.

Haguri *kôri*, Takegahana Village.

A person to whom no letter of attorney has been issued may sometimes assume agency.

Yamagata *kôri*, Takatomi Village.

It is quite natural that there should be a letter of attorney. However, few people issue it.

Mugi *kôri*, Kôzuchi Village.

In a commercial transaction, a person to whom no letter of attorney has been issued can assume agency.

Haguri *kôri*, Kasamatsu Village.

Usually no letter of attorney is necessary.

Fuwa *kôri*, Tarui Village.

A person to whom no letter of attorney has been issued may sometimes assume agency.

Ôno *kôri*, Miwa Village.

A person to whom no letter of attorney has been issued may sometimes assume agency.

Ampachi *kôri*, Gôdo Village.

A person to whom no letter of attorney has been issued may

assume agency.

Tagi *kôri*, Shimada Village.

No answer is given.

Ena *kôri*, Iwa Village.

A person to whom no letter of attorney has been issued can assume agency.

Kamo *kôri*, Hosome Village.

A person to whom no letter of attorney has been issued can assume agency.

Toki *kôri*, Takayama Village.

In this district, agency is usually assumed by persons to whom no letter of attorney has been issued.

Kani *kôri*, Mitake Village.

A person to whom no letter of attorney has been issued may sometimes assume agency.

Ena *kôri*, Akechi Village.

It can be done.

Mugi *kôri*, Seki Village.

If the agent is an executive or an employee, no letter of attorney is necessary. Other persons must have a letter.

Ôno *kôri*, Takayama Township.

In a commercial transaction, a person to whom no letter of attorney has been issued can assume agency. If the agent is sent far away, he will carry a letter of confidence in place of a letter of attorney.

Motosu *kôri*, Kitagata Village.

In a commercial transaction, a person to whom no letter of attorney has been issued can assume agency.

Kamo *kôri*, Ôta Village.

In a commercial transaction, a person to whom no letter of attorney has been issued can assume agency.

Kaisai *kôri* and Kami-ishizu *kôri*.

A person to whom no letter of attorney has been issued can usually assume agency. In such a case, however, some people may doubt about the transaction, if they are not shown any authorization. Then something will be offered as evidence.

Gujô *kôri*.

In a commercial transaction, a person to whom no letter of attorney has been issued may sometimes assume agency.

Topic 2: In a Business Transaction in Which an Agent Is Acting on Behalf of His Principal,[1] Which One of the Two, the Agent or the Principal, Is Supposed to Assume Directly the Rights and Obligations toward the Other Party?[2]

In the Case of the Other Party Concluding a Transaction with an Agent without Knowledge of the Status of the Latter, What Rights and Obligations Should the Principal Assume toward the Other Party?

TOKYO METROPOLIS

Soy Wholesalers.[3]

In answer to the first question, in a transaction in which an agent acts on behalf of his principal, the agent should assume directly the rights and the obligations. As for the second, if a party concludes a transaction with an agent without knowledge of the status of the latter, the principal should assume directly the rights and the obligations.

Sugar Wholesalers.

In a transaction in which an agent is acting on behalf of his principal, we cannot venture to say which one of the two should assume directly the rights and the obligations; a transaction can only be concluded when the other party puts trust in the two. If a party concludes a transaction with an agent without knowledge of his status, the principal should assume directly the rights and obligations toward that party; the transaction can only be concluded when the party puts trust in the agent and the principal.

Dried Bonito Wholesalers.

Even if an agent is acting in a transaction on behalf of his principal, the principal should assume directly the rights and the obligations toward the other party.

Medicine Wholesalers.

In such a case, the agent should assume directly the rights and the obligations. When the other party concludes a transaction with an agent without knowledge of his status, the agent should again

[1] *Honnin.*

[2] *Aitekata.*

[3] *Shôyu-donya-kumiai.*

assume the rights and obligations.

Paper Wholesalers (*Kiu-kumi*).[1]

Since the agent is acting on behalf of his principal, he should assume directly the rights and obligations. The answer to the second question is as stated above.

Oil Wholesalers.

Regarding the first question, the agent should assume directly the rights and obligations. As for the second, the principle assumes no rights and obligations.

Stone Wholesalers.

Since the agent is acting on behalf of his principal, he, the obligor, should assume directly the rights and obligations toward the other party. The answer to the second question is as stated above.

Fuel Wholesalers.

In a transaction in which an agent acts on behalf of his principal, the principal should assume indirectly, and in some cases, directly the rights and obligations toward the other party. The answer to the second question is as stated above.

Porcelain Wholesalers.

The principal should assume directly the rights and obligations. Even if the other party concludes a transaction with an agent without knowledge of the status of the latter, the principal should assume the rights and obligations.

Paper Wholesalers (*Shôkai-kumi*).[2]

The principal should assume directly the rights and obligations toward the other party. When the other party concludes a transaction with an agent without knowledge of his status, the principal should also assume the rights and obligations.

Rice Traders.[3]

Discussions take place between the two as circumstances require. There is no established practice.

Salt Wholesalers.

The agent should assume directly the rights and obligations.

Timber Wholesalers.

Since a letter of attorney has been issued to an agent, the agent

[1] *Kui-kumi kami-donya.*

[2] *Shôkai-kumi kami-donya.*

[3] *Beikoku sangyô-kumiai.*

should assume directly the rights and obligations. The answer to the second question is as above.

Timber Traders.[1]

Since a letter of attorney has been issued to an agent, the agent is supposed to assume directly the rights and obligations. If a party concludes a transaction with an agent without knowledge of his status, the matter will be determined in the manner stipulated by the letter of attorney.

Timber Traders (*Senju*).[2]

As stated above.

Matting Wholesalers.

When an agent acts in a transaction on behalf of his principal, the principal should assume directly the rights and obligations toward the other party. The answer to the second question is as stated above.

Saké Wholesalers.[3]

In general, the agent should assume directly the rights and obligations.

Drapery Wholesalers.

If an agent who is completely in charge of the business has concluded a transaction on his own responsibility, he should assume directly the rights and obligations. If he is only partially in charge of business,[4] the principal should assume directly the rights and obligations. If the other party concludes a transaction with an agent without knowldge of his status, and if he has identified him as legally acceptable, the answer is the same as above.

Tobacco Wholesalers.

Such a practice as this is unknown among us.

Saké Wholesalers.

Both the principal and the agent should equally assume the rights and obligations. The answer to the second question is as stated above.

Lime and Shell Wholesalers.

The agent should assume the rights and obligations. Regarding the second question, since the agent only acts on behalf of his

[1] *Zaimoku-tôsei-kumiai.*

[2] *Senju zaimoku-kumiai.*

[3] *Sake-rui-donya.*

[4] Then he is called "*Buri-dainin.*"

principal, the principal himself will be asked to deal with any difficulties which occur.

Mosquito Net Wholesalers.

When an agent acts on behalf of his principal in a transaction, the principal himself should assume the rights and obligations. The answer to the second question is the same as above.

Copper and Iron Wholesalers.

In a business transaction, the principal and the agent are sometimes seen as equally assuming the rights and obligations. So there is no established practice. It is our practice that there is no difference between the principal and his agent.

Fuel Wholesalers (*Umite-kumi*).[1]

The agent we refer to here is a person called an employee, *tedai*. He is not a person who is temporarily acting on behalf of his principal. In business, therefore, the agent is supposed to assume directly the rights and the obligations. When the other party concludes a transaction with an agent without knowledge of the status of the latter, and if the agent proves to be the principal's employee, *tedai*, stated above, our answer is the same as above.

Kôjimachi Ward.

When an agent acts in a business transaction on behalf of his principal, the latter should assume all the rights and obligations.

Nihombashi Ward.

The agent should assume the rights and obligations. It does not matter whether the other party knows the status of the agent or not. When a transaction is concluded by an agent, our answer is as stated above.

Kyôbashi Ward.

Regarding the first question, the principal himself should assume the rights and obligations. As for the second, in a transaction concluded by a legally identified agent, all the obligations resulting from the transaction should be assumed by the principal himself.

Yotsuya Ward and Ushigome Ward.

If an agent identified as legally acceptable has concluded a transaction, the agent should assume the rights and obligations as long as he retains his position.

Asakusa Ward.

[1] *Umite-kumi shintan-donya.*

Regarding the first question, the principal should assume directly the rights and obligations. As for the second, in this case the principal is not supposed to assume the rights and obligations.

Honjo Ward.

In a commercial transaction in which an agent has acted on behalf of his principal, the agent should assume directly the rights and obligations. In a case when the other party concludes a transaction with an agent without knowledge of his status, the principal should assume the rights and obligations.

Ebara *kôri.*

In a transaction in which an agent has acted on behalf of his principal, the agent, not the principal, should assume directly the rights and the obligations. In a case when the other party concludes a transaction with an agent without knowledge of his status, the principal should assume the rights and obligations.

Higashi-tama *kôri* and Minami-toshima *kôri.*

As long as an agent retains his position as agent, the rights and obligations of the agent are the same as those of his principal. As to whether they should be assumed directly or indirectly, the principal should assume them a little more directly. Even if the other party concludes a transaction with an agent without knowledge of the status of the latter, they are supposed to assume directly the rights and obligations since they have already concluded the transaction.

Kita-toshima *kôri.*

Our answer has already been given in Topic 1.

Minami-adachi *kôri.*

Regarding the first question, the principal should assume directly the rights and obligations. As for the second, the principal does not assume directly the rights and obligations.

Shitaya Ward.

In a transaction in which an agent acts on behalf of his principal, the principal should assume directly the rights and obligations. Even when the other party concludes a transaction with an agent without knowledge of his status, the principal should assume the rights and obligations.

Kanda Ward.

Our answer to the problem of agency has already been given in Topic 1. As for the questions from Topics 2 to 6, which refer to the relations of an agent with his principal and the other party, we have nothing more to say. According to our present practice, the principal, or a shop-keeper, generally concludes a transaction with the help of his employee, acting as agent.

Akasaka Ward and Azabu Ward.

Regarding the first question, the principal, not the agent, should assume directly the rights and obligations. As for the second, the principal should assume directly the rights and obligations.

Hongô Ward.

In a business transaction in which an agent acts on behalf of his principal, the principal should assume directly the rights and obligations. In the case when the other party concludes a transaction with an agent without knowledge of his status, the principal should assume the obligations, but not the rights, unless the other party knows that the agent is acting in place of, and on behalf of, his principal.

Chiba Prefecture

Awa *kôri*, Hei *kôri*, Asai *kôri* and Nagasa *kôri*.

Since the principal has already made his agent act as agent without giving the latter a letter of attorney, he should assume directly the rights and obligations. However, the conclusion of a transaction may under some circumstances be delayed, for instance, when the agent in charge of the business happens at that time to be out of his shop.

Katori *kôri*.

The principal should assume directly all rights and obligations.

Yamabe *kôri* and Muza *kôri*.

The agent should assume directly the rights and obligations.

Unakami *kôri* and Sôsa *kôri*.

If the principal has made his agent act as agent without giving him any letter of attorney, the principal himself should assume directly the rights and obligations.

Higashi-katsushika *kôri*.

The agent should assume directly the rights and obligations. If the other party concludes a transaction with an agent without knowledge of his status, the agent should assume directly the rights and obligations.

Ibaraki Prefecture

Nishi-katsushika *kôri* and Sashima *kôri*.

The agent should assume directly the rights and obligations. If the other party concludes a transaction with an agent without knowledge of his status, and if the agent concludes the transaction with the other party without informing the latter that he is acting as an agent, the principal does not have to assume directly the rights and obligations, even if that agent has since left his employ.

KANAGAWA PREFECTURE

Miura *kôri.*

Regarding the first question, the agent should assume directly the rights and obligations. As for the second, if the other party concludes a transaction with an agent without knowledge of his status, the principal should assume directly the rights and obligations.

Tachibana *kôri.*

The agent should assume directly the rights and obligations. If the other party concludes a transaction with an agent without knowledge of his status, the principal should assume directly the rights and obligations.

Kita-tama *kôri.*

In a transaction in which an agent is acting on behalf of his principal, the latter should assume directly the rights and obligations, as long as the agent remains within the competence granted by his principal. If the other party concludes a transaction with an agent without knowledge of his status, the principal again should assume the rights and obligations.

Ashigara-shimo *kôri.*

While an agent is acting in a transaction on behalf of his principal, the agent should assume directly the rights and obligations. Regarding the second question, the transaction will be concluded according to the wishes of the other party.

Prefectural Industrial Bureau.

In a transaction, the agent seldom acts on his own. Generally speaking, he acts only as his principal pleases. Therefore, the principal should assume directly the rights and obligations. In fact, we have never seen a case where the other party concludes a transaction with an agent without knowledge of his status.

TOCHIGI PREFECTURE

Prefectural Office.

When an agent acts in a transaction on behalf of his principal (just as, for example, that principal's employee or chief clerk does), the principal should assume directly all the rights and obligations. The answer to the second question is the same as above.

Shimo-tsuga *kôri* and Samukawa *kôri*.

As regards the first question, when an agent acts in a transaction on behalf of his principal, the latter should assume directly the rights and obligations. Regarding the second, if the other party concludes a transaction with an agent without knowledge of his status, the principal again should assume directly the rights and obligations.

Ashikaga *kôri* and Yanada *kôri*.

Regarding the first question, as already indicated in Topic 1, our prevailing practice is that an agent is acting on behalf of his principal even without carrying a letter of attorney. Therefore even in the case when the agent is a principal's branch manager who carries such a letter, the principal should assume the rights and obligations. As for the second question, if the other party concludes a transaction with an agent without knowledge of his status, the principal, not the agent, should assume directly the rights and obligations.

MIE PREFECTURE

Suzuka *kôri*.

In a transaction in which an agent acts on behalf of his principal, the latter should assume directly all the rights and obligations. If the other party concludes a transaction with an agent without knowledge of his status, no one can prove whether it is valid or not. Thus we have no established practice.

Ichishi *kôri*.

If not specially provided for, the principal should assume directly the rights and obligations. As to whether the other party knows the status of the agent or not, there is no difference in the rights and obligations.

Nabari *kôri* and Iga *kôri*.

The principal should assume the rights and the obligations. However he does not, if his chief clerk or employee act in their own names. If the other party concludes a transaction with an agent without knowledge of his status, the principal should assume the rights and obligations toward the other party.

Kita-muro *kôri*.

Having confidence in the principal, the other party, who may never have done business with the principal before, will sometimes conclude a transaction with an agent acting on behalf of the principal, although he is carrying no letter of attorney. Therefore, the principal should assume directly the rights and obligations. Even when the other party concludes a transaction with an agent without knowledge of his status, the principal should assume the rights and obligations.

AICHI PREFECTURE

Nakajima *kôri.*

The rights and obligations toward the other party are considered to be directly assumed by the agent. Even when he is not known as the agent himself, he should assume the rights and obligations, depending upon the case.

Nagoya Ward.

In a transaction in which an agent, such as a chief clerk or an employee, acts on behalf of his principal, the latter should assume the rights and obligations. Whether the other party knows the status of the agent or not, the principal should assume the rights and obligations.

Chita *kôri.*

The principal should assume the rights and obligations. If the other party concludes a transaction with an agent without knowledge of his status, the principal should assume the rights and obligations.

Minami-shidara *kôri.*

The agent should assume the same rights and obligations as the principal does. When the other party does not know the status of the agent, the same holds true.

Atsumi *kôri.*

The agent should assume directly the rights and obligations. The rights and obligations toward the other party are considered assumed not by the principal but by the agent.

Kaitô *kôri* and Kaisai *kôri.*

In general, the principal should assume the rights and obligations.

Aichi *kôri.*

The agent, needless to say, is acting in a transaction on behalf of his principal. It is not the agent but the principal who directly assumes the rights and the obligations. Even though the other party does not know the status of the agent, the principal should assume the rights and obligations.

Niwa *kôri* and Haguri *kôri*.

In a transaction in which an agent acts on behalf of his principal, the agent should assume directly the rights and obligations. If the other party concludes a transaction with an agent without knowledge of his status, the principal does not have to assume the rights and obligations.

SHIZUOKA PREFECTURE

Prefectural Office.

Regarding the first question, the agent should assume the rights and obligations. As for the second, if the other party concludes a transaction with an agent without knowledge of his status, the agent should assume the rights and obligations.

Udo *kôri* and Abe *kôri*.

The agent should assume the rights and obligations. The rights and obligations are assumed directly by the agent and indirectly by the principal.

Inasa *kôri* and Aratama *kôri*.

The agent should assume directly the rights and obligations. If a principal directly accepts an offer in advance from the other party, the principal will inform his agent and ask him to act on his behalf. If the other party concludes a transaction with an agent without knowledge of his status, and if the agent has not done it intentionally, the principal will assume the rights and the obligations. However, if the agent has done it intentionally, the principal should be completely free of any rights and obligations.

Kamo *kôri* and Naka *kôri*.

The agent should assume directly the rights and obligations. The principal lets the agent act directly on his behalf.

Saya *kôri* and Kitô *kôri*.

There is no established practice.

GIFU PREFECTURE

Mugi *kôri*.

Regarding the first question, the principal should assume directly the rights and obligations. As for the second, if the other party concludes a transaction with an agent without knowledge of his status, the principal should assume directly the rights and obligations.

Ampachi *kôri.*

According to our practice, the principal should assume the rights and obligations. As for the second question, the principal is completely free of the rights and obligations.

Fuwa *kôri.*

In the first case, the agent shall assume directly the rights and obligations. In the second case, the principal shall assume the rights and obligations.

Atsumi *kôri*, Kagami *kôri* and Katagata *kôri.*

Regarding the first question, the agent should assume directly the rights and obligations. As for the second, in theory, the agent should assume the rights and obligations. In almost every case, however, the principal lets his own chief clerk or employee conclude the transaction. Therefore, it is generally thought to be the principal himself who is acting in the transaction. Judging from the real circumstances, we think that in the second item, too, the principal should assume directly the rights and obligations.

Tagi *kôri* and Kami-ishizu *kôri.*

In a transaction in which an agent acts on behalf of his principal, the agent should assume directly the rights and obligations. Even if the other party has concluded a transaction with an agent without knowledge of his status, the agent who has directly concluded the transaction should assume the rights and obligations. If the principal has his chief clerk or employee act on his behalf, he of course should assume the rights and obligations.

Ôno *kôri* and Ikeda *kôri.*

In a transaction in which an agent acts on behalf of his principal, the agent should assume directly the rights and obligations. Even if the other party concludes a transaction with an agent without knowledge of his status, the agent should assume the rights and obligations.

Haguri *kôri* and Nakajima *kôri.*

Regarding the first question, the principal should assume directly the rights and obligations. As for the second, the agent should assume the rights and obligations.

Ena *kôri.*

The principal should assume directly the rights and obligations.

Kamo *kôri.*

In a transaction in which an agent acts on behalf of his principal, the principal should assume directly the rights and obligations. As for timber traders, however, the agent should assume directly the rights and obligations. When the other party concludes a transaction with an agent without knowledge of his status, the principal should assume the rights and obligations.

Kani *kôri.*

The agents in a transaction can be divided into two groups, according to whether they are completely[1] or only partially[2] in charge of the business. Therefore, this is what we can answer for the present. Regarding the first question, the agent should assume directly all the rights and obligations. As for the second, the principal is supposed to assume them indirectly. Depending on the case, the other party may on occasion regard the agent as the principal himself. In that case, the principal of course should directly assume them all.

Atsumi *kôri,* Gifu Township.

Regarding the first question, the principal should assume directly the rights and obligations. As for the second, the principal should assume directly the rights and obligations.

Ôgaki.

According to our practice, the principal should assume directly the rights and obligations. As regards the second question, the principal is completely free of them.

Ena *kôri,* Nakatsugawa Village.

The agent should assume directly the rights and obligations. Regarding the second question, the principal is completely free of them.

Shimo-ishizu *kôri,* Takasu Township.

With regard to the first question, the agent should assume directly the rights and obligations. As for the second, if the other party concludes a transaction with an agent without knowledge of his status, the agent and the principal should assume them completely.

Haguri *kôri,* Takegahana Village.

The principal should assume the rights and obligations. If the other party concludes a transaction with an agent without knowledge of his status, the agent should assume them completely.

[1] *Sôri.*

[2] *Buri.*

Yamagata *kôri*, Takatomi Village.

Needless to say, a principal is superior to an agent. If the principal, however, uses an agent who is unfamiliar with the other party, and as a result causes any kind of trouble, the principal cannot claim the rights and obligations toward the other party.

Mugi *kôri*, Kôzuchi Village.

The principal should assume directly the rights and obligations. If the other party concludes a transaction with an agent without knowledge of his status, the principal, as well as the agent, is supposed to assume them.

Haguri *kôri*, Kasamatsu Village.

In regard to the first question, in most cases, the principal should assume the rights and obligations. As for the second, the agent should assume them.

Fuwa *kôri*, Tarui Village.

Regarding the first question, the agent should assume directly the rights and obligations. As for the second, the principal should assume them.

Ôno *kôri*, Miwa Village.

The agent, if he is acting on behalf of his principal, should assume directly the rights and obligations. As for the second question, the agent assumes them first, and the principal second.

Ampachi *kôri*, Gôdo Village.

The principal should assume the rights and obligations toward the other party. If the other party concludes a transaction with an agent without knowledge of his status, the principal should assume them.

Tagi *kôri*, Shimada Village.

No answer is given.

Ena *kôri*, Iwa Village.

Regarding the first question the principal should assume them directly. As for the second, the principal[1] should assume them.

Kamo *kôri*, Hosome Village.

In the first case, the agent should assume the rights and obligations. If the other party concludes a transaction with an agent without knowledge of his status, the principal should assume them.

[1] In this answer it is not clear which is meant, the principal or the agent. Judging from the context, "principal" seems to be the proper designation. [Trans.]

Toki *kôri*, Takayama Village.

The person representing the principal[1] should assume the rights and obligations. Regarding the second question, the principal may assume the same rights and obligations as the agent. However, the principal's rights and obligations are limited to the scope of authority.

Kani *kôri*, Mitake Village.

The principal should assume them.

Ena *kôri*, Akechi Village.

The principal should assume directly the rights and obligations.

Mugi *kôri*, Seki Village.

The agent should assume directly the rights and obligations. If the other party concludes a transaction with an agent without knowledge of his status, the principal should assume them directly.

Ôno *kôri*, Takayama Township.

The agent, if he is directly acting on behalf of his principal, should assume the rights and obligations. If the agent has delivered it[2] to his principal, however, the rights and obligations are to be assumed by the principal. Regarding the second question, as stated above, they are to be assumed by the principal, if the agent has delivered it to his principal.

Motosu *kôri*, Kitagata Village.

In a transaction in which an agent acts on behalf of his principal, the principal should assume directly the rights and obligations. If the other party concludes a transaction with an agent without knowledge of his status, the principal is completely free of the rights and obligations.

Kamo *kôri*, Ôta Village.

In a transaction in which an agent acts on behalf of his principal, the agent should assume the rights and obligations. If the other party concludes a transaction with an agent without knowledge of his status, the principal as well as the agent are supposed to assume them.

Kaisai *kôri* and Shimo-ishizu *kôri*.

In a transaction in which an agent acts on behalf of his principal, the agent should assume directly the rights and obligations.

[1] *Dairi-sha.*

[2] His agency.

Regarding the second question, since there may be no proof whether an agent is really acting as an agent or not, the principal can do nothing but claim the rights and assume the obligations.

Gujô *kôri*.

In a transaction in which an agent acts on behalf of his principal, the agent should assume the rights and obligations.

Topic 3: When an Agent Acts beyond His Powers,[1] but the Other Party Is Not Aware of This, Is a Contract Thus Concluded between the Two Parties Valid? If It Is, What Should Be Done about the Loss Incurred by the Principal as a Result of His Agent Having Acted in Excess of His Power?

TOKYO METROPOLIS

Soy Wholesalers.[2]

If the other party is unaware of the circumstances, the contract thus concluded between the two parties will be judged valid. As for the second question, if the loss has been incurred by the principal because his agent has exceeded his authority, it should be paid by the agent.

Sugar Wholesalers.

If an agent exceeds his powers and the other party remains unaware of this, the principal will not be free of his rights and obligations, because a contract is always based on mutual confidence. If a loss is thus incurred by the principal, the agent will be made to pay for it within one year.

Dried Bonito Wholesalers.

If an agent exceeds his powers and thereby causes a loss to his principal, the latter cannot but compensate for the loss since he himself has asked the agent to act on his behalf.

Medicine Wholesalers.

If an agent exceeds his powers, the contract remains valid, if the agent is an employee of the principal. The resulting loss incurred by the principal should be paid by the principal.

Paper Wholesalers (*Kiu-kumi*).[3]

If an agent to whom a letter of attorney has been issued exceeds his authority, the principal should make up the loss.

Oil Wholesalers.

Such an example has not been seen.

Stone Wholesalers.

[1] *Kengen-o-koeru.*

[2] *Shôyu-donya-kumiai.*

[3] *Kiu-kumi kami-donya.*

The answer to the first question is that it can be judged valid. As for the second, according to our practice, the principal should pay the loss, if it is due to any act by his agent.

Fuel Wholesalers.

When an agent exceeds his powers and thereby causes a loss to his principal, the latter will compensate for the loss as long as the agent acts only as a matter of duty. However, the principal on occasion, without consulting his agent, will ask the other party to cancel the contract, if the agent has acted with malicious intent. (For example, if he concludes a contract for money by making the other party believe some goods were in hand and offering the other party an unreasonably low price on them.)

Porcelain Wholesalers.

If the other party is unaware of the circumstances, the contract can be judged valid. Therefore, the resulting loss should be compensated for by the principal.

Paper Wholesalers (*Shôkai-kumi*).[1]

If an agent exceeds his powers (for example, trading in draperies or rice although he is a dealer of paper), the principal is completely free of the responsibilities of the contract, whether the other party is aware of the status of the agent or not. The resulting damage or loss should be compensated for by the agent.

Rice Traders.[2]

We have never heard of such a case.

Salt Wholesalers.

Since the circumstances vary, no definite answer can be given. Regarding the second question, the loss should be paid by the principal.

Timber Wholesalers.

Such a case has never been experienced.

Timber Traders.[3]

Such a case has never been experienced.

Timber Traders (*Senju*).[4]

We have never heard of such a case.

Matting Wholesalers.

[1] *Shôkai-kumi kami-donya.*

[2] *Beikoku sangyô-kumiai.*

[3] *Zaimoku tôsei-kumiai.*

[4] *Senju zaimoku-kumiai.*

Even if an agent exceeds his powers, the contract still remains valid. Unless his act proves unlawful, the principal cannot be freed of his responsibilities.

Saké Wholesalers.

A loss resulting from an agent's acting beyond his powers should be borne by him. However, depending upon the circumstances, the principal will also assume a part of the loss, after talks between the two.

Dry Goods Wholesalers.

Regarding the present topic, when an agent acts beyond his powers and the other party is not aware of the circumstances, the contract thus concluded is still valid.

Tobacco Wholesalers.

There is no established practice, since the matter is settled through deliberation between the two parties, according to the circumstances.

Saké Wholesalers.[1]

If an agent exceeds his powers, the contract remains valid. After a contract has been concluded, if an agent exceeds his powers and thereby causes damage to his principal, the principal of course should be bound to compensate for the loss.

Mosquito Net Wholesalers.

If an agent exceeds his powers, and acts without dishonest intent, it is the principal's duty to pay for the loss.

Fuel Wholesalers (*Umite-kumi*).[2]

According to practices which existed until some fifteen years ago, if an agent exceeded his powers, the contract was judged valid and the resulting loss was considered to fall on the principal. Now, however, many traders seem to have altered their practices. Therefore, there is no established rule.

Copper and Iron Wholesalers.

Even if the other party is unaware of the real circumstances, if the goods in question are those handled by the agent's business circle, the contract is judged valid. The loss incurred by the agent should be compensated for by the principal.

Kôjimachi Ward.

[1] *Sake-rui donya.*

[2] *Umite-kumi shintan-donya.*

If an agent carrying a letter of attorney exceeds his powers, the contract is judged invalid, it is considered to be a mistake by the agent. If the person acting as agent is a chief clerk or an employee, the principal cannot be freed of the responsibilities.

Nihombashi Ward.

There is no established practice.

Kyôbashi Ward.

Regarding the first question, if an agent exceeds his powers, the contract is judged invalid. As for the second, the agent is bound to pay for the loss.

Yotsuya Ward and Ushigome Ward.

In the case of an agent who exceeds his powers in a transaction in which the other party is unaware of this, if the agent has worked for the principal for many years, the principal is bound to compensate for any loss resulting from the transaction.

Asakusa Ward.

Regarding the first question, in a transaction, the commercial shop in the street does not specify the scope of authority of the agent. In most cases, the person acting as an agent is a branch manager employed by his shopkeeper. Therefore, even if the agent exceeds his powers, the shopkeeper, or the principal, cannot declare the contract invalid. Regarding the second question, the loss incurred by the principal should be compensated for by the principal himself.

Honjo Ward.

If an agent exceeds his powers and the other party is unaware of this, the contract is judged invalid.

Ebara *kôri*.

If an agent exceeds his powers and the other party is unaware of this, the contract is judged valid. The resulting loss thereby should be paid by the principal.

Higashi-tama *kôri* and Minami-toshima *kôri*.

Even if an agent exceeds his powers, the contract still remains valid. The loss should be compensated for by the principal. Discussions should be held for settlement between the two parties.

Kita-toshima *kôri*.

As already stated in Topic 1.

Minami-adachi *kôri*.

Regarding the first question, the contract is judged valid. As for the second, the principal cannot demand compensation from the other party, but can from the agent.

Shitaya Ward.

As we have already answered in Topic 1, the agent in business is acting on behalf of the principal. Even if he exceeds his powers, and the other party is unaware of this, the contract is judged valid. The loss incurred by the principal should, of course, be compensated for by the principal.

Kanda Ward.

We have already answered this in Topic 2.

Akasaka Ward and Azabu Ward.

Regarding the first question, if the other party has no knowledge of the real circumstances, the contract remains valid. As for the second, if an agent exceeds his powers and thereby causes damage to his principal, the agent usually seems bound to pay for the loss.

Hongô Ward.

If an agent exceeds his powers and the other party is unaware of this, the contract remains valid. If the principal suffers a loss as a result, he only has the right to sue the agent for the loss.

CHIBA PREFECTURE

Awa *kôri*, Hei *kôri*, Asai *kôri* and Nagasa *kôri*.

Even if an agent exceeds his powers, the contract is judged valid. Generally speaking, the principal seems to be bound to assume the responsibilities. For example, if an agent ordered by his principal to purchase, say, 500 bags of dried sardines has concluded a contract with the other party to purchase 1,000 bags based on an assessment of the general price fluctuation, the principal will not invalidate the contract. Also in a transaction in which an agent exceeds his powers, the principal will not make him pay for any resulting loss.

Katori *kôri*.

If an agent exceeds his powers and the other party is unaware of this, the contract remains valid. Even if the principal suffers a loss, he will compensate for it.

Yamabe *kôri* and Muza *kôri*.

In such a case, the contract is generally judged invalid. Under special circumstances, if the contract cannot be made invalid, the principal will make the agent pay for the resulting loss.

Unakami *kôri* and Sôsa *kôri*.

If an agent exceeds his powers and the other party is unaware of this, the contract is judged valid. The loss thus incurred by the principal should be paid for by the principal.

Higashi-katsushika *kôri.*

In such a case the agent acts only on his own, and not his principal's, behalf. The contract, therefore, cannot be judged valid.

IBARAKI PREFECTURE

Nishi-katsushika *kôri* and Sashima *kôri.*

If an agent exceeds his powers and the other party is unaware of this, the contract will be judged invalid. The answer to the second question is as stated above: the contract is judged invalid.

KANAGAWA PREFECTURE

Miura *kôri.*

Regarding the first question, the contract can be judged valid. As for the second, the loss falls on the principal.

Tachibana *kôri.*

The contract cannot be judged valid. The agent will be made to assume the responsibilities.

Kita-tama *kôri.*

If an agent exceeds his powers and the other party is unaware of this, the principal will judge the contract valid unless the agent exceeds the limits of his job. Since the principal has given the agent the authority to act on his behalf, the principal cannot be freed of the responsibilities toward the other party, even if he has suffered a loss from the agent's act.

Ashigara-shimo *kôri.*

Regarding the first question, the contract cannot be judged valid. As for the second, the agent will be made to pay for the loss toward the other party.

Prefectural Industrial Bureau.

Whether an agent exceeds his powers or not, the other party will be able to judge the contract as valid. If any loss is incurred by the principal as a result of the agent's act of arrogance, it will be paid for by the principal.

TOCHIGI PREFECTURE

Prefectural Office.

If an agent (such as a head clerk, a sales clerk, a salesman,[1] etc.)

[1] *Uri-shi.*

exceeds his powers and the other party is unaware of this, the contract is judged valid, according to our practice. The resulting loss will fall on the principal.

Shimo-tsuga *kôri* and Samukawa *kôri*.

Regarding the first question, if an agent exceeds his powers and the other party is unaware of this, the contract is judged valid. As for the second, the resulting loss will fall on the principal and not on anybody else.

Ashikaga *kôri* and Yanada *kôri*.

Regarding the first question, if a clerk representing a branch office or a manager exceeds the authority granted by the principal and the other party is unaware of this, the contract is judged valid. As for the second, the loss should be paid for by the principal.

MIE PREFECTURE

Suzuka *kôri*.

If an agent exceeds his powers and the other party is unaware of this, the contract remains valid. The resulting loss should be paid for by the principal, not by anybody else.

Ichishi *kôri*.

Regarding the first question, the contract is judged valid. As for the second question, there is no established practice. Sometimes the agent will be made to pay for the loss, but in other cases he will not.

Nabari *kôri* and Iga *kôri*.

If an agent exceeds his powers and the other party is unaware of this, the contract can be judged valid. The resulting loss will fall on the principal.

Kita-muro *kôri*.

If an agent unintentionally exceeds his powers, the contract will remain valid. The loss resulting from the transaction should be compensated for by the principal.

AICHI PREFECTURE

Nakajima *kôri*.

The contract can be judged valid. The loss falls on the principal.

Nagoya Ward.

In all cases where the other party is unaware of the circumstances, the contract is usually judged valid. The resulting loss incurred by the principal should be compensated for by the principal.

Chita *kôri*.

If an agent exceeds his powers and the other party is unaware of this, the contract can be judged valid. The loss incurred by the principal resulting from an agent's exceeding his powers, in theory, should be paid for by the agent himself. However, the principal, usually not issuing a letter of attorney to the agent, usually seems to pay for the loss.

Minami-shidara *kôri*.

In either case, settlement will be made through mutual discussion. There is no established practice.

Atsumi *kôri*.

If the other party is unaware of the status of the agent, the contract cannot be judged valid. The loss resulting from the act of arrogance will fall on the principal.

Kaitô *kôri* and Kaisai *kôri*.

If the other party is unaware of the circumstances, the contract usually seems to be judged valid. The resulting loss usually falls on the principal.

Aichi *kôri*.

If an agent exceeds his powers and the other party is unaware of this, the contract will necessarily be judged valid. The loss incurred by the principal resulting from the agent's acting beyond his powers should be compensated for by the agent.

Niwa *kôri* and Haguri *kôri*.

If an agent exceeds his powers and the other party is unaware of this, the contract cannot be judged valid.

SHIZUOKA PREFECTURE

Prefectural Office.

Regarding the first question, it is judged valid. As for the second, the loss falls on the principal.

Udo *kôri* and Abe *kôri*.

The contract is judged valid. Our answer to the question of agency is already given in Topic 1. If an agent exceeds his powers and the principal thereby suffers a loss, the principal will not make the agent pay for the loss. He must consider that he has made a mistake in his estimate of the agent. If the transaction results in profits, the principal will assume them and encourage his agent with praise.

Inasa *kôri* and Aratama *kôri*.

The contract is judged valid. If the agent acts far beyond his powers, the principal will make the agent compensate for the loss.

Kamo *kôri* and Naka *kôri*.

The contract cannot be judged valid. Since the contract becomes void, the principal will be freed from the loss.

Saya *kôri* and Kitô *kôri*.

There is no established practice.

Gifu Prefecture

Mugi *kôri*.

Regarding the first question, if an agent exceeds his powers, the contract is judged valid. As for the second, it follows quite naturally from the answer given above that any resulting loss should fall on the principal.

Ampachi *kôri*.

The contract made by the agent is judged valid. As for the loss resulting from the agent's act of arrogance, there is no established practice. Generally speaking, however, the principal compensates for the loss.

Fuwa *kôri*.

Regarding the first question, the contract is judged valid. As for the second, the loss falls on the principal.

Atsumi *kôri*, Kagami *kôri* and Katagata *kôri*.

Regarding the first question, the contract is judged valid. As for the second, the agent will be made to pay the loss. In situations where the agent exceeds his powers, the contract still remains valid.

Tagi *kôri* and Kami-ishizu *kôri*.

If an agent exceeds his powers and the other party is unaware of this, the question of validity depends solely upon an agreement between the agent and the other party. This is no different from an ordinary transaction.

Ôno *kôri* and Ikeda *kôri*.

If an agent exceeds his powers and the other party is unaware of this, it is natural that the contract is judged valid. If the agent thus causes damage to the other party, he is bound to compensate for the damage.

Haguri *kôri* and Nakajima *kôri*.

In answer to the first question, the contract is judged valid. As for the second, the loss usually falls on the principal.

Ena *kôri*.

The contract cannot be judged valid.

Kamo *kôri.*

If an agent exceeds his powers and the other party is unaware of this, the decision as to whether the contract is valid or not is made by the principal. Thus there is no established practice. Timber traders, however, judge the contract invalid if an agent exceeds his powers.

Kani *kôri.*

In response to the first question, in the case of a contract which has been officially concluded, nothing can be done to change its validity. In many cases, however, where it is a matter of verbal promise, it is judged invalid. Regarding the second, the loss falls on the agent, with the principal compensating for any remaining amount which the agent does not pay.

Atsumi *kôri,* Gifu Township.

In answer to the first question, the contract is judged valid. As for the second, the loss falls on the principal.

Ôgaki.

The contract made by the agent is judged valid. There is no established practice concerning the loss resulting from an agent's act of arrogance. However, in most cases, it falls on the principal.

Ena *kôri,* Nakatsugawa Village.

A contract which an agent has concluded in excess of his powers cannot be judged valid.

Shimo-ishizu *kôri,* Takasu Township.

If the other party is unaware of the circumstances, the contract is considered valid. Since the contract is judged valid, if the agent exceeds his powers and causes damage of his principal, the agent will not be able to evade the responsibility to compensate for it.

Haguri *kôri,* Takegahana Village.

In such a case, it will be difficult to make the contract valid. If any loss results, the agent will be made to compensate for the loss.

Yamagata *kôri,* Takatomi Village.

The contract can be made valid if the other party wishes it to be. The loss is to be paid by the principal.

Mugi *kôri,* Kôzuchi Village.

If the other party concludes a contract with an agent exceeding his powers, the contract is valid. If the agent causes damage to his principal, it must be paid for by the principal.

Haguri *kôri,* Kasamatsu Village.

The answer to the first question is that the contract is judged valid. Regarding the second, usually the principal seems to compensate for the loss.

Fuwa *kôri*, Tarui Village.

Regarding the first question, the contract cannot be judged valid. As for the second, if a loss is incurred by the principal, it should be compensated for by one of the two.[1]

Ôno *kôri*, Miwa Village.

In such a case, the two parties will negotiate the settlement.

Ampachi *kôri*, Gôdo Village.

If an agent exceeds his powers, the contract becomes invalid.

Tagi *kôri*, Shimada Village.

No answer is given.

Ena *kôri*, Iwa Village.

The contract is judged valid.

Kamo *kôri*, Hosome Village.

If an agent exceeds his powers and the other party is unaware of this, the contract is judged valid. However, it cannot be judged valid if the agent does not carry a letter of attorney issued to him by his principal. If the agent has a letter of attorney from his principal, the principal is bound to compensate for the loss even if the agent has acted beyond his powers.

Toki *kôri*, Takayama Village.

The contract cannot be valid.

Kani *kôri*, Mitake Village.

Regarding the first question, each case differs, so there is no definite practice. As for the second, the agent should pay for any losses.

Ena *kôri*, Akechi Village.

It cannot be valid.

Mugi *kôri*, Seki Village.

If an agent exceeds his powers and the other party is unaware of this, the contract is judged valid. Suppose that an agent has been asked by his principal to collect a loan of ¥100 from a customer and that when he calls at the debtor's home, he finds that the latter has only ¥80 on hand. If all the debtor's properties, movable and immovable, have already been transferred to others and the agent

[1] *Shizen-shômetsu-sezu.*

is compelled to accept the ¥80, we can say that the agent has exceeded his powers and that he had inflicted a loss of ¥20 on his principal.

Ône *kôri*, Takayama Township.

If an agent exceeds his powers, acting without a letter of attorney or power orally authorized, and the other party is unaware of this, the contract can be judged valid. When the agent exceeds the limits of his authority and the other party is aware of this, the contract cannot be judged valid. In such a case the loss falls on the agent. If the agent does not have enough money to cover the entire loss, the principal sometimes makes up the remainder.

Motosu *kôri*, Kitagata Village.

If an agent exceeds his powers and the other party is not aware of this, the contract cannot be judged valid.

Kamo *kôri*, Ôta Village.

If an agent exceeds his powers and the other party is unaware of this, the decision as to whether or not the contract is valid depends solely on the principal. There is no established practice.

Kaisai *kôri* and Shimo-ishizu *kôri*.

If the other party is unaware of the circumstances, the contract is often judged valid. If the contract is judged valid, and if damage is incurred by the principal, the agent is bound to compensate for the damage.

Gujô *kôri*.

We can give no answer to this question.

Topic 4: When an Agent Alone Is Held Responsible for a Business Transaction Which Has Been Conducted in the Name of His Principal, Is the Principal Entitled to Retain the Goods, If Any, Which Have Already Come into His Possession, or May He Be Dispossessed of Such Goods?

Although It Seems Apparent That the Restoration of the Goods to the Other Party Should Be Made by the Agent, Does It Ever Happen That the Other Party Tries to Recover the Goods for Himself?

Tokyo Metropolis

Soy Wholesalers.[1]

The principal may not retain the goods. As for the second question, the agent should carry out the restoration of the goods for the other party.

Sugar Wholesalers.

As we have already stated in Topic 3, the agent is responsible for the loss only within a one-year time limit. There is no further regulation. Any trouble between an agent and a principal has nothing to do with the other party.

Dried Bonito Wholesalers.

The principal may retain the goods.

Medicine Wholesalers.

Such a case has never been seen among us.

Paper Wholesalers (*Kiu-kumi*).[2]

The answer to the first question is that he will be dispossessed of them. As for the second, the other party tries to recover the goods for himself.

Oil Wholesalers.

We have never seen such a case.

Stone Wholesalers.

Such a case has never been seen.

Fuel Wholesalers.

If the goods have come into the principal's possession because of negligence or error on the part of his agent, he may retain the

[1] *Shôyu-donya-kumiai.*

[2] *Kiu-kumi kami-donya.*

goods. The final decision on dispossession depends on the original contract.

Porcelain Wholesalers.

Such a case as this has never occurred.

Paper Wholesalers (*Shôkai-kumi*).[1]

The principal will not try to retain the goods. He will be dispossessed of them. The other party is not allowed to recover the goods for himself.

Rice Traders.[2]

We have never seen such a case.

Salt Wholesalers.

The principal is not allowed to retain the goods. Regarding the second question, the other party recovers the goods for himself.

Timber Wholesalers.

Such a case has never occurred.

Timber Traders.[3]

We have never seen such a case.

Timber Traders (*Senju*).[4]

Such a case has never been seen.

Matting Wholesalers.

The principal may retain the goods. The agent should carry out the restoration of the goods to the other party.

Saké Wholesalers.[5]

Cases vary according to circumstances. We have no established practice.

Drapery Wholesalers.

The principal will be dispossessed of the goods. Regarding the second question, restoration should be carried out by the agent.

Tobacco Wholesalers.

The two parties will reach mutual agreement on the best arrangement. There is no established practice.

Saké Wholesalers.

We have no such business practice.

Mosquito Net Wholesalers.

[1] *Shôkai-kumi kami-donya.*

[2] *Beikoku sangyô-kumiai.*

[3] *Zaimoku tôsei-kumiai.*

[4] *Senju zaimoku-kumiai.*

[5] *Sake-rui-donya.*

The principal may retain the goods. Restoration should be done by the agent for himself.

Fuel Wholesalers (*Umite-kumi*).[1]

As the transaction has been conducted in the name of the principal, and the goods have come into his possession, it seems apparent that the agent alone is held responsible for the transaction, and the principal can retain the goods. As for the dispossession of the goods, there is a variety of ways between the two, according to circumstances.

Copper and Iron Wholesalers.

The principal should be dispossessed of the goods. The agent should carry out the restoration of the goods.

Kôjimachi Ward.

When an agent is solely responsible for the transaction, the goods should be delivered to him.

Nihombashi Ward.

The principal may retain the goods unless otherwise provided.

Kyôbashi Ward.

Regarding the first question, the principal is not allowed to retain the goods. As for the second, the other party sometimes tries to recover the goods for himself.

Yotsuya Ward and Ushigome Ward.

No answer is given.

Asakusa Ward.

Regarding the first question, of course the principal will be dispossessed of the goods. As for the second, the agent should carry out the restoration of the goods.

Honjo Ward.

When an agent is held solely responsible for a transaction conducted in the name of his principal, the principal may not retain any goods which have come into his possession, and he will be dispossessed of them. Sometimes the agent will not carry out the restoration of the goods, but the other party will recover them for himself.

Ebara *kôri*.

When an agent is held solely responsible for a transaction conducted in the name of his principal, the principal will be dis-

[1] *Umite-kumi shintan-donya.*

possessed of any goods which have already come into his possession. Sometimes the agent should carry out the restoration of the goods to the other party, and at other times the other party will recover them for himself.

Higashi-tama *kôri* and Minami-toshima *kôri.*

When an agent is held solely responsible for the transaction, the principal may not retain any goods which have already come into his possession.

Kita-toshima *kôri.*

We have already answered this question in Topic 1.

Minami-adachi *kôri.*

Regarding the first question, the principal should be dispossessed of the goods. As for the second, in principle, the agent should carry out the restoration of the goods. But the principal sometimes recovers the goods for himself.

Shitaya Ward.

As we have already stated in the previous topic, it is very rare that the agent is held solely responsible for a transaction conducted in the name of the principal. If such a case occurs, there is little fear of any trouble between the principal and the other party. The principal will decide whether or not to retain the goods as circumstances require. The other party sometimes recovers the goods for himself rather than having the agent restore them.

Kanda Ward.

Our answer has already been given in Topic 2.

Akasaka Ward and Azabu Ward.

Regarding the first question, as we have already said in the preceding section, such a case cannot be found among us. The answer to the second question is as stated above.

Hongô Ward.

When an agent is held solely responsible for the transaction, the principal will be dispossessed of any goods which have already come into his possession, and the goods should be returned to the other party without delay. If the agent cannot recover the goods from the principal immediately, the other party will negotiate the restoration directly with the principal.

Chiba Prefecture

Awa *kôri,* Hei *kôri,* Asai *kôri* and Nagasa *kôri.*

No answer is given.

Katori *kôri*.

No answer is given.

Yamabe *kôri* and Muza *kôri*.

No answer is given.

Unakami *kôri* and Sôsa *kôri*.

No answer is given.

Higashi-katsushika *kôri*.

When an agent is held solely responsible in the transaction, the principal may retain the goods. There is no established rule as to whether the agent or the other party should recover the goods. This depends on the situation at the time and the kind of articles involved.

IBARAKI PREFECTURE

Nishi-katsushika *kôri* and Sashima *kôri*.

In such a case, the principal should be dispossessed of any goods which have already come into his possession. The agent carries out the restoration of the goods.

KANAGAWA PREFECTURE

Miura *kôri*.

So far such a case has never been found.

Tachibana *kôri*.

The principal may not retain the goods. If there are any goods to restore, the agent will recover them.

Kita-tama *kôri*.

Since the agent is held solely responsible for the transaction, the principal may retain the goods if he pleases. There is therefore no case in which the agent recovers the goods.

Ashigara-shimo *kôri*.

As for us, the principal may retain the goods, because the agent is held solely responsible for the transaction. Regarding the second question, the goods can be restored directly to the other party.

Prefectural Industrial Bureau.

As a matter of fact, we do not know of such a case. In regard to the second question, we have nothing to answer.

TOCHIGI PREFECTURE

Prefectural Office.

According to our practice, when an agent is held solely responsible for the transaction, the principal may retain any goods which have already come into his possession. If he wishes the goods restored, the other party will recover them himself. Although it seems that the agent is completely free of rights and obligations, this business practice has developed because of the idea that a prosperous business is based on mutual confidence.

Shimo-tsuga *kôri* and Samukawa *kôri*.

Regarding the first question, when an agent is held solely responsible for a transaction concluded in the name of the principal, the principal may not retain the goods. As for the second, the other party sometimes recovers the goods for himself.

Ashikaga *kôri* and Yanada *kôri*.

In this area, a case such as described in the first question has never been seen. Therefore, no answer can be given to the second question either.

Mie Prefecture

Suzuka *kôri*.

When a transaction is concluded in the name of the principal, his agent can never be held solely responsible for it.

Ichishi *kôri*.

Whether or not the principal may retain the goods depends on the particular case. The same is true of whether or not he is dispossessed of the goods. There is no established practice. As for restoration of the goods, the other party sometimes recovers them himself.

Nabari *kôri* and Iga *kôri*.

When an agent is held solely responsible for the transaction, he may dispose of the goods which have already come into the principal's possession. But he may not exercise responsibilities which go beyond his powers as a result of his act unless he is entitled to do so. As for the restoration of the goods from the principal, the agent may recover them if he is acting lawfully.

Kita-muro *kôri*.

When an agent is held solely responsible for the transaction, the principal may not retain any goods which have already come into his possession. If necessary, however, he may sometimes retain them. As for the restoration of the goods, the other party may sometimes negotiate their disposition with the principal when the agent is held responsible for the transaction. The decision on whether to accept his wishes or not, however, is taken only through talks between the agent and the other party.

AICHI PREFECTURE

Nakajima *kôri*.

When an agent is held solely responsible for the transaction, the principal may be dispossessed of the goods if the agent pleases.

Nagoya Ward.

When an agent is held solely responsible for the transaction due to his own mistake, the principal will be dispossessed of any goods which have already come into his possession. The agent usually carries out the restoration. Sometimes, however, the other party will recover them for himself if this is more convenient.

Chita *kôri*.

When an agent is held solely responsible for a transaction, the principal may not retain any goods which have already come into his possession. As for the restoration of the goods, it is said that the other party does not recover them for himself.

Minami-shidara *kôri*.

When an agent is held solely responsible for a transaction, apparently the principal may retain the goods. But in some cases he may be dispossessed of them. If any trouble occurs in recovering the goods, the other party may sometimes help, but he seldom undertakes it on his own.

Atsumi *kôri*.

The principal may retain the goods which have already come into his possession. He cannot be dispossessed of them by the agent. Since the goods are already out of the agent's hands, the other party may sometimes recover them for himself.

Kaitô *kôri* and Kaisai *kôri*.

The principal may retain the goods. Therefore, the other party may sometimes recover them for himself.

Aichi *kôri*.

When an agent is held solely responsible for a transaction due to any trouble on the part of the agent, it is quite natural that the principal should be dispossessed of any goods which have already come into his possession. The principal may not retain them. In most cases, the agent carries out the restoration of the goods, although the other party sometimes recovers them for himself.

Niwa *kôri* and Haguri *kôri*.

When an agent is held solely responsible for a transaction conducted in the name of the principal, the principal may retain any goods which have already come into his possession. The agent should compensate for the damage and should carry out the restoration of the goods. The other party never recovers them for himself.

SHIZUOKA PREFECTURE

Prefectural Office.

Regarding the first question, the principal may not retain the goods. As for the second, the other party may not himself ask the principal directly for the restoration.

Udo *kôri* and Abe *kôri*.

Sometimes he may be dispossessed of them. The agent should carry out the restoration of the goods. Sometimes, however, the other party may recover them for himself. Our answer to the second question has already been given above.

Inasa *kôri* and Aratama *kôri*.

The principal may be dispossessed of the goods. The agent carries out the restoration of the goods.

Kamo *kôri* and Naka *kôri*.

When an agent is held solely responsible for a transaction, the principal may retain the goods which have already come into his possession. In such a case, the other party may not recover the goods for himself.

Saya *kôri* and Kitô *kôri*.

There is no established practice.

GIFU PREFECTURE

Mugi *kôri*.

Regarding the first question, when an agent is held solely responsible for a transaction conducted in the name of the principal, the principal may be temporarily dispossessed of any goods which have already come into his possession, leaving them in the agent's hands. As for the second, the agent himself will carry out the restoration of the goods.

Ampachi *kôri*.

In such a case, the principal will be dispossessed of the goods. Regarding the second question, depending on the extent of the agent's responsibility, the other party will recover the goods for himself.

Fuwa *kôri*.

In answer to the first question, the principal may be dispossessed of the goods. As for the second, the agent carries out the restoration. According to circumstances, however, the other party sometimes recovers the goods for himself.

Atsumi *kôri*, Kagami *kôri* and Katagata *kôri*.

Regarding the first question, the principal may not retain the goods. As for the second, the other party will sometimes recover them for himself.

Tagi *kôri* and Kami-ishizu *kôri*.

When an agent is held solely responsible for a transaction conducted in the name of the principal, the principal will not be dispossessed (unless the agent agrees with him about it) of any goods which have already come into his possession.

Ôno *kôri* and Ikeda *kôri*.

In such a case the principal may not retain the goods. As for the restoration of the goods, there is no established practice. Either the agent will do it or the other party will do it for himself.

Haguri *kôri* and Nakajima *kôri*.

In response to the first question, the principal may usually retain the goods. As for the second, the other party usually recovers the goods for himself.

Ena *kôri*.

Regarding the first question, the principal will sometimes be dispossessed of the goods. As for the second, the other party will sometimes recover the goods himself.

Kamo *kôri*.

When an agent is held solely responsible for a transaction conducted in the name of the principal, the principal will be dispossessed of any goods which have already come into his possession. The agent will carry out the restoration of the goods.

Kani *kôri*.

As for the first question, the principal will be dispossessed of the goods. Regarding the second, the agent will carry out the restoration of the goods.

Atsumi *kôri*, Gifu Township.

There is no established practice.

Ôgaki.

In such a case, the principal will be dispossessed of the goods. Regarding the second question, according to the extent of the agent's responsibility, the other party can sometimes recover the goods.

Ena *kôri*, Nakatsugawa Village.

Even if the principal has already received the goods, he should be dispossessed of them. Regarding the second question, the agent should carry out the restoration of the goods, never the other party.

Shimo-ishizu *kôri*, Takasu Township.

According to the circumstances under which the agent is held responsible, the principal may sometimes be dispossessed of any goods which have already come into his possession. As for the restoration of the goods, it seems that the agent should carry it out. However in some cases, the other party will recover them for himself.

Haguri *kôri*, Takegahana Village.

In such a case, the principal will be dispossessed of the goods. As regards the second question, in some cases, the other party can recover them for himself.

Yamagata *kôri*, Takatomi Village.

Unless an agent is opposed to it, it is quite natural that the principal should be dispossessed of the goods. The other party can recover them for himself.

Mugi *kôri*, Kôzuchi Village.

When an agent concludes a transaction in the name of his principal, the principal may retain any goods which have already come into his possession. The other party will sometimes recover them for himself.

Haguri *kôri*, Kasamatsu Village.

Regarding the first question, usually the principal will retain the goods. As for the second, usually the other party recovers them for himself.

Fuwa *kôri*, Tarui Village.

The principal will sometimes be dispossessed of the goods. The agent sometimes carries out the restoration of the goods. In some cases, however, the other party recovers them for himself.

Ôno *kôri*, Miwa Village.

In such a case the principal will be dispossessed of the goods. The agent carries out the restoration of the goods, but sometimes the other party recovers them.

Ampachi *kôri*, Gôdo Village.

Any goods which have come into the principal's possession should be delivered to the agent. The other party will never recover the goods directly himself.

Tagi *kôri,* Shimada Village.

No answer is given.

Ena *kôri,* Iwa Village.

As regards the first question, the principal will be dispossessed of the goods. As for the second, the other party may not recover the goods for himself.

Kamo *kôri,* Hosome Village.

When an agent is held solely responsible for a transaction concluded in the name of the principal, the principal will be dispossessed of any goods which have already come into his possession. Although it appears that the agent should carry out restoration himself, the other party often recovers the goods for himself.

Toki *kôri,* Takayama Village.

The principal will be dispossessed of the goods. The other party will never recover them for himself.

Kani *kôri,* Mitake Village.

Regarding the first question, the principal cannot refuse to be dispossessed of the goods. As for the second, the other party will not recover the goods for himself.

Ena *kôri,* Akechi Village.

In answer to the first question, the principal will often be dispossessed of the goods. As for the second, the other party will sometimes recover them for himself.

Mugi *kôri,* Seki Village.

When an agent conducts a transaction in the name of his principal, he cannot be held solely responsible for it; the agent's responsibility is also the principal's. The principal sometimes carries out the restoration of the goods himself rather than having the agent do it. The other party will sometimes recover them for himself.

Ôno *kôri,* Takayama Township.

Although the agent is held responsible, goods already in the principal's possession should be retained by the principal, and he should be dispossessed of them. At that time, the other party can on occasion recover the goods for himself if the agent so desires.

Motosu *kôri,* Kitagata Village.

When an agent is held solely responsible for a transaction conducted in the name of his principal, the latter cannot refuse to be dispossessed of any goods which have already come into his possession. It seems that the agent should make the restoration of the goods, but sometimes the other party recovers them for himself.

Kamo *kôri*, Ôta Village.

When an agent is held solely responsible for a transaction conducted in the name of the principal, the latter will be dispossessed of any goods which have already come into his possession. The agent will make the restoration of the goods.

Kaisai *kôri* and Shimo-ishizu *kôri*.

When an agent is held solely responsible for a transaction conducted in the name of his principal, the latter may sometimes retain any goods which have already come into his possession. In such a case, the principal will make a thorough investigation of the damage, and will sometimes share the loss. When the goods are already in the principal's hands, he can retain them. When the principal may not be dispossessed of the goods for some reason, the other party will sometimes recover the goods for himself.

Gujô *kôri*.

No answer can be given.

Topic 5: Does the Delegation of Authority[1] (to an Agent) Terminate Automatically When the Principal or the Agent Dies?

TOKYO METROPOLIS

Soy Wholesalers.[2]

It terminates automatically when the principal or the agent dies.

Sugar Wholesalers.

The delegation of authority itself terminates automatically when the principal or the agent dies. However, the contract which has been already concluded should be fulfilled without any trouble.

Dried Bonito Wholesalers.

The commission of authority terminates automatically when the principal or the agent dies.

Medicine Wholesalers.

It terminates when the agent dies, but not when the principal dies.

Paper Wholesalers (*Kiu-kumi*).[3]

When the principal dies, his family members will fulfill the contract. When the agent dies, the principal will.

Oil Wholesalers.

The delegation of authority terminates automatically when the principal or the agent dies.

Stone Wholesalers.

It terminates automatically when either of them dies.

Fuel Wholesalers.

Such a case has never been seen among us.

Porcelain Wholesalers.

It is supposed to terminate temporarily when the principal dies. However, his heir will fulfill the contract. It terminates automatically when the agent dies.

Paper Wholesalers (*Shôkai-kumi*).[4]

It terminates automatically when either of them dies.

[1] *Dairi-no-inin.*

[2] *Shôyu-donya-kumiai.*

[3] *Kiu-kumi kami-donya.*

[4] *Shôkai-kumi kami-donya.*

Rice Traders.[1]

Such a case has never been seen among us.

Salt Wholesalers.

It terminates automatically when the principal or the agent dies.

Timber Wholesalers.

We think that it will terminate automatically when the principal or the agent dies.

Timber Traders.[2]

We have not seen such a case.

Timber Traders (*Senju*).[3]

Such a case has never been seen among us.

Matting Wholesalers.

The delegation of authority terminates automatically when the principal and the agent both die.

Saké Wholesalers.[4]

Yes, it does.

Drapery Wholesalers.

It terminates automatically when either of the two dies.

Saké Wholesalers.

We have no such business practice.

Lime and Shell Wholesalers.

Yes, it does, but sometimes it does not terminate when the principal dies.

Mosquito Net Wholesalers.

The delegation of authority terminates automatically when both of them die.

Copper and Iron Wholesalers.

It does not terminate automatically when the principal or the agent dies.

Fuel Wholesalers (*Umite-kumi*).[5]

The delegation of authority terminates automatically when the principal or the agent dies.

Tobacco Wholesalers.

The two parties will negotiate when necessary. There is no estab-

[1] *Beikoku-sangyô-kumiai.*

[2] *Zaimoku-tôsei-kumiai.*

[3] *Senju zaimoku-kumiai.*

[4] *Sake-rui-donya.*

[5] *Umite-kumi shintan-donya.*

lished practice.

Kôjimachi Ward.

Yes, that is right.

Nihombashi Ward.

It terminates automatically.

Kyôbashi Ward.

It terminates at that time.

Yotsuya Ward and Ushigome Ward.

Even if the principal or the agent has died, the principal or the heir must fulfill a contract which has already been concluded.

Asakusa Ward.

It terminates automatically when the principal or the agent dies.

Honjo Ward.

The delegation of authority terminates automatically when the principal or the agent dies.

Ebara *kôri*.

The delegation of authority does not terminate automatically when the principal dies. It does terminate automatically when the agent dies.

Higashi-tama *kôri* and Minami-toshima *kôri*.

The delegation of authority terminates automatically when the principal or the agent dies. However, the principal's heir will sometimes name the same agent once more, or appoint another man as agent. With the death of the principal, the contract sometimes cannot be left unfulfilled. In such a case it may be left untouched.

Kita-toshima *kôri*.

The delegation of authority terminates automatically when the agent dies. The same is true when the principal dies.

Minami-adachi *kôri*.

When the principal dies, it terminates automatically if fulfillment of the contract has not begun, but it does not terminate if it has begun. It terminates naturally when the agent dies.

Shitaya Ward.

In either case, the delegation of authority does not terminate. The contract will be fulfilled by the principal's heir if the principal dies, or by another person as agent if the agent dies.

Kanda Ward.

We have already answered this in Topic 2.

Akasaka Ward and Azabu Ward.

It terminates automatically when the principal or the agent dies.

Hongô Ward.

The delegation of authority usually terminates when the principal or the agent dies. When the transaction cannot be left partially completed, it must be continued by the dead person's heir. When an agent concludes a contract with another party without knowledge of the death of his principal, or when the other party concludes a contract with an agent without knowledge of the death of his principal, the heir of the dead person must fulfill the contract.

Chiba Prefecture

Awa *kôri*, Hei *kôri*, Asai *kôri* and Nagasa *kôri*.

The delegation of authority does not terminate automatically when the principal or the agent dies. It will remain valid as long as the transaction goes on.

Katori *kôri*.

The delegation of authority terminates automatically when the principal or the agent dies.

Yamabe *kôri* and Muza *kôri*.

The delegation of authority terminates on the day the agent dies. In some cases it remains valid for a while after the principal dies.

Unakami *kôri* and Sôsa *kôri*.

The delegation of authority terminates automatically when the agent dies. However, it does not terminate when the principal dies as long as the transaction continues.

Higashi-katsushika *kôri*.

Yes, that is right.

Ibaraki Prefecture

Nishi-katsushika *kôri* and Sashima *kôri*.

The delegation of authority terminates automatically when the principal or the agent dies.

Kanagawa Prefecture

Miura *kôri*.

It terminates automatically when the agent dies, but not when the principal dies.

Tachibana *kôri*.

It terminates automatically when he dies.

Kita-tama *kôri*.

The delegation of authority terminates temporarily when the

principal dies, and another person may be named as agent by the heir of the dead principal. Needless to say, the agent is released from the post when he dies.

Ashigara-shimo *kôri*.

Yes, that is right. It terminates automatically.

Prefectural Industrial Bureau.

The delegation of authority terminates automatically when the principal or the agent dies.

TOCHIGI PREFECTURE

Prefectural Office.

It terminates automatically when he dies.

Shimo-tsuga *kôri* and Samukawa *kôri*.

The delegation of authority terminates automatically when the principal or the agent dies.

Ashikaga *kôri* and Yanada *kôri*.

The delegation of authority terminates automatically when the agent dies. But does not always terminate when the principal dies.

MIE PREFECTURE

Suzuka *kôri*.

The delegation of authority terminates automatically when the agent dies, but not when the principal dies.

Ichishi *kôri*.

Yes, it terminates.

Nabari *kôri* and Iga *kôri*.

The delegation of authority terminates automatically when the agent dies. But sometimes it does not when the principal dies.

Kita-muro *kôri*.

The delegation of authority terminates automatically on the day the principal or the agent dies.

AICHI PREFECTURE

Nakajima *kôri*.

Yes, that is right.

Nagoya Ward.

The delegation of authority under which a manager or a sales clerk acts in a transaction terminates at that time. However, the transaction or the contract which has resulted from the delegation of authority does not terminate as long as the store continues in business.

Chita *kôri*.

It terminates automatically when the principal or the agent dies.

Minami-shidara *kôri.*

It terminates automatically.

Atsumi *kôri.*

It terminates automatically.

Kaitô *kôri* and Kaisai *kôri.*

The delegation of authority remains valid for the period agreed on in the contract.

Aichi *kôri.*

Yes, that is right.

Niwa *kôri* and Haguri *kôri.*

The delegation of authority terminates completely when the principal or the agent dies.

SHIZUOKA PREFECTURE

Prefectural Office.

Yes, that is right.

Udo *kôri* and Abe *kôri.*

Yes.

Inasa *kôri* and Aratama *kôri.*

It terminates automatically when he dies.

Kamo *kôri* and Naka *kôri.*

The delegation of authority terminates automatically when the agent dies but not when the principal dies.

Saya *kôri* and Kitô *kôri.*

There is no established practice.

GIFU PREFECTURE

Mugi *kôri.*

The delegation of authority terminates automatically when the principal or the agent dies.

Ampachi *kôri.*

It terminates automatically when the agent dies but not when the principal dies.

Fuwa *kôri.*

Even if the principal dies, an agent to whom a letter of attorney has been issued is able to continue business. When the transaction is based only on a verbal promise and the agent dies, it terminates automatically.

Atsumi *kôri,* Kagami *kôri* and Katagata *kôri.*

Yes, that is right.

Tagi *kôri* and Kami-ishizu *kôri*.

The agent described here does not seem to be an official agent to whom a letter of attorney has been issued. In that case, he can act in the transaction only within the sphere of a single kind of business.

Ôno *kôri* and Ikeda *kôri*.

Unless specially otherwise provided beforehand, it terminates automatically as stated here.

Haguri *kôri* and Nakajima *kôri*.

Needless to say, it terminates automatically.

Ena *kôri*.

Yes.

Kamo *kôri*.

The delegation of authority terminates automatically when the agent dies but not when the principal dies.

Kani *kôri*.

Of course the delegation of authority terminates automatically when the agent dies. However, it does not when the principal dies unless the agent is released from his position by the dead principal's heir.

Atsumi *kôri*, Gifu Township.

It terminates automatically.

Ôgaki.

It terminates automatically when the agent dies but not when the principal dies.

Ena *kôri*, Nakatsugawa Village.

It terminates automatically when either of them dies.

Shimo-ishizu *kôri*, Takasu Township.

It terminates automatically.

Haguri *kôri*, Takegahana Village.

It terminates automatically when either of them or the other party dies.

Yamagata *kôri*, Takatomi Village.

The delegation of authority terminates automatically when the agent dies. But it does not terminate when the principal dies as long as the transaction remains uncompleted.

Mugi *kôri*, Kôzuchi Village.

It terminates automatically.

Haguri *kôri*, Kasamatsu Village.

Needless to say, it terminates automatically.

Fuwa *kôri*, Tarui Village.

The delegation of authority to the agent does not terminate automatically when his principal dies if a letter of attorney has been issued to him. If the transaction is only a verbal promise, it terminates automatically when the agent dies.

Ôno *kôri*, Miwa Village.

It terminates automatically when the principal or the agent dies.

Ampachi *kôri*, Gôdo Village.

It terminates automatically when the agent dies but not when the principal dies.

Tagi *kôri*, Shimada Village.

No answer is given.

Ena *kôri*, Iwa Village.

It terminates automatically when either of them dies.

Kamo *kôri*, Hosome Village.

As stated here it terminates automatically when both of them die.

Toki *kôri*, Takayama Village.

Yes. It terminates automatically when the agent dies but not when the principal dies. The agent must fulfill the contract to the end.

Kani *kôri*, Mitake Village.

The delegation of authority does not terminate when the principal dies unless it is declared null by the dead principal's heir.

Ena *kôri*, Akechi Village.

Yes.

Mugi *kôri*, Seki Village.

It terminates automatically.

Ôno *kôri*, Takayama Township.

The delegation of authority does not terminate as long as the agent remains an employee of the shop. It terminates automatically when he is dismissed. When the principal dies, it does not terminate if his heir succeeds him. It terminates automatically when the agent dies.

Motosu *kôri*, Kitagata Village.

The delegation of authority terminates automatically when the agent dies. The principal's heir, however, must succeed to the business when the principal dies if the business remains unfinished.

Kamo *kôri*, Ôta Village.

The delegation of authority terminates automatically when the principal or the agent dies.

Kaisai *kôri* and Shimo-ishizu *kôri*.

The delegation of authority terminates automatically when the principal or the agent dies as stated here.

Gujô *kôri*.

Yes, that is right.

Topic 6: Is It Possible for an Agent to Delegate to Somebody Else the Authority Which Has Been Committed to Him? Is This Possible Only When Consent of the Principal Is Obtained?

TOKYO METROPOLIS

Soy Wholesalers.[1]

It is possible for an agent only with the consent of the principal.

Sugar Wholesalers.

A principal who has committed the authority to an agent will not allow sub-agent to act in his own name without his own consent.

Dried Bonito Wholesalers.

Only with the consent of the principal may an agent delegate his authority to somebody else.

Medicine Wholesalers.

Such a case cannot be found among us.

Paper Wholesalers (*Kiu-kumi*).[2]

It is possible only with the consent of the principal.

Oil Wholesalers.

Such a case can sometimes be found among us.

Stone Wholesalers.

It is possible only with the consent of the principal.

Fuel Wholesalers.

Apart from the employment of laborers, etc., an agent may delegate his authority to somebody else only with the consent of the principal.

Porcelain Wholesalers.

It is possible only with the consent of the principal.

Paper Wholesalers (*Shôkai-kumi*).[3]

An agent may delegate his authority to somebody else only with the consent of the principal.

Rice Traders.[4]

Such a case cannot be found among us.

Salt Wholesalers.

[1] *Shôyu-donya-kumiai.*

[2] *Kiu-kumi kami-donya.*

[3] *Shôkai-kumi kami-donya.*

[4] *Beikoku sangyô-kumiai.*

An agent may do so only with the consent of the principal.

Timber Wholesalers.

An agent may delegate his authority to somebody else only with the consent of the principal.

Timber Traders.[1]

Such a case has never been seen among us.

Timber Traders (*Senju*).[2]

Such a case has never been seen among us.

Matting Wholesalers.

An agent may delegate his authority to somebody else only with the consent of the principal.

Saké Wholesalers.[3]

It is possible only with the consent of the principal.

Drapery Wholesalers.

It is possible only with the consent of the principal.

Saké Wholesalers.

It is possible for an agent only with the consent of the principal.

Lime and Shell Wholesalers.

An agent may not delegate his authority to somebody else. The authority by a branch manager is an exception.

Mosquito Net Wholesalers.

An agent may not delegate his authority to somebody else. It is possible for him to do so only with the consent of the principal.

Copper and Iron Wholesalers.

It is possible for him to do so only with the consent of the principal.

Fuel Wholesalers (*Umite-kumi*).[4]

An agent may never delegate his authority to somebody else. But it is sometimes possible for him if he obtains the consent of the principal.

Tobacco Wholesalers.

Talks will be held between the two when necessary. There is no established practice.

Kôjimachi Ward.

It is possible for him only with the consent of the principal.

[1] *Zaimoku-tôsei-kumiai.*

[2] *Senju zaimoku-kumiai.*

[3] *Sake-rui-donya.*

[4] *Umite-kumi shintan-donya.*

Nihombashi Ward.

An agent may sometimes delegate his authority to somebody else. But this is not recognized as a common practice.

Kyôbashi Ward.

It is possible for him only with the consent of the principal.

Yotsuya Ward and Ushigome Ward.

An agent may delegate his authority to somebody else only with the consent of the principal.

Asakusa Ward.

When the consent of the principal is not obtained, he may sometimes delegate his authority to somebody else.

Honjo Ward.

An agent may not delegate his authority to somebody else. It is possible for him only with the consent of the principal.

Ebara *kôri*.

An agent may not delegate his authority to somebody else.

Higashi-tama *kôri* and Minami-toshima *kôri*.

An agent may not delegate his authority to somebody else as he pleases.

Kita-toshima *kôri*.

In minor matters, an agent is able to do so if he wishes, but in major matters, it is possible for him only with the consent of the principal.

Minami-adachi *kôri*.

It is possible for him only with the consent of the principal.

Shitaya Ward.

It is impossible for him when the consent of the principal cannot be obtained.

Kanda Ward.

We have already answered this in Topic 2.

Akasaka Ward and Azabu Ward.

It is possible for him only with the consent of the principal.

Hongô Ward.

An agent may not delegate his authority to somebody else.

Chiba Prefecture

Awa *kôri*, Hei *kôri*, Asai *kôri* and Nagasa *kôri*.

An agent may not delegate his authority to somebody else. However, if an employee has been ordered by his principal to go to a place and buy some amount of goods, he may delegate part of his authority to somebody else for purchasing the goods conveniently.

Katori *kôri*.

An agent may delegate his authority to somebody else only with the consent of the principal.

Yamabe *kôri* and Muza *kôri*.

Even without the consent of the principal, the agent sometimes delegates his authority to somebody else.

Unakami *kôri* and Sôsa *kôri*.

Without the consent of the principal, an agent may not delegate his authority to somebody else.

Higashi-katsushika *kôri*.

An agent may not delegate his authority to somebody else. But it is sometimes possible for him when the consent of the principal is obtained.

IBARAKI PREFECTURE

Nishi-katsushika *kôri* and Sashima *kôri*.

An agent may not delegate his authority to somebody else without the consent of the principal.

KANAGAWA PREFECTURE

Miura *kôri*.

It is possible only with the consent of the principal.

Tachibana *kôri*.

It is possible only with the consent of the principal.

Kita-tama *kôri*.

It is frequently possible for an agent to delegate a part of his powers in a single day to somebody else. If the agent wants to delegate his entire authority to somebody else, however, he must first obtain the consent of the principal.

Ashigara-shimo *kôri*.

An agent may not do so when the consent of the principal cannot be obtained.

Prefectural Industrial Bureau.

An agent may delegate his authority to somebody else, only with the consent of the principal. In minor transactions, however, it is possible for him to do so.

TOCHIGI PREFECTURE

Prefectural Office.

An agent may not delegate his authority to somebody else. If the principal or the agent encounter unavoidable difficulties, either can release the others from the position any time.

Shimo-tsuga *kôri* and Samukawa *kôri*.

An agent may not delegate his authority to somebody else. He must always obtain the consent of the principal.

Ashikaga *kôri* and Yanada *kôri*.

The principal is responsible for the business as a whole. An agent may delegate his authority only with the consent of the principal.

Mie Prefecture

Suzuka *kôri*.

An agent may not delegate his authority to somebody else.

Ichishi *kôri*.

According to our practice, unless specially provided in the contract, an agent may delegate his authority to somebody else only with the consent of the principal.

Nabari *kôri* and Iga *kôri*.

It is not always possible for an agent to delegate to somebody else the authority only when the consent of the principal is obtained.

Kita-muro *kôri*.

An agent may delegate his authority to somebody else only with the consent of the principal.

Aichi Prefecture

Nakajima *kôri*.

An agent is able to do so only with the consent of the principal.

Nagoya Ward.

Only a manager or a sales clerk may be an agent in a business transaction. No one unrelated to the shop will be named as an agent.

Chita *kôri*.

An agent may not delegate his authority to somebody else when the consent of the principal cannot be obtained.

Minami-shidara *kôri*.

An agent may do so only with the consent of the principal.

Atsumi *kôri*.

An agent may do so only with the consent of the principal.

Kaitô *kôri* and Kaisai *kôri*.

He may do so only with the consent of the principal.

Aichi *kôri*.

An agent may delegate his authority to somebody else only with the consent of the principal.

Niwa *kôri* and Haguri *kôri.*

It may appear possible for an agent to delegate his authority to somebody else, but he should obtain the consent of the principal.

SHIZUOKA PREFECTURE

Prefectural Office.

It is possible only with the consent of the principal.

Udo *kôri* and Abe *kôri.*

An agent may not delegate his authority to somebody else.

Inasa *kôri* and Aratama *kôri.*

It is possible only with the consent of the principal.

Kamo *kôri* and Naka *kôri.*

It is possible only with the consent of the principal.

Saya *kôri* and Kitô *kôri.*

There is no established practice.

GIFU PREFECTURE

Mugi *kôri.*

An agent may not delegate his authority to somebody else when the consent of the principal cannot be obtained.

Ampachi *kôri.*

An agent may not delegate his authority to somebody else.

Fuwa *kôri.*

An agent may not delegate his authority to somebody else when the consent of the principal cannot be obtained.

Atsumi *kôri*, Kagami *kôri* and Katagata *kôri.*

It is possible only with the consent of the principal.

Tagi *kôri* and Kami-ishizu *kôri.*

An agent may not delegate his authority to somebody else when the consent of the principal cannot be obtained.

Ôno *kôri* and Ikeda *kôri.*

An agent may not delegate his authority to somebody else when the consent of the principal cannot be obtained.

Haguri *kôri* and Nakajima *kôri.*

It is possible only with the consent of the principal.

Ena *kôri.*

It is possible only with the consent of the principal.

Kamo *kôri.*

An agent may delegate his authority to somebody else.

Kani *kôri.*

Although we cannot be absolutely certain, it appears normally impossible for an agent to delegate his authority to somebody else when the consent of the principal cannot be obtained.

Atsumi *kôri*, Gifu Township.

It is possible for the agent. Sometimes the consent of the principal should be obtained.

Ôgaki.

An agent may not delegate his authority to somebody else.

Ena *kôri*, Nakatsugawa Village.

The consent of the principal should be obtained in any case.

Shimo-ishizu *kôri*, Takasu Township.

An agent may not delegate his authority to somebody else. If unavoidable circumstances require it, he must obtain the consent of the principal.

Haguri *kôri*, Takegahana Village.

An agent may not delegate his authority to somebody else when the consent of the principal is not obtained.

Yamagata *kôri*, Takatomi Village.

An agent may delegate his authority to somebody else only with the consent of the principal.

Mugi *kôri*, Kôzuchi Viliage.

An agent may delegate his authority to somebody else only with the consent of the principal.

Haguri *kôri*, Kasamatsu Village.

It is possible only with the consent of the principal.

Fuwa *kôri*, Tarui Village.

In both cases, there is an established practice.

Ôno *kôri*, Miwa Village.

Only with the consent of the principal may an agent delegate his authority.

Ampachi *kôri*, Gôdo Village.

An agent may not delegate his authority to somebody else.

Tagi *kôri*, Shimada Village.

No answer is given.

Ena *kôri*, Iwa Village.

An agent may not delegate his authority to somebody else. It is possible only with the consent of the principal.

Kamo *kôri*, Hosome Village.

An agent may delegate his authority to somebody else.

Toki *kôri*, Takayama Village.

It is possible only with the consent of the principal.

Kani *kôri*, Mitake Village.

An agent may delegate his authority to another agent. The former is responsible for any damage done by the latter.

Ena *kôri*, Akechi Village.

It is possible only with the consent of the principal.

Mugi *kôri*, Seki Village.

An agent may not delegate his authority to another agent. It is possible only with the consent of the principal.

Ôno *kôri*, Takayama Township.

An agent may sometimes delegate his authority to another agent.

Motosu *kôri*, Kitagata Village.

An agent may not delegate his authority to somebody else when the consent of the principal cannot be obtained.

Kamo *kôri*, Ôta Village.

Sometimes an agent may delegate his authority to somebody else.

Kaisai *kôri* and Shimo-ishizu *kôri*.

An agent may not delegate his authority to somebody else. If unavoidable circumstances require it, he must obtain the consent of the principal.

Gujô *kôri*.

Sometimes an agent may delegate his authority to somebody else, without the consent of the principal.

CHAPTER VI
ACCOUNT CURRENT[1]

Topic 1: Is There Any Practice Whereby Merchants Who Are Engaged in Continuous Transactions with One Another, Assuming in Turn the Roles of a Creditor or a Debtor, Settle Their Accounts Not at Each Transaction, but After Several Months or Half a Year of Transactions, Balance and Settle Accounts for the Whole Period, or Carry the Balance over into Next Term's Account?

Is This Method of Balancing Accounts[2] (at One Time for a Whole Period) Practiced Only When It Is Stipulated Beforehand in a Contract, or Is It Observed, Even If There Is No Stipulation to That Effect, When the Mutual Accounts Reach a Large Amount?

When This Practice Is Stipulated in a Contract, What Is the Usual Length of Period for Settling an Account?

Is any Interest Supposed to Accrue on This Account?

Is There Any Special Name by Which This Practice Is Designated?

TOKYO METROPOLIS

Prefectural Office.

Soy Wholesalers.[3]

Accounts are settled in full after each period. The balance, if any, will be carried over into the next term. Regarding the second question, it must be stipulated beforehand in a contract. As for the third, the period for settling accounts is two months or half a year. Regarding the fourth, no interest accrues on the account. The name referred to in the fifth question is *shikiri*.

Sugar Wholesalers.

What is stated here is a common business practice. The period for settling accounts is usually half a year at the longest. Sometimes for convenience the balance is carried over into the next term. This method of balancing accounts is usually stipulated beforehand in

[1] *Kôgo-keisan.*

[2] *Sashihiki-kanjô.*

[3] *Shôyu-donya-kumiai.*

a contract. A verbal agreement to this effect will become invalid if any trouble occurs in the course of the transaction. Even without any contract, the practice is observed between merchants engaged in continuous transactions. No contract is concluded on account settlement. In any case, accounts are settled in cash. There is no special name for this practice.

Dried Bonito Wholesalers.

Usually the period for settling accounts is fifteen days, twice each month. But accounts for several months of transactions may be settled for the whole period and any balance may be carried over into the next term for the convenience of either party. As for the second, third and fourth questions, we have nothing to answer. As for the fifth, the practice is called the "30th" and the "14th."

Medicine Wholesalers.

Usually accounts are settled and balanced after each transaction, but they may sometimes be settled for a whole period after several months for the convenience of either party. A case such as that referred to in the second question has never been seen among us. In answer to the third, the period is one month. As for the fourth, the debtor must pay interest. And regarding the fifth, the practice is called *tsuki-kanjô*, "settlement for each month."

Paper Wholesalers (*Kiu-kumi*).[1]

In regard to the first question, payment is made in full when it is due. As for the second, there is no case in which mutual accounts reach a large amount. Regarding the third, the period for a contract is about thirty days. In answer to the fourth, no interest accrues on the account during the period. As for the fifth, there is no special name.

Oil Wholesalers.

Regarding the first question, such cases can be seen everywhere. As for the second, this method will be stipulated in a contract if it is convenient. Accounts are usually settled in July and December, February and August. As regards the fourth question, no interest accrues. As for the fifth, there is no special name.

Stone Wholesalers.

Regarding the first question, accounts for transactions between regular traders are balanced every month or two. The remainder

[1] *Kiu-kumi kami-donya.*

is sometimes carried over into the next term. In answer to the second question, if necessary, the settlement is made before the due date. As to the third, the matter is settled through talks. Regarding the fourth, no interest accrues. And as to the fifth, there is no special name.

Fuel Wholesalers.

Regarding the first question, in both cases, accounts are balanced and settled for a whole period rather than after each transaction. Any remainder is paid immediately. The time limit for balancing accounts is the 14th and the 30th of the month. No interest accrues on the account, unless specially provided in the contract. In answer to the fifth question, there is no special name.

Porcelain Wholesalers.

Our practice is that payment in full should be made at the time of account settlement. If both parties find it necessary, however, any remainder will be carried over into the next term. The method of balancing accounts is stipulated beforehand in a contract. Accounts are balanced and settled six times a year. In transactions between two widely separated districts, however, accounts are settled two or three times a year. Unless specially provided beforehand, no interest accrues on the account. Regarding the fifth question, the practice is called *sekku-barai* (payment for a season) and *niki-barai* (payment for half a year).

Paper Wholesalers (*Shôkai-kumi*).[1]

Of course payment should be made in full at the time of account settlement for a whole period. However, any balance is sometimes carried over into the next term, if both parties find it necessary. Accounts are generally balanced for a month or two, regardless of whether the mutual accounts reach large amounts. Even if this method of payment is stipulated, the period does not exceed two months, unless specially provided beforehand. No interest accrues on the account. There is no special name.

Rice Traders.[2]

Some accounts are settled after each transaction, but others are settled for half a year. There is no established practice. Sometimes the method of balancing accunts is stipulated, but not at other times.

[1] *Shôkai-kumi kami-donya.*

[2] *Beikoku sangyô-kumiai.*

There is no established practice with regard to interest either; practice varies with each shop. In answer to the fifth question, there is no special name.

Salt Wholesalers.

The accounts are sometimes balanced and settled en bloc after a period of transactions. The balance is sometimes carried over into next period. Regarding the second question, the practice is observed when the mutual accounts reach a large amount. As for the third, the period is agreed upon in a conference between the two. The answer to the fourth is as stated above. In answer to the fifth, no special name exists.

Timber Wholesalers.

Sometimes the remainder is paid immediately after the settlement, but in other cases it is carried over into the next term. This is agreed on in talks. With regard to the second question, everything is settled in talks. The period referred to in the third is as a rule the 14th and the 30th of the month. Regarding the fourth, unless specially provided beforehand, no interest accrues on the account. As for the fifth question, there is no special name.

Timber Traders.[1]

As answered above.

Timber Traders (*Senju*).[2]

Since there is no established practice, agreement is reached only through talks.

Matting Wholesalers.

Accounts are balanced and settled for the whole period after several months. Any balance is usually paid by the debtor to the creditor at that time. But sometimes it is carried over into the next term. The time limit for payment comes thirty or sixty days after the transaction, according to the contract. In answer to the fourth question, no interest accrues on the account. As for the fifth, the popular name is *sashihiki-zankin* (the balance left).

Saké Wholesalers.[3]

Any balance left after settlement will be carried over into the next term. When the mutual accounts reach a large amount, they are balanced for a whole year, and any balance is carried over into

[1] *Zaimoku-tôsei-kumiai.*

[2] *Senju zaimoku-kumiai.*

[3] *Sake-rui-donya.*

the next term regardless of whether a contract is concluded or not. The account does not carry any interest. There is no special name for the practice.

Drapery Wholesalers.

Accounts for goods coming from various places of production are settled after each transaction. Regarding the second question, among us, the period of payment for continuous transactions between a creditor and a debtor is stipulated in a contract as thirty days. The accounts are balanced and settled at every interval of thirty days. In transactions with other fellow traders, such as our buyers, payment is made every two months, according to the contract. Accounts are balanced after six months. The account does not carry any interest. This method of payment is called *kyû-go-sekku-kanjô* (payment by seasonal installments, five times a year).

Saké Wholesalers.

In transactions between a creditor and a debtor, the method of balancing accounts is not always established as a definite practice. Sometimes the accounts are settled after each transaction, and at other times after several months or half a year. And sometimes the balance is carried over into the next term. Whether or not the method of balancing accounts is stipulated in a contract, they may be balanced at any time if the mutual accounts reach a large amount. If stipulated in a contract, it is done according to the contract. No interest accrues on the account. This method of payment is called *chô-jime* (settlement of accounts).

Lime and Shell Wholesalers.

Traders balance and settle all accounts for transactions in a whole period only for a limited period of two months, or six times a year. They sometimes settle accounts in part at the time of each transaction when a promise of payment is scheduled for a later date. The contract stipulates whether or not interest accrues. In general, however, they do not demand interest. No special name exists.

Mosquito Net Wholesalers.

Accounts are balanced and settled for the whole period after several months of transactions. According to our practice, any balance is paid by the debtor at that time. In some cases it is carried over into the next term. Depending on the contract, the period of payment is thirty or sixty days. The account does not carry interest.

The popular name for this is *sashihiki-zankin* (the balance left).

Copper and Iron Wholesalers.

There are various methods of calculation for account settlement. Sometimes, the total accounts are settled for the whole period after several months of transactions. At other times, the accounts are settled four times a year, and the balance is paid without delay. At other times, the balance is carried over into the next term, and payment is made in full when it is due. Whether or not it is stipulated in a contract, payment, sometimes in part, will be requested when the mutual accounts reach a large amount. Any contract which is concluded includes promises of various kinds. But the period of payment should not be longer than half a year. The accounts do not carry any interest. There is no special name.

Fuel Wholesalers (*Umite-kumi*).[1]

After a month or several months of transactions, accounts are very often balanced and settled for the whole period, and any balance is carried over into the next term. In theory, payment should be made in cash. In some circumstances, however, the balance is carried over into the next term, as stated above. There is no established practice for the period of payment. But as a general rule, the time limit is the 14th or the last day of a month, unless specially provided. There is no general practice on whether or not to demand interest; this depends on the circumstances at that time. Since there are many different kinds of transactions, for instance, purchase from a producing center, selling to Tokyo and other areas, and so on, no special name can be given.

Tobacco Wholesalers.

There is no established practice, since the matter is settled through the talks between the two, depending upon the circumstances.

Kôjimachi Ward.

For transactions between two parties of long standing, the balance is sometimes carried over into the next term. If not stipulated in a contract, accounts will sometimes be balanced for a whole period. If it is stipulated beforehand, the period of payment will be one month, half a year, or one year. Interest accrues on the account. The special name is *sashihiki-kanjô* (balancing accounts).

[1] *Umite-kumi shintan-donya.*

Nihombashi Ward.

We have a business practice called *tana-oroshi-kanjô* (term-end settlement of accounts), by which accounts are settled for a period ending in July or in December. Any balance will be paid at that time. Regarding the second question, this method is done regardless of whether or not it is stipulated in a contract. As for the third, in general, the year consists of two periods ending in July and in December. Regarding the fourth, no interest accrues on the account. And in answer to the fifth, no special name exists.

Kyôbashi Ward.

Regarding the first question, in continuous transactions between a creditor and a debtor for several months or half a year, the accounts are balanced and settled for the whole period, and the balance is paid or carried over into the next term. As for the second, this method of balancing accounts is observed when the mutual accounts reach a large amount. As regard the third, no established practice can be given. As for the fourth, no interest accrues. And in answer to the fifth, the term is *kiritsuki* (the last month of a period of payment).

Yotsuya Ward and Ushigome Ward.

In general, the total accounts are balanced and settled in full after a certain period. According to the original contract, however, any balance may be carried over into the next term. No stipulation beforehand in a contract is necessary for balancing accounts. Payment is made on the day stipulated in the contract. Unless specially provided beforehand, no interest accrues on the account. This method of payment is usually called *sashihiki* (the balance), since there is no special name established.

Asakusa Ward.

Regarding the first question, accounts are settled every thirty days or six months. After settling the accounts, the two parties pay or receive the balance. As for the second question, even without a previous contract, the accounts will be balanced and settled. Regarding the third, the period of payment is at least one month and at most half a year. In answer to the fourth question, no interest accrues on the account. As for the fifth, there is no special name, but we use such popular names as *tsukibarai* (payment for a month), *go-sekku* (payment for each of five seasons),[1] or *niki-barai* (payment for each half a year).

Honjo Ward.

Accounts for transactions between two parties of long standing are sometimes balanced and settled in total after several months or half a year rather than after each transaction. Any balance is paid by the debtor to the creditor, or is carried over into the next term. Accounts are balanced when stipulated in the contract or when they reach a large amount. The period of payment usually is not stipulated in a contract. Sometimes interest accrues, but at other times, it does not. This method of payment has no special name.

Ebara *kôri*.

Accounts for transactions between two parties of long standing are balanced and settled in total, not after each transaction, but after a period of several months or half a year, and any balance is paid without delay. No balance will be carried over into the next term. Accounts will be balanced only when stipulated beforehand. They will not be balanced when it is not so stipulated even if they reach a large amount. In a transaction under a contract, the period of payment is as a rule sixty days. The account does not carry any interest. There is no special name for this method of payment.

Higashi-tama *kôri* and Minami-toshima *kôri*.

When accounts are balanced, any balance is usually paid without delay. Prior to a transaction, the method of balancing accounts is stipulated in a contract in outline. The period of payment usually ends in July or December, although there are minor differences according to the kind of business. However, the two parties sometimes agree on extraordinary balancing of their accounts, when the mutual accounts reach a large amount. No interest accrues on the account. There is no special name for this method of payment.

Kita-toshima *kôri*.

In transactions between a creditor and a debtor, no account is balanced and settled after each transaction. Usually the total accounts are balanced in July or December. The two parties will reach a decision through talks as to whether the balance should be

[1] Recently it seems that the name *go-sekku* has gone out officially, but it is still widely used.

paid at that time or carried over into the next term. Even before the time limit, the total accounts may be balanced and settled when the mutual accounts reach a large amount. Then the account of balance carries no interest. The method of payment is named *bon-kanjô* (payment in mid-summer) or *kure-kanjô* (payment at year's end).

Minami-adachi *kôri.*

In answer to the first question, no amount left after the account has been balanced can be carried over into the next term. As for the second, payment is made at *bon* (mid-summer) and *kure* (year's end). In rural districts, *bon* refers to the 15th of August, but in urban districts, the 15th of July. As for the third question, the time limit is the last day of the month. In answer to the fourth, no interest accrues. As for the fifth, the term is *sashihiki-kanjô* (the balancing of accounts).

Shitaya Ward.

In answer to the first question, our merchants do not settle accounts after each transaction. After a certain period of transactions, they balance and settle the total accounts for the whole period. The period is long or short depending on the kind of business, but usually it is half a year or a year. The balance, as a rule, should be paid in full. It is said to be unusual for it to be carried over into the next term. Regarding the second question, the method of balancing accounts is stipulated beforehand in a contract or is decided upon according to common practice. With regard to the third, as we answered at the beginning, the period of payment is half a year or a year. A month is rare. Regarding the fourth, unless provided beforehand in a contract, no interest accrues on the account. And in answer to the fifth, in most cases, the practice is called *sô-shikiri-kanjô* (total balancing of accounts).

Kanda Ward.

The total accounts are balanced and settled after several transactions, and any balance is carried over into the next term. Accounts are not balanced according to a contract, but when the mutual accounts reach a large amount. The period of contract is usually two months. For example, the accounts will be settled by the last day of next month for a transaction that takes place on any day of this month. The total accounts for half a year are balanced and settled in July and December. No interest accrues. The total debts for a period may be rewritten into an official document if the accounts reach a large amount. At that time, no interest accrues. This practice is called *uri kake-kin* (credit).

Akasaka Ward and Azabu Ward.

Regarding the first question, there are two methods of balancing accounts, paying the full balance without delay, and carrying it into the next term. As for the second question, whether or not it is stipulated in a contract, the accounts may sometimes be settled when they reach a large amount. Regarding the third, these periods are the 14th and 30th of the month, at the five annual festivals, *bon* (mid-summer) and *kure* (year's end). The two parties will choose the day through talks. In regard to the fourth question, no interest accrues. As for the fifth, the practice is called *sashihiki-kanjô* (balancing accounts), and *kaisai-kanjô* (total payment of accounts), or *kanjô* (accounts).

Hongô Ward.

In continuous transactions between a creditor and a debtor, the total accounts are balanced and settled for a whole period, and the balance is usually paid in full immediately. Sometimes the accounts are balanced and settled according to a contract concluded beforehand, or when the accounts reach a large amount. The time limit for balancing accounts is the 14th and 30th of the month. No interest accrues on the account. There is no special name.

Chiba Prefecture

Awa *kôri*, Hei *kôri*, Asai *kôri* and Nagasa *kôri*.

In transactions between a creditor and a debtor, the accounts are not settled after each transaction. In most cases, they are balanced for half a year or a whole year. Any balance is paid in full immediately or is carried over into the next term. When the accounts reach a large amount, they will be settled before the due date. It is unusual to promise a specific period of settlement. However, according to common practice, the accounts are balanced and settled on July 13 and December 31 of the old calendar. No interest accrues on balanced accounts which are settled between fellow merchants.

Katori *kôri*.

A year is divided into two terms for balancing accounts. After several transactions, the accounts are balanced and settled for the whole period. Any balance is carried over into the next term. When the accounts reach a large amount, they are balanced and settled before the due date. Usually no definite promise is made. The regular period is three months. In principle the account does not carry interest.

Yamabe *kôri* and Muza *kôri*.

When the accounts are balanced, any balance is usually paid in full. Sometimes it is carried over into the next term. The method of balancing accounts is stipulated in a contract beforehand, the period for settling accounts being indicated. In some business circles, however, no promise is made. When the accounts reach a large amount, they are balanced and settled. The period is usually half a year or six months. In some circles, however, the period is one to three months. Unless specially provided, no interest accrues on the account.

Unakami *kôri* and Sôsa *kôri*.

Accounts for regular transactions of long standing are balanced and settled for the whole period of one year or for six months. Any balance is carried over into the next term. In this case a definite length of period is shown. Usually the accounts are settled twice a year, on July 13 and December 31 of the old calendar. The two parties will not demand interest from each other.

Higashi-katsushika *kôri*.

After several transactions, the accounts for the whole period are balanced and settled after several months or half a year. Any balance is paid in full immediately, it is rarely carried over into the next term's account. The accounts will be balanced and settled in accordance with the contract, but if stipulated in the contract, they will be settled when they reach a large amount. When stipulated in a contract, the period of settlement is one month, or six months, the latter period ending just before *bon* (mid-summer) in July, or *kure* (year-end) on December 31. In this case, no interest accrues on the account. The popular name for this kind of settlement is *tsuki-kiriage* (payment for a month) or *bon, kure-kiriage* (payment in mid-summer and on December 31).

IBARAKI PREFECTURE

Nishi-katsushika *kôri* and Sashima *kôri*.

According to our practice, after the accounts have been balanced and settled, any balance should be paid in full. The accounts are settled at the time stipulated in the contract. Usually the period of payment is half a year long. The account does not carry interest. It is called *bon-kanjô* (payment at the time of the Bon Festival) and *kure-kanjô* (payment on December 31), usually according to the old calendar.

KANAGAWA PREFECTURE

Miura *kôri*.

In answer to the first question, total accounts for transactions between merchants of long standing are balanced and settled for the whole period after several transactions of half a year. Any balance is paid in full in July or December. Sometimes, if it is more convenient, the balance is carried over into the next term. Regarding the second question, the accounts are balanced every month on the last day of the month, whether stipulated in the contract or not. As for the third, the accounts are settled as described above if the transactions are regular, but they are settled on the last day of every month if the transactions are irregular. Regarding the fourth, no interest accrues on the account. As for the fifth, the balance carried over into the next term is called *kake* (credit).

Tachibana *kôri*.

The accounts are balanced and settled twice a year. Any balance will be paid at that time. It is carried over into the next term when the accounts reach a large amount. In a contract, the period of payment is half a year, ending in June or December. No interest accrues. This is called *niki-kanjô* (payment twice a year).

Kita-tama *kôri*.

In answer to the first question, since cases differ, no definite answer can be given. Regarding the second, the accounts can be balanced and settled any time when they reach a large amount. However, they are usually settled twice a year in July (during the first ten days) and December (the last day, or the 31st). As for the third question, the length of the period is not fixed, so no definite answer can be given. Regarding the fourth, no interest accrues. And as for the fifth, no special name exists.

Ashigara-shimo *kôri*.

Each case described here will be settled through consultation between the two parties. There is no established practice.

Prefectural Industrial Bureau.

When merchants are engaged in continuous transactions with

one another, alternating in the roles of creditor or debtor, the method of balancing total accounts for a whole period is not always practiced. Some merchants settle accounts after each transaction, but others settle the accounts and pay any balance for the whole period after several months or half a year of transactions. Sometimes the balance is carried over into the next term. The method of balancing accounts is observed when the mutual accounts reach a large amount. We think we need not answer this; we have already given the answer earlier in this topic. The account does not carry interest. There is no special name, but *sashihiki-kanjô* (accounts balanced) is popularly used.

Tochigi Prefecture

Prefectural Office.

When merchants are engaged in continuous transactions with one another, alternating in the roles of creditor or debtor, the accounts are rarely balanced and settled after each transaction. Instead they are settled for the whole period on the 15th of the month, or after a month, or half a year. The method of balancing accounts is practiced when the merchants are engaged in continuous transactions. Otherwise, the accounts are settled after each transaction. The accounts are settled at the time stipulated beforehand. The accounts can be balanced and settled any time when they reach a large amount, if the matter is not stipulated beforehand in a contract. When stipulated beforehand, the accounts are settled every fifteen days or every month, whether the balance is to be paid or received. The account does not carry interest. There is no special name for this method, but some merchants call it *yori-kanjô*, while others call it *tsukijime-kanjô* or *torihiki-kanjô*.

Shimo-tsuga *kôri* and Samukawa *kôri*.

In answer to the first question, when merchants are engaged in continuous transactions with one another, alternating in the roles of creditor or debtor, the accounts are balanced and settled for the whole period after several months or half a year of transactions, and any balance is carried into the next term. Regarding the second question, whether stipulated beforehand or not, this method of balancing accounts is practiced when the mutual accounts reach a large amount. As for the third, when the practice is stipulated in a contract, the period for settling accounts ends in June or December, twice a year. Regarding the fourth question, no interest accrues on the account. And regarding the fifth, this method is called *niki-kanjô* (payment twice a year).

Ashikaga *kôri* and Yanada *kôri*.

In answer to the first question, as we have already said in Topic 10 of Selling and Buying Title IV (Book I & II),[1] our trade practice prohibits anyone from keeping a debt. Merchants usually show their books to each other to settle their accounts in part, so that there will be no large balance left. Every half-year they balance and settle their accounts, and pay or receive the balance in full. In some cases, however, the balance is carried over into the next term. Regarding the second question, the accounts are settled when the time limit stated in the contract arrives. As for the third, the time limit for settlement is June 30 and December 31. Regarding the fourth question, no interest accrues on the account. And as for the fifth, there is no special name to indicate this method.

MIE PREFECTURE

Suzuka *kôri*.

When merchants are engaged in continuous transactions with one another, alternating in the roles of creditor or debtor, the accounts are not balanced and settled after each transaction, but for the whole period after several months or half a year of transactions, and any balance is paid in full. It is never carried over into the next term. The method of balancing accounts is practiced only when stipulated beforehand in a contract. However, it may be practiced when the mutual accounts reach a large amount, even if there is no contract. Depending on the contract, the period of settlement is one month, or half a year. The account does not carry interest. The method is called *torihiki-kanjô* (credit).

Ichishi *kôri*.

In answer to the first question, such a practice can be seen here. Regarding the second, the accounts are settled at the end of each season, and when the mutual accounts reach a large amount. As for the third question, usually it is observed at the end of each season. Regarding the fourth, no interest accrues. As for the fifth, no special name exists.

Nabari *kôri* and Iga *kôri*.

Accounts are balanced and settled for the whole period after

[1] *Baibai-hen.*

several months or half a year of transactions, and any balance is paid. Even if there is no contract, the accounts are balanced when the two parties feel the need to settle accounts. There is no definite period established for the fulfillment of a contract. Accounts are settled after half a year, or each term for business. The business term is a period, for example, a tea producing season, during which merchants and brokers are busily engaged in tea transactions. The amount of interest depends on each party's share of the expenditure. But no interest accrues on the account when the two parties buy from and sell to each other. The period of payment is half a year or sixty days. There is no special name for the method of balancing accounts.

Kita-muro *kôri.*

In answer to the first question, in transactions between two parties who have long been engaged in business with each other, the period of balancing accounts is half a year. Any balance is then carried over into the next term for convenience. Regarding the second question, even when the time for settlement is stipulated beforehand in a contract, the accounts are sometimes settled on a special basis if they reach a large amount. Our answer to the third question is as stated above half a year. Regarding the fourth, no interest accrues. As for the fifth, as long as a transaction continues, it is called *sashihiki-kanjô* (balancing accounts).

Aichi Prefecture

Nakajima *kôri.*

After a whole year of transactions, the accounts are balanced and settled for the whole period. Sometimes, however, the balance is carried over into the next term. If there is no stipulation in a contract, the accounts are settled twice a year, that is, in July and December. The account does not carry any interest. This method of settlement is called *kanjô* (balancing accounts).

Nagoya Ward.

Sometimes the accounts are balanced and settled after each transaction, but at other times they are settled for the whole period after a year or half a year (July and December). Any balance is paid immediately or carried over into the next term, which starts in July and January. Accounts in business transactions must be settled without fail, whether stipulated in a contract or not. Methods of settling accounts differ according to the kind of business, the amount of money and the local practice. Thus there is no established practice. No interest accrues on the account. The name by which settlement is generally referred to is *sashihiki-kanjô* (balancing accounts). Settlement of accounts in July and December, however, is specially named *sekku-no-sashihiki-kanjô* (balancing accounts for each business season).

Chita *kôri*.

The balance should be paid after each transaction. Sometimes, however, the accounts are balanced and settled after several months of transactions. The accounts are settled according to a contract agreed upon beforehand. Sometimes, however, they are settled when they have reached a large amount, although it is not stipulated in a contract. The accounts are settled twice a year in June and December. The accounts do not carry interest, unless specially provided in a contract. This method of settlement is called *niki-no-keisan* (balancing accounts twice a year).

Minami-shidara *kôri*.

Generally speaking, the accounts are balanced and settled after each transaction. In some continuous transactions, however, the balance is sometimes carried over into the next term. The accounts are sometimes settled at a time not stipulated beforehand in a contract. If the price offered by one merchant is higher than that offered by the other, the former may ask the latter for an additional payment. The period of balancing accounts is generally three months. Unless specially provided in a contract, no interest accrues on the account. There is no special name here for the method of balancing accounts.

Atsumi *kôri*.

In answer to the first question, there are two different ways of balancing accounts. No definite practice can be given. Regarding the second question, the method of balancing accounts is practiced not only when it is stipulated beforehand in a contract, but also when it is not if the accounts reach a large amount. As for the third, the periods for settlement are at the end of the month or the year. Regarding the fourth question, in business transactions, no interest accrues on the account. As for the fifth, there is no special name.

Kaitô *kôri* and Kaisai *kôri*.

According to our practice, after the accounts have been balanced and settled by the two parties, any balance will be paid in full. Even if there is no stipulation in a contract beforehand, the accounts are usually balanced and settled in July and December. If there is a stipulation to that effect in a contract, the steps described above will be taken. The account carries no interest. There is no special name.

Aichi *kôri.*

In business transactions between merchants, the total accounts are balanced and settled after a specified period of transactions. The balance will be paid in full at that time. It will never be carried over into the next term. The method of balancing accounts is practiced only when stipulated beforehand in a contract, or when the mutual accounts reach a large amount, even if there is no stipulation to that effect. When the practice is stipulated in a contract, the usual period for settling accounts is sixty days, or two months. The account does not carry interest. There is no special name to indicate the practice.

Niwa *kôri* and Haguri *kôri.*

When merchants are engaged in continuous transactions with one another, assuming the roles in turn of creditor or debtor, they balance and settle their accounts over into the next term. This is only a matter of convenience. So far there has been no contract in which the method of settling accounts has been stipulated. There is no practice here to stipulate the period of settlement. Whenever the accounts run up into a large amount, the accounts are balanced and settled, usually, at the end of the month or the year. According to our practice, interest does not accrue on the account. The method of balancing accounts is called *tachiai-kanjô* (mutual credit).

Shizuoka Prefecture

Prefectural Office.

In answer to the first question, after balancing accounts, some people settle the account to the last yen, but others carry the balance over into the next term. As for the second, regardless of whether it is stipulated beforehand in a contract or whether the accounts reach a large amount, the accounts are settled for reasons of convenience. Regarding the third question, when it is stipulated beforehand in a contract, the usual length of period for settling accounts is about three months. As for the fourth, no interest accrues. Regarding the fifth, in general, it is called *sashihiki-kanjô* (balancing accounts).

Udo *kôri* and Abe *kôri.*

In answer to the first question, in most cases the balance is carried over into the next term. Regarding the second, the accounts are settled when they reach a large amount. As for the third, no answer is given. In answer to the fourth question, no interest accrues. As for the fifth, there is no special name.

Inasa *kôri* and Aratama *kôri.*

When the accounts are balanced and settled, the balance, if any, will be immediately paid up completely. The accounts are settled when they reach a large amount. Then interest accrues on the account. The period for settling accounts begins from the time the last accounts were settled.

Kamo *kôri* and Naka *kôri.*

In answer to the first question, the balance, if any, will be paid up at each transaction. Sometimes, however, it may be carried over into the next term. Regarding the second, the accounts will be balanced and settled when it is stipulated beforehand in a contract, or, occasionally, when the accounts reach a large amount. As for the third question, the time of settlement is usually in the months of January and July. Regarding the fourth, no interest accrues on the account. As for the fifth, the method is called *sashihiki-kanjô* (balancing accounts).

Saya *kôri* and Kitô *kôri.*

When the accounts are settled by merchants, the balance, if any, should be paid up immediately. However, the creditor, granting his debtor's request, may carry it over into the next term due to some unavoidable circumstances. The accounts are usually balanced and settled only when it is stipulated beforehand in a contract. But there are also cases when accounts are balanced and settled although it is not stipulated beforehand in a contract when the accounts reach a large amount. The accounts are settled every month, twice a year, or even yearly. In business transactions, no interest accrues on the account. In rural districts, however, the debtor, lending his creditor some daily necessities in exchange for tea, may sometimes pay interest on the account. The accounts are balanced and settled on the 30th of the month, or twice a year, at the time of the Bon Festival or on December 31. The popular name for the method of payment is *sekki-kanjô* (seasonal balancing of accounts), etc.

GIFU PREFECTURE

Mugi *kôri.*

In answer to the first question, the payment is usually made in full after a whole period at the time of settling accounts. If it becomes necessary to postpone payment, the balance will be carried over into the next term. As for the second questions, regardless of whether or not it is stipulated in a contract, if the accounts run up into a large amount, the creditor sometimes asks his debtor to settle the accounts. Regarding the third, the length of period for settling accounts depends on the contract. As for the fourth question, no interest accrues on the account. Regarding the fifth, the popular name is *tachiai-kanjô* (mutual credit).

Ampachi *kôri.*

The balance, as a rule, is paid up. The accounts are balanced and settled when it is stipulated beforehand in a contract, or when the accounts reach a large amount. The usual length of period for settling accounts is six months, although there is no established practice for convenience's sake. Unless specially provided beforehand in a contract, no interest accrues on the account. In general, the method of balancing accounts is called *sekki-kanjô* (seasonal settlement).

Fuwa *kôri.*

The accounts are balanced and settled at each transaction. Sometimes, however, the balance, if any, is paid up twice a year, in February and August. The accounts are balanced when it is stipulated in a contract or in exceptional cases, when the accounts reach a large amount. The length of period for settling accounts is always stipulated in a contract. The account carries no interest. There is no special name.

Atsumi *kôri,* Kagami *kôri* and Katagata *kôri.*

In answer to the first question, after a month or half a year of transactions, the accounts are balanced and settled for that period. Sometimes, however, the balance, if any, may be carried over into the next term. As for the second question, the accounts are balanced and settled when it is stipulated beforehand in a contract. However, the accounts are also balanced and settled on prior demand by the creditor, even when it is not stipulated in a contract, when the accounts reach a large amount. The settlement is made twice a year, in June and December. Regarding the third question, the usual length of period is one to six months. As for the fourth, no interest accrues on the account. Regarding the fifth question, this practice is called *tachiai-kanjô* (mutual credit).

Tagi *kôri* and Kami-ishizu *kôri.*

According to the practice here, merchants engaged in continuous transactions do not settle their accounts at each transaction, but rather after half a year of transactions, usually in February and August. In some rural districts, however, the accounts are settled in June and December of the old calendar, according to the practice prevailing in each district. The account does not carry any interest. There is no special name to indicate the method of settling accounts.

Ôno *kôri* and Ikeda *kôri.*

The accounts are balanced and settled through discussions between the two parties. There is no established method of balancing accounts. In some cases the accounts are settled at each transaction but in others, at the end of a period. The accounts are usually settled in February and August, but also at times stipulated beforehand in a contract or when the accounts reach a large amount. The length of period for settling accounts is not always specified. Unless specially provided beforehand in a contract, no interest accrues on the account. There is no special name to indicate the method of balancing accounts.

Haguri *kôri* and Nakajima *kôri.*

No definite practice can be given for any of the questions asked here.

Ena *kôri.*

Regarding the first question, both cases are found here. As for the second also, both cases are found. Regarding the third, the accounts are balanced and settled twice a year. As for the fourth, no interest accrues on the account. And regarding the fifth, the practice is called *sashihiki-kanjô* (balancing accounts).

Kamo *kôri.*

Merchants who are engaged in continuous transactions with one another do not balance and settle their accounts at each transaction, but after a month or half a year of transactions. Sometimes, however, they will not carry the balance over into the next term. The method of balancing accounts is not practiced unless it is stipulated beforehand in a contract, except when the mutual accounts run up into a large amount. Usually the accounts are settled semiannually, in January and July. The account does not carry any interest. The method of settlement is called *tachiai-kanjô* (mutual credit).

Kani *kôri*.

In answer to the first question, the methods of settling accounts differ according to the type of goods. After several months or half a year of transactions, merchants balance and settle their accounts for the whole period. Regarding the second question, if settlement is not made at each transaction, the accounts are balanced and settled as agreed upon beforehand in a contract. As for the third, business agreements differ according to the circumstances, for example, the size of the business or the type of goods. We have never heard of any established practice. Regarding the fourth question in most cases, no interest accrues. As for the fifth, formerly the practice was called *sashihiki-kanjô* (balancing accounts), but it is now called *kiyome-kanjô* (final balancing of accounts). However, there does not seem to be any special established name.

Atsumi *kôri*, Gifu Township.

In answer to the first question, depending on the type of transaction, the accounts are balanced and settled after a month or after several months. The balance, if any, may be paid up immediately or may be carried over into the next term. Regarding the second question, the debtor will be asked by the creditor to pay up the amount of money which is already agreed upon beforehand in a contract, not only when it is stipulated beforehand, but also when the mutual accounts reach a large amount. The accounts are usually settled in June and December. As for the third question, the length of period is one month or half a year. Regarding the fourth, no interest accrues on the account. As for the fifth, the practice is called *tachiai-kanjô* (mutual credit).

Ôgaki.

Usually the balance, if any, is paid up at the time of settling accounts, although sometimes it is carried over into the next term. The accounts are settled when it is stipulated beforehand in a contract, or when the mutual accounts reach a large amount. Since it is done at the convenience of the two parties, there is no established practice. The period of settling accounts is usually six months. Unless specially provided beforehand, no interest accrues on the account. The method of settling accounts is generally called *sekki-kanjô* (seasonal settlement).

Ena *kôri*, Nakatsugawa Village.

Unless a contract stipulates that the payment of the balance should be made at the time of settling accounts, payment is made on June 30 or December 30. In the case of wholesale transactions, interest accrues, but in the case of retail sales, it does not. The time of settlement, June 30 or December 30, is called *niki-kambi* (semi-annual date of settlement).

Shimo-ishizu *kôri*, Takasu Township.

According to prevailing practice, the balance should be completely paid at the time of settling accounts. Through talks between the two parties, however, it sometimes may be carried over into the next term. The accounts are balanced and settled when it is stipulated beforehand in a contract or when the mutual accounts reach a large amount. If stipulated in a contract, the accounts are settled twice a year, on the last days of June and December, and this settlement time is called *dai-sekki* (date of settlement). When the balance is fairly small, no interest accrues on the account. If there is a big difference in the amount, some interest may be agreed upon by mutual consent. There is no special name to indicate the method of settling accounts. The popular name is *nakama-kanjô* (settlement of accounts between fellow merchants) or *sô-kanjô* (total settlement for a whole period).

Haguri *kôri*, Takegahana Village.

There is no established practice. Some merchants settle their accounts at each transaction, but others do so after several months or half a year of transactions. Some merchants pay up the balance in total at the time of settling accounts, but others carry it over into the next term. In ordinary transactions, the date of settlement is the 30th of the month. In the case of balancing accounts, settlement, unless specially provided beforehand in a contract, is made twice a year, on February 28 and August 31, times called *dai-sekki* (the date of settlement). In business world loans, there is no practice of paying interest, unless stipulated beforehand in a contract.

Yamagata *kôri*, Takatomi Village.

After a period of transactions, the accounts are totally balanced and settled for the whole period. When it is not stipulated beforehand in a contract, but when mutual accounts reach a large amount, the accounts are balanced. The usual length of period for merchants whose business is prosperous is a month, the month beginning on the fifth of one month and ending on the fifth of the next. In business practice, the balance does not carry any interest. However, by mutual consent it may carry some interest, if the business fails to increase efficiency or if the balance reaches a large amount.

Mugi *kôri*, Kôzuchi Village.

In transactions in which merchants assume both the role of creditor and debtor, the accounts are usually balanced and settled, not at each transaction, but after several months or half a year. How the balance, if any, is settled is a matter decided between the two. When it is not stipulated beforehand in a contract, but the mutual accounts reach a large amount, the accounts are settled. When stipulated in a contract, the period for settling accounts is half a year. No interest accrues on the account. There is no special name to indicate the method of settlement, since one case differs from the other.

Haguri *kôri*, Kasamatsu Village.

No definite answer can be given for any of the questions asked here, since cases differ.

Fuwa *kôri*, Tarui Village.

In answer to the first question, some merchants balance and settle their accounts at each transaction, but others, only after several months of transactions. Regarding the second, the accounts are balanced and settled when circumstances require, either when it is stipulated beforehand in a contract, or when the mutual accounts reach a large amount. As for the third question, the length of period for settling accounts is a matter to be established in a contract between the two, so a fixed answer cannot be given. Regarding the fourth question, no interest accrues on the account. As for the fifth, there is no special name to indicate the method of settlement.

Ôno *kôri*, Miwa Village.

When merchants are engaged in continuous transactions, they balance and settle their accounts at each transaction, or after a month or half a year of transactions. They usually settle the balance to the last yen, but sometimes, after paying only part of it, they carry it over into the next term. There is no established practice. In balancing accounts, too, there is no established practice. Some people settle the accounts when the mutual accounts reach large amounts. The length of period for settling accounts is not specified. No interest accrues on the account, unless agreed upon beforehand between the two. There is no special name to indicate the method.

Ampachi *kôri*, Gôdo Village.

When the accounts are balanced and settled, in some cases the balance is paid up to the last yen, and in others it is carried over into the next term. Sometimes it is paid when it is stipulated beforehand in a contract, or when the mutual accounts reach a large amount. The length of period for settling accounts will be decided on through discussions between the two parties. The account does not carry any interest. There is no special name to indicate the method of settling accounts, but there is a popular name, *sashihiki-kanjô* (balancing accounts).

Tagi *kôri*, Shimada Village.

When merchants are engaged in continuous transactions, they balance and settle their accounts after three months or half a year of transactions. The balance, if any, is paid up at that time, or is carried over into the next term. There is no established practice.

Ena *kôri*, Iwa Village.

In answer to the first question, at the time of settling accounts, the balance, if any, is paid up, or is carried over into the next term. Regarding the second, when it is not stipulated beforehand, but the mutual accounts reach a large amount, the accounts are settled. As for the third question, the accounts are settled twice a year, in June and December. Regarding the fourth, no interest accrues on the account. As for the fifth, there is no special name to indicate the method.

Kamo *kôri*, Hosome Village.

When the accounts are balanced and settled, the balance, if any, is paid up, or is carried over into the next term. Regardless of whether or not it is stipulated beforehand in a contract, the accounts are settled when the mutual accounts reach a large amount. When it is stipulated beforehand in a contract, the length of period for settling accounts ranges from one month to half a year. According to our practice, no interest accrues on the account. The popular name to indicate the method of settling accounts is *niki-no-kanjô* (semiannual settlement), and these settlements are made in midsummer and at the end of the year.

Toki *kôri*, Takayama Village.

In answer to the first question, after half a year of transactions, the accounts are balanced and settled, and the balance, if any, is paid up. Regarding the second, it is a matter of contract. As for the third, the accounts are settled twice a year, in June and December. Regarding the fourth question, yes, that is right. As for the fifth, no special name exists.

Kani *kôri*, Mitake Village.

In answer to the first question, the balance, if any, will be paid up. It is never carried over into the next term. Regarding the second question, when it is not stipulated beforehand in a contract, the accounts may be settled if any special circumstances require. As for the third, if stipulated in a contract, the settlement is made in July and December. Regarding the fourth, in some cases interest accrues, but not in others, it depends upon the contract. As for the fifth, in general, the practice is called *sashihiki-kanjô* (balancing accounts) or *seisan-kanjô* (settlement). No special name is known.

Ena *kôri*, Akechi Village.

In response to the first question, both cases can be found. Regarding the second, both cases can be found. As for the third, the accounts are settled twice a year. Regarding the fourth question, no interest accrues on the account. As for the fifth, the practice is called *sashihiki-kanjô* (balancing accounts).

Mugi *kôri*, Seki Village.

After a month or half a year of transactions, merchants engaged in continuous transactions balance and settle their accounts for the whole period, settling the balance, if any, at that time, or carrying it over into the next term. The accounts are balanced and settled every month or every three or six months. In such cases no stipulation to the effect is necessary. Sometimes, however, it may be stipulated beforehand in a contract, but the usual manner is as stated above. Sometimes the account carries interest, but at other times it does not, it depends upon the contract. There is no special name to indicate the method.

Ôno *kôri*, Takayama Township.

In business transactions the accounts are balanced and settled, depending upon the type of goods handled, at each transaction, or after one month or half a year of transactions. The balance, if any, will be carried over to other transaction. Each transaction has a contract stipulating the settlement of accounts. According to our practice, even if it is not stipulated beforehand in a contract, the accounts should be settled for each transaction. There is no established rule for interest. If the transaction is between traders, the manner of settlement will be indicated beforehand, but if it is between a trader and a customer, it will not be.

Motosu *kôri*, Kitagata Village.

When merchants are engaged in continuous transactions with one another, they do not balance and settle their accounts at each transaction, but after several months or half a year of transactions. Sometimes they pay up the total balance, but at other times they carry the balance over into the next term's account. The accounts are settled when it is stipulated beforehand in a contract, or, if it is not, when the mutual accounts reach a large amount. When it is stipulated beforehand, the usual length of period for settling the account is six months (twice a year, in June and December). No interest accrues on the account.

Kamo *kôri*, Ôta Village.

When merchants are engaged in continuous transactions with one another, they do not balance and settle their account at each transaction, but after a month or half a year of transactions. Sometimes they pay up the total balance, but at other times they carry the balance over into the next term's account. The accounts are settled when it is stipulated beforehand in a contract, or, if it is not, when the mutual accounts reach a large amount. The usual length of time for settling accounts is every month or every six months. No interst accrues on the account. The method is called *bon-kure-niki-no-kanjô*, according to the practice here.

Kaisai *kôri* and Shimo-ishizu *kôri*.

Regarding the present matter, when merchants are engaged in continuous transactions with one another, assuming the roles in turn of a creditor and a debtor, they do not balance and settle their accounts at each transaction, but after two months or half a year. Whether the balance is to be paid or carried over into the next term's account is decided in talks between the two. The accounts are settled when it is stipulated beforehand in the contract, or, if no agreement has been made, when the mutual accounts reach a large amount, for the convenience of the two parties. According to the practice here, when stipulated, the accounts are settled on the last day of June and December, called *dai-sekki*, with regard to the account, interest does not accrue when the balance is a trifling amount. It does accrue, however, when the balance reaches a substantial amount. There is no special name to indicate the present method, but it is often called *nakama-kanjô* or *sô-keisan*.

Gujô *kôri*.

When merchants are engaged in continuous transactions with one another, alternating in the roles of creditor or debtor, they settle their accounts after each transaction, or balance and settle the accounts for the whole period after several months or half a year of transactions. They will settle the balance in full at that time or carry it over into the next term. Whether or not it is stipulated beforehand in a contract, they will settle accounts when the mutual accounts reach a large amount. There is no special name to indicate this method. If there is a big difference in the amount of money owed by the two parties, it is possible for the creditor to charge some interest on the account.

Appendices: (a) Time limit for initiating a lawsuit[1] (Chiba Prefecture).

Awa *kôri*, Hei *kôri*, Asai *kôri* and Nagasa *kôri*.

According to present law, the time limit for initiating a lawsuit over accounts of credit sales is only six months. After this period, we can do nothing. As a matter of fact, this appears to be quite inconvenient. If a wholesaler, or a retailer, has failed to settle accounts for a short while, the creditor can not start a lawsuit, for if he is severe enough to start a lawsuit immediately, he will lose every chance in business. If he allows his debtor some time to make the payment, however, he will find the time limit of six months has already expired. This will enable the debtor to grow all the more selfish. Such circumstances can also be seen in day-to-day transactions. When a merchant cannot make his debtor settle accounts, he cannot start a lawsuit against him each time such a case occurs. By being generous, he is forced to give up his legal

[1] *Shusso-kigen.*

right. We consider the law very unreasonable, to say nothing of its inconvenience for merchants. Credit should be the first consideration for every merchant who wants his business to be prosperous. Merchants would rather devote themselves to their business than contest against others in court over small amounts of money. However, their rights should be protected. We are taking advantage of this response to these questions to express our own opinions frankly.

Appendices: (b) Conditions for the circulation of bills[1]; Advantages of bills; Disadvantages of bills (Tochigi Prefecture).

Ashikaga *kôri* and Yanada *kôri*.

The bill circulating in the Ashikaga area is not a licensed one but a credit one. It was formerly called *kinu-kai-fuda* (bill for buying silk goods). The amount of money is written in large-sized characters on a piece of *Hikoma* paper[2] folded in eight, and a tally impression is affixed to the top of the paper. Expressions related to the date for payment, such as "the term of repayment is within 30 days", or "repayment is due in 20 days", are not shown, such things being decided in the nature of the transation. In place of the name of the year, one of the twelve horary signs, such as *uma* (horse) or *hitsuji* (goat), is written. Instead of his own full name, the issuer affixes his official seal[3] and writes the acceptor's trade mark, or an initial. These days more and more merchants are using new bills made of foreign paper carrying the date of repayment or the name of the acceptor. But the old bill is very convenient and there is little fear of its being forged. What counts with respect to these bills is not the seal impression but the style of writing. In contrast with the old bill, which is written in large-sized characters which are difficult to copy, the new bill of today has some blanks where a few small-sized characters can be written in by hand, making it very easy to forge.

The bills usually issued by textile brokers circulate among weaving shopowners, thread makers, dyers, etc. When a broker

[1] *Tegata*.

[2] This paper is a product of Hikoma Village, Aso *kôri*.

[3] *Shikiri-ban*.

wants to buy textiles, he hands the bill over to a weaving shopowner. Next, the weaving shopowner hands it over to a thread maker or a dyer to buy materials. And the dyer in turn hands it over to an indigo producer. Thus the bill circulates all over the business world. It has no established period, but usually circulates for at least one *ichi* (term), or five days, or for at most six *ichi*, or thirty days. The bill can be discounted by subtracting interest by the day. A bill for ¥100 with a time limit of twenty days and a daily interest rate of ¥0.10 can be discounted to ¥98 by subtracting ¥2. If he is an influential businessman, a merchant can make his bank discount his bill by the above rate. Very recently in Ashikaga, as well as in Kiryû,[1] store employees are said to be enjoying opportunities for speculation. This is due to the situation described above. Apart from the resulting evils, the system has an advantage. An economic depression will have an immediate influence upon the discount rate, reducing the price of ¥100 to ¥70 or ¥80, so merchants can quickly estimate their business in the future. Even if they fail in business and go bankrupt, it is said that they are able to avoid serious damage.

Printed in April, the 17th Year of Meiji (1884).

[1] The practice is observed in Kiryû, too.

Topic 2: What Degree of Care Must Be Exercised in Commercial Transactions in Order to Protect the Interests of Another Party?

TOKYO METROPOLIS

Prefectural Office.

Paper Wholesalers (*Kiu-kumi*).

In the case of trade with merchants in the Tokyo metropolis, the buyer and seller are to be held responsible for the 70 percent of the damage in transit, the forwarding agent[1] 30 percent.

Oil Wholesalers.

When the seller is in charge of the carriage of goods, damage in transit is made good by him. If the buyer is in charge, the responsibility rests with him.

Stone Wholesalers.

Suppose a merchant has sold a customer a total of 100 stone pillars, and some damage to a few pillars occurs in transit. The seller is sometimes willing to exchange the damaged pillars for new ones. Needless to say, however, the seller is completely free from any responsibility if he delivered the merchandise to the buyer at his own shop.

Medicine Wholesalers.

According to the practice prevailing here in the Tokyo metropolitan area, any loss should be covered by the seller himself.

Sugar Wholesalers.

As long as the seller has not yet received from the buyer an acknowledgement in writing that the goods were received, the loss should be covered by the seller himself. If the delivery of the goods has been made at the seller's shop, the seller, needless to say, is not responsible for damage in transit.

Dried Bonito Wholesalers.

If the seller is in charge of delivering the goods to the buyer's shop,[2] the seller is to bear responsibility for any damage done to the goods in transit. If the buyer has received the goods at the seller's shop,[3] the buyer is to bear the damage. According to the circum-

[1] *Shafu.*

[2] *Okuritsuke-buppin.*

[3] *Kaitsuke-buppin.*

stances, there will also be negotiations between the two as to how to divide the responsibility. A forwarding agent, or a conveyer, will sometimes bear some of this responsibility.

Soy Wholesalers.

Suppose a seller has concluded a contract with a buyer, and the seller has promised to deliver the goods by a convenient means. If the cart for this use is the seller's, the seller is to be blamed for damage done to the goods in transit. If the cart belongs to the buyer, the buyer will bear responsibility. If there is a third person, a broker, acting for the two, he is to bear the damage.

Timber Wholesalers.

Suppose some cargo has been damaged in transit—at sea, for instance. If the buyer has not received the cargo yet, the responsibility for the damage rests with the seller. However, if the buyer has already received the cargo, he is to bear the responsibility. The conveyer, a boatman or a cartman, occasionally will be held responsible according to the degree to which he caused the damage, or according to the degree to which the consignee has agreed to share such responsibility.[1] In the case of unavoidable damage, a special meeting will be held between the seller, the buyer and the forwarding agent, with a view to making some joint settlement.

Timber Traders.[2]

Timber traders all make it a guiding principle to do business with sincerity, and to do their best in handling goods and making transactions. As timber is not easily damaged, there are few cases such as those questioned here. If cargo should be damaged in transit, either by cart or by ship, the loss will be borne as follows: if the cargo has not yet passed to the buyer's hands, the responsibility is solely upon the seller. According to some special circumstances, however, talks will be held to reach a joint settlement between the two. In some cases, the conveyer, a boatman or a cartman, is to be blamed.

Timber Traders (*Senju-kumi*).[3]

Even after concluding the contract to sell the cargo to the buyer, the seller should be responsible for damage in transit. However, if the cargo is being carried by the buyer's cart or ship, the respon-

[1] *Ukeai.*

[2] *Zaimoku-tôsei-kumiai.*

[3] *Senju-kumi zaimoku-tôsei-kumiai.*

sibility is solely with the buyer. Boatmen or cartmen are free of any responsibility. But sometimes they will be blamed for the loss, in keeping with the conditions set down by the consignee.[1]

Fuel Wholesalers.

The delivery of the goods usually is made at the wholesaler's yard. However much it may cost to bring the goods there from the place of production, and however much damage may occur by accident, at sea, for instance, the responsibility is solely upon the consignee and the boatman, and not upon the wholesaler. If the goods are found short when landed at the port of arrival, the boatman will be told to pay for the damage. All the money from the boatman will later be handed over to the consignee at the time of settling the accounts. If the goods are found short in great quantity, the final settlement for the loss will be arrived at through the old practice of discussions between the consignee and the wholesaler. The delivery of goods to a retail dealer has also long been made at the wholesaler's yard, a practice called *niwa-barai*. If the goods are waterdamaged, lost, or found short due to shipwreck, collision, or theft, etc., while being transported by the wholesaler (seller), the responsibility rests solely with the seller. If the goods are being transported by the buyer, he is solely liable for the kind of damage mentioned above. Unless such damage is the result of intentional carelessness, the conveyer will not be blamed.

Porcelain Wholesalers.

The obligations arising from a contract are to be written into the contract itself. It is thus quite impossible to lay down any rule of thumb in advance. Let us give you, however, a few examples. In a case where goods in bags are to be delivered from merchant A to merchant B, a discount of 7, 5, or 3 percent of the original price will occasionally be allowed in anticipation of damage in transit. The discount rate, however, is fixed according to the case and there is no established practice. If the goods suffer any damage in transit due to shipwreck, etc., the loss should be divided between the two, although sometimes only one of them bears it. This is also a matter to be settled between the two, and there seems to be no definite practice.

[1] *Futansha.*

Paper Wholesalers (*Shôkai-kumi*).[1]

When goods in transit from a seller to a buyer under an agreement made beforehand between the two (of the same trade, in the same metropolis) suffer any damage, the loss is solely upon the seller, although in some cases the conveyer must accept a part of the responsibility. If a contract of sale is formed with a customer from the provinces of many years (a trader coming from a distant village, town, or province to renew his stock), the seller is obliged to convey the goods to a place of landing in the metropolis on the instructions of his buyer. (The form of delivery is called *ibarai* in referring to goods sold, and *niwa-chaku* in referring to goods bought.) When a contract is made with a merchant from a provincial district,[2] damage from any accident at sea or on land should be covered as stipulated in the contract. It thus depends on the particular case. Responsibility is generally divided, 60 to 70 percent being borne by the consignor, and 30 to 40 percent by the buyer. Even when not clearly stipulated, the division of responsibility seems to fall within the above guidelines. If the damage is small, it will be borne by the boatman.

Rice Traders.[3]

Upon concluding a contract with a buyer, or his agent, with some agreement on the unit of measurement,[4] the seller should, among other things, deliver the goods to the buyer either at the very building where the goods are in stock, or in front of the seller's own shop. Whatever loss may occur thereafter due to accidents aboard a ship or on a cart, the seller is free of responsibility. If the rice sold turns out to be short of weight, the damage will be shared by the two, each assuming half of the loss. As for the retail dealer, the seller sometimes permits him to take away a little more, if there is some hope that the price will go up.

Salt Wholesalers.

We need not take such responsibility.

Saké Wholesalers.[5]

[1] *Shôkai-kumi kami-donya.*

[2] A person coming from the district where paper is produced who makes a contract of sale with a wholesaler.

[3] *Beikoku sangyô-kumiai.*

[4] *Masu-mawashi.*

[5] *Sake-rui-donya.*

Theoretically, the cartman should assume such responsibility. However, being unable in most cases to do so, he discusses the settlement in a meeting with the seller or the buyer, or sometimes with both of them. In general, the consignor assumes the responsibility.

Tobacco Wholesalers.

If there is any damage in transit, the two parties will deliberate on how to settle the matter.

Kudari Saké Wholesalers.

With the signing of a contract, the ownership of the goods passes into the hands of the buyer. Theoretically, therefore, there should be no claim against the seller. If there is any accidental damage in transit aboard a boat or a cart, however, the seller and the buyer jointly bear the loss, which would otherwise have to be borne by the conveyer, on a fifty-fifty.

Mosquito Net Wholesalers.

According to Article XIV of our Code, when goods are sold and delivered, all damage in transit should be covered by the buyer, not the seller.

Lime and Shell Wholesalers.

Any damage in transit to goods already sold should be covered by the party responsible for chartering the cart and seeing to it that the goods are delivered. There is, however, no established practice. Sometimes the two share the damage. Damage suffered at sea or on a river should be borne by the shipowner if the loss is due to an error on the part of his boatman. If a ship goes down and loses its cargo in rough seas, the seller, as stated above, will have the buyer take the responsibility. However personal interrelationships sometimes demand that the seller and buyer split the loss fifty-fifty. If the transaction has taken place in cash, the seller is completely free of responsibility.

Copper and Iron Wholesalers.

Suppose an order has arrived from a customer of long standing, whether in or out of the prefecture. The goods, chosen and packed as carefully as possible, are to be sent by ship or by cart, and the buyer informed of the current prices. The transaction is made in cash, sometimes with only partial payment, or with a time limit for settling the accounts. We traders in the so-called *kyûten-kumi* hold that goods are to be handed over immediately after the deal is concluded to a forwarding agent for sea or land transport. Goods may also be sent on a cart chartered by the buyer. Whatever the case, once the goods leave our hands (*niwa-barai*), the buyer assumes full responsibility. Accidental damage in transit should be borne by the buyer. In special cases, however, the seller, or the forwarding agent, shares a portion of such losses.

Matting Wholesalers.

Article XIII of our Code states: "Whatever loss may occur in transit, if it occurs after the goods have been sold and delivered, it is solely the buyer's responsibility." The buyer, therefore, should bear the total loss.

Drapery Wholesalers.

Regarding the loss referred to in the present topic, full responsibility rests with the buyer. However, the seller shares some responsibility with the buyer, as the case may be. If the damage is the fault of the forwarding agent, he bears the loss.

Fuel Wholesalers (*Umite-kumi*).[1]

Accidental damage in transit is to be borne by the party who is in charge of the transportation. In special cases, however, a seller and a buyer may share the responsibility. The circumstances being different from one case to another, a definite rule cannot be established. If the damage is due to the intent or negligence of the forwarding agent, he bears the responsibilities.

Kôjimachi Ward.

The responsibility of a seller to take care of the goods ends when he completes delivery of the same to the buyer.

Nihombashi Ward.

There is no definite, established rule, but a seller has the responsibility to inform his customer that, for example, the goods in transit are well packed, the ship carrying them is free from danger, and the time by which they must be sold, if they are perishable.

Kyôbashi Ward.

There is a great variety of customs in such dealings, so a definite rule cannot be established. We cannot give any definite answer.

[1] *Umite-kumi shintan-donya.*

Yotsuya Ward and Ushigome Ward.

Answer missing.

Asakusa Ward.

No definite rule can be established, the circumstances differ according to the situation.

Honjo Ward.

Sincerity should be a guiding principle for all merchants in trading their goods.

Ebara *kôri*.

No definite rule can be found. Duties vary according to the circumstances under which people are placed.

Higashi-tama *kôri* and Minami-toshima *kôri*.

No definite answer can be given. If the prices are about to rise, we will buy, and if not, we will sell. What should be done is left to the judgement of each merchant.

Kita-toshima *kôri*.

If a pawnshop loses something by fire, the pawnbroker will lose the money which otherwise he would have gotten, and the borrower will lose his article. This is an established practice and applied when a person borrows some money by placing something for security which is later lost.

Minami-adachi *kôri*.

No definite answer can be given.

Shitaya Ward.

We hardly know to what degree we should take such responsibility. It is left to the individual's judgement.

Kanda Ward.

In the case of a transaction involving, dangerous or perishable goods, the seller must store the goods with caution and deliver them to his buyer with a clear statement about their condition.

Akasaka Ward and Azabu Ward.

The goods of others should be dealt with in the same way we treat our own goods.

Hongô Ward.

In general, the responsibility rests with the seller until the time when the goods are delivered to the buyer. The extent of responsibility differs according to the time and the place.

Chiba Prefecture

Awa *kôri*, Hei *kôri*, Asai *kôri* and Nagasa *kôri*.

Answer missing.
Katori *kôri*.
No answer.
Yamabe *kôri* and Muza *kôri*.
Answer missing.